# THE GOOD, THE BAD, AND THE JUST

*Riël Vermunt's book provides a thoughtful explanation of our understanding of the psychology of fairness, as it has emerged over the last half-century, and it gives an exciting new perspective on how and why people act fairly (or unfairly). It is a wonderful work for anyone interested in the topic.*

E. Allan Lind, Duke University, USA

*What do people think is just? How do ideas of justice shape actual allocations? What is the magnitude of the injustice associated with specified discrepancies between the actual reward and the just reward? What are the reactions to injustice? In this broad-ranging and stimulating book, Riël Vermunt addresses these questions, examining the three protagonists in justice processes—allocator, rewardee, observer—the goods and bads that are allocated, and the unfolding of the sense of justice. The pages are alive with the thoughts, sentiments, and actions of the justice life.*

Guillermina Jasso, New York University, USA

Riël Vermunt holds the Lifetime Achievement Award for 2014, awarded by The International Society for Justice Research (ISJR).

# Law, Ethics and Economics

*Series Editors:*
Christoph Luetge, Technische Universitaet Muenchen, Germany
Itaru Shimazu, Chiba University, Japan

Law, Ethics and Economics brings together interdisciplinary books which deal with at least two of the three constituents. Among other subjects, this series covers issues in ethics and economics, law and economics, as well as constitutional issues in law, economics, philosophy and social theory. The focus is on theoretical analysis that goes beyond purely normative considerations, thus aiming at a synthesis of the desirable and the feasible.

*Also in the Series:*

**Power and Principle in the Market Place**
**On Ethics and Economics**
*Edited by Jacob Dahl Rendtorff*
ISBN 978 1 4094 0717 1

**Absolute Poverty and Global Justice**
**Empirical Data – Moral Theories – Initiatives**
*Edited by Elke Mack, Michael Schramm, Stephan Klasen and Thomas Pogge*
ISBN 978 0 7546 7849 6

**Corporate Citizenship, Contractarianism and Ethical Theory**
**On Philosophical Foundations of Business Ethics**
*Edited by Jesús Conill, Christoph Luetge and Tatjana Schönwälder-Kuntze*
ISBN 978 0 7546 7383 5

**Public Reason and Applied Ethics**
**The Ways of Practical Reason in a Pluralist Society**
*Edited by Adela Cortina, Domingo García-Marzá and Jesús Conill*
ISBN 978 0 7546 7287 6

**Globalisation and Business Ethics**
*Edited by Karl Homann, Peter Koslowski and Christoph Luetge*
ISBN 978 0 7546 4817 8

# The Good, the Bad, and the Just

## How Modern Men Shape Their World

RIËL VERMUNT
*Leiden University, The Netherlands*

ASHGATE

Published by
Ashgate Publishing Limited
Wey Court East
Union Road
Farnham
Surrey, GU9 7PT
England

Ashgate Publishing Company
110 Cherry Street
Suite 3-1
Burlington, VT 05401-3818
USA

www.ashgate.com

**British Library Cataloguing in Publication Data**
A catalogue record for this book is available from the British Library

**The Library of Congress has cataloged the printed edition as follows:**
Vermunt, Riël.
The good, the bad, and the just : how modern men shape their world / by Riël Vermunt.
pages cm. -- (Law, ethics and economics)
Includes bibliographical references and index.
ISBN 978-1-4094-6845-5 (hardback) -- ISBN 978-1-4094-6846-2 (ebook) -- ISBN 978-1-4094-6847-9 (epub) 1. Social justice. 2. Social exchange. I. Title.
HM671.V47 2014
303.3'72--dc23

2013039373

ISBN 9781409468455 (hbk)
ISBN 9781409468462 (ebk – PDF)
ISBN 9781409468479 (ebk – ePUB)

MIX
Paper from responsible sources
FSC® C013985

Printed in the United Kingdom by Henry Ling Limited,
at the Dorset Press, Dorchester, DT1 1HD

# Contents

# List of Figures and Tables

## Figures



## Tables

# Preface

When I started my academic education at Amsterdam University, the duration of the curriculum at that time was six years. It started with a three-year bachelor program and was followed by a three-year master's program. The feature that appealed to me most about the curriculum was the broad spectrum of courses that was offered in the bachelor phase. Although my major was social psychology, other disciplines were taught as well: sociology, pedagogy, philosophy, political science. The courses were mainly taught as lectures. Examinations in each field were oral, with the teacher posing questions about both the lectures and an additional 2,000 pages of reading material.

It was from these courses that my interest in scientific knowledge grew beyond its original focus of social psychology. This interest in other fields has not left me, and during my academic career I have, from time to time, been able to find outlets for the interests and knowledge I have acquired in related areas.

I developed a growing interest in the study of social justice: describing and explaining people's feelings of justice. I focused on the consequences of unjust behavior, and victims' reactions to injustice. Because feelings of justice have a psychological component as well as sociological, philosophical, legal, and political, the subject of justice was extremely suitable for an interdisciplinary approach. But it was only in one or two publications that I had the opportunity to apply the interdisciplinary approach. Now that I am in the fortunate position where impact factors and the number of publications do not matter so much, I am able to indulge in "interdisciplinarity."

In the past, I made an attempt to approach justice from a genuinely interdisciplinary perspective. Mel Lerner played a major role in my discovery of the justice motive, and focused me on the position justice has for people and for society (Lerner 1980). But my first attempt stalled, and I let it rest. The main issue was that I had no paradigm that could serve as an eventual link between the knowledge bases of the various disciplines. What was left was a chain of facts that lacked coherence. It was a great advance when I discovered the work of Foa and Foa (1974) on social resource theory. It was Kjell Törnblom, my Swedish friend and colleague, who introduced their writings to me. Kjell and I applied social resource theory to the study of social justice. We published articles and chapters in books in which we integrated theories of distributive justice, procedural justice, and social resource theory.

It took some time before I recognized what their work could mean for my thinking. That recognition came when I started to set out a justice model in which the focus is not primarily on people's reactions to others' unjust behaviors but on the active component of people's just or unjust behavior: why and when and how do people act justly or unjustly? To describe this behavior, Foa and Foa's social resource theory was essential. The core of the theory for me is that behavior is viewed as the transmitter of resource allocations. In other words, the relevance of behavior is situated in the allocation of scarce resources.

This book is the result of my thinking. Its realization could not have been achieved without the scientific, pragmatic, and moral support of the people around me: Gezinus Wolters, Leiden University, for explaining neuropsychological phenomena and theories; Jeroen Vermunt, my son, for making the illustrations and figures; the department of social and organizational psychology, Leiden University, for the financial support. And I will not forget the hours with my colleagues in the scientific garden at the Social Science Faculty of Leiden University. I am most grateful to Alison Kirk and her colleagues at Ashgate for their creativity and their efforts to improve the quality of this work.

I have taken the rather unusual decision to offer advice on how best to approach this book. For the impatient reader who would like to have a quick overview, I advise reading the Epilogue first, but only the section entitled "Demonstration." If they are still interested in the rest of the book, I advise them to read the Prologue, and from that text to decide which chapters interest them most. Of course, I would like to believe that readers are as eager as I was when starting this journey of the human adventure and its societal, social, and psychological ramifications, to follow the steps from beginning to end. However, maybe I am asking too much of the reader. Anyway, the advice is well-meant, and I hope that readers will understand it that way.

## References

Foa, U.G. And Foa, E.B. 1974. *Societal Structures of the Mind.* Springfield, IL: Charles C. Thomas Publisher.

Lerner, M.J. 1980. *The Belief in a Just World: A Fundamental Delusion.* New York: Springer.

*I combine well-known ideas and principles in a new way.*

Prof. Dr E. Verlinde, theoretical physicist, *VPRO gids*, 37, 2011 AD

*It is, indeed, no easy task … to give to all a natural manner, and to each its peculiar nature.*

Pliny the Elder, Book I, Dedication, 77 AD

# Prologue: The Justice Model

## A Theoretical Notion of Social Justice

We know that from the beginning of written history, people have asked themselves the question: what is justice? Although Greek philosophers coined the term justice, behaviors and attitudes with regard to the exchange of goods (resources) must have been developed long before that period. For instance, following the period when people settled more permanently in fertile areas and agriculture developed, they produced more food than they could consume and began to exchange this food for other goods. Questions must have come up as to how much should food cost—that is, how much, in terms of goods or services, can be asked for the labor to produce the food? Or how much of a certain type of food should be exchanged for what amount of other goods? All sorts of rules may have been tried out until some were accepted by most of the agents involved in the exchange. The assumption is that the rules that have survived were those that were beneficial for individual members of the group or category, as well as for the group or category as a whole. These accepted rules of exchange were coined "just" rules. The social environment is constantly changing, giving rise to new behavioral and social patterns. How rules of fair exchange and allocation of resources develop, how people decide what is right or wrong in terms of allocation, and how psychological and social processes affect fair allocation of food and other resources in the changing world is the subject matter of this book.

## The Allocation Event

A large part, or for some scholars all, of the interactions between people concern the exchange or allocation of resources, like goods, money, or information. A resource is anything of value for the interacting parties, and can be material, such as money or goods, or immaterial, like love or information (Foa and Foa 1974). These authors distinguish six resource classes, the four classes mentioned already—money, goods, love (affection), information—along with status (respect) and service (giving support). *Love* is an expression of affectionate regard, warmth, or comfort. *Status* indicates an evaluative judgment that conveys prestige, regard, or esteem. *Services* involve activities that affect the body or belongings of a person and that often constitute labor for another. *Information* includes advice, opinions, instruction, or enlightenment, but excludes those behaviors that could be classified as love or status. *Money* is any coin, currency, or token that has some standard unit of exchange value. *Goods* are tangible products, objects, or materials. A specific group of goods is food: a tangible, edible product that increases someone's physical and social mass. Each resource has a positive valence (reward, affection) or a negative one (punishment, hate). Allocation of resources between two interacting parties should be differentiated from exchange of resources. Exchange is defined as a sequence of resource allocations: allocation of resources by one party is followed by or is simultaneous with allocation of resources by the other. The fundamental act is thus allocation of resources, and that will be the focus of this book.

An interaction in which resources are allocated is called an allocation event. An allocation event is instigated by an actor who has discretionary power to allocate a resource between himself and other(s)—recipient(s)—or between two or more recipients mutually. The actor makes decisions to allocate resources to or among recipients. What the actor allocates is labeled here an "allocated resource" or "distribution of the allocation decision"; these terms are used interchangeably. The rules the actor uses to make the allocation decision are labeled "procedure." Distribution and procedure are evaluated in terms of justice or fairness. Examples of allocation events are fathers dividing candy between their children, or a child who, at a birthday party, divides small presents between self and friends. The child who is asked to divide candy could keep all the candy, or could give away all the candy to another. The child could also divide the candy evenly, so that all children get the same amount of candy. It is not only the actor and recipient(s) who are part of an allocation event, other parties can be distinguished as well. Observers of the allocation event, although not actually receiving a part of the resource, may be very important for the final evaluation of the event because they were past recipients, or may become future recipients, or they may be otherwise affected by the allocation decision. Thus, actors may take into account observers' evaluation of the allocation event in their allocation decision. For instance, in many countries, governmental representatives negotiate with representatives of the police unions for the next work agreement for police personnel. The personnel of other governmental agencies, such as the garbage collecting agency, and their unions, will follow the negotiations closely since they are the next in line for work agreement negotiations. But other citizens will also watch the negotiations closely. An efficiently operating and satisfied police force is in the interest of all citizens. Because of the crucial position of the police force in society, the government, as well as the unions, will keep a close eye on public opinion. Another example is the father who offers a present to one of his children at the child's birthday party and takes the (tacit) opinions of his wife and other children in choosing the present into account. All parties will, for instance, compare the present with what others (siblings) received. Not only is it important that the birthday girl is satisfied and feels well treated, but also his wife and his other children. A gift will be given and received with the greatest enthusiasm if all parties have the feeling that everyone is, in one way or another, satisfied.

Allocation decisions are evaluated in terms of justice. The child who gives all other children equal amounts of candy is said to act justly. The child who keeps all the candy is said to act unjustly, or more precisely egoistically, while the child who gives away all the candy acts not justly, but altruistically. The question is, how can just acts be differentiated from egoistic acts and altruistic acts? The answer to this question is given by the social justice model.

## The Justice Model

From the above description of allocation events, it is possible to arrive at the important components of the social justice model. In my view, a social justice model should include four components, reflecting the why, what, and how questions of allocation behavior, as well as the reaction component. The four components are:

i. The justice motive component, which describes and explains an actor's just allocation behavior.
ii. The moral component, which describes and explains an actor's moral decision-making, focusing on respect for the other.
iii. The psychological component, which describes and explains how emotions, cognitions, and social relationships ameliorate or worsen the operation of the justice motive.
iv. The reaction component, which describes and explains recipients' and also observers' reactions to unjust allocation decisions.

Components (i), (ii), and (iii) can be subsumed under what Greenberg (1987) coined "active justice," because they concern the activities of the actor. Component (iv) can be subsumed under "reactive justice," because it concerns the reactions of recipients and observers to received resources. The main focus of the book is on describing and explaining active justice.

In the four above-mentioned components, several terms need to be defined before we can proceed with their elaboration. An allocation decision is taken by the actor in an allocation event. An allocation decision is accompanied by appropriate behavior that directly or indirectly leads to the actual distribution. For instance, one can give flowers personally or through an intermediary like a mail agency. People are involved, which means that people in some way are related to each other or feel related to each other. Let us think of a group or category of people, such as the family, a neighborhood, a work group or people who watch television. In such a setting, in an allocation event in which resources are allocated, three parties are involved: actor, recipient, and observer.

Justice can be studied from different angles. One angle is to view justice as part of morality. It will be contended in chapters 3 and 4 that only resource allocation forms the basis of morality, specifically the allocation of respect (status). Therefore, I will not discuss justice by starting with a study of morality. Another angle is to view justice as motivated by psychological processes: as an individual motive (Vermunt 2002). I will start from the two fundamental motives that play a role in resource allocation processes: egoism or self-love, and altruism or other-love. Justice, as the go-between of egoism and altruism, will be described as the drive to do well to others while taking into account one's own position in deciding about resource allocation (chapters 1 and 2). Attempts to allocate resources fairly may be hindered or advanced by social or psychological processes, as described in chapters 5 and 6.

## The Justice Motive Component

Many people are convinced that human beings are selfish, that is, that their behavior is directed at increasing their own welfare, often at the expense of the welfare of others. For them, selfishness is good, and "otherishness" is bad. For other people, who are more concerned about the welfare of others, otherishness is good and selfishness is bad. But if the observation is correct and people *only* behave selfishly, how could individuals survive the conflict that placed everyone against everyone else that would logically follow from purely selfish behavior? And how could groups develop as they did and still do? In the same vein, one can ask the question how groups of people would survive if their own interests and life were so poor as not to be worth defending? To answer these questions we should first look more carefully at selfishness, or self-love, and its counterpart, otherishness, or other-love.

### *Self-love and Other-love*

Egoism is defined by Batson (1991) as a motivational state with the ultimate goal of increasing one's own welfare. Egoism, or psychological egoism, defends the view that human beings always act from one single motive: self-love. In the egoistic view, what satisfies one's own needs is seen as just. So, it is judged as just when persons satisfy their needs even if this is detrimental to others. But in this view it is also seen as just when persons satisfy their needs by helping others: such an altruistic act satisfies the motive of self-love. Psychological egoism states that all motives are self-regarding, even motives directed at helping or comforting others, because helping others satisfies a personal need. It is obvious that this argumentation has several drawbacks. As Batson and others explain, having pleasure, as a consequence of helping others, does not imply that pleasure-seeking is the ultimate goal of helping. It can be a mere by-product of helping. Moreover, the egoistic view denies the existence of other motives than self-love. And as a methodological consequence, statements about the self-love motive are not testable—they cannot be refuted—and thus are not scientific statements.

Another, more important, objection against the concept of psychological egoism is that even if the origin of a motive is relevant, the direction of the action that is instigated by the motive may be more relevant. Is it directed to increase one's own welfare or well-being, or the welfare or well-being of another? It makes a huge difference in intentionality, as well, if one tries to help another or oneself, whether both motives originate from one and the same origin or not. If there is self-love in helping another, there is less self-interest involved than helping oneself: Helping oneself satisfies a personal need *and* it increases one's own welfare or well-being. Helping another satisfies a personal need, and increases the *other*'s welfare or well-being. The concept of altruism or psychological altruism has the same drawbacks as the concept of egoism.

Self-love, the motive that is seemingly the driving force behind any action, is seen from the psychological egoism point of view as a discrete entity. Batson (1991) differentiates between egoism and altruism, and views egoism and altruism as opposite poles of a dichotomous category. In my view, self-love is not a category but a dimension that can run from total self-love to negligible self-love and all positions in between. The amount of self-love motivation is one component that makes an act more or less selfish. Altruism can be viewed as a dimension as well, running from high altruism to low or zero altruism. The two dimensions form the axes in a two-dimensional space, though the axes are not perpendicular to each other, denoting that high egoism goes together with low altruism and vice versa. The two dimensions are depicted in Figure P.1. The horizontal axis is the egoism dimension running from low to high, and the tilted axis is the altruism dimension, running from high to low. Within this structure, justice can be positioned as an oval that is situated between the altruism and egoism axes—a bit further away. The design of the oval is such that there are positions in the oval in which egoism exceeds altruism. In other words, there may be situations where egoism rather than altruism can be defended on the basis of justice arguments. For instance, in a situation of illness it is considered just that the actor should take more. We may infer from Figure P.1 that altruism, or keeping an eye on the welfare and well-being of others, is sometimes more dominant than one's own well-being or welfare, but that one's own well-being is not forgotten. The oval may be smaller or larger, or may be situated at another position, more to the right or left, or more to the top or to the bottom, but the figure is clear that justice on the one hand and egoism and altruism on the other hand are related, but are not the same.

Viewing egoism and altruism as dimensions is related to Schokkaert's list of motives (Schokkaert 2006) that run from self-interest via reciprocity to pure altruism: a dimension of motives with egoism and altruism as opposite ends of the dimension and mixed motives in between. This seems attractive, but a one-dimensional representation of the two motives gives the impression that egoism and altruism have one and the same underlying principle. And that need not be the case. As is shown on brain image pictures, the operation of each motive occurs at different positions in the brain's physical substrate. Moreover, some authors state that pure altruism brings costs for the individual and is quite a different process from pure egoism. Elster (2006) defines true altruism as "the willingness to incur a loss of material welfare to enhance the welfare (material or not) of others."

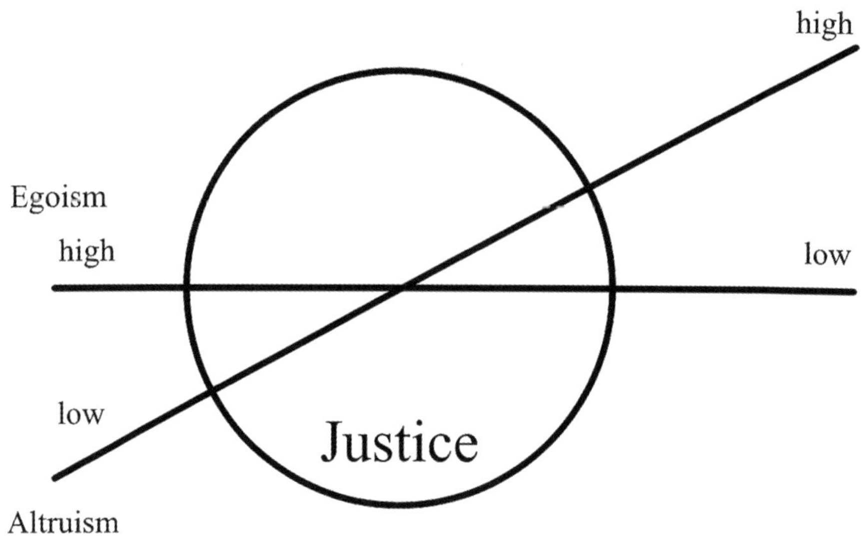


**Figure P.1 Egoism, altruism, and justice**

Incurring costs for oneself and the probably related distress is quite different from pleasure-seeking: helping other to fulfill a personal need. Altruism is also described in terms of utility. To link, for instance, actor's utility to recipients' utility, one can view resource allocation as a sort of gift-giving (Kolm 2006: 7) from the actor to the recipients. A gift is a resource that is given to increase another's satisfaction. In other words, the actor's utility is not achieved by selfishly consuming the resource, but is derived from the consumption of the resource by others. Kolm developed an equation relating the actor's satisfaction to the recipients' consumption.

*Allocation Motive: Intensity, Direction and Content*

For some, a negligible amount of self-love seems to be a natural attitude toward the social environment. It is as if they are easily moved to help others in need without much deliberation or mental calculation. When they see another person in distress their natural reaction is to help the other. Others have a natural attitude of self-love. They show mistrust toward others as if the others are motivated to decrease their welfare and well-being. Selfish people help themselves in the first place and find this behavior a natural and just way of doing things. "Otherish" persons help others without calculating their own costs. Other people show a mixture of self-love and other-love. They will help others, but not at all costs—their own interests are factored into their decisions to allocate resources between self and others. For these people it is a challenge to help another if they only see a small return compensation now or in the near future. Moreover, it is also a challenge when they expect to incur costs by helping another. If they help another, with only a small chance of compensation or moderately high chance of incurring costs, one can label that help as a strong example of fair or just behavior. One cannot label this behavior selfish or otherish. The intensity of a just allocation motive may thus be high or low. Those with a low or weak justice motive ask for more compensation and are not prepared to incur higher costs by helping another. Those acting from justice motivation have to overcome resistance in the sense that their tendency for self-love pulls them toward not acting, while their tendency for other-love pulls them in the direction of indiscriminate acting. For some individuals, their self-love or other-love must be massaged to act in a balanced way. The Good Samaritan acted altruistically in helping the victim, while the Jewish Priest and Levite acted egoistically by refusing to help the victim. Neither act is labeled fair or unfair. The Good Samaritan or the Priest/Levite would be said to act unfairly if they had asked for a large sum of money for the help. However, the Good Samaritan would be said to have acted justly if he had asked the recovered victim for appropriate compensation for the costs he had incurred. Moreover, because the Jewish Priest and Levite did not show respect for the victim, by neglecting him, they acted immorally.

Helping oneself or helping another are opposites with regard to the object the act is directed at: self or other. For high self-love individuals, the perception of people in need is distressing because of the consideration that helping decreases one's own welfare. To evaluate the justice of an act, it is essential to consider whether one acts toward oneself—the act is primarily directed at reducing one's own distress while helping an other—or toward the other—the act is primarily directed at reducing the other's distress. In other words, is the act intended to increase or decrease one's own welfare or the welfare of the other?

In evaluating the selfishness or otherishness of an act, both the direction of the act (to self or to the other) and the content of the act are relevant. One can help another or one can harm another: helping another is generally seen as just, while doing harm to another is not. In this respect, Batson defines altruism as "a motivational state with the ultimate goal of increasing another's welfare." The act is directed at the other and the motivation is to increase the other's welfare or well-being.

An additional element in the evaluation process is what the consequences of an act are. A person may be motivated to harm another, but the outcome might be that the other benefits from the act. For instance, your boss evaluates your work negatively (according to you, the boss did not take all relevant information into account) and designates you to a task which he is convinced you will be unable to complete satisfactorily. He is eager to show that he is right about your incompetence. But if you fulfill the task adequately you will rise in your colleagues' esteem. Was the boss's decision not so egoistic after all? Another example is the person who helps another but with detrimental effects for the other's well-being: You give the support the other asks for, but in the circumstances the effect is to increase the other's distress. Was the support given less altruistic? In both cases, the consequences will probably affect the selfishness/otherishness evaluation of the act. Concluding, evaluation of the type of motive instigating an act may be influenced by the intensity, content, direction, as well as the consequences of the act. Let us look more carefully at the justice view with these concepts in mind.

### *The Justice View*

It seems that justice more than egoism and altruism demands cognitive activity to arrive at the justice evaluation of a certain division of goods. According to the view of psychological and ethical egoism, a just distribution of goods is the one that allocates all the goods to the person him/herself. Therefore, a justice evaluation of an egoistically derived allocation is simple: It is just if the person him/herself receives all that there is to allocate. No reference needs to be made to another. According to the view of ethical altruism, if the term ethical altruism exists at all, a just distribution of goods is the one that allocates all the goods to the other. In the same way, the justice evaluation of an altruistically derived allocated resource is simple as well: It is just if the other receives all there is to allocate. No reference needs to be made to the allocator him/herself. When an evaluation is made about an allocated resource in which both the needs of the allocating person as well as those of the receiver are taken into account, a sort of cognitive algebra is needed to arrive at the evaluation that the allocation process is performed justly. This is called a justice evaluation (see also Jasso 1978).

Thus, the egoistic as well as the altruistic view of human behavior is rather one-sided: The behavior, so it seems, is directed toward oneself, disregarding of the other, or toward the other, disregarding the self. This is not a realistic presentation of people's behavior. People do not often behave in a way that is purely directed at others or purely directed at self. In other words, people are not often purely selfish (egoistic) or purely otherish (altruistic). People mostly take into account the position of others as well as their own position. And it is this taking both subjects into account—me and other—that makes an act, in principle, just. Justice bridges egoism and altruism. In principle, because taking both positions into account does not, in itself, make a just act. As was said before, the motivation is also essential for labeling an act as just. Thus, to help another while taking into account one's own position is a just act when the positions are balanced. An act aimed at helping the self while harming another is not a just act. The agent indeed takes both positions—self and other—into account, but the act is not aimed at helping the other.

Justice may thus be regarded as taking a position in between these two views. It not only takes the "me" (self-love) or the "you" (other-love) into account, but both you and me. But taking both into account can go two ways: One way is that the focus is on the "me" with "other" as a reference point. The vision in which the other is seen as a reference point assumes that helping oneself is only possible if one offers part of the resource to the other. In this view, the focus is on self and the agent is motivated to favor him/herself, but realizes that this is only possible if the other is favored as well. In essence, thus, it is a selfish strategy and is primarily not directed at the well-being or welfare of the other. Allocations with "self" as the focus are based on the weak justice motive: the person is willing to help another, but only because it is beneficial to the self as well. The other way is that the focus is on the "other," with the "me" as the reference point. Allocations with the "other" as the focus are manifestations of the strong justice motive.

### *The Operation of the Justice Motive*

This idea of rational other-love is best realized in the justice motive. As said, according to the justice motive view, a person evaluates the justice of an allocation by taking into account what the other receives as well as what the person receives. Both components of the evaluation process originate from the evaluating person, but the objects of the evaluation are other as well as oneself. According to the psychological egoism view, the person who likes to satisfy both needs of self-love—having pleasure in helping oneself and in helping the other—will be a person who has to make a split. Sometimes this person prefers to help him/herself and sometimes he/she prefers to help the other. Helping is not done primarily from a justice motive but from a hedonic motive.

Just behavior is behavior that is aimed at increasing the welfare and well-being of the recipient (and observer). The actor thus behaves according to what is generally referred to as the justice motive. Some scholars argue that actors have a sense of social responsibility to help and thus to increase welfare and the well-being of the recipient. But, according to Lerner's theory of justice (Lerner 1977), actors only help or allocate justly if they think the recipient deserves it. In Lerner's view, children learn to postpone direct need satisfaction in order to gain more in the future. In a stable environment these experiences lead to the notion that one gets what one deserves and is entitled to: the personal contract. Only if the actor thinks that the recipient deserves it will the actor divide resources justly. If, however, the actor thinks that recipient does not deserve a certain amount of a resource, the actor will not provide the resource. The child celebrating her birthday will give candies to the invited children and not to the uninvited.

Lerner's justice motive explanation is focused on a "deservingness" evaluation of one of the parties in the interaction, for instance, on the recipient's deservingness. Why not take into account the attribution of deservingness and entitlement of the actor, recipient, and observers? The Good Samaritan is focused on the deservingness of the other: is convinced that the victim deserves to be helped. The Jewish Priest does not think in terms of the other's deservingness, but of his own deservingness: he is convinced that he is entitled not to incur costs by helping.

As Lerner has indicated, the growing child learns from being rewarded and/or punished that good consequences follow from good behavior and bad consequences from bad behavior. Lerner assumes that these reward–punishment chains are generalized to the behavior of others as well, resulting in a belief that the world is a just place where people get what they deserve. But if the justice theory, according to Lerner, emphasizes commitment to the personal contract, how can one explain that, for instance, in helping behavior, a recipient's deservingness is taken into account but not the actor's own deservingness? Both of these deservingness considerations should be taken into account in a justice theory. It might result in a more or less balanced decision for the actor to help or not.

Consideration of the deservingness of observers is relevant as well. If the actor has to decide whether to help the neighbor, the actor may take into account that helping now will affect future behavior toward another neighbor. The actor can decide then that in this case the obligation (Folger 2001) toward the first neighbor is less than future obligations when other neighbors may ask the same.

The introduction of own deservingness in transactions may also explain why people offer more resources when a small gift is used, for instance a pencil, to encourage helping. Lerner explains this by referring to societal norms that govern exchange behavior. Offering a small present changes helping into a more generally accepted economic exchange in which altruistic helping becomes an economic activity. Lerner (1980) showed that participants in the study offered more money in conditions in which a small gift (of negligible financial value) was allocated by the actor (the person at the door) than in those conditions where there was no such gift. But receiving a small gift might be interpreted by the participant as compensation for being bothered by the actor's fate and by showing that the actor understands the participant's deservingness: "I understand that you do not deserve to be bothered by me and my project, but with this small gift I would like to offer some compensation." Moreover, it might also be assumed that the participant weighs his own deservingness of becoming involved in and bothered by the actor's fate against the actor's deservingness. And if the participants evaluate the actor's deservingness to be higher than theirs, the participants will offer a gift. If, however, the participants evaluate their deservingness higher than the actor's, they will not be inclined to help. This interpretation of justice theory gives a more important role to deservingness than in Lerner's formulation. It makes the elements of deservingness and entitlement in justice theory—when these assumptions are corroborated—more prominent. Moreover, this view supports the notion that justice is a balance between own interests and others' interests. If this idea is correct, one can ask the question what the Jewish Priest could have done for the victim while still bearing in mind his own interests? Instead of helping directly he could have warned people or paid other people to help the victim. The Priest's status would not have been reduced and it would have shown him to be a man of compassion, which is appropriate for a priest.

Folger's deonance approach (Folger 2001; Folger, Cropanzano, and Goldman 2005) deviates somewhat from Lerner's justice motive approach (Lerner 1980). In Folger's approach, justice is viewed as an ethical standard that creates an obligation to disregard the self-interest of material or immaterial benefits (see also the concept of moral mandate, Skitka and Houston 2001). Turillo et al. (2002) view fairness or justice as "an ethical standard conceived independently of self-interest so that it can act as a constraint against an otherwise unfettered self-interest" (841). According to the deontic approach, justice is a human motive "that can rise above self-interest" (841). In their study, participants observed an actor treating a recipient unfairly by offering only 10 percent and keeping 90 percent of a sum of money. Observers were prepared to accept a loss of money if that guaranteed that no money at all would go to the actor who kept 90 percent for himself (Turillo et al. 2002). The authors explain the observers' self-sacrificing behavior as a demonstration of the operation of the justice motive.

Starting from the definition of altruism, these results can be explained in terms of the operation of the altruistic motive (Batson 1991; Elster 2006). An actor who allocates the financial reward evenly between self and other is relatively disadvantaged (receives $5) compared to an actor who takes 90 percent for himself (receives 6$). An observer is prepared to sacrifice money in order to "compensate" for the misfortune of the 50 percent actor. In the case of punishing an advantageous actor, the observer pays less to an advantageous actor (18/2) then to a less advantageous actor (10/10). That seems rather altruistic.

Interesting in Folger's approach is that fairness as ethical principle acts as a constraint to self-interest. People have an obligation to help when another is in need. The deontic approach "represents a way of understanding fairness-related phenomena that points to the key role of morally accountable conduct" (Folger, Cropanzano, and Goldman 2005: 230). One should add to this statement that people have an obligation toward the self as well—they can be held responsible for what they do to themselves. In the balanced view of justice propagated here, people not only have obligations to others but also to themselves.

## The Moral Component

Morality, in short, concerns the appropriate allocation of the resource status (respect). The justice model thus includes a moral component. This statement is not without risk. Many scholars will fervently defend the theoretical notion that justice is part of morality, rather than morality being part of justice. I agree in this debate with developmental psychologist Kohlberg (1981), who viewed moral development as principally concerned with justice. How then can justice and morality be related? To answer this question I will give the following example that was put forward by Folger (Folger, Cropanzano, and Goldman 2005): "Consider a supervisor who gives an incomplete, 'positive spun' explanation for a key decision, versus one who treats a subordinate rudely and disrespectfully. The latter action would likely be viewed as immoral. The former might be a bit sloppy, but 'immoral' seems too strong a word" (230). Why is one behavior labeled immoral and the other not? The authors do not answer this question. One answer might be that treating people disrespectfully highly reduces others' status and integrity, while giving incomplete information does that to a lesser extent. Receiving complete information tells recipients that the actor evaluates their status highly, while incompleteness of the information reduces it. Attacking others' integrity and status is immoral. Both actions are immoral, the one more than the other.

Haidt (Haidt and Graham 2007) defends the view that morality is more than justice. The author distinguishes psychological foundations of morality, of which fairness/reciprocity and harm/care are only two. The other three foundations are in-group/loyalty, authority/respect, and purity/sanctity. According to Haidt, societies developed virtues based on these five psychological foundations. The psychological foundations run parallel with built-in intuitions. The interesting issue with the five foundations is that the first two refer to the basic principle of equality, while the other three refer to inequality. Respect for authority implies disrespect for subordinates; in-group loyalty implies discrimination to other groups. Purity/sanctity refers to inequality based on opinions about human nature. Moreover, the group value model of justice (Lind and Tyler 1988) and the relational model of authority in groups (Tyler and Lind 1992) are connected, respectively, to Haidt's in-group/loyalty and authority/respect modules of morality. In other words, the first two foundations reflect compassion for human beings in general, while the last three foundations reflect compassion for particular human beings. In my view, a morality should be based on respect for all human beings.

In terms of allocation events in which resources are allocated between parties, status and information are both resources to be allocated. As described earlier, status and information are only two of the six resource classes that parties allocate in interactions with each other. For instance, in the psychology/economy literature, allocation of money and goods and fairness reactions to the received resource are studied. In the procedural justice literature, fairness reactions to allocation of less tangible goods like service (caring about the recipient) and information (giving accurate information) are studied. And as Folger's example shows, rude behavior and a recipient's fairness reaction are also investigated. In all these examples scholars assume that people react in terms of fairness to deserved as well as undeserved outcomes of allocation decisions. But, specifically in the case of status allocation, the term moral seems to be appropriate. Moral behavior, therefore, can best be defined as allocating status (respect, dignity) to another. Morality in this sense has three flavors: respect for persons, social relationships, and groups (society).

### *Allocation Rules and Morality: Respect for Persons*

Recipients react to outcomes of allocation decisions in terms of fairness. But how can actors, recipients, and observers decide whether an act is fair or morally right? The stance defended here, and worked out in detail in chapters 3 and 4, is that allocation decisions should be founded on good argumentation. Actors should underpin allocation decisions with good reasons. Of course, it is sometimes difficult to decide whether an argument is valid, but in furthering groups, organizations, and societies, people developed and develop rules for smooth interactions and to reduce conflict. The Universal Declaration of Human Rights is a set of rules to guide and evaluate the way people should be treated. Although one can observe many violations of this set of rules, its existence gives human rights watchers, governments, and non-governmental organizations important tools for criticizing violations and eventually bringing responsible persons to justice. The process of rule development and acceptance is often accompanied by conflict, and it takes time before rules are generally accepted. Sometimes, catastrophes, war, or severe accidents may lead to new rules and increased acceptance of rules. The ferocities of the First and Second World Wars were the starting point of the development of rules for warfare such as the Geneva Convention for behavior toward captured soldiers, as well as toward civilians. The rules are used as argumentation to legitimize a certain course of action: My act is fair or morally right because it is in line with one of the rules of the Geneva Convention or the Universal Declaration of Human Rights.

Morally wrong or right applies well when it concerns the need rule. The need rule is often applied to people who are in a dependent relationship to others, like children, sick people, the elderly, or captured soldiers. The essence of the need rule is that the need state of the dependent person is the ground for allocation of resources. In other words, the recipient's status (need position) is taken into account. The higher the need, the higher the care should be. Treating someone in need inappropriately harms that person's dignity and is said to be immoral. Haidt and Joseph (2007) relate this behavior to one of the five moral modules, the one prescribing care for the needy and to avoid doing harm to them. Another moral module Haidt and Joseph differentiate with regard to persons is authority/respect, which is subsumed here under status allocation.

In the literature, moral dilemmas are described in abundance to show how difficult it often is to act in a morally right fashion. These dilemmas are discussed in Chapter 3.

### *Allocation Rules and Morality: Respect for Social Relationships*

Aristotle described several rules for maintaining good relationships between citizens, between citizens and state, and between state and citizens. The justice with which Aristotle was concerned has two branches: the distributive one of honors and the like among citizens by the state, and of private property by contract and agreement; and the corrective, the remedying of unfair distribution. The distribution is a question not of equality, but of right proportion; and this applies to retribution, which is recognized as one of its aspects. Later on, these rules of allocation became more detailed. Take the rule of right proportion. Adams (1965) elaborated on this idea by incorporating what A receives (outcome) in relation to what A invests (input) as compared to what B receives in relation to what B invests. When the ratio of inputs and outcomes of A is in proportion to those of B, A's received resource will be evaluated as fair. Research data shows that this rule is widely applied in all kinds of settings where people make investments. For instance, the rule will be applied in the work situation. When an actor allocates resources (a bonus, for instance) in negotiations with group members, the equity rule will serve as guideline for the allocation decision. The actor will presumably argue that a group member has made this level of investment and that a certain reward is appropriate. In other words, the actor offers appropriate arguments for the distribution resulting in a higher justice evaluation of the offer and thus in higher chances of acceptance of the offer than without the arguments. In the case of financial reward, the allocated resource is evaluated in terms of justice or fairness and not in terms of being morally right or wrong.

It is generally accepted that these rules of distribution are not viewed as appropriate under all conditions. Lerner (1980), for instance, assumed that in close relationships the need and equality rule are more dominant than the equity rule, and that in economic transactions the equity rule is more dominant than the equality rule. These distribution rules are, to a large extent, accepted in most Western societies. This means that in distributing resources like salary or goods, reference will be made to the rules. And acceptance of a certain division is greater and people find the distribution more just if actors make explicit reference to the rules. In other words, distribution rules are used as reasons to justify a distribution of resources among recipients. It must be emphasized again that distributions as described are evaluated in terms of justice and not of morality.

Next to distributive rules, in prescribing how much of a resource a recipient should get, the actor may apply rules that prescribe how the relationship between actor and recipient should be. These rules or criteria are not primarily used to give recipients their due, but they are applied to express the quality of the relationship between actor and recipients. In this sense they can be labeled relational values: values by which the relationship between people is evaluated. Tyler and Lind (1992) assume that the three most important relational values indicate how morally right an actor is toward recipient and observers: the actor should be impartial, should respect recipients as well as observers, and should behave in such a way that he/she can be trusted. Haidt and Joseph (2007) would subsume these behaviors under the moral module of authority/respect. Impartiality means that the actor gives equal consideration and attention to the behaviors, opinions, and attitudes of all involved; respect means that the actor highly values the persons displaying the behaviors, opinions, and attitudes, irrespective of how he/she values the persons' behaviors, opinions, and attitudes; trust means that the actor displays the same behavior and opinion toward all involved and in all situations. In many cultures, impartiality (or neutrality), respect, and trust are basic values, and applying these values in allocation processes will elicit positive feelings and just evaluations, while not applying these values in allocation decisions will elicit negative feelings and evaluations of having been treated unjustly. Procedural rules, therefore, are often regarded as more important for assessing justice than distributive rules, except for the allocation of status.

Types of concrete allocation behavior, subsumed under the umbrella of the three abstract values neutrality, respect, and trust, have been developed by researchers in recent decades. Leventhal (1980), for instance, proposed the following criteria for evaluating the fairness of a procedure: consistency, bias suppression, accuracy, correctability, ethicality, representativeness. Further developments of procedural justice focused on criteria for the assessment of interactional justice (Bies and Moag 1986), emphasizing interpersonal sensitivity, such as not asking inappropriate questions.

Because recipients apply these criteria to evaluate the morality and fairness of the allocation event, actors can be motivated to use the criteria to justify their allocation decisions. Implementing, for instance, the accuracy rule, increases a recipient's trust in the actor, and thus increases the recipient's positive feelings, justice and moral evaluations, and acceptance of the allocation decision. Thus, the actor may announce that he/she will allocate the resource in proportion to the hours worked and that he/she will accurately count the worked hours (an indication of trustworthy behavior). In doing so, the actor gave good reasons for their allocation behavior and this behavior will likely be evaluated as just.

When the above-mentioned distributive and procedural rules for resource allocation touch vital parts of the recipient's life, property, integrity, or dignity—that is, the recipient's essential status—neglecting these rules will be evaluated as immoral behavior.

### *Allocation Rules and Morality: Respect for the Group*

Does Cinderella's stepmother have respect for her children? The stepmother and her daughters treat Cinderella with disdain, while she rewards her daughters. Cinderella does not get the same beautiful clothes and treatment as the two daughters. The stepmother neglects Cinderella's essential status. Moreover, the stepmother does not care about creating harmony in the group of children she is responsible for. She makes no attempt to increase happiness and justice for all (in-group/loyalty, Haidt and Joseph 2007). On the contrary, she increases differences in wealth and treatment between her daughters and Cinderella.

Maximization of people's justice experiences, as well as minimization of differences between people with regard to these experiences, is a crucial element of moral and just decision-making (Rawls 1971). Thus, it is not only crucial that the distributing actor has just motivation and proper argumentation for the allocation decision, but the actor should pay attention to the way the decision finds its way through to the receiving group of people.

Rawls (1971) described a social arrangement based on the aggregative–distributive dichotomy. According to Rawls, a just society can be achieved by applying the two principles: "the basic structure of society is to be designed first to produce the most good in the sense of the greatest net balance of satisfaction and second to distribute satisfaction equally" (Rawls 1971: 36). From a social psychological as well as from a justice and moral point of view, the "maximin" principle is highly interesting. From the justice point of view, maximization of justice experiences and minimizing differences in in/justice feelings between group members is widely described as being beneficial for the recipient as well as for the group as a whole. Although this idea has not been worked out fully in the ethics literature, in the justice area some findings point to the detrimental effects of injustice between groups. Urry (1973), for instance, has pointed out that not absolute differences in wealth between groups initiates protest and revolution, but the relative deprivation of one group versus another. The same conclusion can be drawn with regard to members of a group. These observations may lead to the conclusion that, for the "maximin" principle, differences in allocated resource between group members—the relative position with respect to the resource—are more important than the absolute position with regard to the resource. The question is whether these observations apply to allocation of status and respect as well. Or, with regard to status allocation and the moral evaluation of received respect, is the difference between group members in received respect less important than the absolute respect received? Referring to the Cinderella case: Is it the disrespectful treatment of Cinderella that elicits moral outrage or is it Cinderella's disrespectful treatment in relation to the treatment the other daughters received?

Rawls (1971) labeled the notion about group justice—mean justice evaluations as well as deviations between justice evaluations—as a theory of the intuitive type, because one cannot logically derive the precedence of one element over the other. In other words, both elements are of equal importance in assessing the justice of an allocation decision. That is, an allocation decision should result in the highest mean justice experience for all involved, as well as the smallest difference between the justice experiences of all involved. But there may be arguments for giving priority to one of the elements over the other. As already mentioned, an allocation event is considered here as consisting of agents (actor, recipients, and observers), resources, and allocation rules. Actors making the allocation decision will, of course, view their decision as fair or morally correct. Recipients and observers, however, may differ from the actor with regard to the justice and moral quality of the decision and evaluate the allocation decision as less just or less moral. But also, recipients and observers may differ mutually. Recipients, as the most directly affected by the allocation decision, often evaluate the allocation decision as less just or more just than observers. The reason is that observers take into account more or other aspects of the allocation event than recipients. Some would say that observers are biased in their perception of the allocation event. Whatever the attitude of the observers, the end result is that all three involved parties may differ in their evaluation of the allocation event, and that as a consequence the average justice evaluation of the event will not differ much from the theory-derived mean of justice evaluations: a mean that lies in between totally unjust and totally just. Of course, the actor is bound—being a just allocator as he/she sees him/herself—to increase the average level of justice evaluations. But the assumption is that attention will primarily be focused on the differences between the justice evaluations of the agents involved to reduce conflict. Moreover, several social scientists have pointed to the phenomenon that neither absolute poverty nor absolute resource possession give rise to protest and conflict, but relative poverty and possession: poverty in relation to other relevant groups or categories. Translating this observation to the allocation event elements of mean justice experiences and differences in justice experiences adds an argument for the primacy of the differentiation component over the mean component. Therefore, the assumption is that priority can and should be assessed between the two components of group justice: An actor will try to take an allocation decision such that, first, the differences between justice experiences between all involved will be as small as possible, and only second that mean justice experiences will be as high as possible. When both components refer to a group member's status position, they contain a moral component. Not only did Cinderella receive less than her sisters—which is an injustice—but she was treated very disrespectfully in comparison with her sisters—which is immoral.

## The Psychology Component

As already pointed out, an important element of the allocation event is the actor who divides resources among recipients. The actor's role is crucial because he/she is the initiator of the allocation and is responsible for its outcome. In theories and research on distributive justice, the actor has only played a minor role as a background figure who is essential but is kept out of focus. More recently, when research started in the realm of procedural justice, the actor's role became more prominent. Tyler and Lind (1992) formulated the relational model of authority and revaluated the actor's role. In this model, a good relationship between actor and recipient is what recipients strive for, and an indication of a good relationship is the fairness of the actor's treatment of the recipient. Before the formulation of the relational model, other features of the allocation model had the attention of researchers, such as the distributive and procedural rules.

The justice notion described in the present chapter is a continuation of the ideas of Tyler and Lind, but emphasizes even more firmly than these authors do the important role of the actor, focusing on the actor's emotions and cognition, and how they affect the operation of the justice motive. A just actor is one who is motivated to act fairly and, as previously described, this means that the actor not only takes into account the interests of others but also the interests of self. In other words, the actor is constantly weighing what he thinks others deserve and what he/she deserves. This balance can easily sway in one direction or the other, that is, that decisions to allocate resources between self and other can become more self-directed or more other-directed. The actor's mental state can influence the operation of the justice motive, resulting in a more unbalanced allocation decision. Operation of the justice motive is challenged by internal and external conditions.

### *Conditions Affecting the Operation of the Justice Motive*

Operation of the justice motive—its weak as well as its strong form—depends on factors in the actor's personality, the social environment, and on features of the allocated resource.

Some people are more other-oriented and therefore are more inclined to take another's position into account. In the literature, this inclination is related to phenomena such as field dependency. Field-dependent persons (Hakstian and Cattel 1976) need the presence of a "yardstick" in order to orient themselves in the social environment, while field-independent persons do not. Moreover, brain research results show that some people have more so-called mirror neurons (brain cells) than other people. Mirror brain cells play an important role in "reading" the intentions of others. Persons with more mirror brain cells are better able to read others' intentions, and are better able to evaluate another's need state. It is likely that other-oriented people and people with relatively large numbers of mirror neurons are inclined to do good to others. In addition, it is likely that self-oriented people and people with relatively small numbers of mirror neurons are inclined to do good to themselves. Chapter 1 will expand in more detail the evolutionary development of the justice motive.

Emotions may also affect the operation of the justice motive. Self-preservation emotions are differentiated from moral emotions. Positive self-preservation emotions are, for example, happiness or joy; negative self-preservation emotions are, for example, anger or anxiety. Anxiety is a central experience for human beings who realize that they are mortal, and who often feel uncertain during periods of economic and social crisis; the uncertainty elicits anxiety feelings. A third important source of anxiety is formed by the perception or presence of groups of strangers. Anxiety has a large influence on perception and cognition, and may affect operation of the justice motive. Moral emotions are defined by Haidt (2003: 276) as those "that are linked to the interests or welfare of society as a whole or at least of persons other than the judge or agent." Among the positive moral emotions are moral pride, self-approval, elevation and gratitude. Among the negative moral emotions are shame, guilt, and embarrassment. Some people are prone to positive or to negative moral emotions. People easily feel guilty or ashamed after having taken an allocation decision; for example, they think they have offered too low a financial contribution to a program to help children in need. Others easily feel pride in their allocation decision: they value their financial contribution as more than sufficient. It is further assumed that the experience of shame interferes with orientation on others. The person feeling shame turns inward and is less responsive to the needs of others (Tangney et al. 2007). Guilt feelings have the opposite effect on responsiveness to others' needs: a guilty person may be more prone to do good things for others.

The social environment challenges the justice motive as well. The presence of a needy person will move even a selfish person. The behavior of people in economic games reflects what is meant by just behavior: the desire to do well to others as well as to themselves. Perception of a needy other might elicit an actor's helping behavior. When an actor sees another drowning, the first inclination is to help. Some actors jump into the water to rescue the drowning person, others are more cautious and deliberate over whether their action will be successful. Others may seek help in different ways, such as calling an ambulance or the police. In such cases, the other is totally dependent on the actor and this dependency increases the actor's motivation to help. One can observe helping behavior in more controlled settings, as well. This might be the case when the other is totally dependent on the actor, for instance in a Dictator Game (DG). In a DG, the actor offers a bid and the other can only accept the bid. In one of our studies, we made the dependency of the recipient on the actor even greater: the actor knew that the recipient was not aware of the value of the token representing money (Van Dijk and Vermunt 2000)—the actor's token was twice the value of recipient's token. So, the actor could present him/herself as a just person by offering an equal division of tokens. But actually, the actor received twice the amount of money as recipient. What we found, however, was totally different from the predictions of game theory. Actors in the DG did not misuse the recipient's dependency by offering few tokens. Instead, they offered more tokens (money) to recipients than predicted. From these and other findings one may conclude that when a recipient is completely dependent on an actor, the actor is willing to set aside personal gain in order to satisfy the recipient's need. Of course, the actor could have offered the other all the tokens, showing pure altruistic behavior. This was not the case, showing that the person also tried to satisfy their own needs. This behavior is a good example of the earlier description of justice as a bridge between egoism and altruism.

An actor's perceptual focus on the social environment can suddenly change. Discussing trivial (male) issues with a male friend, the arrival of a female friend can change the conversation and the atmosphere: It can be inferred from the content of the conversation between the male friends that the atmosphere was friendly and cooperative, but with the arrival of the female friend the atmosphere between the two male friends becomes more competitive. They both want to show the female friend who is the best—they compete to win her attention.

Allocating a resource to another is also affected by the type of allocation event and by the relationship between actor and recipient. When a recipient gives a gift to an actor, the actor is inclined to reciprocate. Several authors have contemplated the issue of reciprocity. In short, reciprocity is viewed as the motivation that a gift elicits another gift. An actor gives a gift in anticipation of either getting something in return or not. In a work relationship, a gift may be given in order to get something done by the other person; for example, assistance in performing a task. In a friendship relationship, a gift is not given with the idea of getting something back—the gift is given in return for received friendship. Moreover, a gift may be given to a person of the same status or to a person of a different status. A person can give a gift to a higher-status other or to a lower-status other. In both cases they expect to get something in return. The giver must be very careful in offering a gift to a person of a different status. The gift can easily be viewed by the recipient as a bribe or as undue influence. In both cases one expects to get something in return. In all these cases, the initiative starts from one person. He or she is the actor, the other is the recipient. And the other may or may not reciprocate. In fact, reciprocation is a case of resource allocation in which two allocation events follow each other. It is plausible to assume that the increasing complexity of society with its intricate status hierarchies has molded the operation of the justice motive. Chapter 2 will describe the influence of the emerging society on the operation of the justice motive.

In addition, the differentiation between material and immaterial resources will have an effect on the operation of the justice motive. It may be assumed that allocating a material resource makes one's own position on the resource more salient than allocating an immaterial resource: being asked to offer money makes one's own financial position more salient and easier to calculate than being asked to listen to someone. Offering money challenges the justice motive more than making time for listening. This assumption of effect can also be made for a positively valued resource as compared to a negatively valued resource. In the economic literature, reactions to losses (negative outcome of a resource) are not the inverse of reactions to gains (positive outcome of a resource)—people weigh losses heavier than gains (Harinck et al. 2007). Moreover, losses are mostly divided equally, while gains are mostly divided according to contribution or merit (De Dreu 1998).

## The Reaction Component: A Theory of Injustice Reactions

In everyday life, people often experience injustices: they become angry because their salary is less than they think they deserve, or they are not treated with due respect. In the Netherlands, police officers protested against a new salary contract in which, in their view, increased occupational hazards were not sufficiently compensated. They prepared action to show their anger, like refusing to fine civilians for small misdemeanors. In addition, in interviews they showed contempt for the lack of due consideration—a pat on the back—for irregular working hours and for their often difficult work as police officers. They felt undervalued by society for what they do. Hollywood text writers went on strike to protest against the low financial compensation for their work. Many other examples can be given showing the anger and frustration resulting from underpayment and/or undervaluation. But one can also observe that people often do not become angry and start protesting, even though they are objectively in a disadvantaged position. Take, for example, immigrants in the Netherlands. Their income is very low but most do not protest against their miserable situation. Why these differences between groups of people with respect to the evaluation of their situation and their readiness to act? According to Lerner (1977), people will not protest against their bad fate if they think they deserve it. Deservingness is a sufficient and necessary condition of justice evaluations. But what does it mean, that they do not deserve their bad fate? As stated above, deservingness is an evaluation of the situation in which a fairness (but sometimes a moral) component is operative. One compares the present situation with an internal norm—derived from early experiences—and when the present situation deviates (negatively) from that norm then the present situation is evaluated as undeserved and thus as unfair. A major component of unfairness, therefore, is the discrepancy experienced between people's present situation and a simulated situation. Folger (1987) assumed, in this respect, the operation of a simulation heuristic which people use to evaluate their position in the group or society. Folger further assumed that simulation can occur in several ways. One is the internal norm as comparison standard. Other ways are the situation of others in more or less similar conditions, such as others from the same sex, with the same status, from the same profession, and so forth. Another simulation method is to compare one's present situation with one's situation earlier in time. Such a comparison may lead to the conclusion that one's situation is worse than expected, and this discrepancy is accompanied by negative emotions and/or action to overcome the discrepancy. In social psychology, much time and energy is devoted to unraveling the cognitive and emotional mechanisms of justice evaluations, such as research on the role of uncertainty and self-esteem in justice evaluations or the application of cognitive algebra to arrive at equity judgments of one's income.

Knowledge about recipients' evaluations and reactions to allocation decisions is of crucial importance to actors. If actors have knowledge of the precise justice evaluations and reactions of recipients, they can take account of these and eventually adapt their allocation decisions. Some recipients react differently from other recipients to injustice. The same allocation outcome may be evaluated by some people as unfair while others may judge the event as less unfair or even moderately fair. If an actor is motivated to allocate resources as fairly as possible, and if the actor wants to use the fairest arguments for the decision to be made, and if the actor wants to accomplish an allocation that is most fair for as large a group of recipients as possible, the actor needs knowledge about the reactions of the recipients (and observers) to injustice. Most research of recent decades has been conducted to elucidate the conditions of fairness evaluations. Distributive justice theories are developed to predict reactions to unfair resource allocations, and procedural justice theories are developed to predict reactions to unfair application of allocation procedures. In the realm of distributive justice, Adams (1965) has shown that underpayment—compared with the payment of relevant others—is evaluated as unfair and results in, for instance, decreasing work performance. Adams also distinguishes other reactions such as protest and cognitive distortion of performance. In the realm of procedural justice, research showed comparable results: Modde and Vermunt (2007) found that an inaccurate evaluation procedure for academic performance was judged as unfair and increased norm-violating behavior.

The question that remains after all these studies is how unfair the treatment has to be before the recipient decides to take action, and what the likelihood of a certain reaction to the unfairness is as compared to other reactions. Our knowledge, and thus also the knowledge of actors about recipients' reactions, is far from complete, making it difficult to accomplish a fair allocation decision. Chapter 7 will describe—as a new approach based on Törnblom and Vermunt

(2007)—theoretical innovations to predicting reactions to perceived injustice with regard to the magnitude as well as to the type of reaction.

This section will attempt to expand distributive and procedural justice theories using insights from resource theory (see Törnblom and Vermunt 2007). Distributive justice theories and procedural justice theories have already been described in some detail (for further details of the theories, see Chapter 7). Resource theory (Foa and Foa 1974), however, has not, so it will briefly be described here. Within the context of resource theory, *interpersonal behavior* is conceived as "a channel for resource transmission," and *resource* is defined as "any commodity—material or symbolic—which is transmitted through interpersonal behavior" (Foa and Foa 1974: 36).

According to Törnblom and Vermunt (2012: 186):

> The major contributions of resource theory are based on its focus on the *nature* of the objects or resources of exchange. These are categorized into six presumably exhaustive and mutually exclusive resource classes which are then plotted along the two coordinates of particularism (ranging from particularistic to universalistic) and concreteness (ranging from concrete to abstract) … The values of particularistic resources (i.e., love, status, and services) are strongly influenced by the identity of the provider and the relationship between provider and recipient, while the values of universalistic resources (i.e., information, goods, and money) are [to a lesser extent] (money, for instance, is worth the same whomever you get it from). The concreteness dimension concerns the type of behavior that is characteristic for the exchange of a particular resource: providing a good and doing someone a favor are concrete behaviors, conveying status and information are symbolic/abstract behaviors, while love and money may be provided both symbolically (e.g., verbal expressions of affection and as stock or other tokens, respectively) and concretely (e.g., sexual acts and hard currency, respectively). Resource *classes* are defined as '… categories of the *meaning* assigned to actions and not a classification of actions' (Foa and Foa 1974: 82). Thus, a number of different actions may convey the same resource (e.g., the acts of smiling, kissing, hugging, verbal statements, all of which convey love and affection).

But one action may convey different resources as well. For instance, massages may be acts that convey love or service. It is difficult for an outsider observing the act to determine whether it is out of love or out of service.

### *The Fundamental Resources*

In my view, the six resource classes can be partitioned into three fundamental resources each based on (1) the content of the act involved (unit of observation), and (2) intensity of the act (see Figure P.2). One group concerns the resource classes Love and Service, with acts that are specified by the factor *time* spent on the other. With the factor time as specific element, this group of resource classes is differentiated from the other resource classes. The difference between the resource classes Love and Service is the intensity with which the actor performs the act. Love is a resource class subsuming acts that have greater intensity than acts representing Service. Or, in other words, the intensity of the act is greater for acts conveying Love than conveying Service.

The other group of resource classes is that of Money and Goods. The content (results) of the act (decision) is the amount of *currency* allocated. Intensity differentiates allocation of Money from allocation of Goods: Goods are more personal and are therefore a stronger indication of an actor's involvement than allocation of Money.

The third group of resource classes concerns Information and Status. The content of the act that differentiates this group of resource classes from the other two groups is that information—advice, opinion, enlightenment—can be said to be allocated (shared) in terms of bits. Status, in terms of respect, regard, esteem is also conveyed in terms of bits. In fact, it is words that mainly convey Information as well as Status. And words can be translated into bits of information. The two resource classes are differentiated in terms of the intensity of the information conveyed: Status implies a high involvement of actor and recipient, while conveying Information is often less intense.

| **Resource type** | **Unit of observation** |
|---|---|
| Service | Time |
| Love | Time + Intensity |
| Money | Currency |
| Goods | Currency + Intensity |
| Information | Bits |
| Status | Bits + Intensity |

**Figure P.2 Three groups of resource classes and their observables**

1. The unit of observation for Service and Love is Time (and Intensity). The amount of Service can be observed in terms of the time the actor spends on the recipient with a certain intensity. The amount of Love can be observed in terms of time as well as high intensity. Time is measured on a ratio scale, intensity and the accompanying act on an interval scale.
2. The unit of observation for Money and Goods is Currency (and Intensity). The amount of Currency can be observed in terms of the currency the actor spends on the recipient with a certain intensity. The amount of Goods can

be observed in terms of currency as well as high intensity. Currency is measured on a ratio scale, intensity on an interval scale.

3. The unit of observation for Information and Status are Bits (and Intensity). The amount of Information can be observed in terms of the bits the actor spends on the recipient with a certain intensity. The amount of Status can be observed in terms of bits as well as high intensity. Bits are measured on a ratio scale, intensity on an interval scale.

At first sight, time, currency, and bits do not have much in common. Their inherent qualities are very different. People earn money and exchange money, but not time. People increase their wealth but not time. People share bits but not time or money: informing another person does not imply that one loses information. When people offer money or time, they cannot spend it on themselves. Is there no way to make the fundamental resources more in line with each other for comparison purposes? It seems there might be. Let us start with time.

People can save time, can increase time and thus exchange time, more or less like money. Although there are only 24 hours in a day, people increase their time by inviting other people to join, for instance, to do a job. Enterprises, organizations, and employment offices are, in fact, time-increasing bodies. They hire people to augment their time to make a product. They extend their time. It seems that there are time banks today: the work one does for another results not in pay, but is put in a time bank. Doing a service for another earns time which is put in a bank for later use or exchange.

Information needs a different approach to accommodate it with money and time. People exchange information, but the allocator still keeps the information. One pays for scarce information—like scientific information—but the journal receives the money *and* keeps the information. The journal sells it for a fixed price every time others ask for it. That is a remarkable quality of information, and differentiates it from money and time. Sharing of information implies—especially now, with modern communication devices—that any person can emit limitless information without losing it. I imagine a world in which sending information is less free of obligation. Just as each new-born baby gets a nationality, he or she gets a share in an information bank. The amount increases with age up to their eighteenth birthday. The personal information budget increases or decreases with use. By sending out a message, the person loses a part of their personal information budget. Receiving information increases the budget. A person with information that affects other people has a good chance that others send information back, resulting in a larger budget.

These ideas about time, bits, and currency have to be worked out further, but the exercise brings comparison between the fundamental resources nearer. Application of the idea of fundamental resources opens avenues for hypotheses integrating distributive justice theories, procedural justice theories, and resource theory, as shown in Chapter 7, although hypotheses will be stated in terms of Foa and Foa's resource classes.

Time, currency, and bits are labeled fundamental resources because they cannot be split up further. In the now-prevailing view, the fundamental resources differ in some respects from each other. Actors possess currency and often currency is earned; time is not possessed, an actor has time, time can be earned; actors "have" bits of information, and when actors allocate information they do not lose information—actors, therefore, share information. When actors spread negative information about recipients their status is not affected, generally. Currency and time spent on a recipient is lost for the actor: when actors offer goods to a recipient, they do not possess the goods any longer. And when actors spend time on recipient, they cannot spend that time on themselves. Moreover, currency and bits can have a negative valence, but time does not. An actor can give recipient a fine, or steal goods from a recipient; an actor can show contempt for a recipient, which is negative information. Acts spent on a recipient in a certain time period can have a positive or negative valence: Helping is positive, while beating a recipient is a negative service.

From this analysis it can be concluded that, to some extent, resource classes characterize the type of relationship between actor and recipient, but also that resources are allocated through interaction between actor and recipient. If, in a love relationship, money is allocated, the act of giving or receiving money is not specific for a love relationship. It might even be concluded that the act of allocating money makes the love relationship—for a moment—a business-like relationship. The resource, in other words, determines the type of relationship between parties, or for how long the relationship lasts. And although the allocation of money determines the type of relationship, the intensity factor will probably differentiate a business-like allocation event in a love relationship from a business-like allocation event in a business relationship.

The fundamental resources differ in one important way: they differ from each other in scarcity. In general, for a busy person time is more scarce than for a retired person. Similarly, money is more scarce for a beggar than for a well-paid employee. People prefer to reciprocate resources which are evenly scarce, as explained in Chapter 7.

### *Resource Classes and Justice*

Resource classes are viewed as "categories of the *meaning* assigned to behaviors," and different behaviors may convey the same resource. It is important to know the cognitive and emotional processes when actors and/or recipients decide what kind of behaviors represent which resource class (Vermunt and Törnblom 2007). For instance, does hugging represent love, status, or service? To answer this question, individuals need knowledge of the context in which the hugging occurs. If the hugging takes place in a situation in which a man and a woman stand before a priest who asked them whether they want to become man and wife, the observer may be confident that the hugging is an expression of love. In a board meeting of a large company, hugging between members of the board becomes more ambiguous.

It may convey appreciation (status), affection (love), or helpfulness (service). In the boardroom, an observer needs more information about the meaning of the action of hugging than in the church. If the hugging person is a member and the other is the chairman, the hugging can be an expression of all three classes. When the two huggers are common members, hugging most likely represents affection.

The difference between the church event and the boardroom event is quite clear: both have different chains of appropriate behaviors. Observers have learned the difference between the two events. Maybe they have experience with both events or have read or heard about them, and have developed what is commonly labeled a script: the marriage script and the boardroom script. In a script, players each have their role and act according to behavioral rules. In a restaurant, for instance, there is a certain order of behavioral sequences. Seeking a table, asking for the menu, deciding about what to eat and drink, eating, asking for the bill, paying, and leaving—a simple script, in which client and personnel have their specific roles. The waiter leads the client to the table, asks what they wish to eat, brings the food, and so on.

Because parts of a script may not be well defined, room is left for interpretation. In the boardroom, members greet each other when they arrive. But how and whom they greet—partly—is up to each member's personal decisions.

An actor's deviation from the boardroom script has an impact on the recipient. A pattern of expectations has been broken, initiating a state of alertness in the recipient. If he or she concludes that the actor deliberately broke the script, the recipient may feel unfairly treated whether the behavior is subsumed under status, love, or service. If the discrepancy is experienced as undeserved, experience of injustice is imminent. The recipient perceives the discrepancy as an injustice related to status, or love, or service. An injustice that is based on lack of respect for the recipient is experienced as the most negative because it lowers the recipient's self-esteem. Lack of affection will be experienced as less unjust than lack of respect; lack of helpfulness will be experienced as unjust, but less so than with lack of affection. The reason is that, in the boardroom script, lack of respect is more central to the conception of the recipient's self than lack of helpfulness.

In fact, recipients view justice—as the above-mentioned example shows—as an indication of their own emotional state (e.g., do I feel resentment?). Further, recipients conceive of justice as an indication of their cognitive state (how much of this emotion do I have?). And finally, justice can be viewed as an indication of the recipient's position in relation to others/group/society (how far am I from the "good guys?"). The meaning the recipient attributes to an actor's specific behavior—is it interpreted as status, love, or service—is of great relevance for the experience of justice and the accompanying intrapersonal processes (emotional and cognitive processes).

*Justice as emotional state*

In justice research, affect and emotion have received considerable attention. One type of research focused on the emotional consequences of unfair treatment, while another type of research focused on emotion as precursor of evaluating the fairness of treatment (see Mullen 2007).

In equity research, Adams studied the effects of unfair payment on emotional, cognitive, and behavioral reactions (Adams 1965). Unfair treatment, for instance, in the form of underpayment, activates emotions like anger. It is assumed that the most effective reaction to unfairness, which also helps to reduce negative emotions, is to restore it. Restoration can be accomplished, for instance, by protesting against unfair payment or by reducing the amount of effort in subsequent production events, or even by destructive actions. Protesting and reducing may be tricky because of a high personal risk of being fired. If that is the case, the recipient can apply cognitive strategies to reduce anger. Reduction may be accomplished by cognitive reappraisal, for instance, through devaluating salary, or through re-evaluating the content of the job. Other researchers have shown that unfair treatment may result in feelings of resentment. Research on relative deprivation (Crosby 1976) has shown that when workers receive outcomes that are less than they desired, they experience anger and resentment. Folger and Martin (1986) showed that people experiencing unfair procedures in resource allocation also developed feelings of resentment. Moreover, when people are asked to describe their emotions in relation to times in the past when they were unfairly treated, the majority mentioned emotions like anger and resentment (Mikula 1986, 1987; Frijda et al. 1989).

Mullen (2007) states that not only do perceptions of fairness or unfairness lead to positive or negative emotions, but that emotions are probably more primary than fairness judgments. Mullen argues that emotions elicited while experiencing fair or unfair outcomes or treatment influence people's perceptions of fairness. I would like to go one step further, as I will show in Chapter 5, and state that experiencing an event as fair or unfair is instigated by emotions: the moral emotions. But I agree with Mullen that specific emotions influence perceptions of fairness. Van den Bos (2003), for instance, has convincingly shown that a positive as well as a negative affective state affects evaluation of subsequent received outcomes or procedure. Participants in a negative mood rated the outcome they received as less fair than participants in a positive mood. Thus, in sum, justice experiences are strongly related to emotions and form an indication how emotionally aroused a person is (see also Vermunt et al. 2001).

*Justice as cognitive state*

Much research has been done to pin down Adams' equity formula, culminating in the volume edited by Messick and Cook (1983) in which attempts are made to formulate equity more precisely in terms of a mathematical equation. These attempts partially succeeded. It made clear that a kind of cognitive algebra to predict the amount of injustice and distress experienced after receiving an unfair outcome resulted in ordinal data, and not in so-called ratio data. In other words, correlations were high between, on the one hand, discrepancy between expected outcome as compared to actually received outcomes and, on the other hand, feelings of injustice and of distress. But this relationship was not on a ratio scale: discrepancy was not a one-to-one relationship with feelings. A discrepancy that was twice as large did not result in feelings twice as strong. But as such, the high correlation between discrepancy and feelings of injustice was a very important finding that was replicated many times. It showed that recipients of resources (salary) seemingly first calculated the discrepancy between expected and actually received outcomes, which resulted in accompanying feelings of injustice. The "calculations," however, were rather imprecise, giving rise to other ideas about cognitive mastering of people's experiences after being exposed to allocation events. Moreover, researchers assumed that people often do not go into lengthy accounts of calculating discrepancies, partly because they have insufficient information about an allocation event or they are not motivated to do so. In these instances, they use shortcuts (heuristics) to arrive at evaluations of allocation events. Folger (1987) introduced the simulation heuristic in justice research. Instead of calculating the discrepancy between expected and received outcomes, people generate alternative outcomes with the information they have available and compare these alternative outcomes with the actual outcome in a more or less loose way. Van den Bos et al. (1997a) showed that information about the fairness evaluation of the outcome of an allocation event is used as a proxy for evaluating the fairness of the applied procedure, and vice versa. Lind (2001) developed fairness heuristic theory. The concept of a "fairness heuristic" is defined as "a psychological shortcut used to decide whether to accept or reject the directives of people in positions of authority" (Lind et al. 1993: 225). Fairness heuristics are formed quickly using whatever information is available (Van den Bos et al. 1997b). People confronted with the decisions of authorities have to decide whether they comply with the authorities, to obtain valued outcomes, or not, because of the risk of exploitation. Thus, fairness heuristic theory explicitly raises the question "How much of this characteristic do I have?" In other words, how much power do I have in relation to the authority? If a recipient has little power, exploitation is not far away, but if a recipient has some power to retaliate, the risk of being exploited is further away.

*Justice as group state*

Justice says "something about the nature of one's group and one's particular place in it" (Colquitt et al. 2005: 40). In the group-value model, Lind and Tyler (1988) assumed that personal gains or self-interest explain only part of the success of procedural fairness, as was postulated and tested by Thibaut and Walker (1975): Having a say after an actor had decided about allocation of resources drastically changed the recipient's justice evaluations of the outcome (Lind et al. 1990). The outcome was judged fairer when the recipient had a say after the decision than when the recipient received no opportunity to have a say. As Lind and Tyler explained, this effect cannot be attributed to the operation of the self-interest motive because voice was effectuated after the decision was made. There must have been something else that explained the result: the ability to express oneself is viewed as an indication of respect from the actor toward the recipient. And respect reflects, for the recipient, important values of group life. An actor's attitude towards a group member determines in large part how proud the recipient is in the group, whether he or she feels respected by group members, and identifies with the group.

The interesting question, whether justice experiences lead to better relationships with authorities or that better relations with authorities lead to experiencing justice in relation to others, continues to be an open question in the group-value model and its modern version: the relational model of authority. Combining fairness heuristic theory with the group-value model one can expect that fairness is relevant for the affirmation of important group values, like neutrality (in evaluating another's allocation behavior one should look at different sides of the issue), trust, and standing. Because these values are difficult to judge because of their complexity, fairness is a proxy yardstick for the presence of the values. In this instance, fairness is a shortcut for these values. But in a more specific sense in which a recipient continuously monitors allocation events in the group when the leader or another group member is allocating a resource, fairness evaluations are probably the first to arise. The valence of the evaluation is an indication of whether the recipient can trust the actor. In this explanation of the event, fairness judgments precede other characteristics of the relationship between actor and recipient. To adequately interpret the relationship between attitudes and fairness, it is important to view the entire allocation event in which the distribution, procedure, resources to allocate, actor, and recipient are all taken into account. Chapter 7 will go into this issue in detail.

In the allocation process in which an actor allocates a resource between self and other or between different others, justice satisfies several roles. For the actor, justice is the moral standard during the entire allocation event. Justice prescribes what kind of resource is allocated, to which recipients, and to what amounts: How much time will the actor spend on the recipient, as indications of Love and Service? How much money will the actor spend on the recipient, as indications of Money and Goods? How many bits of information will the actor offer to the recipient, as indications of Information and Status?

For recipients, justice is an indication of their emotional state, of their cognitive state, and of their group state. Let us take the example of a judge punishing a recipient for a misdemeanor. A punishment is the allocation of a negative service to the recipient. The justice evaluation and acceptance of the punishment is higher when the judge gives recipients the opportunity to give their views on the matter: the judge allocates status (shows respect) to the recipient. The judge as actor is guided by legal rules used in the courtroom session, but also by moral principles to do justice to the recipient. Experience of the judge's fair behavior affects the recipient's perception of the neutrality of the judge, trust in the judge, and regard for the judge, and thus of the recipient's position in society.

## The Further Content of the Book

The justice model, as described here, consists of four components: the justice motive component, the morality component, the psychology component, and the injustice reaction component. The *justice motive* component describes how the justice motive is related to egoism and altruism; the *morality* component of the justice model describes and explains how justice and morality are interrelated to make a just society; the *psychology* component of the model describes and explains how an actor's psychological make-up ameliorates or deteriorates the operation of the justice motive. Finally, the *injustice reaction* component describes how, when, and to what extent people react to unjust behavior.

The justice model applies social resource theory to link the components of the social justice model; that is, that human behavior can be characterized as chains of resource allocations in which an actor divides material or immaterial resources between (among) recipients, resulting in an allocated resource or distribution (distributive justice), using procedures (procedural justice, interactional justice).

In this book, the focus is on the *actor* as provider and allocator of resources, and to a lesser extent (see, however, chapters 7 and 8) on the recipient.

The four components find their counterparts in the four parts into which the book is divided: Part I, justice motivation: about human allocation motives and justice; Part II, morality: about people's allocation of status and respect; Part III, mental states, about actors' emotions, cognitions, and social relationships in shaping (un)just allocation decisions; Part IV, reactions: about recipients' reactions to (in)justice.

An Epilogue summarizes and comments on the proposed justice model, and opens avenues for further research.

*Part I The Justice Motive*

*Chapter 1 Origins of the justice motive: Between egoism and altruism*
This chapter is concerned with one of the most intriguing resources to allocate: food. Not only because food allocation can be studied in all people, but also in the distant past and in animals as well. By comparing food allocation behavior past and present, in different peoples and in primates and humans, much can be unraveled about the relationship between the three motives: egoism, justice, and altruism. It is stated that the justice motive is typically human and its development is strongly related to the transition from hominin[1] to *Homo*. Using the allocation behavior of primates and hunter-gatherer groups as proxies for, respectively, pre-hominin and hominin groups, some evidence has been found for the transition hypothesis.

1 Here I use the term hominin and not hominid.

*Chapter 2 Climate change, social change, and the justice motive*
This chapter describes the period when hunter-gatherers became farmers and settled themselves in groups and villages. Allocation of material resources became more salient to differentiate oneself from the still-existing hunter-gatherers, but also from other groups of farmers and other village dwellers. People developed new allocation rules to protect private property and to exchange new types of goods, and laws on how and how much to punish perpetrators and how to divide goods and property among family members. Hunter-gatherers and farmers form a social figuration in which farmers as newcomers challenged the way of existence of the settled: the hunter-gatherers. The waxing and waning of social figurations (the virulence of social figurations) indicate changes with regard to culture, structure of social groups and of society, and of personality. Looking more carefully at relatively sudden breaks in the relationships between social groups shows the impact of climate change and technological innovations.

*Part II Morality and Justice*

*Chapter 3 Resource allocation, justice, and morality*
This chapter defines morality as equal allocation of the immaterial resource respect (status) between self and other. Justice is defined as equal allocation of all other resources between self and other, and among others. Several forms of anxiety thwart equal allocation of respect between self and other. Unequal respect allocation is only acceptable (permissible) if all involved in the allocation process (actor, recipient, and observer) accept the justifications with love and respect. Some ideas to generate an encompassing theoretical system of moral behavior are brought forward.

*Chapter 4 Resource allocation and justice in society*
Starting from Rawls' theory of justice, in this chapter his idea about the veil of ignorance resulting in equal allocation of civil liberties and material goods is challenged. It is asserted that the veil robs the subject of the most essential characteristics of being human, resulting in basic anxiety leading to extreme instead of moderate judgments of distribution of resources. The "waiting room" metaphor attempts to find other forms of social arrangement to allocate resources justly. Equality and (small) justified inequality—not only of material resources but also of immaterial ones—lead to a just society. The mathematical tools I use here are simple and should be followed by more precise tools: linear models as well as non-linear.

*Part III Justice-Related Mental States*

*Chapter 5 The psychology of just resource allocation.*
*Part I: Emotions and cognitions*
As stated previously, this book focuses on the actor's just allocation behavior. It is postulated that all individuals have an urge to allocate resources fairly. This urge is modulated by fear, and by egoism as well as altruism. Positive and negative self-preservation emotions often struggle with positive and negative moral emotions resulting in (un)fair behavior. Neurophysiological correlates of the struggle are discussed and physiological assessments can be used to detect this struggle.

*Chapter 6 The psychology of just resource allocation.*
*Part II: Relationships*
This chapter describes the relationship between actor and recipient as crucial for the course and direction of the allocation process. To put it simply, resource allocation when actor and recipient are of the same group runs rather smoothly: the more the recipient contributes, the more the actor will reward the recipient. In the case where the actor and recipient are of different groups, threat is imminent and allocation does not run smoothly but is characterized by abrupt changes: the catastrophe. Knowledge of these abrupt changes is essential for understanding allocation processes and how justice works.

*Part IV: Reactions to Unfair Decisions*

*Chapter 7 Reactions to unfair allocation behavior.*
*Part I Role of recipient and observer*
Unfairness and frustration are experienced when recipient perceives a discrepancy between actual received resource and expected resource. Discrepancies are the driver for alertness, and set into motion the self-preservation and moral emotions required to face adequately the threat triggered by the discrepancy experience. Recipients' reactions are physiological, psychological, and behavioral. Several reactions to restore justice or reduce frustration are applied, such as attempts to get compensation and justification, as well as self-directed attempts to (re)appreciate and mitigate components of the allocation event. Mild and severe forms of retaliation can be expected when the former reactions do not restore justice sufficiently. Observers of an allocation event experience discrepancy between the expected and received resources for the recipient as well, and they sometimes react with the offended recipient.

*Chapter 8 Reactions to unfair allocation behavior.*
*Part II: Actor's role*
This chapter describes how experience of discrepancy leading to feelings of injustice and frustration causes stress, often resulting in chronic stress. The prevalence of stress among workers is high. According to the Injustice Stress

model (Vermunt and Steensma 2005), injustices in the allocated resource (focal resource) or procedure (additional resource) cause stress. Actors have a strong influence on the onset of a recipient's stress process and, therefore, play a crucial role in reducing or even preventing stress. A crucial condition is the actor's identification of the recipient's stress via facial expression, bodily posture, speech, but also writings.

*Epilogue*
This summarizes the most important features of the justice model, evaluating them and speculating about future directions of both theory and research in the justice area.

## References


Adams, J.S. 1965. Inequity in Social Exchange, in *Advances in Experimental Social Psychology*, edited by L. Berkowitz. New York: Academic Press, 267–99.

Batson, C.D. 1991. *The Altruism Question. Toward a Social-Psychological Answer*. New York: Lawrence Erlbaum Associates.

Bies, R.J., and Moag, J.F. 1986. Interactional Justice: Communication Criteria of Fairness, in *Research on Negotiations in Organizations*, edited by R.J. Lewicki, B.H. Sheppard, and M.H. Bazerman. Greenwich, CT: JAI Press, 43–55.

Colquitt, J.A., Greenberg, J., and Zapata-Phelan, C.P. 2005. What is Organizational Justice? A Historical Overview, in *Handbook of Organizational Justice*, edited by J.A. Colquitt, and J. Greenberg. Mahwah, NJ: LEA, 3–58.

Crosby, F. 1976. A model of egoistical relative deprivation. *Psychological Review*, 83, 85–113.

De Dreu, C. 1998. Gain-loss-frame in outcome-interdependence: Does it influence equality or equity considerations. *European Journal of Social Psychology*, 26(2), 315–26.

Elster, J. 2006. Altruistic Behavior and Altruistic Motivations, in *Handbook of the Economics of Giving, Altruism, and Reciprocity*, edited by S.-Ch. Kolm and J. Mercier Ythier. Amsterdam: Elsevier, 183–206.

Foa, U.G., and Foa, E.B. 1974. *Societal Structures of the Mind*. Springfield, IL: Charles C. Thomas Publisher.

Folger, R. 1987. Reformulating the Preconditions of Resentment: A Referent Cognitions Model, in *Social Comparison, Justice, and Relative Deprivation: Theoretical, Empirical, and Policy Perspectives*, edited by J.C. Masters, and W.P. Smith. Hillsdale, NJ: LEA, 183–215.

Folger, R., and Martin, C. 1986. Relative deprivation and referent cognitions: Distributive and procedural justice effects. *Journal of Experimental Social Psychology*, 22, 531–46.

Folger, R. 2001. Fairness as Deonance, in *Research in Social Issues in Management*, edited by S.W. Gilliland, D.D. Steiner, and D.P. Skarlicki. Charlotte, NC: Information Age Publishing, 3–31.

Folger, R., Cropanzano, R., and Goldman, B. 2005. What Is the Relationship between Justice and Morality? in *Handbook of Organizational Justice*, edited by J. Greenberg and J.A. Colquitt. Mahwah, NJ: Lawrence Erlbaum Associates, 215–46.

Frijda, N., Kuipers, P., and Ter Schure, E. 1989. Relations among emotion, appraisal, and emotional action readiness. *Journal of Personality and Social Psychology*, 57, 212–28.

Greenberg, J. 1987. A taxonomy of organizational justice theories. *Academy of Management Review*, 12, 9–22.

Haidt, J. 2003. Elevation and the Positive Psychology of Morality, in *Flourishing: Positive Psychology and the Life Well-Lived*, edited by C.L. Keyes, and J. Haidt. Washington, DC: Am. Psychol. Assoc., 275–89.

Haidt, J., and Graham, J. 2007. When morality opposes justice: Conservatives have moral intuitions that Liberals may not recognize. *Social Justice Research*, 20, 1, 98–116.

Haidt, J., and Joseph, C. 2007. The Moral Mind: How Five Sets of Innate Intuitions Guide the Development of Many Culture-Specific Virtues, and Perhaps Even Modules, in *The Innate Mind*, edited by P. Carruthers, S. Lawrence, and S. Stich. Oxford, UK: Oxford University Press, 367–92.

Hakstian, A.R., and Cattell, R.B. 1976. *Manual of the Cognitive Abilities Battery (CAB)*. Champaign, IL: The Institute for Personality and Ability Testing.

Harinck, F., Van Dijk, E., Van Beest, I., and Mersman, P. 2007. When gains loom larger than losses: Reversed loss aversion for small amounts of money. *Psychological Science*, 18(12), 1099–105.

Jasso, G. 1978. On the justice of earnings: A new specification of the justice evaluation function. *American Journal of Sociology*, 83, 1398–419.

Kohlberg, L. 1981. *Essays on Moral Development, Vol. I: The Philosophy of Moral Development*. San Francisco, CA: Harper and Row.

Kolm, S.-Ch. 2006. Introduction to the Economics of Giving, Altruism and Reciprocity, in *Handbook of the Economics of Giving, Altruism, and Reciprocity*, edited by S.-Ch. Kolm and J. Mercier Ythier. Amsterdam: Elsevier, 1–122.

Lerner, M.J. 1977. The justice motive in social behavior: Some hypotheses as to its origins and forms. *Journal of Personality*, 45, 1–52.

Lerner, M.J. 1980. *The Belief in a Just World: A Fundamental Delusion*. New York: Springer.

Leventhal, G.S. 1980. What Should Be Done with Equity Theory? New Approaches to the Study of Fairness in Social Relationship, in *Social Exchange: Advances in Theory and Research*, edited by K. Gergen, M. Greenberg., and R. Willis. New York: Plenum Press, 27–55.

Lind, E.A. 2001. Fairness Heuristic Theory: Justice Judgments as Pivotal Cognitions in Organizational Relations, in *Advances in Organizational Justice*, edited by J. Greenberg and R. Cropanzano. Redwood City, CA: Stanford University Press, 56–88.

Lind, E.A., and Tyler, T.R. 1988. *The Social Psychology of Procedural Justice*. New York: Plenum.

Lind, E.A., Kanfer, R., and Earley, P.C. 1990. Voice, control, and procedural justice: Instrumental and noninstrumental concerns in fairness judgments. *Journal of Personality and Social Psychology*, 59, 952–9.

Lind, E.A., Kulik, C.T., Ambrose, M., and de Vera Park, M.V. 1993. Individual and corporate dispute resolution: Using procedural fairness as a decision heuristic. *Administrative Science Quarterly*, 38, 224–51.

Messick, D.M., and Cook, K.S. 1983. *Equity Theory: Psychological and Sociological Perpectives*. New York: Praeger Publishing.

Mikula, G. 1986. The Experience of Injustice: Toward a Better Understanding of its Phenomenology, in *Justice in Social Relations*, edited by H.W. Bierhoff, R.I. Cohen, and J. Greenberg. New York: Plenum, 103–23.

Mikula, G. 1987. Exploring the Experience of Injustice, in *Issues in Contemporary German Social Psychology*, edited by G.R. Semin, and B. Krahe. London: Sage, 74–96.

Modde, J., and Vermunt, R. 2007. The Effects of Procedural Unfairness on Norm-Violating Behavior, in *Distributive and Procedural Fairness: Research and Social Applications*, edited by K. Törnblom, and R. Vermunt. Hampshire: Ashgate Publishing Limited, 111–24.

Mullen, E. 2007. The Reciprocal Relationship between Affect and Perceptions of Fairness, in *Distributive and Procedural Fairness: Research and Social Applications*, edited by K. Törnblom, and R. Vermunt. Hampshire: Ashgate Publishing Limited, 15–37.

Rawls, J. 1971. *A Theory of Justice*. London: Oxford University Press.

Schokkaert, E. 2006. The Empirical Analysis of Transfer Motives, in *Handbook of the Economics of Giving, Altruism, and Reciprocity*, edited by S.-Ch. Kolm and J. Mercier Ythier. Amsterdam: Elsevier, 127–81.

Skitka, L.J., and Houston, D. 2001. When due process is of no consequence. Moral mandates and presumed defendant guilt or innocence. *Social Justice Research*, 14, 305–26.

Tangney, J.P., Stuewigg, J., and Mashek, D.J. 2007. Moral emotions and moral behavior. *Annual Review of Psychology*, 58, 345–72.

Thibaut, J., and Walker, L. 1975. *Procedural Justice: A Psychological Analysis*. Hillsdale, NJ: LEA.

Törnblom, K., and Vermunt, R. 2007. Towards integrating distributive justice, procedural justice, and social resource theories. *Social Justice Research*, 20, 222–35.

Törnblom, K., and Vermunt, R. 2012. Towards integrating distributive justice, procedural justice, and social resource theories, in *Handbook of Social Resource Theory*, edited by K. Törnblom, and A. Kazemi. New York: Springer, 181–205.

Turillo, C.J., Folger, R., Lavelle, J.J., Umphress, E.E., and Gee, J.O. 2002. Is virtue its own reward? Self-sacrificial decisions for the sake of fairness. *Organizational Behavior and Human Decision Processes*, 89, 839–65.

Tyler, T.R., and Lind E.A. 1992. A Relational Model of Authority in Groups, in *Advances in Experimental Social Psychology*, edited by M.P. Zanna. San Diego, CA: Academic Press, 115–91.

Urry, J. 1973. *Reference Groups and the Theory of Revolution*. London: Routledge and Kegan Paul.

Van den Bos, K. 2003. On the subjective quality of social justice: The role of affect as information in the psychology of justice judgments. *Journal of Personality and Social Psychology*, 85, 482–98.

Van den Bos, K., Lind, A., Vermunt, R., and Wilke, H. 1997a. "How do I judge my outcome when I don't know the outcome of others?": The psychology of the fair process effect. *Journal of Personality and Social Psychology*, 5, 1034–46.

Van den Bos, K., Vermunt, R., and Wilke, H. 1997b. Procedural and distributive justice: What is fair depends more on what comes first than on what comes next. *Journal of Personality and Social Psychology*, 72, 95–104.

Van Dijk, E., and Vermunt, R. 2000. Sometimes it pays to be powerless: Strategy and fairness in social decision making. *Journal of Experimental Social Psychology*, 36, 1–25.

Vermunt, R. 2002. The Justice Motive in Perspective, in *The Justice Motive in Social Life: Essays in honor of Melvin Lerner*, edited by M. Ross and D. Miller. New York: Cambridge University Press, 63–78.

Vermunt, R., and Steensma, H. 2005. How can justice be used to reduce stress in organizations, in *Handbook of Organizational Justice*, edited by J. Greenberg and J. Colquitt. Mawah, NJ: LEA, 383–410.

Vermunt, R., and Törnblom, K. 2007. Distributive and Procedural Justice: Introduction, in *Distributive and Procedural Justice. Research and Social Applications*, edited by K. Törnblom and R. Vermunt. Hampshire: Ashgate Publishing Company.

Vermunt, R., Van Knippenberg, D., Van Knippenberg, B., and Blaauw, E. 2001. Self-esteem and outcome fairness judgments: Differential use of procedural and outcome information. *Journal of Applied Psychology*, 86(4), 612–18.

# PART I
# The Justice Motive

# Chapter 1
# Origins of the Justice Motive: Between Egoism and Altruism

## Introduction

In everyday life, one can often observe people helping others. Parents help their children to grow up, and children help their parents when they grow old. Brothers and sisters support each other when necessary. Are these behaviors manifestations of altruism? It is claimed by many that helping behavior between close relatives has nothing to do with altruistic motivation but is the result of age-old genetic processes in which the survival of one's own genes has formed an innate urge to help relatives. Dawkins (1976), in this respect, assumes the operation of the "selfish gene" for which human beings only seem to be carriers, and which drives human beings to behave in such a way as to increase the chances of the gene's survival; one of those behaviors is to help one's offspring or close relatives. Economists, in addition, argue that all human behavior is directed to increasing pleasure and reducing pain. Helping close relatives is not seen as an act of altruism but as an act of self-interest: the more I help my children, the more likely it is that they will help me.

Other observations and interpretations of human behavior, however, run counter to such an egoistic or self-interested explanation of behavior. It is often observed that, during a disaster, bystanders will rescue victims even at the cost of their own health or of their own life. And not only family members engage in these behaviors—people who are complete strangers to those in need help them to get out of the dangerous situation. One can think of members of the fire brigade, rescuing people who are trapped in a fire, or a bystander who rescues a drowning person. Less dramatic are the gifts people offer to improve the living circumstances of the poor. People they have never met and will not meet in the future. Of course, it is easy to bring these behaviors under the umbrella of egoistic behavior by emphasizing the positive effects of such actions for one's own mood or conscience. But many of these decisions to help occur in a split second, apparently without any deliberation. It is an act that immediately springs to mind, and people sometimes have decided before they realize what they have done, but feel afterwards that it was well done.

Can we disregard the altruism-like behaviors and interpret them as instigated only from an egoistic motivation? That is too simple and does not do justice to the many observations of helping behavior. That is why human beings have developed a series of gestures and facial expressions that express orientation to others, consideration with others, and support of others. Human beings have the ability to empathize with others, and to understand the situations in which others find themselves. Every human being has that ability, to a greater or lesser degree; the animals who are the close relatives of the human species, the primates, also have this capacity, as illustrated by de Waal's well-known observation of a young gorilla who tries to comfort a male after he has lost the fight for the first position in the group. The comforting gesture of the young gorilla presupposes the youngster's ability to recognize the sad state of the adult gorilla from posture and facial expression. And it presupposes a motivation to somehow relieve the other's loss, as well as the youngster's ability to carry out the appropriate behavior.

The antithesis between egoistic motives and altruistic motives for behavior has divided scholars around the world and in all periods of history. Some scholars are fervent proponents of egoistic motives while others are fervent proponents of altruistic motives in explaining behavior. In reading articles and chapters about egoism and altruism from authors of different disciplines, one gets the impression that the antithesis is based on ideology. This is highly visible in the scholars' interpretations of the results of their own empirical research, or in comments on the research carried out by opponents—some examples of this bias will be shown later in this chapter. One important reason for the ideological antithesis is the dichotomous character of egoism and altruism. Altruism and egoism are viewed as two mutually exclusive opposing entities. If a motive is qualified as egoistic then it is not altruistic, and vice versa.

But how egoistic and how altruistic are behaviors? Might it not be that some behaviors are less egoistically driven than other behaviors but are still not altruistic, and vice versa? If people steal money to feed their children, is that less egoistic than stealing money to buy more goods for themselves? In other words, can we not better define the motive underlying exchange behaviors as a dimensional entity ranging from more egoistic to more altruistic, instead of categorizing them as a dichotomy of motives, egoistic or altruistic, as explained in the Prologue? If one agrees with this idea, one consequence is that motives situated at the extreme positions of the scale can be designated as "pure" egoism or "pure" altruism. Motives at less extreme positions of the scale have egoistic as well as altruistic elements in them. But if we accept this idea, there is a large range of behaviors whose motivations fall in between the two extremes of egoistic and altruistic. And, as described in the previous chapter, the mix of altruistic and egoistic behaviors can be related to what is commonly labeled justice-motivated behaviors.

Egoism and altruism are assumed to motivate behavior in situations of resource allocation. A large part of our daily activities concerns the allocation of goods, such as distribution of food, or services, like repair works. And as historical facts show, allocation of resources has been part and parcel of human activities for a long time. How did these resource allocations develop? What role did egoistic and altruistic motives play in these allocations?

Researchers from different disciplines have tried to find answers to these questions: paleontologists, archeologists and anthropologists, ethologists, sociologists, psychologists, philosophers, and economists have all studied allocation processes to find out how humans, and other species, allocate resources. Since allocation processes are found everywhere and in all phases of life for different species, knowing more about these processes gives us knowledge about the nature of subsistence for different species and about relations between members of these species. And in the case of some species, like humans, allocation processes tell us a lot about how relations are organized between members. For instance, knowing to whom members allocate resources tells us a lot about liking relationships, but also about dominance relationships. Trade measures by developed countries to protect their own industry tell us something about how they judge the dependent position of underdeveloped countries.

If we would like to know more about our present life, knowledge about how our ancestors lived is of crucial significance. Past allocation processes may tell us how we developed as human beings in terms of personality, relationships, culture, and society. However, it is not so easy to investigate allocation processes in the earliest times because hardly any traces of them are left. Moreover, primitive hunting groups had a restricted quantity of artifacts to allocate—for instance, some precious stones. And their remains and their distribution patterns have not, as yet, been related to allocation behaviors. There is one exception: food. Traces of food allocation and food consumption can be found in many places in the world, and in several periods of history. As far back as the Pleistocene period of about two million years ago, traces of food allocation can be found. Moreover, because food is a resource that is used by all species, the study of food allocation processes need not be restricted to the human species. For instance, biologists and ethologists have investigated food allocation practice in primates and other animals.

Specifically, biologists and ethologists were and are interested in *non-kin* food-sharing practice because non-kin food sharing intuitively goes counter to the survival-of-the-fittest goals of animal behavior. Food sharing is regarded by many biologists and ethologists (Hockings et al. 2007; Stevens and Gilby 2004) as a paradox: the recipient gains fitness benefits from the donor. Non-kin food sharing, therefore, became the focus of research activities to find out more about the underlying motives.

This chapter will review studies on primate and hunter-gatherer food-sharing practices to find out how these practices have developed and are related to each other. Primate food-sharing practice is conceived of as a proxy for the food-sharing practice of pre-hominin groups. These groups lived more than two million years ago in the eastern part of Africa: the Great Rift Valley. The food-sharing practices of still-existing hunter-gatherer groups are conceived of as a proxy for the hunting groups that lived from less than two million years ago until now. In the transition period between the Pliocene and Pleistocene eras, between about five and two million years ago, dramatic climate changes took place that greatly affected the lives of hominin groups. They triggered the onset of bi-pedalism, an increase in brain capacity, and the structural use of artifacts. It will be shown that these changes had an impact on food-sharing practice and on the underlying motives as well.

Scientists have studied exchange behavior by focusing on food-sharing practice in primates and (proto-human hominin) hunting groups. Biologists and ethologists like de Waal (1996), investigated primate behavior to unravel food-sharing behaviors in higher animals. They used observational studies and experimental set-ups to study animal food-sharing motives. Food-sharing practice could be traced in paleo-archeological sites in Eastern Africa (2–3 million years ago), as well as, for instance, at the Magdalenian settlement site at Pincevent, France (about 20,000 years ago). At these sites, fossil bones of captured animals and artifacts (tools) were excavated and inferences were made about food-sharing behavior based on the distribution pattern of the discarded artifacts and fossil bones. Food-sharing practice is also studied in existing hunting groups like the Ache in Paraguay and the Hadza in Tanzania. Some studies compared paleo-archeological findings with observations of still-existing hunting groups. Other studies used game-theoretical models to find out how and why people share food with other members of the group. In general, the main conclusion from the analysis of all these studies is that allocation behavior became more complex and could better be explained in terms of justice: from animal behavior to more complex (proto-)human behavior.

## Primate Food-sharing

### *Getting Meat and Fruit*

Goodall (1986) observed in the 1960s that of the great apes (the gorilla, the orangutan, bonobo, and chimpanzee), only chimpanzees eat meat on a more or less regular basis. Chimpanzees hunt, sometimes alone, sometimes in groups, and eat meat more frequently under certain conditions. For instance, when there are female chimpanzees with sexual swellings, and in the dry season, although Gilby et al. (2008) found no evidence for these associations. It was assumed (Stanford 1995) that hunting and eating meat were nutritionally based. Eating meat provides chimpanzees with important micronutrients that are difficult to obtain solely from fruit. It was hypothesized that the more chimpanzees engage in hunting the more prey can be killed, resulting in higher protein consumption. However, a correlation between group size and the nutritional benefits could not be found.

The motivation to join a hunting group of chimpanzees must be strong because hunting costs time and energy, and is risky, thus should result in more food per capita. Although the nutritional benefits of hunting are still an important reason for joining hunting groups, there are clearly other motives as well. One assumption is that joining the group is rewarding in itself, maybe irrespective of the type of activity the group is engaged in. Chimpanzees like to join hunting groups to improve their status position in the group. Recent studies (Gilby et al. 2008) show that hunting is initiated by particular key hunters of the group, and that hunting is rarely done without these key hunters. Although hunting is a group process, these individuals have a large say in when the group starts to hunt. It turns out that these individual chimpanzees show a willingness to hunt and that they are successful in hunting. Meat is frequently shared in hunting chimpanzee communities to nurture alliances and social bonds.

If meat and fruit are so important for chimpanzees, do they share these types of food in the same way? Primates' diet consists for about 95 percent of wild plant foods (the majority from fruit), about 1.5 percent meat, and the rest is insects (Goodall 1986). The sharing of wild plant food is infrequent in chimpanzees (Hockings et al. 2007). Hockings, however, observed that wild chimpanzees shared plants cultivated by humans for human consumption as a means to acquire sex and other commodities. It was assumed that the human-dominated environment offered chimpanzees new challenges, such as crop-raiding. Because crop-raiding is risky, the resulting food is of high value and can be exchanged for other commodities.

### *Food-sharing Motives*

Stevens and Stephen (2002) experimented with other ideas about food-sharing motives. They assumed that sharing food diminishes the costs of defending food against the possible harassment of a beggar. Beggars will engage in costly harassment acts if they can equal the costs of harassment with benefits, such as morsels of food. They tested related and unrelated female chimpanzees and squirrel monkeys in pairs. Half of the primate pairs were tested in adjacent cages with a partition, the other half without a partition—that is, with a hole through which the primates could physically contact each other. One of the primates got food (owner), while the other received none (beggar). Each primate played both roles. The duration and frequency of harassment and sharing were counted for each pair. The results showed, among other things, that when the partition was absent, and thus the benefits of harassment were available, more harassment and more sharing occurred (though not for squirrel monkeys). The authors concluded that selfish acts—avoid costly defense of food—cannot be ruled out as an explanation for food sharing. In a study by Koyama and Dunbar (1996), chimpanzees groomed nearby mates before feeding in order to create an opportunity for tolerated theft to take place.

Stevens and Gilby (2004) developed several hypotheses for food sharing that point in the direction of increased self-interest. Evidence that may support these hypotheses, however, is difficult to get, such as in the case of trading, in which food is exchanged for something less tangible like an increase in status. As Stevens and Gilby state, it is difficult to separate explanations that assume altruism from explanations that assume egoism. There are always other factors that may explain food sharing. De Waal and Luttrell (1986) found evidence of reciprocity in food sharing, but according to Stevens and Gilby sharing could be a by-product of symmetrical attraction: Both animals like each other and share food without accounting what one gives to other or vice versa.

What do these findings of food sharing tell us about the motives for food sharing in animals? Stevens and Gilby (2004) assumed that selfishness lies at the core of food sharing and that this motive can best explain the results of the many studies on animal food sharing. This conclusion does not rule out the possibility that animals under specific conditions share food altruistically, but the common underlying motivation for food-sharing seems to be self-interest.

*Explanations for Non-kin Food Sharing*

Because sharing food with others diminishes one's own fitness while improving the fitness of the recipient, simple survival explanations cannot explain this generous type of behavior. Therefore, several explanations have been proposed for non-kin food sharing in animal groups, some of which have already been discussed: *reciprocal altruism*, stating that food at one point in time is exchanged for food at some later point in time (food now for food later: Kaplan and Gurven 2005; see also Marlowe 2004, Hauser et al. 2003); *cooperative acquisition* or *foraging efficiency*, in which food is exchanged for labor in coordinated efforts to hunt large prey (food for foraging partners); *tolerated theft* or *tolerated scrounging* or *harassment*, which states that the donor is robbed of part of the hunted prey but accepts it because the hunter wants to avoid a fight which he may lose (food for peace); *costly signaling*, in which sharing food is seen as a sign of the donor's good phenotypic qualities (food for non-food benefits); *nepotism*, which is a means to favor one's own kin, and is, in fact, a kin behavior explanation (food for kin); *trait-group selection*, which states that costly food sharing may favor the in-group since the intra-group fitness of altruist groups is higher than the fitness of a group of egoists. The *predation avoidance* explanation states that food is shared to reduce the predation risk: with more members, the risks of being harassed by predators are lower. *Mate provision* explains food sharing by assuming that it gains fitness benefits. The *trade* hypothesis combines food sharing with reciprocation in a resource other than food, for instance, grooming (see Stevens and Gilby 2004).

It seems plausible to assume that some of the above-mentioned explanations contain more egoistic-like elements than altruistic-like elements, such as predation avoidance, while others contain more altruistic-like elements than egoistic-like ones, such as trait-group selection and altruistic reciprocity. Predation avoidance primarily serves self-interest: no risk of being killed by prey. But it might serve altruism as well: the survival of a member of the (kin) group increases the chances of the survival of the (kin) group as a whole. Altruistic reciprocity may be motivated primarily by altruism, but might also serve self-interest: the donor gets something in return later. As de Waal (2000) and others have shown, altruistic reciprocity may be the underlying motive for food-sharing practices. De Waal used captive capuchins to show that if capuchin A shared frequently with capuchin B in one particular trial, then B tended to share frequently with A in the next trial. According to De Waal, this attitudinal reciprocity does not require strict contingency between given and received services and therefore proves less cognitively demanding (de Waal 2000: 260). But what the experiment proves is the operation of some sort of empathy that many animals possess, to a greater or lesser degree. Many studies have shown that some animals show compassion with other animals (see, e.g., De Waal 1996). De Waal describes a female elephant that regularly went back to the place where one of the members of the elephant herd died. Compassion, or the capacity to empathize with others, is viewed as a sufficient condition for altruistic behavior. In other words, every time people are altruistic, compassion is present as well. But compassion or empathy is not a necessary condition for altruism. Every time compassion is shown, altruistic sharing will not always follow: out of compassion, people may punish others. Sharing food but also sorrow for and grievances with others can only fully be understood if one assumes that animals and men are able to see and feel the needs and desires of others. But seeing the needs and desires of others will not always result in altruistic behavior toward those others. In many situations, donors see the needs and the desires of others and have compassion for them, but their sharing is not the same for all others to the same degree.

Reciprocity may also be explained as a type of imitation in which one capuchin imitates the other. Or it can be viewed as an example of imitation of human behavior: captive animals are fed and they need not to do anything for it—this behavior of human food allocation may be copied by animals. Whatever it is, it is difficult to prove that reciprocity and cooperation—altruistically motivated—are an inherent part of primate behavior.

Stevens and Gilby conclude from their review of animal studies that altruistic explanations of food sharing "probably do not account for cooperative behavior in most nonhuman animals" (Stevens and Gilby 2004: 609). Reciprocity is limited by the timing of benefits, because discounting can devalue reciprocated acts. Moreover, other alternative explanations for reciprocity cannot be ruled out, such as mutuality sharing based on time spent with the other. Stevens and Gilby conclude that "[n]o studies have convincingly documented calculated reciprocity" (Stevens and Gilby 2004: 607). I conclude from these studies that animal food sharing is primarily egoistically motivated, with incidental altruistic outliers. Own-need fulfillment in non-kin food sharing is most important, and one cannot speak of a balanced food-sharing practice in which own and others' needs are not taken into account.

Primate brain capacity is probably not sufficiently complex to make allocation decisions in which others' needs as well as own needs are both taken into consideration. Dramatic climate changes urged species to adapt and find new ways to cope with new situations. These adaptations contributed to the development of more complex cognition and a trend to more complex allocation patterns.

## Environmental Conditions and Food Sharing

The inter-tropical convergence zone compressed, so that East Africa at the beginning of the Pleistocene era (about 2–3 million years ago) became locally sensitive to rapid shifts from wet to dry conditions. Estimates have been made that lakes dried out over a period of about 500 years. These periods of extreme climate variability may have provided a catalyst for evolutionary change (Trauth et al. 2007; deMenocal 2011). Food became more difficult to find where before it was there in abundance. Moreover, woodland was replaced by grassland, resulting in migration (Kingston et al. 2007). Forced climate variations had significant effects on biota that may cumulatively have driven speciation and extinction. Speciation is the formation of new species having separate gene pools compared to the old species. Genetic types originate in mutations in DNA: random changes in the sequences of connected strings of the proteins adenine (A), cytosine (C), guanine (G), and thymine (T) that form the double helix. It is estimated that each string or nucleotide has one chance in a billion of mutating to another nucleotide (Orr 2009). It is also suggested that "jumping genes" account for changes in the human genetic make-up (Gage and Muotri 2012). Most mutations are harmful for individual fitness, that is, they reduce fitness. Only a very small minority of the mutations prove to be beneficial and increase fitness. In each generation, mutation brings new genetic variants into populations. Natural selection then screens them to remove unfit variants and favor fit variants. The presence of grassland as well as the deterioration and change of forest in East Africa led to changes in the biota, forcing species to adapt or to become extinct. The common forebear of the *Homo* genus—*Australopithecus afarensis* (*Aa*; but see Wong 2012)—was challenged by these climatic and ecological changes. How *Aa* adapted is hard to say, because fossil findings are scarce. It is certain that some groups of *Aa* developed as *Homo ergaster* and other *Homo* strands.

To better understand the onset of allocation behavior we ought, in fact, to know more about the habits and behavior of the *Aa* and the transformation to the *Homo* genus (Wong 2009), but we have hardly any information about them. The best approximation of the habits and behavior of early *Aa*, however, are the primates as we study them to day. We view, as a thought experiment, primate food-sharing practice as examples of the behavior of early *Aa*. The food-sharing practice of today's primates is not, of course, similar to those of early *Aa*, and we must be cautious in making inferences. Moreover, in line with hominin research, *Aa* left no traces of their ways of subsistence. In our thought experiment, *Aa* (primate) food sharing is transformed to the *Homo* food sharing known through studies of paleo-archeological sites. And knowledge about *Homo* food-sharing practice is complemented with knowledge of food sharing in still-existing hunter-gatherer groups. Enloe (2003) presents evidence that spatial patterning of fossil bones and artifacts, complemented by carcass refitting, are appropriate and feasible methods for investigating food sharing on (paleo)archeological sites.

The traditional savannah hypothesis assumes that grassland replaced forest, and that some groups of *Aa* had to adapt to treeless expanses. Premo (2005) assumes that the ecological shift showed itself as fragmentation of closed habitat rather than as expansion of open habitat. Indirect evidence for the patched habitat hypothesis is found in *Aa* remains in a variety of paleo-habitats like swamps, woodlands, and gallery forests. Moreover, morphological characteristics of *Australipithecus afarensis* (4.2–2.9 million years ago), such as long curved phalanges and a relatively large humero-femoral index, serve as skeletal evidence that *Aa* were still adapted to life in and around trees. The length of the femur is conceived of as an important difference between life in trees and walking upright on the ground. Apes have a relatively short femur and a relatively long humerus. An analysis of three measures of the femur (e.g., length) of several modern humans, apes, and hominin fossils (Richmond and Jungers 2008) shows that the femur in modern humans differs from that of apes and *Aa*. Modern humans differ in the length of the femur, as is the case between apes, and femurs also differ between hominins. The analysis showed that the differences in femur length of members within each of the groups was smaller than the femur differences between members of the three different groups. It could be reliably shown that the modern human femur is longest, the ape femur is shortest, and the *Aa* femur is in between these two. It is assumed that *Aa* lived on the ground but slept in trees, and therefore had femur characteristics in between apes and humans.

However, these findings do not exclude the savannah hypothesis, which states that *Aa* may have had their habitat on the fringes of grassland and forest. Either way, the retreat and deterioration of the forest forced *Aa* to roam the grassland to increase their territory for food acquisition. Bipedalism, developed earlier, may have advanced this tendency. In the struggle for life in the changing habitat, strong *Aa* group members could conquer forest places with the best food. Less strong group members were forced to migrate, searching for other, less attractive, places, eventually to mix with members of other turned away groups and form new bonds. But these less strong groups consisted of members who were already cooperative in their former groups, and were seeking support from others (see, e.g., Chui 2000; for indirect evidence, see Silk et al. 2004). Less strong members always seek support and cooperation. Cooperation-motivated behavior was strengthened by the *Aa* empathy for others' needs that is present in primates, but also in other living animals such as elephants and wolves (Darwin 1859; De Waal 1996). The cooperative tendency was strengthened when the new groups were forced to act on the fringes of woodland and open grassland. Old groups still lived in the forest or went back to the forest, and reverted to being more apelike. Haile-Selassie et al. (2012) have found fossil foot bones of contemporaries of *Aa* with different bone settings from *Aa* which make them more apelike. The owner lived mainly in trees.

The new environment may have led the transition from incidental giving (as in the case of primates) to more structural giving. In other words, the harsh environment of the savannah may have created conditions in which already latent traits became more and more effective. Premo (2005) developed a model of the evolution of cooperative behavior based on multilevel selection theory. According to this theory, natural selection operates at two levels of the biological hierarchy: within-group and between-group. Within-group selection promotes traits that allow an individual to maximize their relative fitness in comparison to other group members, while between-group selection promotes traits that are beneficial to the fitness of other members of the group. Premo assumes that climate changes in Pliocene/Pleistocene epochs led to the retreat of the forest and the increased presence of savannah vegetation. The forest retreat led to savannah with patches of woodland where hominin groups lived. Competition between groups for food increased the chances of more altruistic traits occurring in group members. A preliminary test of the model in which several variables were fixed and some experimentally varied confirmed the hypotheses about the evolution of cooperative and altruistic behaviors. Although application of a multilevel evolutionary model is appealing, it also has some important drawbacks. One is the assumption that hominin groups chose as their habitat the patches of woodland, and from there competed with other groups. But competition between pre-hominin or primate groups living in the forest was common as well, as we know from primate studies, but clearly did not lead to the development of altruistic traits as Premo assumed to be present in patched hominin groups, groups living at the fringes of wood and grassland. Moreover, Premo finds it hard to accept that Pliocene hominins "voluntarily abandoned habitable woodland patches in order to compete for the treeless ecological niche." No, not voluntarily, but the retreating forests made woodland and food scarce, resulting in the least fit group members being driven away. In the savannah, whether patched or not, food was scarce and in order to get it the early hominins were forced to cooperate, an already latent attitude. Folger and Skarlicki (2008) adopted the hypothesis that cooperation was enhanced when hunter-gatherers sought to catch large prey. Defection reduced group effectiveness and was punished, leading, according to Folger and Skarlicki, to the development of deontic-motivated behavior.

## From Hominin to *Homo*

According to Isaac (1978), altruistic behaviors like cooperation and food sharing can be inferred from excavations at two-million-year-old sites in East Africa, when *Aa* was already two million years old. These sites contained artifacts and fossil bones of animals like the hippopotamus. From the arrangement of artifacts and bones, as well as the association of artifacts with broken animal bones, it could be inferred that both recently killed and already dead animals were cut and/or broken into pieces. Artifacts and bones of several different animals in nearby sites, like giraffe, pig, porcupine, waterbuck, and gazelle, suggest that the sites were used regularly and that dead animals were transported to the sites to be cut and/or broken into pieces. Whether food was shared was indirectly inferred from the dispersion of bone fossils. But with the scarcity of findings, family sharing cannot be ruled out. As a firmer basis for the hypothesis of food sharing from these excavations, Isaac referred to the behavior of extant and recently extinct primitive human societies like hunter-gatherer groups.

### *Food Sharing in a Drastically Changing Natural Environment*

#### *Intellectual developments*

In these difficult circumstances, food-for-food exchanges become very urgent. Marlowe (2004) suggests that food-for-food may take two forms: one is in-kind food exchange, in which food is exchanged for the same type of food at a later point in time. Although food-for-food is a specific form of exchange and thus easily applied, it must take into account the operation of the discounting principle (Stevens and Gilby 2004). Food at a later point in time has less value for the donor than at the moment the recipient received food. So, it is a risk for the donor to rely on future exchange, but not sharing is an even bigger risk. Migration made *Aa* more vulnerable to predation, and operating in groups was necessary for survival. A group of *Aa* could defend themselves better against predators than an individual *Aa*. Moreover, the time delay as well as the diminishing return value inherent in future exchange assumes more intellectual capacity than *Aa* had in the beginning, and resulted in the development of expectations about recipients' behavior. Increasing intellectual capacity contributed to survival.

The other form is not-in-kind food exchange, in which food is exchanged for other food or other resources. According to Marlowe, not-in-kind food exchange occurs often in kin relationships, where man and wife bring in different types of food. Marlowe assumes that food is exchanged for other resources as well, such as food for services (grooming) between non-kin members of the group. But, as Stevens and Gilby indicate, exchange of food and non-food resources brings with it currency problems: how much of the food for how much of the other resource? The currency problem does not play much of a role in kin relationships because the man and wife are seen as different and bring in different items. In times of great uncertainty and fear of extinction, not-in-kind food exchange might have extended from a family activity to an inter-family activity and become an important tool for survival.

Studies of primate behavior show that when groups of primates go hunting everyone shares the meat of monkeys who are captured, including those primates that do not participate in the hunting: free-riders are accepted. The explanation is that this sharing strengthens social bonds. But the consequence is that members of the group do not learn to connect effort (participating in a risky hunt) with getting food. Some animals participating in the hunt get food, but so too do those who do not participate in the hunt. It is very likely that in times of scarcity free-riders were forced to participate in the hunt or to engage in harassment-like behavior to acquire food. In other words, efforts have to be exerted in order to get food, and a direct connection between effort and acquiring food gradually became the rule. The

*Aa* learned that doing something and getting something were related; effort was essential for getting food. Sharing among the differently skilled hunters became appropriate. Later on, when hunting groups became more skilled at capturing larger prey, meat was shared with those outside the hunting group as well. These cause-and-effect relationships can be viewed as of essential significance for the onset of sharing, and stand at the basis of justice considerations. A difference between primates and humans is that some considerations of justice, like equity, require a relatively large brain capacity, and it may be doubted that primates and other animals have this capacity. Children before a certain age have difficulty in applying the rather complex equity rule which prescribes that effort and reward between self and other are weighed. Research with first-grade children show that they are unable to cognitively grasp the fine calculations that are required for application of the equity rule (Ter Laak and Aleva 1991). In allocating sweets among children who differed in their efforts on a previous task, young children divided equally while older children took the differences in effort into account. It has been observed that chimpanzee children up to two years of age can match the intellectual capacities of human children, but that after the age of two human children show a large increase in intellectual ability, with language acquisition, for instance, where chimpanzee children are left behind. Smaller brains, clearly, have less cognitive capacity than full-grown brains. Brain size increase in humans went together with complexity of content; justice elicited larger brains.

*Emotional developments*

Early *Aa* not only developed their cognitive abilities but also their emotional make-up during the transition to *Homo*. Although early hominins lived in groups, emotions that foster group life were primarily directed at self-preservation and compassion with others, but were not intentionally directed at maintaining group life. Early *Aa*, confronted with severe scarcity, struggled more and more to find food and to protect themselves from predators at the fringes of the woods. Free-riding became a burden and deteriorated the chances of survival as a group. Behaviors that diminished survival chances became forbidden and could have been the onset of emotions like guilt and shame—emotions that psychologists subsume under the moral emotions. In an interview with Dutch NRC Handelsblad on 3 April, 2013, Frans de Waal stated that primates have no emotions like guilt and shame. I assume that these emotions developed during the transition to *Homo*. It is likely that defense of group life and efforts to get group members' behavior in line with each other resulted in the punishment of defectors. In the course of time these behaviors were internalized and accompanied by feelings of inadequacy, resulting in emotions like guilt and shame.

Empathy, a capacity primates already have, has evolved into the more complex "theory of mind." Empathy is the specific ability to mentally place oneself in the position of another person and to understand what the other experiences. The theory of mind is the ability to understand that others have feelings, thoughts, intentions, and emotions, just like oneself. Being able to link our own intentions, motivations, and feelings to observations of other people is hypothesized to be a general mechanism whereby we are able to generate knowledge of other minds and feelings of empathy (Keysers and Perrett 2004).

*Social developments*

Next to intellectual capacity, social life might also have changed from hominin to *Homo*. As we learn from their behavior, primates are no saints. If they get the opportunity they try to steal food. In each group, and thus also in groups of *Aa*, free-riders are present. They try to harass to get food. Because of inherent constraints in many other explanations of animal food sharing, Stevens and Gilby find the harassment hypothesis the most likely to explain food-sharing practice: "Harassment has very few constraints. Two complete strangers can find themselves in a situation in which harassment can elicit sharing. Simple instrumental learning of aversive stimuli can condition animals to avoid harassment" (2004: 609). Harassment has been observed in many species, including primates. It is, therefore, very likely that primates or their followers the pre-hominins continued with the same behavior that they had shown when they were forest dwellers: scrounging in groups in which food sharing was (sometimes) achieved by harassment (Gilby et al. 2008). But for the forest/grassland dwellers for whom acquisition of food became more problematic, and who thus became more dependent on each other for food acquisition, harassment might have become a burden for group life. Sharing food that was incidental when food was abundant may have evolved into structural behavior when the situation needed it. Potential internal struggle was always avoided by donors giving in, but this reduced the capacity of the group to cope with external threats like the greater vulnerability to predators in the grassland compared to forest life, or the struggle for scarce resources with other groups. In the case of forest dwellers with an abundance of food, food sharing was an incidental phenomenon; it became a structural one when food became scarce and *Aa* became more dependent on each other. Consequently, harassment behavior was punished by necessity in order to survive (see also Gintis et al. 2008). However clumsy or (probably) ineffective the punishment was in the beginning, it was the starting point of a new type of social interaction between group members. Food could not be received without a sort of group-supporting behavior. Reciprocity based on mutual contribution became habitual and set a standard for appropriate group life. Animal bone distribution between fire places at the Magdalenian site in Pincevent showed that the hunters kept the best parts of a killed animal for themselves while other members of the group received the lesser parts (Enloe 2003; Lawson 2004). People may consider the fate of others and empathize with them but support for those others is subject to other, often concurrent, considerations. Studying isolated events of food sharing can easily lead to the conclusion that the donors are altruistic or egoistic, but one must take into account the entire picture of food exchanges over long periods of time. Then one sees that pure altruism or pure egoism are very seldom shown.

## Sharing Food in Hunter-Gatherer Groups

Because hunter-gatherer groups lived for thousands of years, food-sharing must have been part of human (primitive) societies for a very long time. The findings of Isaac and others in East Africa, Olduvai, Laetolil, Koobi For in the Omo Valley, and Hadar suggest that hunter-gatherers were already present two million years ago. Kaplan and Gurven (2005 state that food-sharing between families is universal in present day human societies. Food sharing, thus, is a phenomenon that is assumed to be omnipresent throughout time and space, and is therefore the most important source for studying allocation behavior.

The Magdalenian settlement site at Pincevent in the Paris Basin, France, is one of the very few sites where food sharing has been identified archeologically (Lawson 2004). The remains were preserved in clay and the silts deposited by the river Seine. These remains consist of stone artifacts and bone fragments of killed reindeer, as well as numerous hearths, which may point to repeated occupation by reindeer hunters who lived about 12,000 years ago. The excavations started in 1964 and were carried out very carefully to preserve the distribution of bones. By refitting broken bones that were found at different hearths it was possible to infer the allocation of bones and thus of reindeer meat among the hunters, the providers of the food, and between hunters and other members of the group. The providers occupied so-called provider hearths while the receivers occupied the others. It could be inferred from the available distribution of bones (only the forelimbs could be used for investigation) that equal sharing was prevalent between provider hearths, while unequal sharing of food was prevalent between provider hearths and receiver hearths. Still, imbalances in sharing could be observed even between provider hearths (see also Kaplan and Gurven 2005, indicating that food sharing was more complex than simple equal sharing. The imbalances might be due to the fact that kinship sharing was intermixed with non-kin sharing. Within the group of hunters some may have been relatives while others were not. Kin members may have shared more food with other kin members than with other hunters.

Present-day hunter-gatherer groups share food, as has been observed, for instance, in the Hadza community, an ethnic group that has been living for thousands of years around lake Eyasi in central Tanzania, in the Rift Valley, and in the neighboring Serengeti Plateau (see, e.g., Marlowe 2004; Wood 2006). Other food-sharing groups that have been studied are the Ache people who lived in the rainforests in Eastern Paraguay, but were forced to leave their territory when the rainforest was burned down for agricultural purposes (see, e.g., Kaplan and Gurven 2005. These hunter-gatherer people were mostly organized on an egalitarian basis, with no decisive authority. Moreover, it was observed that food sharing in those societies was associated with a division of labor between the sexes. Females, encumbered with children, gathered plant foods, but also small reptiles, eggs, insects, and the like. The males provided most of the hunted food. Other hunter groups studied intensively were the Inuit in Northern Canada and Alaska (see, e.g., Binford 1991).

To find out more about the relationship between motives and patterns of giving and receiving, Marlowe (2004) showed that Hadza hunters offered less than American students in an Ultimatum Bargaining Game and Dictator Game. In addition, the Hadza strongly rejected unfair offers. Both observations led to the conclusion that the Hadza will share with others but, if an opportunity opens up, they are motivated to take more for themselves. Moreover, sharing is something for others to do, but less so or not at all for oneself. In another study, Wood (2006) interviewed Hadza hunters and presented pictures of two types of fictitious hunters and their families. Pictures were shown in which hunters were depicted who clearly differed in hunting skills: skilled and less skilled. The interviewed hunters were asked their preferences for joining the group for a short period of time. The study investigated two hypotheses for food sharing. One, the show-off hypothesis, suggested that sharing would be repaid with social attention, including increased mating opportunities—this hypothesis would be supported when interviewed hunters chose the picture of the less skilled hunters. The alternative hypothesis is the family provisioning hypothesis, suggesting that hunters share food to receive better provisioning for the family, resulting in a better position in the struggle for survival of the fittest. If this hypothesis was correct, the interviewed hunters would choose to join the skilled groups because of the greater chances of getting food. The findings showed mixed results. The hunters interviewed preferred the skilled group: of the 34 interviewed, 26 chose to join the skilled group and 8 the less skilled group. Splitting the group into Hadza male with dependent family (22) and without dependent family (12), the group without dependent family had no preference for joining the skilled or less skilled hunters. Of the group with dependent family, 20 members choose to join the skilled hunters, and 2 members the unskilled hunters. From these data we can infer that most Hadza choose the less egoistic alternative—extreme egoistic Hadza would have chosen the less skilled group in order to become outstanding and acquire better mating opportunities.

Kaplan and Gurven (2005) evaluated findings on food sharing in four groups: the Yanomano, Hiwi, Ache, and Pilagi in South America. Correlations between resources given and resources received were significant in all cases, offering support for the altruistic reciprocity hypothesis and not for the alternative hypothesis of tolerated theft (allowing not-hunters to scrounge). Kaplan and Gurven, however, observed several imbalances in food sharing. In some cases these imbalances can be attributed to sharing within kin relationships between adult and young members, but also to the often short-term nature of most field studies and the often long time period of reciprocal behavior. Other imbalances may occur due to the immaterial nature of the reciprocated resources, such as is the case with costly signaling (food given for status). Moreover, imbalances should be measured against differences between parties with regard to influence, wealth, or status. Also, the recipients' needs should be taken into account. It has been found among the Ache people that the amount of resources given is a function of the number of people dependent on the food. From a review of many food sharing studies of many hunting groups, Kaplan and Gurven concluded that "there is substantial cross-cultural evidence supporting the view that reciprocal altruism of some sort underlies much food sharing behavior" (105).

The imbalances in food exchange practices and their acceptance can be explained partly by referring to the way hunter-gatherers view their world (Martin 1993). Their animistic view of the world includes seeing themselves as part of that world and not as distinct from it (Ingold 1994). Living in good relationships with group members, with plants, and with animals is a crucial aspect of it. This view makes them less vulnerable to imbalances or inconsistencies in the food exchange process. It is seen as more favorable to have a good relationship and to live together in harmony than to receive more or less food.

The studies described here can easily be supplemented by others, of which some seem to support the egoistic line of reasoning and others seem to support the altruistic line. First of all, studies supporting the altruistic motivation of food sharing are all of a correlational nature. That is, the researchers looked, for instance, at resources given compared to resources received, and a significant correlation was viewed as support for the altruistic reciprocity explanation of food sharing. But as some authors have remarked, a correlation does not mean a causal connection between giving and receiving, implying that other factors may be responsible for the correlation. Experimental studies—the best way to investigate causal relationships—found non-conclusive evidence for either an egoistic or altruistic explanation of food sharing.

### *Studies Based on Game Theory*

Some authors explain food-sharing practice by referring to game-theoretical principles. Binmore (2006), for instance, explains reciprocity in food sharing as the result of trying to reach a Nash equilibrium in a repeated prisoners' dilemma game. A Nash equilibrium is reached when each player is making the best reply to the choice made by the other player. In such a game, the donor chooses a row (Dove or Hawk) and the beggar chooses a column (Dove or Hawk). When both donor and beggar choose Dove, both players receive two units; when the donor chooses Dove and the beggar chooses Hawk, the donor gets nothing and the beggar three units; when the donor chooses Hawk and the beggar chooses Dove, the donor gets three units and the beggar receives nothing; When both players choose Hawk, both receive one unit. The cell (1,1) is a Nash equilibrium: whatever the choice of the beggar (Dove or Hawk), the Donor will always receive something (one unit if the beggar also chooses Hawk, or three units if the beggar chooses Dove). In other words, if the donor gives in (chooses Dove) and the beggar chooses to harass (Hawk), the donor gets nothing and the beggar all. If the donor chooses to resist (Hawk), the beggar gets nothing, but if the beggar chooses to harass (Hawk), both get something. According to Binmore, this result is most likely when the game is repeated: a plausible assumption in hunter communities where hunters repeatedly come back with meat. These findings corroborate the assumption of food sharing where people are best off if they do not strive to take all but give in a little and take as much as the other.

Results from game-theoretical studies show that in a Dictator Game (DG), people offer lower bids than in an Ultimatum Bargaining Game (UBG). In a UBG two players—donor and recipient—divide a sum of money; the donor offers a division and when the recipient accepts the offer both receive the proposed amount. If the recipient refuses the offer, both players get nothing. In such a situation most offers are made close to 50 percent. Offers of 70 percent for self or more are rejected by most recipients. In a DG, the donor makes an offer and the recipient has to accept it. Because, in a DG as compared to a UBG, recipients have no influence on the bidding process, donors offer less in a DG than in a UBG. In other words, the more influence the recipient has on the bidding process the higher the donor's offer will be (Marlowe 2004; Suleiman 1996; van Dijk and Vermunt 2000). But even in a DG people offer more of the resource than can be inferred from game theory, which predicts that donors will offer the smallest amount possible. Game theory predicts that recipients accept any bid, because refusal leaves them with nothing. All studies on DG show that donors offer more than egoism would predict, but less than altruism would predict.

Marlowe taught Hadza males and females to play both UBG and DG. The sum to divide was 2,000 Tanzania shillings (2 Euro), about a day's wage in Tanzania. Some Hadza people played the role of proposer (actor), others were responder (recipient). The games were played anonymously. Marlowe tested three explanations of food sharing: reciprocity, costly signaling, and tolerated scrounging. If reciprocity was the common motivation for sharing in the Hadza community, Marlowe assumed that such a motivation would lead to high offers in UBG and DG, say between 40 percent and 50 percent of the sum, and that low offers would be rejected at high rates. Costly signaling implies that foragers will advertise their qualities by sharing food, resulting in high offers (50 percent or more) in UBG and DG. Tolerated scrounging implies the forager does not really want to give food, resulting in low offers in UBG and DG. The data showed most support for tolerated scrounging, and next for reciprocity. A propensity toward generosity was observed in that there were no zero offers in DG. Marlowe concluded that all three explanations play a role in food sharing, with tolerated scrounging the most important.

By letting the Hadza play UBG and DG, Marlowe's study offers more insight into people's propensity to share than other studies do. But a clear explanation of sharing has still not been given. The author observed egoistic-like motivation as well as altruistic-like motivation to share. And to conclude from the data that people do not like to share but have to is not realistic. No statistical test results of significant differences between numbers of people who propose different offers are reported. One may assume that these differences are too small to be important. Marlowe, thus, bases his conclusions on trends. For instance, in one of the figures (2004: 82, Figure 6), the frequencies of proposers and offers as a percentage of stakes in a DG are presented. Remember, in a DG the proposer knows that the anonymous responder has no say in the proposal. From the 22 male Hadza players, only four showed the predicted offer of zero percent. Eighteen players offered more than zero percent of the resources, while six players even offered 50 percent of the sum of 2,000 shillings, in a situation where there are no costs at all for offering nothing to the other player. Moreover, in the DG—as well as, to a lesser extent, in the UBG—female Hadza proposed lower offers than male Hadza. For instance, in DG, nine woman against five men proposed 10 percent offers; five women against three men proposed 20 percent offers; 10 men proposed offers of 30 percent and higher against four women. Thus, male Hadza hunters showed more generous offers than Marlowe suggests from his data. Marlowe states, in this respect: "Men's foods, such as meat and honey, that do make it back to camp do so with greater variance and tend to be shared more widely outside the household than women's foods" (2004: 78). In UBG, 50 percent of Hadza males proposed offers of 40 percent or more. What does it mean that offers are proposed around 50 percent? It means that the offers are proposed according to norms of fairness. In a situation where someone receives a sum of money and is asked to divide the sum between himself and an anonymous other, both players have in common that their fate is connected and the task is the same: to divide a sum of money. The only difference is that one player proposes an offer and other reacts. Because of the same fate for both players, an equal split is in line with it. Interviews with Western students show that a proposer reasons that it is permitted for them to offer a bit more to themselves than to the receiver because the proposer has the responsibility to make the offer. In other words, a large proportion of the Hadza hunters behave fairly in the games. These studies also show that hunter-gatherers are intellectually able to calculate amounts of given and received resources, a capacity that primates clearly have not, or have to a lesser extent. It might be assumed that the attitudes and behavior related to giving and taking have resulted in shared beliefs about the importance of living in harmony with and showing respect for self and others. These shared beliefs may have affected the behavior and decisions of subsequent allocation events (see Elias 1969).

### *The Social Component of Food Sharing*

But what Marlowe's study clearly misses is the cultural component of allocation processes. Allocation behavior is not an activity that occurs in a vacuum. As researchers have observed, allocation processes occur in a group of people where those people hold beliefs about how they see themselves in relation to other group members, to other groups, and to the natural environment. Shared beliefs exert a large influence on the attitudes and behavior of group members, and in their person-to-person interactions. A donor will be affected by these shared beliefs and will judge and act accordingly. Part of the shared beliefs of hunter-gatherer groups includes the worldview that all things, living as well as non-living, people as well as plants and animals, are part of a harmonious unity. When this harmony is upset by individual action, attempts are made to restore harmony. Punishment of the culpable member or a contest between group members is less important than restoration. In such a context it is difficult to understand the explanation that hunters bringing in food will allow scrounging or theft because of possible loss. Such an explanation applies too much of the nature of a person-to-person conflict, in which both parties weigh their interests. The explanation discards the overarching view of harmony and balance through which a personal attack is out of the question.

In line with this view is the study by Kameda et al. (2003). They developed an evolutionary game model to explain food sharing in (hunter-gatherer) human societies. In this view, uncertain resources are designated as common resources to be shared by other members. The authors object to the risk-reduction hypothesis that explains why people value the communal sharing norm, but fails to explain the maintenance of the norm in the presence of egoistic group members. For these members, free-riding is attractive and keeps them in evolutionary good shape. If egoism proliferates in the group then the sharing norm will collapse. The tolerated-theft hypothesis may explain why there is a need for a communal sharing norm but ignores the fact that tolerated theft reflects a norm of sharing. Moreover, proponents of tolerated theft assume that it often goes pair-wise: from beggar to donor. But, according to the authors, in a community there are more beggar and donor pairs whose behaviors may lead to uncontrollable and costly contests about food. They differentiate between acquirers, who by chance catch an animal, and non-acquirers, who try to designate the food as a common resource which can then be shared by all members of the group. How the resource is processed by the group depends on the strategies of the acquirers and non-acquirers. Four strategies are differentiated: The *communal sharer* shares the food whether acquirer or non-acquirer; the *saint* shares the food as acquirer but allows another acquirer to keep their food; the *egoist* claims private property for their own acquired food but demands communal sharing for food from other acquirers; the *bourgeois* claims private property of the food as acquirer as well as non-acquirer. With the help of computer simulations and social psychological experiments, Kameda et al. showed that communal sharing is a dominant strategy in groups.

## Food Sharing as an Allocation Event

The picture of the allocation behavior of primates and (proto-human) hunters shows a development toward more complex sharing in hunter-gatherer groups than in animal groups. The question scientists try to answer is whether food sharing is a type of behavior attributed to selfish motives or altruistic motives. Some authors (Stevens 2004; Stevens and Gilby 2004; Marlowe 2004) attribute food sharing to the operation of selfish motives, while others (Kaplan and Gurven 2005; De Waal 1996; Kameda et al. 2003; Premo 2005) attribute food sharing to the operation of altruistic motives. In applying the justice motivation model, outlined in the Prologue, it is possible to bridge the gap and to describe food sharing in hunter-gatherer groups more precisely and explain it better. But motivation is only one—important—element of the allocation event. As has been described, an allocation event is an event in which an authority (e.g., the donor) allocates material or immaterial resources among (groups of) recipients, and describes recipients' justice reactions to the allocation outcomes. In the following paragraphs we will first focus on the donor as the allocation authority, then the donor's motives, then describe the types of allocated resources.

### *The Donor as Authority*

Food sharing studies among primates reveal the presence of a hierarchy among male chimpanzees. At the top is the so-called alpha male; lower in the hierarchy one can discern beta males and others. Every now and then, the alpha male has to defend his position against other males who try to challenge it. The hierarchy is rather stable, but on some occasions hierarchies may develop temporarily. Some groups of chimpanzees and other primates, under some conditions, go hunting for meat. It has been observed that one of the males in the group will initiates a hunt for, for instance, small monkeys. The initiator need not be the alpha male. When the prey is killed, the group of chimpanzees divides the meat among all members of the group whether they took an active part in the hunt or not (Newton-Fisher et al. 2002). A hierarchy can always be observed in chimpanzee communities, whether the hierarchy is more or less stable, as is the case with the alpha male, or originates in a hunting situation.

The presence of a hierarchy in primate groups stands in sharp contrast to the opinions of scientists who study still-existing hunter groups. The hunter groups of the Hadza or Ache are seen as egalitarian, with no specific or general leader. The main argument for explaining the absence of a hierarchy in hunting groups is that no one hunter always returns from hunting with meat. Many times the hunt is fruitless and the hunter is dependent on the catches of other hunters, preventing the development of a stable hierarchy based, for instance, on hunting skill. But hunting groups in the Magdalenian seem to show some type of hierarchy: animal bone distribution between fireplaces at the Magdalenian site in Pincevent showed that the hunters kept the best parts of the killed animal for themselves, while other members of the group received the other parts (Lawson 2004). Control over the distribution of food can be viewed as an instance of leadership behavior. Does that mean that in hunter groups, that are assumed to be egalitarian, a hierarchy develops or even exists? Yes, hierarchies do develop, but the question is whether these hierarchies are stable and are led by one individual. Boehm (1993), for instance, observed that hunters who try to command others or who become too proud or too bossy are ridiculed and lose respect in the long run. But a successful hunter who exerts leadership in a moderate way—through food reallocation or conflict resolution, for example—is respected and accepted as leader. The hierarchy that arises may not be effective in all situations the group faces. Therefore, a stable hierarchy may not develop, or may develop only temporarily when all the required skills are united in one person. But from Boehm's observations one can safely conclude that leaders emerge in hunter groups when food is distributed or conflicts arise. So, when a hunter comes back with a catch he will have a great say in how the food is distributed. Although other members of the community share in the meat, the successful hunter keeps control of the meat division. His kin and often other hunters get the better parts of the catch, while other members of the community get the remainder. When one compares primate groups with hunter-gatherer groups, a prominent difference is that in primate groups hierarchical organization is stable while in hunter-gatherer groups the hierarchy is an incidental phenomenon.

### *The Motives of the Donor*

A considerable amount of research has been devoted to unveiling the motives that lead successful hunters to distribute meat among non-kin members of the group. As already summarized extensively above, some authors argue that food sharing is triggered by selfish-like motives such as increased foraging efficiency (sharing food increases support from others in the next hunt), predation avoidance (when sharing food the hunter avoids confrontation with possible predators in future hunts), mate provisioning (increased opportunities for access to females), and harassment avoidance (avoiding possibly costly fights against others by sharing food; see Stevens and Gilby 2004). Others assume that food sharing is the result of altruistic-like motives such as recruitment calling, where a hunter calls others to alert them to the food; reciprocity or reciprocal altruism, which states that a donor may perform a costly act—catching prey—that benefits another if the recipient returns the favor later; group augmentation, which states that sharing increases group size which may provide some future benefit (see Stevens and Gilby 2004).

In the dimensional view of motivation, allocation behavior can be explained partly by egoistic motives and partly by altruistic motives. If one agrees with this idea, one consequence is that motives situated at the extreme positions of the scale can be designated as "pure" egoistic or "pure" altruistic. Motives at less extreme positions of the scale have egoistic as well as altruistic elements in them. So, a motive for food sharing labeled as egoistic, like predation avoidance, has egoistic elements—the hunter has better survival chances—as well as an altruistic element—the hunter's survival has benefits for others as well. A motive labeled as altruistic, like reciprocal altruism, has altruistic elements—the hunter donates food without getting something back immediately—as well as an egoistic element—the hunter is benefited at a later point in time.

In other words, hunters donate food to others while taking into account their own interests. If their own interests are discarded completely then food sharing is altruistically motivated, and when their own interests are taken into account completely then food sharing is egoistically motivated. These extremes, however, are very rare. As theory and research on resource allocations show, people show a mix of egoism and altruism when allocating resources.

### *Food Sharing as Resource Exchange*

As stated before, food sharing can be viewed, to a large extent, as an allocation process in which an authority allocates resources among recipients and between self and recipients according to rules of fairness. It is assumed, and observed, that the type of resource affects the way people divide resources. Adults are motivated to punish children equally severely for wrongdoing, although some of the children play a larger part in the wrongdoing than others. Adults are motivated to reward children according to what each child has contributed to the task. Resources, as Foa and Foa (1974) have indicated, can be differentiated into six classes based on two dimensions. One dimension is the particularistic versus universalistic dimension: resources are particularistic if they apply only for specific situations and/or the specific individuals involved in the exchange. Love, for example, is exchanged only to specific others because love only has value for a specific other, while money can be exchanged to many others because money has the same value for all those others. Love is categorized as a particularistic resource, while money is categorized as universalistic. The other dimension to categorize resources is the materialistic versus non-materialistic dimension. Materialistic resources are tangible, can be held in the hand, while non-materialistic resources are symbolic and cannot be held in the hand. Money or goods are materialistic resources, while love and information are non-materialistic resources.

Studies on food sharing mention the following resources that are exchanged: *food*; *other goods* (like stones used as tools); *sex*; *social bonds*; *cooperation*; *support*; *services*; and *status*. One way or another, receiving these goods has survival value. Some of them are individual-directed while others are group-directed or other-directed. So, food, status, support, and other goods are directed at increasing the survival chances of the individual donor—food and other goods because it makes the donor fitter; status because of the privileges for the donor; support indirectly increases survival chances. So, too, is sex, because it increases the chances for fit offspring. Social bonds and cooperation increase survival chances at the group level, as well as increasing survival chances for the individual (see also Premo 2005). All these resource allocations contribute to the survival of the donor; some directly, while other resources contribute via the group. In this last case, motivation is more altruistic.

Of interest also is the differentiation between materialistic and non-materialistic resources. Materialistic resources like food and other goods contribute directly to the survival chances of the donor, while non-materialistic resources contribute indirectly to the donor's survival chances. The distribution of non-materialistic resources like intimacy, prestige, and status contribute to the harmonization of the group, and a harmonious group has more chance of survival in the struggle for scarce resources with other groups than a group in conflict. Sharing food promotes cooperation, which is beneficial for others as well, and because cooperation is not scarce it is beneficial for all when consumed. Allocation of non-material resources can often compensate for imbalances in the allocation of material resources.

The diet of hunter-gatherers like the Hadza consists of meat (10 percent), 80 percent wild plant food, and 10 percent non-wild plant food (received from others; Marlowe 2002). In a study among Ache and Hiwi hunter-gatherers, Gurven (2006) showed that between families, quantity as well as value of (other) food was exchanged for food delivered. Although imbalances between given and received resources were observed, correlations indicated that reciprocation of food delivered between families could be traced with confidence. The Ache as well as Hiwi showed exchange of labor for food as well. What is remarkable is that no contingency occurred for non-meat transfers. Gurven explains, "[a] combination of high predictability, low variance in return rates, and synchronous acquisition across individuals makes reciprocal sharing of these resources less necessary" (Gurven 2006: 187). It is interesting that the hunters' animistic view of the world corresponds highly with Gurven's conclusion: to live in harmony with the group and the animal world is more important than obtaining more or less resources. According to Gurven, these patterns of reciprocity indicate the application of rules of fairness.

Other forms of exchange, like food for grooming or sex, were not observed in hunter-gatherer groups, in contrast to animal groups.

## Concluding Remarks

The controversy between proponents of the egoistic motive for food sharing and proponents of the altruistic motive has led to a large amount of research. Biologists, ethologists, and economists have carried out field studies and experiments, and have tested several models to explain the reasons for food-sharing practices. The results of studies among primates and other animals show that food sharing as an act of altruism is difficult to prove and that, according to Stevens and Gilby (2004), egoistically motivated behavior fits the data better. Of course, animals may empathize with others when these animals are in a state of distress, but that is different from a food-sharing practice. Gurven and others (Enloe 2003) conclude from analyses of many studies that food sharing in hunter groups is explained well by assuming the operation of a justice-like motive. If we assume that primate food-sharing practice is a proxy for early hominin food sharing, and hunter-gatherer food-sharing is a proxy for early *Homo* food-sharing practice, how can we explain the differences between the two in motivation for food sharing?

Climate change forced early hominin groups to cooperate, and, when combined with their already active empathy, this resulted in justice-like behavior. The more complex cognitive activity of taking into account one's own needs as well as the needs of others may have coincided with larger brain capacity, which in turn may have led to hominins' understanding of more complex issues like appreciation of delayed benefits and non-kind resource exchange (Stevens and Gilby 2004). The resulting fairness motive may have acquired a position in the developing brain.

I assume further that the climate change at the beginning of the Pleistocene formed the impetus for a transition between hominin (e.g., *Australopithecus afarensis*) and *Homo* (e.g., *Homo erectus*). But it is unlikely that this climate change is the only factor that was significant for the further development of the human lineage. I therefore suggest here that, in the course of *Homo* development, more climate changes must also have occurred to encourage the onset of important *Homo* bodily and cognitive adaptations, as well as contributing to the extinction of certain *Homo* species. The extinction of *Homo neanderthalensis* is probably due to a combination of climate change and inability to adapt to these changes (Wong, 2009). The next chapter will show the impact of climate change on adaptation in recent times.

Is there a fundamental difference between animal food sharing and human food sharing, or is it a gradual difference? From animal and hunter-gatherer studies, I conclude that the differences are gradual. Primates show empathy, as do hunter-gatherers; primates exchange food for non-material resources, as do hunter-gatherers; primates show altruistic-like sharing, as do hunter-gatherers; and primates show egoistic-like sharing, as do hunter-gatherers. However, the picture that arises from these studies is that considerations of justice in which altruistic-like motivation and egoistic-like motivation are combined are absent in primate food sharing, but are part and parcel of hunter-gatherer food sharing.

In *Homo sapiens sapiens* (150,000 BC), the more complex cognition required for balanced allocations led to a worldview where people find it important for their well-being to live in harmony with others: plants, trees, and animals, as well as human beings. In the context of this worldview, egoism and altruism as pure instances of allocation and exchange motives are rare phenomena. Balance and harmony give rise to the operation of the justice motive in two ways: (1) emphasis is given to balance with regard to own and other interests; and (2) emphasis lies in giving others respect and due consideration and keeping the group in harmony with the natural environment. These two aspects are not equally important. I think that living in harmony with the natural environment is more relevant than the intra-personal balance of motivations, and consequently the allocation of non-material resources (respect) is more relevant than the allocation of material resources (food).

The reviewed chapters and articles about food sharing differ in many respects. For instance, some studies infer food-sharing behavior from the distribution of fossil bones and artifacts in very old layers (Isaac 1978) or recent layers (Lawson 2004). Other studies focus on food-sharing practices and preferences in existing hunting groups (Kaplan and Gurven 2005; Marlowe 2004), in primates (De Waal 1996; Hockings et al. 2007), and other species. Moreover, the studies reviewed differ in the unity of observation. Some studies focus on pairwise exchange of food (Binmore 2006), while others focus on group exchange (Kameda et al. 2003). Despite these differences in studies of primates and hunter-gatherer groups, primate behavior can be differentiated from hunter-gatherer behavior. In primate communities a stable hierarchy is observed, while a stable hierarchy in hunter-gatherer communities is absent. In both communities, the donor has control over the gift of food, but in hunter-gatherer communities the donor varies with the presence of the catch that he brings home. In exchanging resources primates share food for services like grooming and sex, while these types of exchange are largely absent in hunter-gatherer communities. Furthermore, studies show that egoistic-like motives primarily drive primate food sharing, while justice considerations primarily drive hunter-gatherer food sharing.

What is missing in the food sharing research reported here is the social and cultural context of the food-sharing practice. Justice, being respectful, considerate, and truthful to self and others, explains the food-sharing practices of hunter-gatherers better than emphasizing the egoistic or altruistic behavior motivations. However, egoistic and altruistic motivated behaviors are still passively or actively present. The natural context changes, resulting in processes of adaptation giving rise to different methods of subsistence. The social and cultural context changes as well, resulting in changes in the operation of the justice motive. These topics will be the focus of the next chapter.

## References

Binford, L.R. 1991. When the Going Gets Tough, the Tough Get Going: Nunamiut Local Groups, Camping Patterns and Economic Organization, in *Ethnoarchaeological Approaches to Mobile Campsites: Hunter-Gatherer and Pastoralist Case Studies*, edited by C.S. Gamble, and W.A. Boismier. Ann Arbor: International Monographs in Prehistory, 25–187.

Binmore, K. 2006. Justice as a natural phenomenon. *Analyse and Kritik*, 28, 1–12.

Boehm, C. 1993. Egalitarian behavior and reverse dominance hierarchy. *Current Anthropology*, 34, 227–54.

Chui, M.M. 2000. Effects of status on solutions, leadership, and evaluations during group problem-solving. *Sociology of Education*, 73(3), 175–95.

Darwin, C.R. (1859, 2008). *On the origin of species by means of natural selection, or the preservation of favoured races in the struggle of life*. London: John Murray.

Dawkins, R. 1976. *The Selfish Gene*. Oxford: Oxford University Press.

deMenocal, P. 2011. Climate and human evolution. *Science*, 331, 540–42.

De Waal, F.B.M. 1996. *Good Natured. The Origins of Right and Wrong in Humans and Other Animals*. Boston: Harvard University Press.

De Waal, F.B.M. 2000. Attitudinal reciprocity in food sharing among brown capuchins. *Animal Behavior*, 60, 253–61.

De Waal, F.B.M., and Luttrell, L.M. 1986. The similarity principle underlying social bonding among female Rhesus monkeys. *Folia Primatologica*, 46, 215–34.

Elias, N. 1969. *Über den Prozess der Zivilisation. Soziogenetische und Psychogenetische Untersuchungen*. Bern: Francke Verlag.

Enloe, J.G. 2003. Food sharing past and present: Archaeological evidence for economic and social interactions. *Before Farming*, 1, 1–23.

Foa, U.G., and Foa, E.B. 1974. *Societal Structures of the Mind*. Springfield, IL: Charles C. Thomas Publisher.

Folger, R., and Skarlicki, D.P. 2008. The Evolutionary Basis of Deontic Justice, in *Justice, Morality, and Social Responsibility*, edited by S.W. Gilliland, D.D. Steiner, and D.P. Skarlicki. Charlotte, NC: Information Age Publishing, 29–62.

Gage, F.H., and Muotri, A.R. 2012. What makes each brain unique? *Scientific American*, 306(3), 20–25.

Gilby, I.C., Eberly, L.E., and Wrangham, R.E. 2008. Economic profitability of social predation among wild chimpanzees: Individual variation promotes cooperation. *Animal Behavior*, 75, 351–60.

Gintis, H., Henrich J., Bowles, S., Boyd, R., and Fehr, E. 2008. Strong reciprocity and the roots of human morality. *Social Justice Research*, 21, 241–53.

Goodall, J. 1986. *The Chimpanzees of Gombe: Patterns of Behavior*. Cambridge, MA: Harvard University Press.

Gurven, M. 2006. The evolution of contingent evolution. *Current Anthropology*, 47(1), 185–92.

Haile-Selassie, Y., Saylor, B.Z., Deino, A., Levin, N.E., Alene, M., and Latimer, B.M. 2012. A new hominin foot from Ethiopia shows multiple Pliocene bipedal adaptations. *Nature*, 383, 565–9.

Harvey, G. 2005. *Animism: Respecting the Living World*. London: C. Hurst and Co.

Hauser, M.D., Chen, M.K., Chen, F., and Chuang, E. 2003. Give unto others: Genetically unrelated Tamarin monkeys preferentially give food to those who altruistically give food back. *Proceedings of the Royal Society*, 270, 2363–70.

Hockings, K.J., Humle, T., Anderson, J.R., Biro, D., Sousa, C., Ohashi, G., and Matsuzawa, T. 2007. Chimpanzees share forbidden fruit. *Plos One*, 9, 1–4.

Ingold, T. 1994. Introduction, in *What is an Animal?* edited by T. Ingold. London: Routledge, One World Archaeology, 1–16.

Isaac, G. 1978. The food-sharing behavior of protohuman hominids. *Scientific American*, 238, 90–108.

Kameda, T., Takezawa, M., and Hastie, R. 2003. The logic of social sharing: An evolutionary game analysis of adaptive norm development. *Personality and Social Psychology Review*, 7(1), 2–19.

Kaplan, H., and Gurven, M. 2005. The Natural History of Food Sharing and Cooperation: A Review and a New Multi-Approach to the Negotiation of Norms, in *Moral Sentiments and Material Interests: Foundations of Cooperation in Economic Life*, edited by H. Gintis, S. Bowles, and E. Fehr. Cambridge, MA: MIT Press, 75–111.

Keysers, C., and Perrett, D.I. 2004. Demystifying social cognition: A Hebbian perspective. *Trends in Cognitive Sciences*, 8, 501–507.

Kingston, J.D., Deino, A.L. Edgar, R.K., and Hill, A. 2007. Astronomically forced climate change in the Kenyan Rift Valley 2.7–2.55 Ma: Implications for the evolution of early hominin ecosystems. *Journal of Human Evolution*, 53, 487–503.

Koyama, N.F., and Dunbar, R.I.M. 1996. Anticipation of conflict by chimpanzees. *Primates*, 37, 79–86.

Lawson, M. 2004. Interpretations of food sharing practices at the Magdalenian settlement at Pincevent. *Online Archaeology*. Available at http://www.online-archaeology.co.uk/contribute/archaeologyarticles/tabid/85/articletype/articleview/articleid/5/default.aspx [accessed 19 November 2013].

Marlowe, F.W. 2002. Why the Hadza Are Still Hunter-Gatherers, in *Ethnicity, Hunter-Gatherers and the Other*, edited by S. Kent. Washington, DC: Smithsonian Institute Press, 247–75.

Marlowe, F.W. 2004. What explains Hadza food sharing? *Research in Economic Antropology*, 23, 69–88.

Martin, C.L. 1993. *In the Spirit of the Earth*. Baltimore: Johns Hopkins University Press.

Newton-Fisher, N.E., Notman, H., and Reynolds, V. 2002. Hunting of mammalian prey by Budongo forest chimpanzees. *Folia Primatol*, 73, 281–3.

Orr, H.A. 2009. Testing natural selection. *Scientific American*, 300(1), 30–36.

Premo, L.S. 2005. Patchiness and Prosociality: Modeling the Evolution and Archaeology of Plio-Pleisctocene Hominin Food Sharing, in *Multi-Agent and Multi-Agent-Based Simulation. Lecture Notes on Artificial Intelligence*, edited by P. Davidson, K. Takadam, and B. Logan, 3415. Berlin: Springer-Verlag, 210–24.

Richmond, B.G., and Jungers, W.L. 2008. Orrorin tugenensis femoral morphology and the evolution of human bipedalism. *Science*, 319(5870), 1662–5.

Silk, J.B., Alberts, S.C., and Altmann, J. 2004. Patterns of coalition formation by adult female baboons in Amboseli, Kenya. *Animal Behavior*, 67, 573–82.

Stanford, C. 1995. Chimpanzee hunting behavior and human evolution. *American Scientist*, May/June.

Stevens, J.R. 2004. The selfish nature of generosity: Harassment and food sharing in primates. *Proceedings of the Royal Society*, 271, 451–6.

Stevens, J.R., and Gilby, I.C. 2004. A conceptual framework for non-kin food sharing: Timing and currency of benefits. *Animal Behavior*, 67, 603–14.

Stevens, J.R., and Stephens, D.W. 2002. Food sharing: A model of manipulation by harassment. *Behavioral Ecology*, 13, 393–400.

Suleiman, R. 1996. Expectations and fairness in a modified Ultimatum Game. *Journal of Economic Psychology*, 17, 531–54.

Ter Laak, J., and Aleva, L. 1991. Distributive Justice in Children: Social Psychological and Developmental Psychology Perspectives, in *Social Justice in Human Relations*, edited by R. Vermunt, and H. Steensma. New York: Plenum Press, 151–68.

Trauth, M.H., Maslin, M.A., Deino, A., Strecker, M.R., Bergner, A.G.N., and Dühnforth, M. 2007. High- and low-latitude forcing of Plio-Pleistocene African climate and human evolution. *Journal of Human Evolution*, 53, 475–86.

van Dijk, E., and Vermunt, R. 2000. Strategy and fairness in social decision making: Sometimes it pays to be powerless. *Journal of Experimental Social Psychology*, 36, 1–25.

Wood, B.W. 2006. Prestige or provisioning? A test of foraging goals among the Hadza. *Current Anthropology*, 47(2), 383–7.

Wong, K. 2009. The human pedigree. *Scientific American*, 300(1), 46–9.

Wong, K. 2012. First of our kind. *Scientific American*, 306(4), 20–29.

# Chapter 2
# Climate Change, Social Change, and the Justice Motive

## Introduction

A major topic in the study of social justice is the description and explanation of why people behave justly. In many discussions, people view the justice motive as the opposite of the egoistic motive, but also as different from the altruistic motive. Many economists believe that: (1) individuals strive to maximize their own profit; and that (2) the egoistic motive drives social behavior. Some sociologists and psychologists state that individuals strive to maximize their own profit but in doing so realize that unrestricted egoism leads to a war of all against all and, therefore, behave more altruistically (Walster et al. 1978). Other social scientists have tried successfully to show that social behavior is not only governed by self-interest (Montada 1998), but that individuals are also motivated by rules of fairness and justice. Despite the overwhelming evidence to the contrary, the myth of individuals as profit maximizers still exists in the minds of broad categories of people, including scientists, in Western societies (Miller and Ratner 1996). To unravel the intricate threads leading to the complexities of the justice motive, Mel Lerner (1980) has made a major contribution. His definition of the justice motive in terms of deservingness and entitlement received much attention in the literature. Moreover, the operations of the justice motive made visible phenomena that had previously been poorly understood, such as blaming innocent victims. It turned out that the justice motive offers a good explanation of people's justice beliefs and behavior, and empirical evidence supports this explanation.

Chapter 1 described how the justice motive might have originated from the egoistic- and/or altruistic-motivated actions of members of hominin hunting groups. The present chapter will go into the social background of the justice motive. One can imagine that the way individuals seek solutions for survival creates social arrangements, and that these social arrangements in their turn affect the behavior of the members of that society. Asylum seekers who fled their country to escape from torture and killings live in European countries. It was fair that these people received help. However, the allowance, relief, and naturalization of increasing numbers of asylum seekers in many countries changed our conception of what a fair distribution of rights is, and what a fair income for different groups is. In the Netherlands, for example, asylum seekers easily received allowances, and all received a stipend whether they worked or not. However, increasing numbers of asylum seekers brought about a nationwide discussion about the appropriateness of more restricted rules of allowance, relief, and naturalization. Some people view asylum seekers as a threat to Dutch society with regard to access to jobs. People judged as fair that asylum seekers had to work for the stipend they received. What people judged as fair in the beginning they evaluated as less fair as the stream of asylum seekers grew. Because of the changed attitudes, the stream of asylum seekers decreased and some asylum seekers already in the Netherlands went underground. The attitudes toward asylum seekers, many from Moslem countries like Turkey, Morocco, Iraq, and Iran, became more negative and many people saw the Moslem culture as hostile to the Dutch way of living. Most Moslems were willing to learn the Dutch way of life while honoring their origins. A very small fraction of the Moslems developed an extreme negative attitude toward Dutch culture and institutions, and started a fighting group.

This example complements many others in which changes in ways of subsistence modified people's behavior and attitudes. The history of humankind is full of changes that occurred because of changes in the physical as well as social environment. Some of these changes are more dramatic than others, and some have more impact on people's lives than others. A major change in the way people lived together occurred when hunter-gatherer groups became farmers, and settled themselves more permanently in small villages. They developed agricultural methods and gradually created a more hierarchical and differentiated society with rules of how to behave toward group members of higher or lower status, or toward group members with different vocations and trades. I will try to prove in this chapter that the transition from hunting to agriculture also had significant consequences for the way people view justice and how to act justly.

In order to describe and understand the changes that took place in people's way of subsistence, a theoretical framework is indispensable. The framework should describe and explain how individual action plans affect the way people live together and how these arrangements in their turn influence individual ideas and behaviors. The theoretical framework that I will apply to describe and explain the transition from hunter/gatherer to farmer (the Agricultural Revolution) and the transition from a class-ridden society into an industrialized society (the Industrial Revolution) is Elias' civilization theory, and specifically the concept of social figuration (Elias 1969).

The issue raised in this chapter, therefore, is how the justice motive developed when hunters became farmers, settled themselves and created a relatively complex society. The chapter will show how the justice concept also changed under the influence of changes during the Industrial Revolution. First, it will describe the concept of social figuration and present a revised version of it. Then it will go into the transition from hunting to farming in terms of changing relationships between groups within the agricultural community. After that, the societal, cultural, and personality changes that took place during the Industrial Revolution will be described, along with the consequences for justice conceptions.

**Social Figuration**

The description and explanation of social phenomena is the intrinsic task of sociologists and social psychologists, among others. It took a long time in the history of both disciplines before a theoretical framework was developed that could do justice to the complex interplay, and its development, between individual and society. The hypothesis here is that the introduction of the concept of social figuration is very well suited to explaining phenomena at the individual level as well as at the societal level, and to explaining how these phenomena and their interactions change over time. Moreover, we will see that this conceptualization gives us more insight into the justice motive.

According to Elias (1969), people participate in social figurations. Goudsblom (1987) defines a social figuration as "a make-up of individuals who are mutually dependent on each other" (19). More specifically, and in line with the resource allocation model, a social figuration is a make-up of individuals who struggle for dominance over scarce resources. The main characteristics of the concept of social figuration are the presence of two or more parties—the established and the outsiders—who struggle for dominance (Elias and Scotson 1994). The outsiders challenge the position of power (a position based on control over scarce resources) of the established party. The established party tries to maintain their position by counter-force, and by distinguishing themselves culturally (by cultivating new manners) or psychologically (by developing stereotypes about and prejudice toward the outsiders; Tajfel and Turner 1986) from the other party. Social figurations can exist only for a short time, such as the social figuration of the established and the outsiders in an English town (Elias and Scotson 1994); or they can exist for longer, such as with the nobility and the bourgeoisie in France (Elias 1969), or the social figuration of nobility and peasantry in France and England (Moore Jr. 1966. The settled Dutch community view asylum seekers as newcomers. As long as the number of asylum seekers was not too large and their position in the Dutch community not too visible, they were received openheartedly. The attitude toward asylum seekers changed as the number of asylum seekers increased and when economic refugees entered the country along with political refugees. Many groups of citizens saw asylum seekers as competitors in the welfare market, and began to see them as a threat to their jobs and cultural beliefs, although, often, the newcomers did work which Dutch workers did not like. The refugee–Dutch citizenship relationship is a social figuration in which one group seeks to enter into the group of settled people and try to establish a good position. The settled group develops negative attitudes and prejudice toward the newcomers, and discriminates against them.

By introducing the concept of social figuration, Elias wanted to be able to describe the dynamics of social processes. Elias states that constellations of individuals change over time, and that these changes are crucial to understanding social life, individually and collectively. The most important aspect of this analysis is that the actions of individuals lead to changes in the social make-up—structure:

hierarchical relations between groups of people based on differential access to social resources; and culture: amount and type of shared social resources (such as shared beliefs and opinions of a group or society). The created make-up in turn affects the beliefs and behaviors of individuals. Later, generations may experience the make-up as a given entity: a reified social fact. A very important feature of social figuration is that changes are unplanned, and as such are unpredictable. The consequences of these changes, however, lead, according to Elias, to modifications in personality such as increasing restrictions on several types of behavior, like sexual behavior, table manners, or behavior toward strangers.

### *The Nobility–Bourgeois Figuration*

In investigating changes in the social make-up of society, Elias studied the changes in cultural beliefs in several domains of social life in different parts of historical Europe. The use of the term "civilized" marked the most important changes in people's behavior and attitudes. What "civilized" meant changed dramatically over time from medieval to modern Europe. The changes in the definition of the word went hand in hand with changes in the beliefs about what is appropriate in interactions with others. With many examples extracted from books on manners, Elias shows how beliefs and behaviors about what was appropriate at dinner, in the public bathroom, when dating, have changed over time. In the last part of his monumental book, Elias describes the changes in society's make-up that coincide with the changes in cultural beliefs and individual behavior, specifically in the relationship of the two dominant categories in society: the nobility and the bourgeoisie.

The feudal period had divided most land in Europe into small territories where a noblemen reigned. The noblemen were masters of their territory, fought their wars, and could do with their serfs what they wanted: the serfs were dependent on the nobles for their safety. Religion was the main thread in life of noblemen and serfs. The serfs worked the soil, and produced what they and their master needed. Life was not easy, with frequent wars, and people's mood changed from great joy to great sadness (Huizinga 1949) knowing that the reward for living in poverty and sincerity would come in the hereafter. During the ninth century, dramatic changes took place in Europe. The increase in population meant that the land around the castle no longer produced enough food. People could no longer live quietly in the vicinity of the castle, work on the soil, and worship God. They had to seek new venues for farming and raising cattle. The noblemen's sons no longer received parcels of land from their parents because the territory became too small to split up. Instead, the situation forced noblemen to enlarge their territories in order to keep their power and to support their serfs. The continuous succession wars, legacies, and marriages resulted in territories growing larger and larger until eventually the entire area was in the hands of a continually decreasing group of families. In this way, larger areas became pacified and developed longer chains of trade. Because the feudal lord was not able to feed them anymore, serfs became free, began to work for themselves, and, with the help of monks, developed new agricultural methods (Braudel 1989; Landes 1998). Many of the serfs went into handcraft, and gradually a new category of people arose: the bourgeoisie, citizens living in towns. The use of coins for the exchange of goods advanced the advent of the bourgeois, and made this category, the citizens, economically more and more powerful. To protect themselves from attacks from the outside, the town dwellers linked themselves to the noblemen, many of whom were now devoid of income. Both categories became more and more dependent on each other and achieved, with the nobility sinking and the bourgeois rising, a dynamic balance.

The noblemen looked down on the up-coming bourgeoisie, but their own fate and that of the bourgeoisie were intertwined. To differentiate themselves from the bourgeoisie, the noblemen cultivated their manners and viewed themselves as civilized compared to the bourgeoisie. The bourgeoisie copied the nobles' new manners. The term "*courtois*"—hence courtesy—represented the standard of "good behavior" in the feudal period. An example of courtesy or feudal court behavior was that people did not dip bitten-off bread into the communal dish as farmers did. In the Renaissance, the standard of good behavior was represented by the term "*civilité*." The use of a knife replaced the no longer appropriate act of breaking the bread. Later on, in the eighteenth century, the term "civilization" represented appropriate behavior. The use of the knife during dinner was only appropriate when one cut meat or vegetables. Otherwise, one should lay down the knife. People also developed standards for behavior in the bathroom, sexual behavior, and behavior in other domains. According to Elias, parents taught their children the new manners; the children thus internalized the underlying norms and values. In this way, people learned to behave more in line with what etiquette prescribed.

In short, Elias' civilization theory includes the notion of how culture (e.g., manners), structure (e.g., the positions in terms of power and status of the nobility and the bourgeoisie), and personality (e.g., internalization) develop and mutually affect each other. Before discussing the importance of social figuration for the justice motive, let us first briefly consider Elias' thinking in a theoretical perspective.

With the term "social figuration," Elias emphasizes the dynamic aspects of social life. In contrast to famous sociologists like Talcott Parsons (1951), Elias was more interested in changes in society than in the status quo. As Elias wrote in the foreword for the second edition of his work (in 1969), sociology has for too long been interested in continuity, viewing change only as an anomaly of the system, as a disequilibrium. Elias conceived of change as an inherent part of life in society. Under the pressure of new economic, technical, or demographic conditions, individuals change their behavior, causing social institutions to change as well, resulting in changes in behavior and in the personality make-up of individuals. With the idea of cycles of action and reaction, Elias circumvents the pitfall of determinism and reification, and at the same time accommodates the relativism of symbolic interactionism (Berger and Berger 1972): what people define as real is the result of their interaction with others.

### *Social Figuration Revised*

Despite the advantages of Elias' approach of societal and individual changes, the theory has some serious disadvantages with regard to the origin and development of behavior in general and just behavior in particular. One major disadvantage is its strong reliance on Freud's theory of psychodynamics. In line with Freud, Elias assumes that human beings possess drives, of which one of the most important is the libido or sexual drive. In the course of the civilization process, requirements and rules of society restrict the uncontrolled expression of the libido. Elias' main idea is that the more civilization progresses, the more restricted people's behavior will become. The psychological mechanism that is responsible for the suppression of the drives is the superego. The dos and don'ts that society enforces (*Fremdzwang*) are incorporated into the self; specifically, into the superego (*Selbstzwang*). The superego is the gatekeeper that guards the thoughts and actions prompted by the drives (the id). A critical revision of Elias' ideas is necessary in order to deal with some of the weak parts in it: three issues will be discussed here briefly.

Elias describes personality as consisting of drives and mechanisms to restrict the behavior resulting from those drives—specifically, the id, ego (the reality principle), and superego—while he predicts that the development of society and personality inevitably results in behaviors corresponding to Freud's psychodynamic theory. This sounds like circular reasoning.

Moreover, according to Elias, history is an unplanned process that reflects an increasing restraint of inherent behavior drives. This reasoning seems to be logically inconsistent. It is hard to believe that unplanned processes that start and end randomly can produce linearly increasing restraints on individuals. In addition, Duerr (1988) offers convincing evidence that a linear process of increasing restraints in sexual habits is very unlikely. Duerr's historical overview of the sexual preferences and behaviors of individuals in Europe over the last 700 years shows clearly that the dos and don'ts with regard to sexual behavior vary from time period to time period and from class to class. In some periods, sexual restraints are less severe than in earlier periods, while these restrictions should be more severe, according to Elias.

A third issue of the theory to reflect on has to do with Elias' emphasis on the struggle between the nobility and bourgeoisie in France. The continual struggle for dominance between nobility and bourgeoisie was, according to Elias, most visible in what is now the country of France, and he bases his theory of civilization mainly on what happened between the nobility and bourgeoisie in that country. Although the histories of other countries in Europe are in some aspects different from and in other aspects the same as that of France, Elias is justified in restricting his analysis mainly to the developments in France. What happened in other countries may be different from what happened in France, but that does not invalidate the theoretical premise. However, even in France, the growing interdependence between nobility and bourgeoisie was not the only social figuration that arose. This social figuration was probably not even the most important one. From time to time, other figurations became visible which had a notable influence on societal processes as well as on the beliefs and actions of individuals. One such important social figuration is that between the gentry and the peasantry, which Moore Jr (1966) described as operating during the period analyzed by Elias. Moore described the struggle between these classes in society, and showed that the way it proceeded resulted in either revolution from above (Germany and Japan), revolution from below (Russia and China), or in a democratic regime (England, United States, and France). Moore did not go into changes in personality of the citizens of the countries studied, but a thorough look at citizens from these countries shows that they are rather different with regard to openness and attitudes toward freedom, and these differences continue today. Another important struggle in Europe during the last millennium is that between the clergy and dissidents. In many periods in European history, clashes erupted between clergy and dissidents, with the Inquisition being the most famous institution of the dominant group to repress the deviants (Eco 1984; Goudsblom 1987). For instance, in several countries in Europe the Catholic Church persecuted Jews for their religious beliefs. Jews had to flee from Spain and settle in northern countries like Holland and Germany.

It seems to me that a refinement of Elias' ideas on continuity and change in human society and human life is necessary to accommodate recent findings and analyses. One refinement is the recognition of the transient character of social figurations (Vermunt 2002). Social figurations always exist, in the sense that categories of individuals always strive to increase (respectively, decrease) the power distance between themselves and the other group, but in certain times this struggle is stronger than in others. It is even possible that the social figuration almost disappears, as in the case of the nobility–bourgeois figuration. Moreover, new social figurations originate and coexist with established figurations, although they may differ in their strength. The working class and capitalist class still form a figuration, but nowadays the strivings for power are less obvious, and certainly far less so than they were in the 1960s and 1970s. The working class and capitalist class figuration is less in evidence than the figuration that presently exists between settled Dutch citizens and the political and economic refugees from other countries, the so-called asylum seekers. In conclusion, the intensity of conflict between parties in a social figuration can vary across time, and can vary from figuration to figuration within a particular time.

An important aspect of the theory of social figuration that needs attention concerns the aspect of intergroup relations and its consequences for the attitudes groups of people develop toward each other. In detail, Elias (1969) describes how the behavior of the nobility changes over time because of their diminishing status in society, how their cultural habitat changes, for example with the use of the word *civilité*. He describes the manners of the upcoming bourgeoisie as an imitation of those of the nobility (see, e.g., Molière's *Le Bourgeois gentilhomme*). What Elias does not describe in his monumental work of the civilization process is how the nobility and bourgeoisie perceive each other. In a later work (Elias and Scotson 1994), in which he describes the relationship between the established people in a community and outsiders, Elias pays more attention to these intergroup relations and perceptions. In general, one may conclude from studying a community that the more the established judge outsiders as a threat to their position, the more negatively they perceive and talk about outsiders. The more the status position of the two groups converges, the more negative their mutual attitudes become. In other words, it is likely that the convergence of the status position of two (or more) groups results in the development of stereotypes about each other. A revision of Elias' figuration theory of social change may incorporate this aspect of intergroup relations: that stereotyping and negative attitudes are an indication of the presence of a virulent social figuration. Folk ways, fairytales, and epic stories form expressions of the residues of such negative attitudes and stereotyping. The epic story of *The Three Musketeers* by Alexandre Dumas describes the virulent relationship between nobility and bourgeoisie in France. Dumas wrote the story in the nineteenth century, well after the French revolution, marking the end of the virulent nobility–bourgeoisie controversy.

Another addition to Elias' definition of social figuration is that parties in a social figuration differ in their control of scarce resources. Established and outsiders can be more precisely defined by emphasizing the scarce resources one group—the established—controls and the other—the outsiders—challenges. The nobility wielded power using military force that the bourgeois did not have. The increase in the bourgeois' wealth (money and goods) increased their power, resulting in a dynamic balance between nobility and bourgeois. The established also use non-material resources to increase their power. In the nobility's case, they developed manners to differentiate themselves from the—in their eyes—uncivil bourgeois manners. For instance, in *Le Bourgeois gentilhomme*, first shown in 1670, Molière mocks a rich town dweller who likes to imitate the behavior and manners of the aristocracy. In other words, the nobility tried to get a higher position with respect to the resource "status." The bourgeois imitated the manners in an attempt to close the status gap. More important, however, than imitating manners was the bourgeois' attempt to differentiate themselves from the nobility, by developing a philosophy about appropriate behavior: an ethic. The nobility held the belief that the divine king, the highest authority, prescribes what is right or wrong. Bourgeois thinkers introduced the concept of *ratio* (reason) as highest authority of judgment (Descartes 1637; Kant 1780). In *Discourse on Method*, Descartes, explored the origins of knowledge and how one differentiates between true and false knowledge. Kant investigated the boundaries of absolute knowledge. One can say that a rigorous shift occurred from dependency on divine knowledge to knowledge that originates from human intellectual activity. An early, successful, though highly controversial, attempt in this respect was Galileo's discovery—through observation of the planets—that the earth circles around the sun and not the sun around the earth as the Bible text—inspired by God—implied.

The virulent figuration of nobility and bourgeoisie implies, according to Elias, that behaviors in many domains became more restricted because of the nobility's drive to differentiate itself culturally from the bourgeoisie and the bourgeoisie's drive to close this gap; the restrictions formed the superego. In my view of the civilization process, things went differently: The nobility achieved differentiation mainly by cultivating new standards of behavior, derogating the bourgeoisie's emphasis on work and by highlighting the value of loyalty and a military way of life. The bourgeoisie closed the gap by imitating this behavior, but differentiated themselves by engaging in handcraft and trade and by highlighting their financial gains. This process resulted in behavioral and cognitive adaptations to live in line with the newly developed standards. Not to live in accordance with the new standards meant that one became a ridiculed outsider. People learned to accommodate their behavior in such a way that positive outcomes came within reach as much as possible. People learned to anticipate certain outcomes, and to achieve those outcomes by performing the appropriate behaviors. In other words, the nobility as well as the bourgeoisie learned from their strivings to differentiate themselves from each other to give attention to action–outcome chains: If I do this than I will get the desired outcome. For instance, the nobility cultivated their warfare ability, but also poetry and manners to prepare for court life. The bourgeoisie cultivated their manners as well, partly to imitate the nobility for successful interaction with them, but partly to accommodate to the steadily growing circle of trade partners to increase wealth. They learned to interact with people from geographical areas far away and to negotiate with them. To be successful in trade, members of the bourgeoisie had to accommodate to "strange" manners and tongues. People mastered these cognitive abilities because of the interdependent relationship between the groups, and made it part of their children's education.

In this respect, Furby (1986) may be cited: "the fundamental fact about our world is the correlation between the actions we take and the events we experience" (180). Furby developed the action–outcome model of learned expectations (Vermunt 1989). She states that parents teach their children that certain actions will lead to certain outcomes. By trial and error, and by principles of social learning such as positive and negative reinforcement (reward and punishment), the growing child learns that they receive valued outcomes by performing specific actions. Parents teach their children to pay attention to the things they are doing. Children learn to pay attention to efficient behavior by emphasizing the consequences of their actions. The feeling of becoming respected, hard work, and trying to get rich strengthened the bourgeoisie's motivation for cognitively linking acts to outcomes. People improved their cognitive ability more and more, and it became part of the cognitive equipment of individual citizens.

The important question, of course, is why parents teach their children to be attentive to their actions and to care about behavioral outcomes? The most likely answer is that parents believe that it is a social requirement to raise their children in this way. Apparently, parents find it necessary to teach their children to behave in such a way that their actions will lead to predictable outcomes as far as possible. The social environment must have given parents reasons to teach their children to be attentive to the consequences of their actions. The motivation to distinguish oneself from other groups, for instance the nobility from the bourgeois, prompted the nobility to become more "civilized," and they raised their children accordingly. One may safely assume, therefore, that changes in how parents raise their children have a social origin, in that parents have perceived these changes, have anticipated them, have modeled them, and act accordingly. The social origin of child-rearing practice is also visible nowadays. Drastic changes in China during the last two decades from a communist-Confucianist to a capitalist country brought many parents and schoolteachers to teach the children to become more competitive, autonomous, and individualistic, qualities that were unacceptable in the communist-Confucianist tradition. The capitalist newcomers evaluated these qualities higher than the settled communist people (Chen 2009). So, newcomers learned completely different attitudes and behaviors which infected the settled people in an increasing rate.

The action–outcome model of cognitive and behavioral anticipation to social change explains the empirical fact that (1) restrictions are also observed outside the realm of sexual behavior on which Elias' model is strongly based, and (2) periods of restricted behavior are followed by periods of more unrestricted behavior, while Elias' model predicts a linear process.

The concept of social figuration is a useful tool for studying societal change, its roots, its process, and its consequences. We now use the revised version of the civilization theory to study many situations where people become more dependent on each other. A very important situation in this respect occurred during the transition from a predominantly hunter-gatherer way of subsistence to an agricultural way of subsistence.

## From Hunter-Gatherer to Farmer: A Social Figuration Approach

In the Pleistocene (from two million to about 12,000 years ago) and part of the Holocene period (from 12,000 years ago until now) the general way of subsistence for hominins and humans was a combination of hunting, scavenging, foraging, and gathering. Otzi, the Iceman, who lived about 5,300 years ago, was found by hikers at an altitude of about 3,200 meters in the Alps, on the border between Austria and Italy; he carried a bow, a quiver of arrows, and a copper ax. He also carried a small box for making fire. His last meal was one of venison and ibex (*Capra ibex*) meat. He was probably shot in a skirmish with a rival tribe. Although Otzi's last meal consisted of meat, a hunter's diet consisted of about 20 percent meat and about 80 percent plant food. In comparison, the diet of farmers was made up of meat (10 percent), plant food (80 percent), and eggs, milk, and cheese (10 percent). When prey was absent, hunter/forager groups had to depend completely on plant food.

Humans lived in groups, of which most were mobile, moving from one place to another, dependent on prey, while others were more permanent. Some were highly mobile, small in number, subsistence-based, and egalitarian. Others were sedentary or semi-sedentary, populous, produced a surplus of food, and had a hierarchical structure. Apart from some Indian bands in north-west North America, most hunter/forager groups had few possessions: weapons, simple equipment to divide prey and to process wild plants, and some material for shelter (Barker 2006). Many groups lived in caves as a semi-permanent residence, and found shelter there. They used bows and arrows for catching animals and axes or knives of stone, later of bronze and iron, to cut the prey into pieces. The question is, how did they divide prey to non-kin members of the band? Chapter 1 has already discussed this issue; the discussion will continue here in somewhat more detail in order to describe the transition to farming.

### *Hierarchy in Hunter-Gatherer Groups*

Despite the importance of gathering and foraging activities, hunting and bringing in prey was the most important activity. Caribou bone distributions found in the excavations in Pincevent, France (Enloe 2003) supports this view. From the distribution of animal bones, one can infer that the hunters divided the best parts of the animals among themselves, while the other members of the group received the remainder. Females, children, and the senior members of the band carried out most of the foraging/gathering activities, although on occasion hunters did forage as well. Indirect evidence of hunters having higher prestige in the group than females and children appeared in the results of studies among the Ache (Kaplan et al. 1984) and the Hadza (Marlowe 2002). In both groups, meat from large hunted prey was allocated more to non-kin consumers than to kinfolk (87 percent), while honey and fruit were, to a lesser degree, allocated more to non-kin consumers than to kinfolk (80 percent, respectively 62 percent). Food acquired as mission-brought resources, hunters allocated only a relatively small amount to non-kin consumers (50 percent). In other words, the more risk and effort involved in acquiring the food, the more it is allocated to people who do not belong to the family. The food has high value, and allocating meat to non-kin consumers gives higher prestige to the acquirer. It gives rise to status differences between hunters and the rest of the group.

The scientific community agrees that hunter-gatherer groups are rather egalitarian (Marlowe 2002; Enloe 2003; Kaplan and Gurven 2005). This observation contradicts other observations indicating that hunter/gatherer groups have some type of hierarchy. The subject of observation bridges the difference. The scientific community looks at individual status differences within the hunter/gatherer community, instead of looking at status differences between sub-groups in the community. As research of hunter/gatherer communities shows, hunters do not always come back with prey, which prevents the build-up of a permanent status position in the group as well as in the community. However, the group of hunters has a higher status position compared to other groups or categories in the community. In addition, Werner (1981) showed in a study among the Mekranoti Indians of central Brazil that hunters and artisans have higher status than other groups based on prestige, but not based on wealth. According to Keeley (1996), bands are small, politically autonomous groups of 20 to 50 people with an informal headman. Typically, bands are hunter-gatherers or foragers (26). From these findings, I conclude that individual hunters sometimes and hunter sub-groups more permanently had a say in how to allocate meat among themselves and among other members of the band, and thus had higher status. Hierarchical differences based on material possessions between sub-groups were small in hunter/forager groups, as well as between individual members.

*Culture and the Allocation Process in Hunter-Gatherer Groups*

Allocation processes take place in the context of people's culture and their beliefs about how they relate themselves to the natural world, to other people, and to their material possessions. A crucial aspect of hominin and human hunter groups is the way they see themselves in relation to the plant and animal world. As animal pictures made more than 30,000 years ago in caves (Chauvet) in southern France show, prehistoric hunters apparently saw themselves as part of the plant and animal world and not as distinct from it. The natural world was full of "kinfolk," the plants and animals they seek. The foraging way of life was as much a mode of spirituality as a mode of subsistence. Their relationship with others was one of trust, not domination (Ingold 1994; Martin 1993). These beliefs are labeled animistic beliefs. The term animism comes from the Latin word *anima* meaning *breath* or *soul*. Animism is probably one of man's oldest beliefs, with its origin most likely dating to the Paleolithic age. From its earliest beginnings, it was a belief that a soul or spirit existed in every object, even if it was inanimate. In a future state, this soul or spirit would exist as part of an immaterial soul. The spirit, therefore, was a universal one. Animism includes "the attempt to live respectfully as members of the diverse community of living persons (only some of them are human) which we call the world or cosmos" (Harvey 2005). To live in harmony with other group members and with plants and animals is a great good. Even in hunter groups, infanticide is not uncommon in order to keep the group manageable with regard to the available resources and thus to live in harmony with the natural environment. Animistic belief thus includes good relationships with others. To restore harmony in the group, the group of chiefs solves the conflicts that inevitably arise. In doing so, trespassers are treated in such a way that their prestige and status is least affected. An example is how Indian tribes settled the shooting of Spotted Tail in 1881. Spotted Tail took Light-in-the-Lodge away from her disabled husband and took her as his second wife. Crow Dog then acted as a representative of the wronged husband. In the altercation between the two, Crow Dog shot Spotted Tail. The matter was resolved between the clans by using peacemakers. Crow Dog's clan had to compensate Spotted Tail's clan with a payment of $600, eight horses, and one blanket. This decision had the consent of both clans and restored harmony to the tribe (French and Picthall-French 2007). The solution of this problem was in accordance with the American Indian Harmony Ethos. According to French and Picthall-French (2007), this is: "the restoration of group balance and not individual culpability [that] drove the aboriginal system of justice" (185). Intervention aims to restore the group's harmony. Thus, as Benson (1989) has stated, enforcement need not come from a central government. Many primitive societies nominate a go-between to settle disputes. Tribe sanctions are so severe when the accused does not agree with the settlement that members do not trespass. The tribe sanction is so severe because they want to preserve good mutual relationships and live in harmony with the other tribe. The primitive societies Benson studied were sedentary and had property in the form of land or fishing areas; some had an extensive irrigation system, so there were resources to lose. Looking with our materialistic and Western legal eyes at a phenomenon like tolerated theft, we concentrate too much on the allocation of material goods and individual culpability, while prehistoric hunters would probably be more concerned with harmony in the group. To treat others respectfully is essential, and this includes distribution of non-material resources (respect given to others). Group members in hunter communities will, therefore, take into account the relationships within the group as well as the group climate when evaluating allocation events (see also Tyler and Lind 1992). In this sense, the group of leader's behavior resembles that of the alpha male intervening sometimes when a conflict breaks out in the group (de Waal 1996).

Most hunter-gatherer studies, as described in Chapter 1, do not take distribution of non-material goods, such as status, prestige, or harmony into account, while distribution of non-material goods relates to the animistic beliefs of prehistoric hunters. We understand food distribution and justice better when culture—the number and types of shared social resources—is included in analyses of allocation processes.

Harmony between tribes is, however, not common in primitive societies. Battles involving large numbers of fighters are rare in tribal warfare; according to Keeley (1996), the usual form of tribal war is continuous low intensity action—ambushes, raids on enemy villages, destruction of crops, and so forth. Male enemies are seldom taken prisoner, but killed on the spot (or taken for ritual torture or cannibalism), while females and children are taken as wives or slaves. "Primitive … warfare consists of war stripped to its essentials: the murder of enemies; the theft or destruction of their sustenance, wealth, and essential resources, and the inducement in them of insecurity and terror" (Keeley 1996: 75). This situation mainly occurs when tribes compete with each other for scarce resources. In cases of interdependence between two tribes—for instance, when a third party threatens both—peaceful dispute resolution is preferred. However, compared to other economies, like intensive agriculture or animal husbandry, hunter-gatherers have a low frequency of continuous warfare (hunter-gatherer: 20 percent; intensive agriculture: 47 percent; animal husbandry: 89 percent) and a high frequency of no warfare (respectively, 30 percent, 6 percent, 11 percent). So, hunter-gatherer bands lived in relative peace compared to agricultural societies (Keeley 1996: Table 1.2, 186).

This was the situation at around 12,000 years ago, when dramatic climate changes took place.

## After the Ice Age

The end of the Pleistocene period—the beginning of the Holocene—was marked by dramatic climate changes: Ice that covered most parts of the Northern and Southern regions of the earth melted, resulting in heavy rainfall in some parts of the earth, rising sea levels, and higher temperatures (Butzer 1995).

For the Near East, the period from the years 9000 to 3000 BC was moist in the lowland deserts, making it suitable for prehistoric settlements. The transition from hunter-gatherer to farmer did not start at the same time, at the same level, or with the same pace for each hunter-gatherer band. Some hunter-gatherer groups started early, experimenting with more permanent forms of farming. They picked wild barley, made some sort of dough from it and let it dry in the sun. They domesticated goats and sheep, and took them with them when they moved to other areas. Other groups gathered fruits, tubers, and other vegetables from the woods, but did not pick wild grain and process it. They hunted for meat and had no domesticated animals. The transition from hunting to farming was not a linear process. Some groups started to experiment with farming but changed back to hunting when it turned out to be too costly in terms of time and energy (Barker 2006; see also Marlowe 2002). However, in south-west Asia, around 5000 BC, hunter groups were still present but were exceptions; most groups lived in permanent residences and performed a system of mixed farming, that is, the cultivation of wheat and barley and the herding of sheep and goats.

The question as to why hunters changed their way of subsistence and became farmers is hard to answer. Barker warns over after-the-fact reasoning, and cites Diamond (1997) with approval: "what actually happened was not a discovery of food production, nor an invention … food production evolved as a by-product of decisions made without awareness of their consequences" (106). Moreover, some forms of husbandry (the care of animals and plants) were already present far earlier than the late Pleistocene, and are as old as the history of *Homo sapiens*, that is about 100,000 years. However, it did not lead to farming as a systematic method of food production: that occurred at the transition from the Pleistocene to the Holocene period.

Barker (2006) states that any theory explaining the transition from mainly hunting activities to farming activities should take into account not one but several driving factors. One is that climate change is a key driver of the subsistence change. Lamb (1982) finds it helpful to think of climate and climate change as a catalyst or trigger of change (see also Rosen 2007). Lamb is struck by "the many coincidences of the more catastrophic events in both" (the climate record and the course of human history; Lamb 1982: 4). A correlation between the climate record and dramatic changes in human history, therefore, is very likely. It led to changes in the distributions, densities, and predictability of animal and plant resources, and presented people with great challenges and opportunities. Some of these responses had far-reaching consequences for the intensification of food production. Scientists generally accept that climate change often reduced the availability of higher-ranked resources and increased efforts in husbanding lower-ranked resources, although some forager groups acted differently to the climate change. Another factor is the type of resource that was part of the main source of subsistence. Some plants and animals were more suited to domestication than others. People had long recognized cereals as a useful food resource, and it turned out that animals like sheep, goats, cows, pigs, and others were all successful at living with humans. In addition, some places, such as near rivers and lakes, were more suitable for residence than other places, and people came back to these places and often settled there. A third important factor Barker mentioned is that gathering and producing food are activities which not only reflect a relationship between humans and the physical environment, but are social as well. Findings indicate that the acquisition of domesticated plants or animals was often driven by social factors. The question is, which social factors are crucial in this respect? Barker assumes that "foods that we regard now as staples—wheat, sorghum, rice, maize, cattle, sheep, and so on—must often have been attractive to foragers in the phase of initial contact with farmers because they were exotic, their acquisition bringing prestige and status to the owner" (405). What Barker observes here about the prestige and status effects of resource acquisition is not something that comes unexpectedly, but is the result of a long process of valuation of these resources and activities. It remains to be explained why these resources and activities became so attractive for hunters/foragers. By applying Elias' social figuration theory, I will try to answer this question (Elias 1969; Goudsblom 1987, 1992).

### *Reactions to Climate Change and Social Factors*

Climate change affected the flora and fauna of many places on earth, including those of south-west Asia, the hilly flanks of the Fertile Crescent—the arc of hill country to the west of the Syrian Desert and to the north and east of the Tigris and Euphrates valleys. The climate records from isotopic analysis of Greenland ice cores show that the transition from Pleistocene to Holocene was characterized by large and sudden temperature fluctuations. About 15,000 years ago, there was a sudden increase in temperature and moisture in south-east Asia. These changes favored woodland, as well as annual grasses such as wild cereals. The Natufian people (13,000 BC) emerged relatively suddenly throughout the Levant. For the early Natufian people it was relatively easy to hunt and gather cereals—their diet was good, and the Natufian people increased in number. A sudden drop in temperature around 11,000 BC—lasting until 9,500 BC—confronted the rising population with declining returns from foraging and hunting. Some people moved, as a reaction to the climate change, while others diversified their subsistence system and some intensified it. The different reactions to climate change resulted in communities that increasingly differed in their way of subsistence. Some probably continued with hunting while other communities became more dedicated to gathering plants and cereals, and other groups concentrated on horticulture. The communities that diversified and intensified their subsistence system engaged in a mode of subsistence where women had specific tasks. It is assumed (Barker 2006) that in these communities women undertook most of the cereal work, and that the men hunted and then, later on, became more and more involved in ground preparation and related activities. According to Elias' social figuration explanation of social change (Elias 1969), the differences augmented the development of new ways of subsistence in those communities, which differentiated themselves from traditional hunter communities by engaging in other cultural activities as well, like improving ways of producing art as well as agriculture. This finding led Henry (1989) to conclude that Natufian society was matrilocal, with women remaining in the community while men went hunting. In the newly developing communities, women contributed in their own way to the community and became less dependent on the male members' contribution. The development of more efficient modes of subsistence resulted in more leisure time, which was used partly for bone artifact production, emphasizing their and their community's prestige and status.

This is a situation quite different from the one before. The high-status members of the hunter communities were, at first, the hunters. Although they gathered only 20 percent of the daily diet, hunting was a high-status activity. Other members of the community gathered plants and fruits as well, but because they carried out these activities near the temporary settlement and without much risk, these activities were not very well valued. However, the hunters' diminishing returns made other modes of subsistence necessary, with women as driving force. In the new communities, the women's status increased, while the hunters' status decreased. The hunter's role decreased even more when animals were domesticated and meat production was under the control of the whole community. In the meantime, hunting carried on and meat was exchanged with other valuable resources.

The new situation gave rise to increasing networks of exchange between communities, over longer distances, and a greater concern with prestige and rank. This suggests the development of community-wide positions of status and systems of decision-making.

### *Cultural Changes*

The transition from predominantly hunting to predominantly farming brought with it changes in social relationships as well as in material and immaterial culture. Hunter communities had no possessions beyond those they could carry with them when moving to other locations. The settlement dwellers, however, paid great attention to possessions as a way to differentiate themselves from hunters and from other communities. Comparing oneself with others with regard to material resources became a cognitive activity (see also Lane 1991). Competence-in-hunting comparison was probably practiced by hunters, but people in farmer communities compared themselves with regard to their possessions: How big is my wealth compared to that of others? Moreover, people from farmer communities as well as members of hunter bands – coexisting in the same area - developed perceptions and stereotypes of each other. The farmers, in the beginning, were outsiders while the hunters were the established and the hunters developed stereotypes about the newcomers to distance themselves from them. In epic stories, produced much later, traces of these perceptions and stereotypes are present, as in the epic story of Gilgamesh, translated into Dutch by Theo de Feyter (2001). Gilgamesh, king of Uruk, has tyrannical traits and the people complain about it. The gods hear these complaints and seek a friend for Gilgamesh in order to divert his energies. Enkidu is a creature who lives among the animals in a primitive state. He is ignorant about civilized ways of behaving, is respectful to animals, and has straightforward ideas about honesty. When confronted with the king's privilege to sleep with just married women, he is outraged and starts a fight with the king. This stereotypical image of a primitive man – ignorant of our high-standing manners, and to settle a conflict with fighting - might come from farmers' perceptions of hunters when both groups were struggling for dominance.

Farmers sought to impress hunters and began differentiating themselves by initiating activities on the cultural level. People in settlements built houses and decorated them. Of course, hunters competed with others as well, for instance, in the search for good hunting areas. However, these differences related not to differences in wealth or to attempts to increase them. Settlement dwellers, however, were immobile and had to find other areas of differentiation, like possessions—jewelry, pottery, house decoration. The graves of the deceased became richer in decoration; they plastered their houses and made pottery with exclusive prints. All of which were aimed at confirming and strengthening their identity, status, and wealth.

Changes in the immaterial culture took place as well. Religious beliefs shifted from animism—the belief seeing oneself as part of the natural world (Segal 1999)—to theism, or more specifically polytheism—the belief that natural and other phenomena (thunder, war) are represented by a god one has to worship. Each town had its own god. The transition from animism to polytheism relates to the transition from forager to agriculture. The development of agricultural modes of subsistence must have had a tremendous influence on people's relationship with the natural world. No longer were human beings only dependent on what Nature offered them. Domesticating cereals and animals brought part of Nature under control. For subsistence, people no longer depended on risky hunting but on what they produced themselves. This resulted in the belief that one was not part of the natural world but that one was master of (part of) the natural world. This belief must have boosted humankind's confidence. However, at the same time, these experiences might have originated the idea that there should also be a master who controlled human beings and their activities—a being who weighed the positive and negative acts of human beings, punishing the negative acts and rewarding the positive ones. Offering the fruits of their activities had a positive effect on the god's opinion of the people's acts. People made offerings to the war god for a good result when starting a war against an enemy. They made offerings to the city god, the rain god, to the god of the harvest, and of the household. In pre-dynastic Egypt, the gods took on human forms and personalities. Also, in Mesopotamian mythology, gods had anthropomorphic characteristics.

The transition from foraging to agriculture, thus, resulted in changes in the appreciation of material as well as immaterial culture. People in the hamlets, later cities, gradually valued material possessions as representations of their prestige and status. Comparing oneself with others in terms of wealth and status became a cognitive activity that was part of the daily routine of perception of and communication with others. People became increasingly more capable in estimating status differences between self and others and between others mutually, because being wrong in estimating these differences was detrimental for one's own social position. People tried to close the gap between their status position and the status position of those a bit higher in the status hierarchy, resulting in attempts by those positioned higher to enlarge the gap (Elias 1969). This continuous social struggle is often a catalyst for changes in material culture, as developments in housing decoration, pottery, jewelry, and other materials show.

Leisure time was filled differently from the leisure time hunters had. Some authors state that hunter communities were constantly engaged in bringing in food, but studies of the !Kung people in the Kalahari desert show that—even in this difficult environment—it only takes about two hours of the day to gather food. The !Kung spend the rest of the time cooking and in social meetings. The !Kung and other hunter-gatherers had no need to seek to differentiate themselves from others to confirm their status—status differences were temporary rather than permanent. In the cities of Sumer in Mesopotamia, and for other peoples, status became a subject of comparison and people tried to differentiate themselves from others by creating different modes of existence as necessary, like becoming a scribe or a judge. They created professions, making social arrangements even more complex. People became more sensitive to differences in the social order. One could claim that the striving to differentiate oneself from others (newcomers from the settled, and vice versa) could be better achieved if the differentiation could be reproduced simply; for instance, a material object: property. In other words, from my analyses it might be inferred that inequality bred the notion of property and not, as Rousseau claimed, that property created inequality (Rousseau 1754, translated by G.D.H. Cole). Rousseau asserts that "[t]his was the epoch of a first revolution, which established and distinguished families, and introduced a kind of property, in itself the source of a thousand quarrels and conflicts" (Rousseau 1754, translated by Cole, 31).

### *Impact on Justice*

Changes in the social order gave rise to fairness considerations that were different from those in the hunter/foraging cultures. People considered animals as unequal to men, contrary to what hunter-gatherers believed. People treated them with less respect. Animals became part of the livestock of the city dwellers, viewed as part of their wealth. In addition, people based fairness considerations on status and prestige. Community members allowed higher-status people more latitude than lower status people. Text on the Cappadocian tablets in the British Museum shows the operation of fairness beliefs: "Meir and Ilia bring an application against Zuba on the plea that the present division of their father's house has not been a fair division among them, that is, the mother and the brothers. Much silver, silver jewellery and bronze has disappeared from their father's house" (Tablet 114392). The text of this and other tablets deals with commercial and legal transactions of a settlement of Semitic traders who flourished in the region of Caesarea, in the neighborhood of Mount Argaeus, in the twenty-fourth century before Christ. Although there is no evidence that the cuneiform text used the term fair, from the text I infer that the pleading parties, Meir and Ilia, have a notion of what they think they are entitled to receive from their father's house. Implicitly, the pleading party has formed expectations of what they regard as an appropriate allotted resource amount. What they have received is clearly different—and to their disadvantage—from what they expected based on their status position in the household. Meir and Ilia compared the amount they received with the amount they expected to receive in relation to what Zuba received. The assumed comparison processes of amounts of material resources that underlie the plea in the text of Tablet 114392 reflect a social as well as a psychological process. A social process in that Meir and Ilia value material goods greatly, and that they share this belief with other members of the community. Property rights are accepted and the community has clearly developed a procedure to settle property rights disputes like this one. It implies also that people who make a plea accept the outcome of the dispute resolution and thus that an authority can sanction the eventual enforcement of the agreement.

The practices with regard to allocation and reciprocity as exemplified in the Cappadocian tablets amounted to a set of justice rules. Application of justice rules depended on the social class to which a person belonged. The Code of Hammurabi (~1700 BC) reveals a society of strict justice. Penalties for criminal offenses were severe and varied according to the wealth of the individual. According to the Code, there were three social classes in Babylon: an upper class of nobles (government officials, priests, and warriors), the class of freemen (merchants, artisans, professionals, and wealthy farmers), and a lower class of slaves. Society punished an offense against a member of the upper class with more severity than the same offense against a member of a lower class. The principle of retaliation ("an eye for an eye, a tooth for a tooth") was fundamental. The community retaliated in cases where members of the upper class committed criminal offenses against their own social equals. However, for offenses against members of the lower classes, the community allowed a financial fine. In other words, operation of the Code suggests that there was no equality in the law for every citizen.

As can be inferred from the Code of Hammurabi, the existence of status groups, trades, and professions made the operation of justice considerations rather complex. Appropriate allocation decision-making requires accounting for small differences in status between categories of people and between different trades. People have to carry out these decisions and the appropriate behaviors with caution in order to prevent embarrassment and loss of status or respect. Thus, the cognitive processes with regard to justice considerations became more and more differentiated. However, probably even more important was the emergence of inequality of allocation of immaterial resources like respect and dignity given to other groups. Status differences gave rise to attempts to increase one's own group status and to decrease the status of other groups, by developing prejudice, in-group favoritism, and derogation of other groups. Showing respect and dignity for everyone irrespective of their contribution to the community, which was a common practice in foraging societies, had broken down in the emerging agricultural societies. The justice motive that in hunter-gatherer groups was directed toward not decreasing another's status probably changed into a motive for increasing own status as compared to the status of the other. It speaks for itself that these preconceived ideas hamper solutions when conflicts arise about allocation of material resources between status groups.

### *Impact on Cognition and Emotion*

The Cappadocian text reflects the operation of a psychological process as well. People developed cognitive abilities to evaluate the appropriate amounts that they think belong to themselves and to others. Lane (1991) cites Berry (1976) who showed that members of hunter-gatherer societies can better differentiate parts from wholes and figures from background than members from more advanced—agricultural—societies, which is thought to be related to a larger degree of independence and autonomy for members in primitive societies. However, according to Lane, Gamble and Ginsberg (1981)found that members of hunter-gatherer societies showed a lower degree of cognitive differentiation than members of agricultural societies. Moreover, Lane cites Lloyd (1972) who showed that members of primitive societies are less able to imagine alternatives, to "shuffle things around in their heads," than members of Western societies. These findings seem to suggest a lower degree of cognitive independence and autonomy, in that the absence of alternatives makes people more dependent on presented or perceived material. One may conclude, therefore, that members of hunter-gatherer groups are better than those of more advanced societies in differentiating the physical environment but are cognitively less complex and thus less able in the social arena.

In addition to changes in the structure of our cognitions when society becomes more complex, the content of our cognitions also changes. According to Fiske (2007), status differences and cooperation/competition between groups give rise to preconceived ideas about the other group, such as the assumed warmth and competence of the group. The preconceived ideas elicit emotions like envy (not warm and competent; rich people), disgust (not warm and incompetent; drunks), pity (warm and incompetent; elderly), and pride (warm and competent, in-group), and may ultimately end in negative actions toward other groups, like discrimination.

## The Little Ice Age and its Consequences

According to Lamb (1982), analyses have revealed five major post-glacial periods of climate change and five periods of cultural change. One of the major climate changes started at the end of the thirteenth century and lasted until the end of the eighteenth century. People felt the climate change in England, Europe, and in other parts of the world. According to Lamb (1982), the estimated temperatures in England from 900 AD until 1900 AD show large differences. Scientists derived the temperatures from tree ring analysis, Arctic ice core analysis, and daily weather reports in monastic chronicles and government papers. Over the period studied, the average temperature dropped dramatically, although for some years low temperatures and high temperatures alternated, culminating in the lowest temperatures in the last part of the seventeenth century and the second part of the eighteenth century—the Little Ice Age.

The consequences of this climate change were dramatic. Records from several sources show shorter summer periods, stronger western winds in England and western Europe, high rainfall, and consequently low agricultural productivity and high prices for food. Famine and infectious diseases like the Black Death were common, and the health level of the general population was rather low. A study of the registers of births, marriages, and deaths in the parish of Colyton, near Exeter, UK, showed that, after a steady growth from about 1550 until about 1640, the number of burials exceeded the number of births from the 1660s until about 1730. People abandoned their farms and communities. They tried to challenge the problematic situation by adopting successful agricultural methods like horses for plowing and three-course rotation: sowing and harvesting three times in two years. The improved agricultural methods needed less labor, and the superfluous people tried to find work in the towns. The presence of the guilds made finding work very difficult. Moreover, when wool became a profitable commodity, landowners enclosed new pastures to raise sheep. The process of enclosure, which began in the sixteenth century, reached its height in the nineteenth century, with thousands of tenant farmers thrown off the land in order to make room for the more profitable sheep (Heilbroner 2008).

### *The Industrial Revolution*

At the end of the eighteenth century, the most severe period of the Little Ice Age became history. Warming set in, but erratically, sometimes interrupted by cold winters. Temperatures rose gradually, agricultural productivity increased, and people's health improved, resulting in population growth after the 1780s. Although agriculture and small-scale industry, like mining in Germany and England, absorbed some workers, the growing population lived in poverty.

The benevolent climate change coincided with cultural changes. Climate change was not the one and only cause of the onset of the industrial revolution, but it was the trigger for the application and spread of technical inventions. The so-called Industrial Revolution, beginning at the end of the eighteenth century, also brought with it the mechanization of the mining industry, while the introduction of railways, canals, and better roads improved trade.

Population growth increased the demand for food, clothing, housing, and all sorts of equipment. The application of the steam engine in textile manufacturing as well as in trade (ships and railways) ensured that industrialization dealt with these demands. Some authors (Mumford 1963) argue that the technical revolution was in fact not a revolution but an evolution that started in the Middle Ages with the invention of the clock and the printing press (see also Clark 2001). The Protestant Ethic, emerging after the beginning of the sixteenth century, was the driving force for the creation of financial markets and the accumulation of capital. The growing financial markets facilitated the development of the industrial revolution by providing financial support. Moreover, developments in astronomy, physics, and chemistry from the Middle Ages and Renaissance on also added impetus to the industrial revolution.

### *Societal Changes*

Until the end of the eighteenth century, England and the rest of Europe can best be characterized as a class-ridden society. In towns, the working population consisted of professional groups or guilds, which had an enormous influence on people's lives. They determined the admission of new members to the guild, the levels of wages, and the quality of the products they made. In the Netherlands, 69 guilds operated, among them the goldsmiths' and silversmiths' guild, the butchers' guild, and the artists' guild. Being a member of a guild largely determined a person's income. Within a guild competition was very rare—some guilds maintained a monopoly and it was difficult to break through it. Some historians and economists argue that the existence of guilds hampered economic growth (e.g. Landes 1988), although Feinstein (1998) as well as Clark (2001) estimated a growth in income per capita during the guild period. The estimated wages of carpenters compared with the estimated population of England during the Middle Ages (500 AD till 1500 AD) and the Early New Period (1500 AD till 1800 AD) is interesting in this respect: It shows a gradual increase in both population and carpenters' income from the thirteenth century (about six million people) to the nineteenth century (about 16 million people), but a sharp drop in carpenters' income at the beginning of the Industrial Revolution (end of the eighteenth century). In that period, many people fell into unemployment as a result of the mechanization of the wool and cotton industries in England and the policy of enclosure. During the nineteenth century, the growth in income recovered for the carpenters and correlated again with population growth.

The first country where the monopoly of the guilds was broken down was England during the Industrial Revolution. The development of machine tools facilitated the manufacturing of production machines in many industries. The new industries, especially textile manufacturing, could accommodate many workers, but the work conditions were bad, wages low, work injuries high, and the health and job security of workers were not cared for. For the poor, conditions were abominable. Men, women, and children, stripped to the waist and stooped over in semi-darkness, worked in dark mineshafts. Many people struggled for a meager existence (Heilbroner 2008).

*People's Responses to Societal Changes*

Despite an increase in production capacity, unemployment grew, as did the dissatisfaction of large groups of people. In the nineteenth century this development culminated in two categories of people who were strongly antagonistic: the haves and the haves-not. Although a new middle class arose as well (of doctors, lawyers, and others), a new figuration came to the fore: between factory owners and landowners on the one side and the unemployed and low-earning and unhealthy workers on the other. Industrialization made many artisans unemployed, among them the weavers. A group of them, the Luddites, started to destroy machines and factories and gained in popularity. The militia and the army treated these people badly. These riots, along with those in agricultural areas, led to the formation of unions in the middle of the nineteenth century. In the 1830s and 1840s, the Chartist movement was formed which campaigned for political equality and social justice. The unions organized the activities of their members and their main weapon for effecting change was strike action.

The situation in England (as well as in Germany) formed the basis for Marx and Engels' analysis of capitalist society. Marx and Engels (1848) collaborated to produce *The Communist Manifesto*, which became the program of the Communist League, a loose organization of discontented workers who desired fundamental political and economic changes. The International Workingmen's Association replaced the League. A principle that contemporary capitalists choose to ignore was Smith's concept of labor value. Most economists contradicted the observation that labor is the only real standard of values, but it was widely adopted by socialist writers. Later, Karl Marx expanded upon this idea, building it into the theory of "surplus value." Marx stated that labor was of prime importance for the social and cognitive development of humanity. Men learned to manufacture tools, and that implied developing ideas of the physical appearance of the tool, grasping the different steps of tool making, organizing the order of activities to make the tool, and using the tool when it was finished. Tool making implied planning of activities and control over the natural environment. For instance, making a stone fist ax implied learning to choose the right type of stone, learning how to use wood or other stone to work on the stone, to make the stone sharp by slashing, and learning how to use the sharpened stone. According to historic materialism, labor improved men's intellectual abilities. Labor freed men from the harsh conditions put forward by the natural environment, and men could improve their fate by labor. Labor was the prime impetus for social relations between men as well as. Cooperation between men was often necessary, for instance, in the hunt for and killing of large prey, and in building huts. Other writers doubt whether labor had such an impact on intellectual development and social relations (Lane 1991), but as argued earlier in this chapter and in Chapter 1, foraging was a complex activity involving many men and women that had to be planned and coordinated. The steady mastering of these activities may have triggered or may have coincided with intellectual progress.

When property relations changed—and this happened, as argued earlier in this chapter, during the agrarian revolution—some people became property owners while others had no property rights at all: as Marx and Engels (1848) put it, one could distinguish patricians and slaves, feudal lords and serfs, bourgeoisie and proletariat. Historic materialism states that history is a succession of antagonistic groups or classes and views class struggle as the most important trigger for social change. However, according to historic materialism, the bourgeoisie versus proletariat antagonism disappears through class struggle and the new socialist society which arises will be free of class struggle. The communist revolution formed a short transition period that would end in a society of equals, according to Marx and Engels (1848). The relevant feature of Marx's analysis is the emphasis on the value of labor. This concept, and the societal and cultural changes during and after the Industrial Revolution, had tremendous influence on the thinking about human cognitive development and about justice.

*Implications for Cognitive Development*

Lane (1991) asserts that people are engaged in the labor market a couple of times in their life. They have assets, in the form of education and experience, that they can sell on the labor market. The more education and experience they have, the greater their assets and the more chances to sell their labor for a high price. Lane states that the market experience—the fact that people are engaged in the labor market—has many positive benefits. It has positive effects on cognitive complexity, self-attribution, and self-esteem. Cognitive complexity contains the properties of abstractness in handling information, flexibility of thinking, differentiation and integration of information. Self-attribution emphasizes personal responsibility for actions, and self-esteem: the belief that one is a person who deserves respect. I will add that labor has, generally speaking, the same effects on these three aspects as does market experience. Next to it, people are occupied with work and things not related to the market. What is relevant is that labor forms human capital and has value for the people (see also Locke 1982). Because people are engaged in work more frequently and for longer (such as accomplishing a task, creating chances for promotion, getting an income), the effects of labor on the three aspects might even be larger than those of the market experience. Both phenomena contribute to cognitive development. Society challenges people to make plans for the future, and to decide—for themselves as for their children—what kind of education or training is necessary to reach that goal. A certain job or higher position requires certain skills and experiences. Potential employees and employees who are motivated to get a better position have to differentiate the job requirements, combine them to a meaningful whole, and tune their education and training accordingly. Potential employees compare the content of jobs in order to find the best one. They compare themselves with other potential candidates in the competition for jobs and positions, and estimate their skills. In a previous, class-ridden, society, these skills were hardly necessary to find a job. A carpenter's son became a carpenter, learning the skills from his father, and continued with it. When the influence of the unions became stronger, they protected workers' employment and their salaries; they gradually achieved a less unfree labor market, but did not achieve a full free labor market.

### *Implications for Justice*

In the period of the upcoming figuration of haves and have-nots, labor was not valued highly for a large category of people. As Heilbroner (2008) noted, men, women, and children had to work under abominable conditions for too-low wages, and many died from illness and starvation. The Protestant Ethic (Weber 1934; Lerner 1977), claiming that hard work will lead to a decent income, was clearly not applicable for many workers. A decent reward for hard work did not automatically arise from the rules of ethics that were dominant in the protestant countries of that time, like England and Germany. For those groups of people, expectations about the future were low, their situation was hopeless, and action–outcome-frame thinking was poorly developed. People did not experience that a good life resulted from hard work, living economically, and devotion. Children did not learn that certain actions result in certain outcomes (Furby 1986,) and that it is often better to give up an immediate reward in order to get a larger one later (Lerner 1978, 1980). Children did not learn to anticipate alternative actions and their consequences; they did not learn to expect certain outcomes when circumstances are appropriate. These expectations, however, form the basis for concepts like "deservingness" and justice (Lerner 1980).

Thus, large parts of the population in the Industrial Revolution period in England experienced no relationships between actions and their consequences, although their conditions were stable. Whatever they did, however hard they worked, and however economically they lived, their miserable fate did not change. How could they learn what justice is?

The haves, or the established group (Elias and Scotson 1994), preferred to continue this situation and kept the masses down, although some entrepreneurs improved the fate of the workers by offering them decent wages, and by building houses and public facilities like baths and health services. The have-nots, or outsiders, organized themselves to enforce better working and living conditions and to try to close the economic gap between them and the established. In a long struggle, the outsiders won many points in the battle and gradually received better work and living conditions. In this battle, the skilled workers initiated many strike actions. Although they received relatively good wages, they compared their situation with those better off and felt relatively deprived (Runciman 1966). It is often not objective poverty that forms the onset for action, but relative poverty (see also Urry 1973). There are, in my view, two forces for action to change the situation of the poor. There is action by a relatively well-to-do group of workers experiencing that they are worse off than comparable groups of workers. These actions may form the trigger for the poor to act as well. Some authors (e.g., Moore Jr 1964) claim that the actions of well-to-do farmers in the Condé, who feared that under the new economic system their income would decrease, instigated the French revolution of 1789. They foresaw a situation of relative deprivation. This revolt resulted in the actions of the poor in Paris, and in the siege of the Bastille. A vanguard made the poor aware of their miserable working and living conditions, compared to better-off groups, and instigated the poor to take action.

After much struggle, in 1833 and 1844 the first general laws against child labor, the Factory Act, passed in England. The Act prohibited children younger than nine to work, and limited the working day of workers under the age of 18 to 12 hours. These developments led to a more balanced market economy in which human capital (Lane 1991) is valued more than before.

The struggle led to another conception of the justice motive. In the beginning of the Industrial Revolution, when there was a large surplus of labor available and one worker replaced another easily, wages were at a bare minimum—entrepreneurs did not pay workers appropriately for their effort. By fighting for a better reward for work and for better working conditions, workers emphasized that work, that is, the human activity involved in making a product, has economic value next to the physical capital of buildings and machines. By uniting, workers could achieve a better price for their work activities. They enforced by united action that they should receive what they thought they deserved, and thus what they judged as just. Justice was no longer based on the assumption that only status was important for the allocation of wealth (the haves got all and the have-nots nothing). In other words, entitlement (see also Mikula and Lerner 1994) was not the dominant basis for a just allocation, as was the dominant strategy in the class-ridden society, but deservingness, and thus effort at work. When both parties settled this issue and recorded it legally, people became more confident that hard work and good education will lead to better outcomes, and that it became profitable to give up an immediate reward in order to get a higher reward later. One might say, therefore, that societal changes resulted in a fundamental shift in thinking about the justice motive.

## Conclusions

Shifts in people's natural environment prompted them to modify their habitats in order to adapt to the new situation. The climate change that took place around the fourteenth millennium before Christ resulted in higher temperatures, more rain, and more abundant flora and fauna. The population grew and people became healthier. Around the ninth millennium before Christ, the sudden drop in temperature and moisture created obstacles for finding food. It was necessary to tap new sources of subsistence or to intensify already existing sources. Farmers practiced new methods of crop management that gave other members of the group than hunters a prime task in the food chain. The social figuration that came into being between the newcomers (agricultural groups) and the settled (hunter groups) resulted in differentiating behaviors: It was the most important impetus for the creation of new techniques and customs, the emergence of status groups, professions, and trades. It led to cognitive efforts to compare oneself with others in order to determine one's own status and wealth. Allocation of material resources like houses, pottery, and jewelry became salient activities and people learned to appreciate allocations in terms of them being just or unjust, as in the example in the text of the Cappadocian tablets. Differentiating behaviors also led to changes in cognitive content: in-group favoritism and out-group derogation. Hunter/gatherer groups were far less interested in the material side of their living. Their concern was mainly the allocation of immaterial resources like dignity, respect, and trust. Nomadic groups have few possessions that are worth comparing with others. Consequently, the transition from hunting to farming not only had huge effects on the modes of subsistence but also on social relations and cognitive structure (cognitive differentiation and integration), content (prejudice), and processes (social comparison).

Lamb (1982) conceived of five periods of climate change and five periods of cultural change after the last Ice Age ended. One of them was an increase in temperature starting around the eleventh century. This period of higher temperature coincided with the immigration of several peoples, among them the Vikings. It was also the period of the breakdown of the feudal system, the development of towns, and an increase in artisanship. It resulted in the formation of a figuration of nobility and bourgeoisie and all the consequences described in this chapter, such as the increased complexity of the action–outcome chains.

Action–outcome chains, or thinking in terms of causal relationships, considerably restrict people's behavior. They make some behaviors less appropriate for fulfilling one's own social needs: becoming an accepted member of a desired status group. It explains why people adopted certain habits in food consumption, like using forks and spoons, not spitting on the ground while eating, appropriate dress, and so on. The habits became part of their cognitive repertoire. The action–outcome chains explain the restricted behavior that Elias observed and that resulted in a psychodynamic type of personality in which unwanted desires are stored in an unconscious operating reservoir (the id or *das Es*) and kept there by the operation of a superego (*das Über-Ich*). Elias saw in the history of human society a decrease in "free" behaviors and an increase in restricted behavior. Relevant studies challenged this idea. The theory of action–outcome chains explains these irregularities better: Dependent on social need satisfaction, action–outcome chains may lead to behaviors opposite from their original direction.

Climate changes were often the trigger for human adaptive activities to deal with the modified situation. These activities often led to changes in social relations, cognitive development, and personality. More important in the context of this book, these changes had a deep influence on conceptions of justice. The Pliocene/Pleistocene climate change led to the development of hominin groups that roamed around the vicinity of the great forests to find a new way of subsistence. Very gradually, it led to a more harmonious operation between selfish and altruistic motivated behaviors of group members. Group needs formed justice considerations and reflected the animistic belief of unity with all features of nature. It was necessarily restricted to group life. Groups lived in permanent war with each other.

The climate change at the end of the Pleistocene marked the beginning of the Agricultural Revolution, the origins of permanent settlements, the start of material possessions and status groups based on them. The justice conception arose from the rights one had as member of a status group. The next climate change discussed here coincided with the Industrial Revolution and marked the beginning of a justice conception based on deservingness resulting from individual effort.

In the present period, at the start of the twenty-first century, humanity probably faces a severe climate change. Human activities cause climate change, according to the Intergovernmental Panel on Climate Change (IPCC). If the analyses described in this and the previous chapter are correct—and in my view, they are—humanity may expect that social relations will undergo drastic modifications, new social figurations will become virulent, and our beliefs about ourselves and others will change, as will our personality and cognitive and emotional qualities. In addition, our conceptions of justice will change. Is deservingness, and, to a lesser extent, entitlement, the main basis of the justice motive? Or should humanity learn from earlier conceptions of justice as reflected in animistic beliefs? Or will other conceptions of justice arise? Are justice conceptions of material resources like money and goods different from those of immaterial resources like respect? What are, in the present societal context, respectful or appropriate behaviors, and what are fair or acceptable differences in wealth between groups? These issues will be described in the next part of the book: Morality.

## References

Barker, G. 2006. *The Agricultural Revolution in Prehistory. Why Did Foragers Become Farmers?* Oxford: Oxford University Press.

Benson, B.L. 1989. Enforcement of private property rights in primitive societies: Law without government. *The Journal of Libertarian Studies*, 9, 1, 1–26.

Berger, P.L., and Berger, B. 1972. *Sociology*. New York: Basic Books.

Berry, J. 1976. *Human ecology and cognitive style*. Beverly Hills: Sage.

Braudel, F. 1989. *Beschaving, economie en kapitalisme (15de–18de eeuw). Deel 2. Het Spel van de Handel* (Civilization, Economy and Capitalism; 15th–18th century. Part 2. The Game of Trade). Amsterdam: Uitgeverij Contact.

Butzer, K.W. 1995. Environmental Change in the Near East and Human Impact on the Land, in *Civilizations of the Ancient Near East*, edited by J.L. Sasson et al., Vol. 1, Part 2. New York: Scribners, 123–51.

Chen, X. 2009. Socialization and socioemotional development in the changing Chinese society. *Bulletin of the International Society for the Study of Behavioral Development*, 55, 1, 2–5.

Clark, G. 2001 *The Secret History of the Industrial Revolution*. University of California Davis. Available at http://www.econ.ucdavis.edu/faculty/gclark/papers/secret2001.pdf [accessed 21 November 2013].

de Feyter, Th. (trans.). 2001. *Gilgamesh epos*. Amsterdam: Ambo Klassiek.

Descartes, R. 1637. *Discourse on Method*. Cambridge: Cambridge University Press.

De Waal, F. 1996. *Good Natured. The Origins of Right and Wrong in Humans and Other Animals*. Boston: Harvard University Press.

Diamond, J.M. 1997. *Guns, Germs, and Steel*. London: Jonathan Cape.

Duerr, H.P. 1988. *Nacktheit und Scham. Der Mythos vom Zivilisationsprozess* (Nudity and Shame. The Myth of the Process of Civilization). Frankfurt am Main: Suhrkamp Verlag.

Eco, U. 1983. *De naam van de roos* (The Name of the Rose). Amsterdam: Bert Bakker.

Elias, N. 1969. *Über den Prozess der Zivilisation. Soziogenetische und Psychogenetische Untersuchungen*. Teil 1 und Teil 2. Bern: Francke Verlag.

Elias, N., and Scotson, J.L. 1994. *The Established and the Outsiders*. London: Sage.

Enloe, J.G. 2003. Food sharing past and present: Archaeological evidence for economic and social interactions. *Before Farming*, 1, 1–23.

Feinstein, C.H. 1998. Pessimism perpetuated: Real wages and the standard of living in Britain during and after the Industrial Revolution. *Journal of Economic History*, 58(3), 625–58.

Fiske, S. 2007. *Social Cognition: From Brains to Culture*. Boston: McGraw-Hill.

French, L.A., and Picthall-French, N. 2007. Social Injustice in Indian Country: Historical Antecedents of Current Issues, in *Distributive and Procedural Justice. Research and Social Applications*, edited by K. Törnblom, and R. Vermunt. Aldershot: Ashgate Publishing Limited, 159–83.

Furby, L. 1986. Psychology and Justice, in *Justice. Views from the Social Sciences*, edited by R. Cohen. New York: Plenum, 153–204.

Gamble, Th., and Ginsberg, P. 1981. Differentiation, cognition, and social evolution. *Journal of Cross-Cultural Psychology*, 12, 445–59.

Goudsblom, J. 1987. *De sociologie van Norbert Elias* (The Sociology of Norbert Elias). Amsterdam: Meulenhoff Informatief.

Goudsblom, J. 1992. *Vuur en beschaving* (Fire and Civilization). Amsterdam: Meulenhoff.

Harvey, G. 2005. *Animism: Respecting the Living World.* New York: Columbia University Press.

Heilbroner, R.L. 2008. *The Worldly Philosophers*. London: Penguin Books.

Henry, D.O. 1989. *From Foraging to Agriculture: The Levant at the End of the Ice Age*. Philadelphia: University of Pennsylvania Press.

Huizinga, J. 1949. *Herfsttij der Middeleeuwen.* Verzamelde Werken III: Cultuurgeschiedenis. Haarlem: Tjeenk Willink and Zoon N.V.

Ingold, T. 1994. Introduction, in *What is an Animal?* edited by T. Ingold. London: Routledge, One World Archaeology, 1–16.

Kant, I. 1780. *The Metaphysical Elements of Ethics*. Translated by T.K. Abbot.

Kaplan, H., and Gurven, M. 2005. The Natural History of Food Sharing and Cooperation: A Review and a New Multi-Approach to the Negotiation of Norms, in *Moral Sentiments and Material Interests: Foundations of Cooperation in Economic Life*, edited by H. Gintis, S. Bowles, and E. Fehr. Cambridge, MA: MIT Press, 75–113.

Kaplan, H., Hill, K., Hawkes, K., and Hurtado, A. 1984. Food Sharing Among Ache Hunter-Gatherers of Eastern Paraguay. *Current Anthropology*, 25, 113–16.

Keeley, L.H. 1996. *War before Civilization*. New York: Oxford University Press.

Lamb, H.H. 1982. *Climate, History and the Modern World.* London: Methuen.

Landes, D.S. 1998. *The Wealth and Poverty of Nations. Why Some Are So Rich and Some So Poor*. New York: Norton and Co.

Lane, R.E. 1991. *The Market Experience*. Cambridge: Cambridge University Press.

Lerner, M.J. 1977. The justice motive: Some hypotheses as to its origins and forms. *Journal of Personality*, 45, 1–52.

Lerner, M.J. 1980. *The Belief in a Just World*. New York: Plenum.

Lloyd, B. 1972. *Perception and Cognition*. Harmondsworth, UK: Penguin.

Locke, J. 1982. *Two Treatises on Government*. London: Everyman's Library.

Marlowe, F.W. 2002. Why the Hadza are Still Hunter-Gatherers, in *Ethnicity, Hunter-Gatherers and the Other*, edited by S. Kent. Washington: Smithsonian Institute Press, 247–75.

Martin, C.L. 1993. *In the Spirit of the Earth*. Baltimore: Johns Hopkins University Press.

Marx, K., and Engels, F. 1848. *The Communist Manifest*. London: Burghardt.

Mikula, G., and Lerner, M.J. 1994. Justice in Close Relationships: An Introduction, in *Entitlement and the Affectional Bond*, edited by M.J. Lerner and G. Mikula. New York: Plenum, 1–10.

Miller, D.T., and Ratner, R.K. 1996. The Power of the Myth of Self-Interest, in *Current Societal Concerns about Justice*, edited by L. Montada and M.L. Lerner. New York: Plenum Press, 25–48.

Montada, L. 1998. Belief in a Just World: A Hybrid of Justice Motive and Self-Interest? in *Responses to Victimizations and Belief in a Just World*, edited by L. Montada, and M.J. Lerner. New York: Plenum, 217–46.

Moore, B. Jr. 1968. *Social Origins of Dictatorship and Democracy. Lord and Peasant in the Making of the Modern World.* Harmondsworth: Penguin Books.

Mumford, L. 1963. *Technics and Civilization*. Orlando: Harcourt Brace and Company.
Parsons, T. 1951. *The Social System*. Glencoe, IL: The Free Press.
Rosen, A.M. 2007. *Civilizing Climate: Social Responses to Climate Change in the Ancient Near East*. London: Rowman Altamira.
Rousseau, J.-J. 1754. *Discourse on the origin of inequality: What is the origin of the inequality among men, and is it authorised by natural law*. Translated by G.D.H. Cole. Zurich: ETH Zurich.
Runciman, W.G. 1966. *Relative Deprivation and Social Justice*. London: Routledge and Kegan Paul.
Segal, R.A. 1999. *Theorizing about Myth*. Amherst: University of Massachusetts Press.
Tajfel, H., and Turner, J. 1986. The Social Identity Theory of Intergroup Behavior, in *Psychology of Intergroup Relations*, edited by S. Worchel. Chicago: Nelson Hall.
Tyler, T., and Lind, E.A. 1992. A relational model of authority in groups. *Advances in Experimental Social Psychology*, 25, edited by M. Zanna, 115–91.
Urry, J. 1973. *Reference Groups and the Theory of Revolution*. London: Routledge and Kegan Paul.
Vermunt, R. 1989. Happiness and justice. A social psychological view on ultimate reality and meaning. *Ultimate Reality and Meaning, Interdisciplinary Studies in the Philosophy of Understanding*, 12(4), 272–82.
Vermunt, R. 2002. The Justice Motive in Perspective, in *The Justice Motive in Social Life: Essays in Honor of Melvin Lerner*, edited by D. Miller, and M. Ross. New York: Cambridge University Press, 64–77.
Walster, E., Walster, G.W., and Berscheid, E. 1978. *Equity: Theory and Research*. Boston: Allyn and Bacon.
Weber, M. 1934. *Der Protestantische Ethik and der Geist des Kapitalismus*. Tübingen: JCB Mohr.
Werner, D. 1981 Are some people more equal than others? Status inequality among Mekranoti Indians of Central Brazil. *Journal of Anthropological Research*, 37(4), 360–73.

# PART II
# Morality and Justice

# Chapter 3
# Resource Allocation, Justice, and Morality

## Introduction

The origin of the justice motive has a long and intricate history. As stated in the foregoing chapters, it has likely been developed out of the operation of the selfish motive and the altruistic motive (see also Kant 1900: 63/64; Verplaetse 2008). The motivation to do good to oneself and another is an important element of treating self and other in a correct way. Philosophers label doing good to self and other moral behavior. In my view, moral behavior is a component of resource allocation behavior, specifically of the resource status (respect) which takes place in an allocation event. An allocation event consists of an actor who allocates resources to other(s) or between self and other(s). Resource allocation behavior is behavior toward others through transfer of something tangible or intangible that has value for both parties: actor and recipient. The actor is the party with the discretionary power to allocate resources and can be a person (e.g., father, pupil, category of people, citizen), a private person (e.g., owner of private property, political party, entrepreneur) or a public person (e.g., government, MP). The recipient can be a person, group, private person, or public person. Observers are also part of the allocation event. Allocation can take the form of giving or taking, committing or omitting. One can offer a service or withhold a service to another. Resources have a positive valence (e.g., money) or a negative valence (e.g., punishment). It is in the nature of (it is intrinsically good; Hurka 2001) positive-valenced resources for one to desire more of them, and it is intrinsically evil to desire negative-valenced resources. People try to increase positive resources—information, status, service, love, material goods, and money (Foa and Foa 1974).

A recipient's reaction to the allocation by allocating something back is labeled exchange behavior. This chapter (and book) will focus on one part of the exchange and will show that moral behavior can be adequately described and explained in terms of resource allocation behavior.

## Importance of Allocation Events

The first question is, why is allocation such an important component in the existence of living beings in general and human beings in particular? Although living beings differ from inanimate objects with regard to (degree of) conscience, both share the characteristic that they take up space. Inanimate objects, as well as living beings, fill space. They possess the quality of extensiveness. Also, objects, and thus living beings, cannot occupy the same position in space at the same time. They have a certain mass and are susceptible to the rules of inertia. Living beings must orient themselves toward other objects and other living beings.

Moreover, objects and living beings exist in a certain time, from which they cannot escape. They are prisoners of time. The only escape human beings have is in imagining the future and scrutinizing the past. However, they cannot exist in all three regions of time in person, but only in one: the present. These restrictions make human beings aware of the presence of others. In addition, human beings are immersed in the sea of space and time so that, according to Kant (1998), they have a priori knowledge of them. Living beings derive knowledge about other objects or beings from the movements of those objects and beings. Human beings enter each other's personal space or move away from it. In both cases, the accompanying feelings and cognitions are complex. Human beings estimate the physical distance between self and other as more critical to self-esteem than the physical distance between other and self (Tversky 1977; Codol 1987; Vermunt and Extra 1993). Moreover, strangers keep more distance from actors than from relatives or family members. Moving away initiates feelings of solitude.

Taking gravity as an analogy, just as we know the mass of an object from its velocity in orbit around another object, we know the qualities of other human beings from their circling around us. Objects attract or repulse each other. Attraction and repulsion are not the consequence of our knowledge about objects in the world, but are the origin of our knowledge.

Human beings, therefore, meet certain constraints when confronted with time and space. Because human beings cannot escape either to the past or to the future, and cannot occupy the same space, they circle around each other like stars and planets in outer space. Or as electrons do around the atom's nucleus. Human beings attract each other like objects of opposite electrical charge and repel each other like objects with the same electrical charge. They constantly increase their "mass" by trying to "absorb" other human beings: to bring others under their influence, to make others dependent on them. They lose "mass" when others attract them and make them dependent. What gravity is for physical mass, status position is for social "mass."

In this psychological force field of attraction and repulsion (Lewin 1964; Deutsch and Krauss 1965), allocation of resources constitutes a crucial way to find a balance between the two forces. Giving something positive to another makes the other more dependent on the actor, but makes the actor less "massy." Because the actor's status position is always more salient than that of the other, human beings are inclined to allocate more to themselves than to others. This concerns only allocation of positive resources, not negative resources—allocation of negative resources decreases the other's mass but creates distance between the actor and the other.

Allocation events in which resources are allocated between actor and other, or by actor between others mutually, are significant in the actor's life: in such events, one's "mass" or (status) position is at stake. Anticipated outcomes of allocation decisions create tension and, therefore, are closely observed with great interest and evaluated by all involved. Reactions from the actor, the recipients, but also from the observers, to an actor's allocation decision involve judgments about behavior, that is, about the actor's allocated resources (outcomes).

Judgments about allocation outcomes are not absolute, but contain the perception of a difference—the social "mass" of one human being compared with the "mass" of another. For instance, God shows respect for Abel's offer and not for Cain's offer. For God, Abel's social "mass" weighs more than Cain's social "mass." In this example, scientists prefer to speak of a status difference between individuals. Sociologists denote status differences between categories of people in a social system as status inequality.

Differences between the states of one entity exist over time. For example, the difference in status or income of a person perceived before and after the loss of a job, or the physical condition of a person before and after an aggressive attack by hooligans (difference in the negative resource service). Social scientists (e.g., Folger 1986; Jasso 2007) differentiate another type of difference: the difference between individuals' expectation of an outcome or just reward and the actual outcome of an allocation decision or actual reward. For instance, during a disaster people expect others to help victims. If people offer less help (service) then others expect from them, they evaluate the help as insufficient. The perception of a difference between entity states is dominant in comparison with the perception of other features of an allocation event.

## Simple and Complex Allocation Events

### *Types of Allocation Events*

To influence their social mass, human beings are constantly engaged in allocating resources to others. In other words, allocation behavior is a central feature of an individual's daily activities. Examples of allocation behavior are the following: parents give a present to one of their children (allocation of goods); teachers explain a language rule to one of their pupils (allocation of service or information); bosses divide a bonus among their subordinates (allocation of money); a citizen does volunteer work for the Red Cross; a hunter divides food between himself and his fellow hunters; political party members divide their respect between immigrants and settled citizens (allocation of status); a surgeon decides to perform an operation first on wounded person A and then on wounded person B (allocation of service); a committee decides that a movie is not suitable for persons younger than 16 years (status), a girl loves John more than she loves Peter (allocation of love); a girl divides candies between herself and the other children (goods); a citizen decides not to rescue a drowning person (omitting service); the administration decides to tax groups of citizens (allocation of a negative resource: money); a jury (judge) decides that the accused person is guilty (allocation of a negative resource: status).

One of the earliest descriptions of allocation behavior is Genesis 4:1–7 (King James Version). The Bible phrases it as follows:

> 1 And Adam knew Eve his wife; and she conceived, and bare Cain, and said, I have gotten a man from the LORD.
>
> 2 And she again bare his brother Abel. And Abel was a keeper of sheep, but Cain was a tiller of the ground.
>
> 3 And in process of time it came to pass, that Cain brought of the fruit of the ground an offering unto the LORD.
>
> 4 And Abel, he also brought of the firstlings of his flock and of the fat thereof. And the LORD had respect unto Abel and to his offering:
>
> 5 But unto Cain and to his offering he had not respect. And Cain was very wroth, and his countenance fell.
>
> 6 And the LORD said unto Cain, Why art thou wroth? And why is thy countenance fallen?
>
> 7 If thou doest well, shalt thou not be accepted? And if thou doest not well, sin lieth at the door. And unto thee shall be his desire, and thou shalt rule over him.

God gave Abel's offer respect, but not Cain's offer. Cain's reaction to God's decision was horrible: he killed his brother Abel (Dijkhuis 1999). This description is an example of an allocation event: An actor (authority: God in this example) has discretionary power to allocate an immaterial (or material) resource (respect, which is related to the status of a person; Foa and Foa 1974) to two recipients (Cain and Abel). The outcome of this allocation decision (accepting Abel's offer and rejecting Cain's offer) brings with it the reaction of the recipients (Cain's anger and the deed of killing Abel, and Abel worshipping God). In terms of allocation behavior, God took a decision that resulted in an unequal allocation of respect for the two recipients in which Cain received no respect and Abel all the respect from God.

The allocation examples I gave, including the one of God, differ in many respects, like resource type, resource amount, allocation type, and allocation behavior. One aspect I would like to emphasize here is type of allocation behavior. The other one is the number of resources involved in the allocation event: one resource, like candies for friends (goods), or parents' presents (goods) and care (service) for their child. The child allocates one resource, the parents two resources. A third aspect is allocation type: allocation between self and other or among others. To describe and explain moral behavior, these aspects are of crucial importance.

*Allocation behavior*
An actor performs an act to help the recipient, or to punish the recipient. To help the recipient is an example of a positive service, while punishment is an example of a negative status. In some allocation events, the actor commits, does something. The actor can also abstain from action (not rescuing a drowning person): the actor omits, does not do something. In moral dilemmas, committing and omitting an act are strongly related: doing something for one person often means doing nothing for another. The child, however, gives sweets to all other children at her party and each person receives a part of the resource. Moreover, the resource is divisible. In other allocation events, resources may be scarce and/or not divisible. In the example of Cain and Abel, the resource status is not scarce and it is divisible.

*Number of resources*
Philosophers confine descriptions of behavior that is subject to moral judgments to the allocation of only one resource: a person handling a railroad switch to rescue people; a citizen deciding not to rescue a drowning person; a doctor who has to decide whom to help first. These are also the examples ethicists use to illustrate their way of thinking about ethical issues: Kant (1785b) used a suicide case to illustrate the maxim of ethical behavior.

However, a large number of events ask for complex decisions from the actor's side. Let us take the example of an actor confronted with a rape victim. The actor can opt for different types of action that all, in one way or another, relate to helping, but differ in their moral quality. The actor may comfort the victim, or try to catch the perpetrator, or offer money to the victim so that she can go to the hospital, or call an ambulance. In order to evaluate the moral quality of the actor's action, philosophers should investigate all the alternatives. The study of these events can answer the question of whether actor should take one action or another. I will illustrate the complexity of allocation events in relation to morality with the following example. The philosopher Dr Van der Horst gave this example in his lecture about Kant and Sartre in 1967. During WWII, Sartre has to decide whether to stay with his mother, who is mentally and physically in a rather bad way, or to join the Allied Forces to fight against the German troops to honor (avenge) his father who died in the war. The example describes an allocation event in which the actor has to decide between allocating service (care for his mother) or status (honoring his father). The moral question is whether to help the mother and forego the opportunity to honor the father, or to go into battle and leave the mother in a bad condition. In the Cain and Abel case, actors, recipients, and observers easily detect God's unequal treatment, but in the WWII case, comparable differences are absent. More than that: an even allocation in the WWII case is not possible—that is, to spend time with the mother and fight against the enemy. As I shall explain later, when an equal division of time is not possible, the actor should use justifications to deviate from equal division.

Another question is whether it is possible to derive a moral rule from the characteristics of both resource types (respectively, status and service). For instance, that service always weighs more than status. If that is the case, actors would feel more obliged to stay with their mother than to fight. Although this idea is attractive, it is not the core of the allocation model of morality advocated here. The core of this model—as we shall argue in this chapter—is that people (actor, recipient, observers) evaluate the actor's justifications for the allocation decision. The difference in resource type may be an important argument in the discussion for preparing such a decision, but other arguments are relevant as well. For instance, one could argue that service refers more directly to the well-being of the recipient than status, and another's well-being is often salient in moral discussions (Scanlon 1998, 2008; Hurka 2001).

May we ask of the actors in this case to give up their own strivings and focus only on the recipient's well-being? Kant would conclude that to go against his own strivings and do his duty is what actor should do. The question in the Sartre example is that referring to duty does not solve Sartre's problem: maybe the duty to stay with the mother is stronger (well-being of mother) than going to war (well-being of self), but who decides it. Scanlon (1998) would conclude that the claim to stay with the mother asks too much of the actor, and I agree. What can one claim from an actor, then? One must claim that the actor weighs the actor's, recipients', and observers' evaluations of the justifications when deciding on a course of action, and weighing implies active information inquiry in the social world and/or in the mind.

*Allocation type*

A further differentiation of allocation events is that between allocations in which the actor allocates resources between self and recipient or between two or more recipients (allocation type). In a Dictator game, the actor divides money between self and recipient (Actor–Recipient or A–R allocation). An example of the other type of allocation is the child dividing candies between friends at a birthday party (Actor–Recipient–Recipient or A–RR allocation). The differentiation between these types of allocation highlights what I label justice considerations and moral considerations. In A–R allocations, self-interest is always at stake and the outcomes elicit moral considerations. A–RR allocations are subject to justice considerations while self-interest is not at stake, except in those cases where one of the recipients is closer to the actor than the other recipients are.

Applying the above three aspects results in Figure 3.1, where A–R denotes allocation between actor and recipient, and A–RR denotes the actor's allocation between two or more recipients.

The allocation event approach presented here and the classification scheme derived from it offer insight into moral issues, as will be shown in this chapter. Moreover, the classification of allocation events is of tremendous help in organizing and evaluating the many examples of moral dilemmas philosophers use to illuminate their way of thinking regarding moral issues. Presenting the following moral dilemmas, used by Scanlon to critique the "double effect" doctrine (the rule

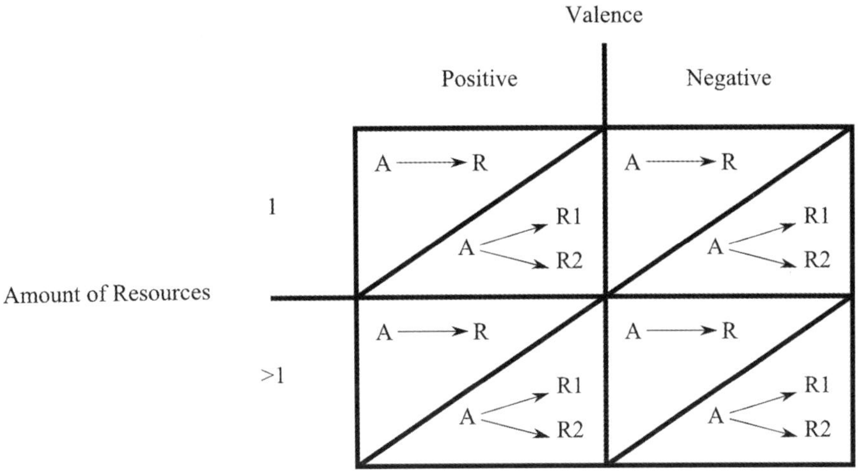


**Figure 3.1 Classification of allocation events according to three aspects: Valence, amount of resources, and allocation type**

that states that effects are intentionally caused or a by-product of behavior), shows the significance of the allocation event approach.

*Drug Shortage (Scanlon 2008: 14–15)* There are five people in Room B, and one person in Room A, all of whom have the same disease, and all of whom will die if not treated soon. There is enough medicine on hand to cure all five of the people in Room B, but since the person in Room A has a more advanced case, it would take all the available drugs to save just him. According to Scanlon, it is permissible to allocate the drug to the five people: The death of the person in Room A is a by-product of the treatment decision. Than Scanlon gives the following example:

*Transplant* The five people in Room B are in need of organs—one needs a heart, two people need a lung, and two need a kidney—and they will all die if they are not given transplants soon. Unfortunately, no organs are available. However, there is a person in Room A, in for a checkup, who could be given a lethal injection instead of the inoculation he is expecting, thereby making the organs available to save the five others.

According to Scanlon, it is not permissible to deliver a lethal injection to the person in Room A to save five lives. The death of the person in Room A is intentional.

Scanlon compares the Drug Shortage case and the Transplant case with each other, implying that both cases have common characteristics. However, are both cases comparable? No, they are not comparable. In the Drug Shortage case, the physician is the actor who can decide to allocate the drug to the five persons in Room B and not to the one person in Room A. The decision based on medical grounds prescribes that it is better to save five lives than one. He does not need the consent of the persons involved. In the Transplant case, the allocation event is as follows. There is also one actor but that is the person in Room A. The physician can deliver the lethal injection to the person in Room A only if he has the consent of the person in Room A to give him the lethal injection. Moreover, the physician is not the owner of the five organs. The owner is the person in Room A. So, the physician cannot allocate the organs without the consent of the patient in Room A. Because the physician is not an actor in the case of the organs, his action is not subject to permissibility judgment. In the Drug Shortage case, the physician is the factual actor, and in the Transplant case, the person in Room A is the actor. The two cases are therefore not comparable. In addition, the dilemma of the physician in the Drug Shortage case is not a moral problem but a justice problem. In the Transplant case, the person in Room A faces a moral dilemma: Shall I give permission to receive the lethal injection so that five persons in Room B can survive, or not, so that I survive?

In both cases, the type of behavior as well as the type of resources delivered is different. In the Drug Shortage case, the resource is a drug with a positive valence: it cures people; in the Transplant case, the resource is in the first instance a negative one: a lethal injection.

## The Actor

The actor has reasons to allocate resources to the recipient. The reasons can be the wishes of the actor to allocate or the perceived need of the recipient. The actor's wishes can be valid reasons to allocate resources, as in the case of the child at her birthday party who divides candies among her friends unequally, or in the case of God allocating respect between Cain and Abel unequally. In these examples, the unfairness lies in the unequal allocation of the resource. Equal allocation is a good in itself. Recipient and observers evaluate the outcome of the allocation decision not in terms of morality but in terms of justice.

In the case of the recipient's need as instigator of the actor's allocation behavior, the situation is quite different. The actor can decide to fulfill the recipient's need, or not. The actor can decide to help the drowning person, or can decide not to do it. Or the actor can decide to help the recipient's financial need, or not. Whether the actor acts or not, or how the actor fulfills the needs will be evaluated in terms of morality.

Recipients' needs are manifold, and a complete typology of needs is hard to make. What is relevant is to divide the needs into categories according to the resources that are lacking. Consequently, one can differentiate between financial needs (related to the resource money); material needs (related to the resource goods); affiliation needs (related to the resource love); information needs, bodily and psychological needs (related to the resource service); and social needs (related to the resource status). The present typology shows some resemblance to Maslow's hierarchy of needs (Maslow 1954), especially the deficiency needs. The type of need state of actor and recipient is an essential feature of the allocation event, in that it triggers the actor's considerations to start a specific resource allocation process. The considerations have to do with whether and how to allocate the resource(s).

Whether the actor allocates resources between self and recipient (moral quality) or allocates resources among recipients (justice quality), equal allocation of resources is an end in itself—it is intrinsically good (see Hurka 2001; see also the concept of moral modules: Haidt and Graham 2007).

Being the actor in an allocation event signifies that the recipient(s) and observers hold the actor responsible and accountable for resource allocation decisions. Being responsible means that the recipient and observer can ask the actor to carry out and stick to the allocation decision. Being accountable means that actors are cognizant of the choices they make and open to recipients' and observers' challenges.

### *The Actor's Fear*

The core of moral and just behavior lies in the allocation of resources. Human beings are constantly engaged in allocating resources to self and others, motivated by justice considerations, which developed out of egoistic and altruistic tendencies (see Prologue of this volume; see Chapter 5 for further elaboration on the motives).

Behind these considerations and tendencies, whether they are egoistic, altruistic, or just, lies fear. It is the fear not to survive or to lose social "mass" or status position. The fear-reducing force can operate at two levels: one is the individual level and the other is the group level. At the individual level, the fear-reducing force motivates individuals to increase their status position and thus their survival chances by, for instance, allocating more to themselves than to others. However, improving one's own status position results in larger differences between self and other, and the increasing difference induces fear as well. To reduce that fear, actors are motivated to decrease differences. Moreover, the egoistic tendency to indiscriminately increase one's status position (survival) is counteracted by actors' understanding that others contribute to their survival, and this motivates actors to regulate or reduce differences between them and others (the justice motive). Human beings need others for maintaining or increasing their status position, to the extent that human beings can only survive if their group has good chances of survival. Each individual has to contribute to the group for group survival. However, group contribution need not to result in "mass" loss. A group member operates optimally if he/she is able to promote group survival, and thus the other's survival, while maintaining his/her own status position. A group member operates sub-optimally if he/she contributes too much to the other and to the group so that the differences become too large, which can be detrimental for individual survival. In other words, allocation as a fear-reducing strategy is the result of a delicate balance between egoistic and altruistic tendencies. Human beings who strive to create and maintain large differences between themselves and others experience much fear, and the more they increase those differences the more they experience fear.

The fear of the rich that they will not survive is as genuine as the fear of the poor that they will not. The rich employ strategies to reduce that fear. They build huge fences around their homes, and use bodyguards and electronic equipment to secure their homes, money, and goods. However, they do more: they often engage in programs to help the poor, raising funds for educating them and improving their chances for a better life. The poor employ other legal as well as illegal strategies to survive: they steal from the rich; they undertake training to get a better income; they invent new technologies; they engage in the drugs and weapon trades. People do their best to reduce the fear of losing "mass," and one of the strategies is to attempt to decrease the differences between self and other.

Concluding, the best strategy to reduce fear is to promote the altruistic tendency while maintaining the same level of the egoistic tendency and to create equality or a minimal difference between self and other. Thus, the direction of difference reduction is to move the others' status position to one's own position, and not moving one's own status position in the others' direction. The following maxim expresses this argumentation:

**Maxim 1**: To reduce fear of "mass" loss effectively, the actor allocates resources to reduce or to equalize differences between self and others by moving the others' "mass" to self and not self to others.

Why mention a "minimal difference" between self and other rather than actual equality? One argument is that equality requires an actor to perfectly maintain the egoistic tendency and to perfectly promote the altruistic tendency. As stated before, human beings weigh their own interests more than others' interests. Maintaining the egoistic and promoting the altruistic tendencies leads mostly to an equilibrium that lies somewhat closer to the egoistic part than to the altruistic part of the motivation dimension. In line with this natural tendency is the self-serving bias: to perceive and interpret positive outcomes as the result of our own efforts and negative outcomes as the result of others' (lack of) effort. Human beings, therefore, maintain a small difference between self and other even while their justice strivings encourage being equal.

The maxim that leads allocation behavior is, therefore, that the actor allocates resources to the recipient so that the actor's fear reduces most. If an actor, for instance, sees a drowning person, he/she can decide to help or not to help. In allocation terms, the actor can decide to deliver a service to another, or not. In the drowning case, one could argue that the actor is moving toward the recipient and not vice versa. How can one explain the actor's movement towards the recipient as "moving the other's 'mass' to self?" The essential movement in this case is that the actor prevents the recipient from drowning, thus from being dead. The actor brings the recipient back to the living, thus back to the actor's own "position." It is not that the actor tries to put himself into the recipient's position. Of course, in trying to rescue the recipient, the actor experiences fear—fear of drowning, a feeling that is not illusory because the recipient's fight to stay alive can affect the actor's attempts at rescue. The struggling might end in the death of both. However, the fear that is aroused by letting the recipient drown can be stronger than the actor's fear of drowning.

### *The Actor's Definition of the Event*

This maxim implies the operation of a cognitive and emotional process. The actor, promoting the altruistic tendency, must have learned the ability to take the perspective of another. The actor has developed this skill during previous allocation events, for instance, while interacting with parents, gaining information about: (1) what kind of needs others have; (2) how important these needs are for actor and other; and (3) how actor and other will react to certain allocation outcomes. Actors arrive at these types of information by asking themselves the question: What would another think, feel, and do in this (allocation) situation? Based on previous experiences, and on extrapolating these experiences to the actual allocation event, the actor may arrive at a rather specific idea about the other's needs. However, actors express their knowledge in conditional or if/then judgments: actors have no objective knowledge about their and the other's situations. Therefore, actors are uncertain about the correctness of their knowledge about their and the other's situation. This lack of objectivity or truth in the knowledge is complemented with the feelings actors have about their ideas about themselves and others. People often become more sure about their knowledge because their feelings "tell them" that what they think is right. For instance, an actor may think that the other in the water is attempting to commit suicide.

Reason gives human beings the capacity to imagine what rational human beings will accept or reject (Barne-Holmes, McHugh, and Barne-Holmes, 2004). Individuals have reason to want certain things (resources; Scanlon 1998: 140). Scanlon also refers to the capacity of individuals to imagine what rational human beings would accept or reject. Scanlon argues: "although we cannot say in advance what will promote the well-being of the particular individuals who will be affected by a principle, we do know that individuals have reason to value well-being abstractly defined, and the principles they have reason to accept will therefore be ones that include this notion in their content" (Scanlon 1998: 140). In other words, Scanlon admits that individuals have the capacity to value the well-being of others and thus to imagine what others' needs are. However, taking the perspective of others, as well as knowledge about others' needs, leads only to partial knowledge. Taking the perspective of another is only possible if the actor has experience of it; but still, the actor is biased.

Actors must also have a view of their own needs, their importance, and their reactions when imagining what might happen when the other allocates resources in return. Because an actor's perception of their own needs, their importance, and their reactions are subjective, knowledge biases slip in easily, as the egocentric and self-serving bias hypotheses predict. An actor, for instance, can fool himself/herself that the other's drowning is a suicide attempt and consequently decide not to help the other. The same biases also operate when knowledge about the recipient's character, intentions, and behavior are processed. Therefore, taking the perspective of the other should be free of bias. That can be supported by the actor's formal position (like judge, or parent), or the bias-free position can be approached by the actor's ostensible effort to conquer the egoistic or altruistic tendencies. If God is asked why he disrespected Cain, God would answer that Cain's character was bad. Would that answer represent the action of a bias-free actor? For many religious people God is bias-free; his position is viewed as the judge who is impartial and benevolent and puts the spiritual well-being of humankind, and thus also of Cain, to the fore. However, even for God the next question would be what the behavioral or other indications are from which God inferred that Cain had a bad character? Is that because Cain dislikes God? Or is it Cain's agricultural way of subsistence? Or that he dislikes his brother Abel? Or dislikes his parents? In the first two representations of Cain's bad character God's position is clearly involved, while in the latter two representations God's position is not, or is less deeply, involved. In the first two alternatives, self-serving and egocentric biases slip in more easily than in the latter two alternatives. By explicating the reasons for their judgment, actors disclose their partiality in the allocation process.

### *The Actor's Justifications*

Is perception of difference absolute, in the sense that cognition (the precipitation of processed perception) has access to it without reference? For instance, perceiving the differences between one's own and another's need state. The perception of difference has a biological basis because it warns living beings of danger. In the natural environment of even the most primitive life forms, a (sudden) change in the environment may indicate danger and may be the trigger for a reaction that may safe life. This alert system is present in the biological systems of all living beings, and even in higher life forms the system often operates at a subconscious level. Individuals perceive a difference immediately: our brain evolved in such a way that it perceives changes in the environment immediately and relates them to danger. In an allocation event in which recipients receive a resource, an observed difference between expected and actual allocation outcome that threatens their (status) position is experienced immediately.

It is not only recipients who are sensitive to differences in the environment—actors are also aware of the salience of differences in the environment, such as differences in allocation outcomes. Actors have an aversion for differences. An actor's behavior resembles, in some way, that of a predator trying to capture prey. Just as predators try to conceal their attack, by hiding themselves or by approaching from a direction against the wind, actors try to conceal a difference in outcomes by applying methods of distraction as well. Actors try to conceal a difference like the unequal allocation of resources by referring to the differential circumstances, behavior, or character of recipients. Actors use deception: when the recipient was not aware of the true value of the chips provided by the actor, the actor took more for himself/herself (Van Dijk, De Kwaadsteniet, and Koning 2012). God, in the example, communicates that Cain's character is bad and Abel's character is good. In other words, God gives reasons for the decision to reject Cain's offer and accept Abel's offer. Stressing the badness of Cain and the goodness of Abel, God's unequal treatment is justified. Using good reasons, the initial inequality becomes an equality. Based on the equal treatment principle (of God), unequal treatment that was wrong became an action that was not wrong, as Baron (2005) would put it. According to Baron, an allocation decision is justified if one can say "that although the action is of a type that is usually wrong, in these circumstances it was not wrong" (389). It was wrong that God treated Cain so badly, but given the circumstances—Cain's bad character—God's act is justified and thus not wrong. Two issues in this reasoning merit attention. The first is that Baron uses the expression: "usually wrong." It means that in "normal" circumstances people judge the action as wrong. However, the question is, who will evaluate the action as wrong in the "normal" circumstances? The actor? It is less likely that the actor will evaluate the act as wrong. The recipient? The recipient will probably judge the action as wrong, as Cain did. Moreover, how will observers evaluate the action, in this case Abel, Adam and Eve? Will they evaluate the action as not wrong? That is the question. In other words, there will likely be a difference in opinion between parties in the allocation event about the wrongness of the act.

Related to this issue is a second one: will all parties involved accept the justification. The evaluation that a justification makes an allocation decision not wrong is not made by some general rule, but is made by the actor, recipient(s), and observer(s) in mutual agreement (as far as possible).

### *Justification and excuse*

Another issue is whether reasons given for an allocation decision are defined as justification or excuse, and whether the definition depends on the actor's, recipient's, or observer's evaluation. Baron's differentiation between justification and excuse ("to say that an action is excused … is to say that it was indeed wrong … but the agent is not blameworthy") I agree with, but whether the differentiation is a priori known, as Baron seems to imply, I would not like to defend. According to Baron, God would be excused if he performed the allocation action under duress or "because of some peculiarity about the actor" (390). Making a decision under duress is a justification, because it is something in the outside world that causes the actor to decide as he/she did. So, in the case of God, the difference in character between Cain and Abel was so overwhelming that God could not decide otherwise than to decline Cain's offer. In this case, an excuse resembles a justification. When, however, some peculiarity of the actor comes into play, a wrong allocation decision will still be wrong, but excuses the actor. However, who attributes a peculiarity to an actor? A peculiarity that some people might attribute to an actor, others will attribute to the environment. A prosecutor may attribute a wrong act in a felony case to the defendant's reaction to the victim's behavior, while the defender pleads for the diminished responsibility of the defendant. Thus, whether the reasons given for an allocation decision are a justification or an excuse depends on the evaluation of the parties involved.

Justification and excuse differ with regard to the actor's responsibility and accountability as well. Justification for an unequal allocation does not absolve the actor of their responsibility and accountability. However, an excuse for an unequal allocation does not absolve the actor of their responsibility, but does absolve the actor of their accountability.

Baron uses the strong and absolute term "wrong." For allocation decisions, I would prefer the term "not permissible." It is often not wrong to allocate more to oneself than to another, but it is less or not permissible.

According to Scanlon, reasons are considerations in favor of something (Scanlon 1998: 18). In the case of justifications and excuses, reasons are considerations in favor of disguising differences.

It is up to recipients and observers to accept or reject the justification or excuse and to unveil the distraction. Recipients' reactions and the question of whether discrepancy is a sufficient and necessary warning condition will be discussed in chapters 7 and 8. In the present chapter, the emphasis is on the actor's behavior.

In the foregoing paragraphs, I used the terms "permissible" and "accept" or "acceptable." An act is permissible or not, while a justification is acceptable or not. Both terms include a boundary: within the boundary is an area of permission and acceptance; outside the boundary, there is neither.

### *Justification and inequality*

A simple look at the social world reveals many indications of differences in consumption between people, showing huge differences in wealth. How then can I maintain that people strive to decrease differences between self and other in order to reduce fear? The answer is that the well-to-do conceal their wealth by bringing in arguments as to why they deserve their wealth. They create justifications and use them to convince others that the differences between self and other are small when the other takes into account, for instance, the huge sacrifices the rich actor has undergone to reach the present "mass" or status position. The actor in fact suggests that if you, the recipient, do the same as I do, then you will become as I am now. Of course, it is a myth, but the myth reflects the basic idea of equality. And justifications are crucial to concealing differences. In addition, the well-to-do behave as much as possible as standard citizens and try not to be too different from them. Many sitcoms show the plainness of the rich and very rich. Moreover, well-known citizens appear in advertisements showing that they too encounter the same problems as ordinary people do. Do those justifications mean that the rich will actually become ordinary citizens? No, they do not, with regard to the allocation of the resource money or status, but they (try to) do so with allocation of other types of resources, like love, service, information, and eventually goods.

To reduce fear, the well-to-do must work on the ordinary citizen's acceptance of the justifications. Often, in rather new allocation events, it is not certain whether the ordinary citizen will accept the justifications. A good example is the bankers' defense of the huge bonuses their employees received during the financial crisis of 2008/2009. Although public money supports the bankers, they give huge bonuses to themselves and their employees. The argument they use is that these employees generate money as well as work, which is beneficial for others. Without the bonuses, these employees will exert less effort and consequently not facilitate the creation of jobs or economic activity. However, the citizens were not convinced of the correctness of the justification and asked governments to work on principles to curb the huge bonuses.

Many rules or principles that people apply as justifications need no public discussion about their acceptance. Allocation of resources is, more or less, performed automatically. This is the case when an actor allocates resources according to accepted rules, like the rules in most countries for rewarding work. The actor takes into account the characteristics of the status position of the other and allocates resources between them accordingly. It seems that in many allocation events differences and even large differences between self and other or between others are generally accepted. This is seemingly so because the accepted allocation rules are used as justifications for the differences. Justifications conceal differences: if we all take the difference in training into account, then the difference in reward will disappear. The justifications used in those events are learned, and are thus culturally related (Lerner 1980; Vermunt 2002). In collective societies, for instance, actors are more inclined to allocate resources to others based on the success of all the individuals involved than in individualistic societies (Hofstede 1980).

**Maxim 2**: When an actor does not achieve factual similarity (equality) of allocation outcomes, the actor applies justifications to conceal differences between self and other.

People view the bankers' call for high bonuses generally as unethical: In this allocation event, bankers allocate too-large financial rewards among their employees at the expense of others in need. The main reason that people label the bankers' call unethical is that the justifications given are not accepted; even more, are rejected (Scanlon 1998). An actor's behavior cannot be evaluated as unethical or ethical as such, but the ethicality of an act can only be assessed by the acceptance or rejection of the given justifications of the act (see also Mill 1987; Scanlon 1998). The acceptance or rejection of the justifications of an allocation outcome are the result of a discussion between actor, recipient, and observer.

The discussion between the three parties starts only when the following conditions are met: (1) The actor (or another person) communicates his/her own and the recipients' allocation outcomes to the public; (2) those involved perceive a difference (inequality) between the intended or realized allocation outcome and what is already accepted; (3) the actor communicates justifications for the allocation decision; and (4) the issue is very important for one or more of the parties.

In publishing the intended allocation decision, the actor clearly anticipates possible disagreement between the parties. Bonuses for bank employees are accepted to a certain extent, dependent on the actual economic situation. When an allocation outcome is done according to rules that are already accepted in the specific social, economic, and political environment then there is no need to explicitly announce the allocation decision. A salary increase, for instance, according to already accepted rules and in a favorable economic climate, needs no additional justifications beyond the ones already accepted. Of course, there is already inequality in the case of bank employees, but the public generally accepts the operative justifications. A swimming instructor who rescues a drowning pupil needs no justification, but the same man who does not rescue a drowning pupil does. In rescuing the drowning pupil, the instructor creates equality between self and pupil: both stay alive. Not rescuing the pupil creates a huge inequality between actor and recipient. In the first instance, observers will be outraged by the instructor's decision not to help the pupil and let him/her die. However, the instructor's justifications for not rescuing the pupil will be discussed by the pupil's family, by the public, and by experts, and they may be convinced to accept them. This discussion, sometimes concluded in a lawsuit, may end in a public rejection (acceptance) of the instructor's and banker's justifications, and condemnation (clearance) of their behavior. A husband lying to his wife about his whereabouts the previous night creates an inequality of the resource information between himself and his wife. The husband has information he will not tell his wife. An observer may be tempted to condemn the husband's behavior, but has to consider the husband's justifications before judging: The husband may have good reasons for his lie, but the question is whether his wife and the observer will accept them.

In all cases of unequal allocation, whether the resource is money, service, or information, the actor, recipient, and observer evaluate, accept, or reject the actor's justifications.

Is it always realistic that there is public discussion about the acceptance of justifications? And if not, is it then reasonable to expect that the ethicality of the behavior can be established? In the case of material resources like money, goods, and information, public discussion is plausible and acceptable. The same goes for the behavior of people in public positions such as politicians, medical personnel, or teachers. For other cases it is less plausible and acceptable that public discussion will always be held. Is a public discussion plausible and acceptable in the case of the husband's lie? The lie may be motivated from egoistic or altruistic motives, and this aspect seems to me not a subject for public discussion, but if other people are deeply involved in the husband's behavior, the behavior may be discussed publicly. Moreover, lying is conveying false information to the other, whether in the case of husband to wife or supervisor to subordinate. It is the allocation of a resource that is not confined to specific actors. Consequently, lying may be subject to public discussion. Observers may have an opinion about lying even in the private setting of a marriage.

Let us further assume that the husband communicates justifications which unveil aspects of the intimate relationship between him and his wife. Is it plausible and acceptable that the public discusses the justifications? Or should the discussion be confined to people that are closely related to the husband and wife? It is plausible and acceptable that the husband and wife confine the circle of observers to the closely related people. And that is what the wife probably will do: discuss the justifications with her close friends. If the justifications are unexpected, the wife has to decide whether to accept them. Acceptance or rejection can be the result of discussion with close relatives. I would call this local ethics.

**Maxim 3**: The ethicality of an actor's allocation behavior depends on the acceptance by the actor, recipient(s), and observers of the communicated justifications.

The moral implications of allocation behavior are most salient in events in which an actor allocates between self and other. In the self–other allocation event, the actor allocates, consciously or through automatic inclination, more to self than to the other. This egoistic tendency relates to what is called the self-serving bias: the tendency to attribute positive outcomes to one's own efforts. So, the actor has to make a deliberate effort to take account of the recipients' interests: that is, moving the other closer to oneself. However, in allocation events in which the actor allocates resources between others mutually, moral considerations can also be salient: for instance, in the situation where one of the recipients is a close relative or family member and the other is not, or in the situation in which one of the recipients is a member of the actor's own group and the other is from a different group. In both allocation events, the actor has to promote the altruistic tendency to allocate resources equally between close and far-off other.

## Justice and Morality

When actors have the formal position of an impartial agent—a judge, for instance—they judge allocation outcomes in terms of justice and not in terms of morality. People do not say that the judge has given an immoral verdict: they say that the judge decided unfairly. A blindfolded Lady Justice and not a blindfolded Lady Morality represents the administration of justice.

However, what then is the difference between justice and morality? The answer to this question is not easy. If one looks at the examples that appear in the literature about moral behavior, they almost all have to do with helping others. In terms of allocation events, morality is related to allocation of the resource service: operating a switch to rescue people, rescuing a drowning person, giving a lethal injection. So it seems that in the case of helping others people evaluate acts towards others more in terms of morality than in terms of justice. In the case of other resources, evaluation in terms of justice is more appropriate than evaluation in terms of morality. However, will people evaluate the money that a person offers to a beggar as a morally right action or as a just action? If the act satisfies the beggar's need, it is probably better to speak of a moral act than of a just act. A parent who gives her child some money to buy chips because the child is hungry satisfies the child's need as well, but it is not a moral act, nor a just act, but a love act or a duty. Thus, although there may be some overlap, in the case of service resource allocation it is appropriate to use the term moral, while in other cases it is appropriate to use the term just.

## Some Examples

With the knowledge described so far we are now in a better position to examine Scanlon's examples of (non-)ethical behavior. Reexamination of the examples makes our position more clear with regard to the difference between justice and morality, and the operation of the egoistic and altruistic motives.

*Drug Shortage (Scanlon, 2008: 14–15)*

There are five people in Room B, and one person in Room A, all of whom have the same disease, and all of whom will die if not treated soon. There is enough medicine on hand to cure all five of the people in Room B, but since the person in Room A has a more advanced case, it would take all of the available supply to save just this patient.

Scanlon states that in this case it is at least permissible to use all of the medicine to save the five people in Room B. However, why is it that everyone regards this solution as permissible? According to the maxim of equal allocation, it would be better to allocate the medicine equally between all persons in both Room A and B. Equal division leads to fear reduction because the actor does not need to discriminate between people. However, the decision not to deliver the medicine equally to all is because an equal division does not save lives, while an unequal division does save the lives of five people (for a comparable interpretation, see also Rawls 1971).

In addition, the actor's decision about the allocation of the medicine activates the egoistic as well as the altruistic motive, but only to a small degree: egoistic in so far as it swells the doctor's pride to save as many lives as possible, and altruistic in so far as saving five people gives joy to more recipients than saving one. However, the actor needs to not maintain the egoistic and to promote the altruistic tendencies, and both tendencies can be satisfied to the same small amount. The actor's decision is not a moral one, but it is an allocation decision and people will evaluate the decision in terms of justice and not in terms of morality.

*Transplant*

The five people in Room B are in need of organs—one needs a heart, two people need a lung, and two need a kidney—and they will all die if they are not given transplants soon. Unfortunately, no organs are available. But there is a person in Room A, in for a checkup, who could be given a lethal injection instead of the expected inoculation, thereby making the organs available to save the five others.

According to Scanlon, it is not permissible to deliver a lethal injection to the person in Room A to save five lives. Killing one person to save five is not permissible. The cases are not comparable, as indicated earlier. But still, this case is interesting from a moral point of view. The decision to give the lethal injection needs the consent of the person in Room A (let us assume that the person in Room A is allowed to take a decision like that; let us also assume, to simplify the language, that he is male). The physician requests the person in Room A to allow the lethal injection. If he says yes, he saves the lives of the five people in Room B. If he says no, he saves his own life but not the five other lives. The question is whether the person in Room A decides egoistically or (extremely) altruistically? Can he conquer the altruistic motivation? If he says no, do the physician, the people in Room B, and any observers regard his decision as egoistic?

The interesting question is whether the physician will give the lethal injection after the person in Room A has given his consent? Is that permissible? I think it is, because the justification is that the physician, in giving the lethal injection, saves five lives: a result contrary to Scanlon's evaluation of the case.

*Drug/Transplant*

The people in Room B are the same as in the previous example, and the person in Room A is the same as in the first example. If the person in Room A dies of his illness, his organs are undamaged and can save the lives of the five people. Is it permissible to withhold the drug from him? From the doctrine of double effect (effect as intended versus effect as foreseeable), it follows that it is not permissible to withhold the drug, because the death of the one is intended and not just foreseeable as in the Drug Shortage case. With these examples, Scanlon shows that it is not tenable to base the permissibility of an act on the doctrine of double effect.

In the Drug/Transplant case, the person in Room A has the disposal of organs to allocate but is very ill. The physician can withhold the drug from this person, whose death saves the life of the five in Room B. Only the consent of the person in Room A allows the physician to withhold the drug. If the person in Room A gives consent for the transplant of his organs, the physician may carry out the necessary steps. Seen from the physician's point of view his action is permissible, contrary to what Scanlon states. Different from the Drug Shortage case, and similar to the Transplant case, the physician is not an actor but an executioner. And the moral dilemma is preserved for the person in Room A.

Scanlon (2008) mentions an example of a moral dilemma that is critical for the allocation explanation of these dilemmas. Judith Thomson gave the example. A patient is fatally ill and in great pain. The only course of medication will also cause the patient's death. In other words, the service to the body of the patient has a positive outcome (pain relief) as well as a negative outcome (causing death). Scanlon and Thomson ask themselves whether the delivery of the drug depends on the physician's intentions, and they conclude that it is clearly not. From an allocation point of view, I have a somewhat different view. The allocation event concerns the simultaneous delivery of a positive resource (service: pain relief) and a negative resource (status: death). The doctor is primarily concerned with the well-being of the patient—pain relief—but the fatal status loss is so vital that the doctor is not able to decide. With the injection, the doctor causes the patient's death, creating an inequality between self and other. Such an inequality must be justified. The justification is the relief of the patient's pain. However, the question is whether the patient will accept the justification. If the patient does not accept the justification then the doctor is not allowed to give the injection. If the patient accepts the justification, the doctor is allowed to give the injection. It depends on the patient's decision to accept the drug. The physician is not merely the means of delivering the drug, he is part of the decision-making process.

I conclude from Scanlon's examples that only in one case—the Drug Shortage case—is the physician the actor in an allocation event, and the dilemma is not a moral dilemma (he need conquer neither egoistic nor altruistic motivations). The other examples are moral dilemmas for the person in Room A.

### *Other Examples*

To make the argument about how to combine the egoistic and altruistic motives stronger, I will work out the example of an actor who decides whether to rescue a drowning person or not. In allocation terms, the actor has to decide whether to allocate resources to the person in the form of service (Foa and Foa 1974). The resource service involves activities that affect the body and belongings of a person, and that often constitute labor for the actor. Rescuing a person surely affects the body and constitutes labor in favor of that person. Whether the actor acts or not depends on the actor's definition of the situation: is the actor capable of rescuing the other? Can the actor overcome the egoistic motivation of staying dry or the danger of drowning? How strong is the altruistic motivation, the desire to do something for the person? Can the actor live with the public scorn if he/she does not jump into the water (egoistic)? Can the actor live with the feelings of guilt for not rescuing the person (egoistic)? Will the actor employ other ways of helping the drowning person without jumping into the water, for instance, cry for help or call the police? If the observers know that the actor cannot swim, not rescuing the drowning person by springing into the water can be permissible. That is, the observers accept the given justification. However, that does not discharge the actor from trying other types of action to bring the rescue of the drowning person nearer. Omission of action, in this case, is morally not permissible.

An example of what some people have labeled a moral dilemma is the following (Hauser 2009). A man is standing at a switchboard on a railroad track. If he does not act, an incoming train will follow the main track; if the man operates the switchboard, the train will follow a side track. A train is coming and cannot stop. Five people are walking on the main track. If the train continues on the main track, the train will run over the five people and they will die. A very fat man is walking on the side track. The mass of the man is such that he can stop the train; he would die, but would save the five men on the main track. What should the man at the switch do? Should he operate the switch to send the train to the side track, causing the death of one person, or do nothing, resulting in five deaths? According to Hauser, it is permissible to operate the switch and save five people with the sacrifice of one (see the Drug Shortage case).

Hauser and others label this dilemma a moral dilemma. However, is it a moral dilemma? Following my own definition of a moral act—delivering service to another—the question is whether the man at the switchboard faces a moral dilemma. Or is it a justice dilemma? The man at the switchboard is confronted with the question of how to save the most lives. That seems to me more an efficiency issue than a moral one. It would be quite a different dilemma, and a true moral dilemma, if one asks the fat man to decide. The fat man can undertake one of two actions. He can continue to walk on the side track and stop the train at the cost of his own life, and so rescue five lives. Or he can step aside and rescue his own life but not the lives of the five other people. The fat man faces a moral dilemma as I have defined it and as it should be defined. Moreover, in this case, no one will blame the fat man if he steps aside. In other words, there are limits to activating the altruistic motive.

For the man on the switchboard, it is a justice dilemma: The man has to decide whether to allocate a negative service to one person or to five persons. It is very likely that observers will blame the man on the switchboard if he lets the five men die.

## Commission and Omission

Is omission—not doing anything and walking away—always not permissible? Imagine the following event. An actor sees a rich person being robbed by beggars. The actor can deliver information about the event or do service to the rich person. For instance, the actor can call the police, help the rich person, go after the robbers and bring back the stolen money, or do nothing and walk away. The question is, what is morally the best thing actor can do? The first thing the actor can do is to estimate the need state of the robbed person. The actor knows from the clothes the person is wearing that he is rich. Financial need is probably not the need that has to be fulfilled. Thus, going after the robbers and trying to bring back the money is not the most appropriate action. The (need) state of the victim can be better described as being bodily and psychologically harmed. The victim is probably wounded, and may be in shock. Comforting the victim and thus delivering service will fulfill this need better than bringing back the money. The resource service is more scarce for the victim than money is, and the correspondence between the victim's need state and the resource allocated (giving comfort) makes service a morally correct act. Moreover, it is aimed at restoring the previous health state of the victim.

Doing nothing in this case will be evaluated as the least morally correct option, or even as immoral. With the not-action, the actor does not try to restore the previous situation of the rich man: the actor does not restore equality between himself and victim with regard to health. As the allocation theory of moral behavior prescribes, the actor must give reasons for the refusal to go after the robbers, to offer service, or to inform the police. If the actor gives good reasons for not helping the rich person, the omission may be permissible (Scanlon 2008)—for instance, if the actor has to deliver service to another person in greater need than the rich person. Permissibility depends on the love and respect the actor, recipient, and observers attribute to the given justifications. For instance, would it be permissible for the actor to walk away because the man is rich and the beggars are poor, so that what the beggars do is to decrease slightly the inequality between the two parties by robbing the rich man? No, that is not permissible, because the need state of the rich man is his damaged health. Is it permissible to walk away because the actor is afraid of retaliation from the beggars? No, because of the need state of the victim, and because alternative ways of intervening—calling the police—are also possible. Calling the police is an act that reduces the anxiety concerning retaliation drastically. Intervention often requires courage, and one may not assume that all people have courage to the same degree. Jan Extra (personal communication) carried out a study investigating courage that touches on people's moral quality. During their training, professional marines experienced a situation while they took an important exam. In the room where only two of them were present, two workers (in fact professional actors) entered the room, each of them carrying a gas cylinder. They apologized for the short interruption and disappeared through a door to another room. Noise came from the other room. After some time smoke entered the examination room from under the door, and the marines clearly heard screams of agony. One of the workers pushed open the door and crawled into the examination room shouting that an accident had occurred with handling the gas cylinder and that his mate was very seriously wounded. Fire came from the back of the adjacent room. The question was what the marines would do in that situation. Would they end their examination and help the victims, or continue with the examination that was very important for their training and further career? Would the marines, selected to operate in circumstances where their life was often at stake, lend support or not? Is it morally permissible for the marines to abstain from helping? Would the marines' justifications that the examination is important for their career be accepted? One can phrase the dilemma as follows: Does continuing with the examination and thus improving one's own status weigh more than lending support (service) to others? Equality weighs heavy in this case: the actor brings the wounded person back to his/her own health state, or tries to.

## Resources

A resource is defined as "any commodity—material or symbolic—which is transmitted through interpersonal behavior" (Foa and Foa 1974: 36). They classified commodities into six resource classes: money, goods, services, information, status, and love. Resource *classes* are defined as "categories of the *meaning* assigned to actions and not a classification of actions" (Foa and Foa 1974: 82). Each of their resource types has a valence running from positive to negative. A positive valence implies that the more a person has of the resource, the more satisfied the person is. A negative valence implies that the more a person has of the resource, the less satisfied the person is (see also, Jasso 2007). The above-mentioned example of rescuing a drowning person assigns a positive valence to the resource service. Not rescuing a drowning person, thus withholding a service, assigns a negative valence to the resource service. Stabbing a person with a knife is delivering a service with a negative valence. Withholding a negative service is not, by definition, evaluated as positive.

A resource is transferred through interpersonal behavior. A fundamental feature of human life is need fulfillment through interpersonal behavior. One can differentiate between actor, the one who initiates the behavior, and recipient, the one to whom the behavior is directed. The actor's initiative is triggered by the other's need state as well as by their own need state: reduction of fear. Maintaining the egoistic, promoting the altruistic, or, in other words, just resource allocation, reduces fear. The other reacts to the outcome and accepts or rejects the perceived allocation outcome. This interaction ends with need fulfillment for the actor as well as the recipient. Fulfillment may be full or partial.

Interpersonal behavior conveys messages with regard to the perceived need state of self and other. Allocation behavior is intended to change the perceived need state. A mother gives food when her child is hungry, and the child accepts it and smiles at her. By offering food (allocating goods) the mother fulfills the need of her child. Giving food reduces the mother's fear of not being a good mother. The child's smile endorses the mother's good behavior. Mother and child have performed a full interaction circle.

Actors fulfill their need through interpersonal behavior, and also develop a conception of mutual understanding. Actors as well as recipients learn from the interaction. In the case of mother and child, the child learns to trust the mother while the child's reaction encourages the mother to continue with the care. Because the mother–child relationship is crucial for the further development of the child, a good bond between mother and child results in the child's positive view of the world.

In order to transfer resources, people must have resources at their disposal. What does that mean? It means that people own something, that that something is their property. Property is any (physical or intangible) entity a person, or a group of people jointly, owns. Owning a property means that the owner has the right to sell, consume, rent, mortgage, transfer, exchange, and even destroy the property. Important types of property include real property (land), personal property (physical possessions belonging to a person), private property (property owned by legal persons or business entities), public property (state-owned or publicly owned and available possessions), and intellectual property (exclusive rights over artistic creations, inventions, information, etc.). People own material resources like money and goods, but also the resources services and information, or people have property rights and exert control over them. People, thus, own financial means, and they own material goods, like computers. Money and goods are tangible or material resources. Food, for instance, is a material resource, it is tangible, but it is not lasting. Food can be sold, consumed, rented, mortgaged, transferred, exchanged, and destroyed by the owner. Renting and mortgaging food is probably not widespread, but it is possible in principle. In our example, one may say that the mother owns the food and she has the right to transfer it to her child. Property is tangible or intangible: a house is a tangible resource, and information is not.

With regard to the six resource classes proposed by Foa and Foa, four of them are more or less easily defined as property: money, goods, information, and services. For money, goods, and information, it is clear how these commodities relate to property. Actors have the right—based on education and training—to carry out services defined as activities that affect the body or belongings of a person. Their intellectual and practical skills are defined here as intellectual property. A surgeon carries out activities on the patient's body. The surgeon's knowledge and skills are learned, and the profession of surgeon is protected in that not everyone may call themselves a surgeon. The same argument is used for nurses, therapists, and others in a service profession.

Family and friends carry out activities on the body of another without training or education. The question is whether these activities can be subsumed under the heading of service. It may be more fruitful to subsume the activities of laypersons on the body of another under the heading of love. Laypersons carry out activities on the body of another out of sympathy, friendship, or affection for the other.

However, how can one define love and status as property? Love is a feeling that a person has toward someone or something. Does a person possess love? Can one say that? No, but still actors have control over their feelings: actors can transfer love, or can exchange love, can destroy it, for instance. Can one say that a person has the right to transfer love? No. The same argument can be made for status. In other words, one cannot define love and status as property in the strict sense. To overcome this problem is to look at how these two resources are controlled. How can a person sell, transfer, or destroy love? One way is that the person conveys that he/she loves another; that is, the person gives information.

And information can be defined as intellectual property, not in the formal sense but in the informal one. Another way to show love is that the actor gives something to another. Flowers can be defined as a material good and thus as property. Thus, the way a person handles love relates to commodities labeled as property. The same argument applies for status.

Each resource or property has a material as well as a symbolic component. Offering money not only encompasses the transfer of the (physical) sum of money but also the symbolic value of it. It may convey respect to the recipient of the allocation. Love is not only an intangible or symbolic resource but also encompasses the transfer of tangible goods, like giving flowers.

### *Love and Respect*

#### *Love*

Social science researchers view love as an important resource that an actor allocates (Foa and Foa 1974). Love is an expression of affectionate regard, warmth, or comfort. According to Swanton (2003: 117), love has the following features: It is a form of becoming close; it is particular, universal, impartial, and unconditional. Particular in so far as love is directed at specific individuals, as Foa and Foa (1974) have defined it. For these authors, love is particularistic because one can allocate love only to those individuals one can identify and with whom one has a special relationship. Love is particularistic and therefore people allocate love unequally among others. Love creates inequality between people. However, in principle, each individual human being can fall in love with each other human being. And out of the total pool of candidates, a person chooses one. This creates the inequality. The inequality is not intended, but is the result of the choice. Still, individuals do not view the resulting inequality as unjust or immoral. Applying the allocation model of justice and morality, people must give reasons to justify the inequality. The standard justification in modern Western society is that feelings find their way irrespective of the person's will.

Swanton distinguishes self-love from universal love and stresses the importance of self-love: a healthy self-love has a positive effect on the exercise and enjoyment of one's rational powers. Rational powers regulate our passions (Plato) or sentiments (Hume). Universal love, in this view, is a resource that one gives to others, but differs greatly from the boundless compassion Schopenhauer (2001) describes. In his view, self-love as well as universal love has the feature of boundlessness. People give it or receive it in limitless amounts. This may be the case in the abstract, but practically it will be impossible. Showing love costs time and money and, because time and money are scarce, a person cannot show love in these limitless amounts. Love is a scarce resource and an actor must decide how much love to give to others and to self. The characteristic of universal love is that people give it in equal amounts to others irrespective of the characteristics of those others.

*Respect*

Kant (1785a) defines respect as follows: "Act in such a way that you always treat humanity, whether in your own person or in the person of any other, never simply as a means, but always at the same time as an end" (Hinman 2001: Slide 4). The opposite of respecting people is to treat them merely as means to an end. According to Hinman (2001), treating people with respect means: (1) not denying them relevant information, and (2) allowing them freedom of choice. Kant distinguishes between a partial form of respect—respect owed to others of differential status—and an impartial form of respect owed to all humans by virtue of their inherent dignity (Swanton 2003: 104, note 9). Respect is keeping distance, as Kant claimed.

*Love and respect*

Kant argues that love and respect are opposite to each other as attraction and repulsion are. He views love as coming close and respect as keeping a distance. Baron (2002) states that love and respect are not opposing forces, as some scholars (Kant) claimed. According to Baron, love and respect are different: duties of love put others under obligation, while duties of respect do not. Love defined as coming close connects it to love as defined by Foa and Foa (1974): coming close implies a particular relationship between actor and recipient. One cannot come close to anyone, but only to specific others one can identify. Love implies experience with another. With respect, it is different. Respect implies status, reputation, information one has heard. Although love and respect are viewed as different, would love not also imply that correct information should be conveyed? Can one call it love when an actor denies another relevant information? And is it also conceivable that someone respects another without loving them? And is it possible to hate someone and still respect that person?

People not only express love and respect in terms of information they convey, but also with regard to services offered, or money, or goods. Love is the amount of time an actor devotes to another, or the amount of money or goods that actor offers. Respect is expressed in these other resources as well. In both cases, showing respect or love, one can ask the question: should a large amount of love and respect coincide with a large amount of other resources, or not? Probably the answer is yes. Moreover, love as a particularistic resource elicits particularistic operationalizations like service (*services* involve activities that affect the body or belongings of a person and that often constitute labor for another). Respect, as a more universalistic resource, elicits universalistic operationalizations, like information (*information* includes advice, opinions, instruction, or enlightenment but excludes those behaviors that could be classed as love or status). Kant states that respecting another implies that one does not lie to the other, and connects respect with information.

Combining love and respect results in other feelings or emotions, like pity or compassion. Compassion includes certain amounts of love and respect. People have compassion for another person or group of people, and they mean that those others merit love and respect. People feel empathy with some others—for instance, victims of a disaster—but for one or two persons who behaved bravely, people have respect. Brave victims are pitied for the condition they are in and admired for their courage: coming close as well as keeping a distance. For others, people feel pity, empathy but with less respect; pity has a somewhat negative connotation. Compassion includes love and respect in sufficient amounts.

*Love, respect, and justice*

Swanton asks herself how love and respect—but specifically love, because it is particularistic—can be an aspect of such broader virtues like justice. "For though justice as a virtue is primarily concerned with respecting status and honoring (legitimate) rules and procedures, rules and procedures have to be made and interpreted, and making and interpreting them with a loving eye will enhance or 'perfect' justice" (Swanton 2003: 116). This idea coincides well with social justice theories. The justice literature makes a distinction between distributive justice and procedural justice. Distributive justice concerns the justice evaluation of the allocated resource, while procedural justice concerns the justice evaluation of the applied rules and procedures. Both types of justice reflect respecting someone's status. However, a recipient's treatment reflects respect but also love. An example of an interpersonal procedural rule is the appropriateness rule: an actor should not ask inappropriate questions of the recipient. An actor who conforms to this rule acts justly procedurally, and will earn love and respect from others. Consequently, if the application of a procedure will receive love and respect from recipients as well as from observers, the rule must be applied correctly procedurally as well as interpersonally.

Foa and Foa view love and respect as resources that an actor allocates to another or exchanges with another. Love and respect—Foa and Foa label it status—are resource classes that an actor allocates, just like money, goods, services, and information. If one adopts Kant's vision that love and respect are the basis for moral behavior, I add to it that these resources form the basis for a just allocation as well. This vision implies that Foa and Foa's resource classes are not, as these authors assume, of equal relevance for interpersonal allocation behavior, but assume a hierarchy between love and status (respect) on the one hand and money, goods, information, services on the other hand. Hinman (2001) supports the idea of a hierarchy of resources. Hinman (2001) suggests that respect shows itself in the information given to the other. To be respected persons means that they are not denied relevant information. Denying relevant information is an operationalization of disrespect, as if the other is not an end in itself but a means to obtain something for oneself. Hinman points to the use of participants in medical or other research. He argues that researchers should respect participants and thus should inform them fully about the purpose and procedures of the experiments in which they participate. By not conveying correct information about purpose and procedures, researchers are sure of people's participation and of receiving sufficient data for analysis. Researchers use participants only as a means to get data, and Kant argued that such use of human subjects is immoral.

The justice motive coincides with respect for human beings, for other living creatures, and also for the world of inanimate objects. Respect, therefore became an important mode of allocation. The agrarian revolution (see Chapter 2) triggered changes in the beliefs on how to allocate resources: a person's status position entitled him/her to have a right to a certain amount of resources. The Industrial Revolution brought with it an emphasis on the person's desert as a basis of allocation. All these bases—respect, entitlement, and deservingness—are still operating when an actor allocates resources, with respect and deservingness as dominant in the Western (post-)industrialized world. The way these bases are applied—interpersonal treatment—reflects love for recipient.

## The Allocation Event and Morality

### *Resource Type and Moral Behavior*

Foa and Foa (1974) differentiate between six types of resources: love, service, status, information, goods, and money. The resources differ in their degree of concreteness and latitude of applicability. Particular love, for instance, is abstract but also confined to specific persons. Its expression is dependent on the relationship between actor and recipient while money is not. Service requires specific actions with respect to the person or body, while delivering goods does not. The issue I would like to raise now is whether resource type elicits or conditions different forms of moral behavior. Is, for instance, the impact on moral behavior of providing a service to another different from donating a monetary gift? An actor's appropriate behavior—the moral quality of the behavior—depends on the perceived need state of the recipient and the kind of comparison made: (1) comparison between recipients; or (2) comparison of self—actor—with recipient. Recall the example discussed previously. An actor sees a rich man robbed by beggars. Going after the beggars and trying to bring back the money is a less appropriate action. Moreover, this is an Actor–Recipient–Recipient action and not an Actor–Recipient action: Actor tries to reallocate money from the beggars to the owner. If the actor starts to run after the beggars, people will probably evaluate the behavior as courageous, as more or less just behavior, but not as moral behavior (except when actor's life is at stake). If the victim was a poor man, the actor's action to try to bring back the money is more just than when the victim is a rich man: the actor decreases the inequality between the beggars and the poor victim, but hardly between the beggars and the rich victim. Robbing a rich person (an Actor–Recipient action) is morally less inappropriate (because it decreases the inequality between the beggars and rich man) than robbing a poor person, because it increases inequality. The correspondence between the victim's need state and the resource allocated is in all likelihood the best criterion for helping: it aims to restore the previous state of the victim and bring it back to the actor's own state. Because of the correspondence, observers evaluate the service delivered as morally higher than going after the money. Doing nothing in this case is least permissible, and thus least moral. Thus, allocating service in this event is a more appropriate action than allocating money.

The actor is often not able to provide service from a distance. Bodily contact is often required to deliver service, such as mouth-to-mouth resuscitation to an accident victim. Asking help from others, as in the marine case, is permissible. In other cases, donating money is simpler and needs no bodily contact. A financial gift is easier to give than offering service. In addition, rendering a service costs time and energy, which may be converted into money, but are often not counted as such. So, at the end the actor is not poorer than at the beginning of the service. Donating money is different. The actor is poorer after the allocation than before. Calculation of "costs" for the actor is easier for material resources than for immaterial resources. The ease of calculation may be a hindrance when the actor decides to donate money or goods compared to delivering love or service. In general, one may argue that immaterial resources "cost" energy (the actor acts on the recipient) from the actor which is difficult to calculate, while material resources are relatively easy to deliver and the costs can easily be calculated. Moreover, actors allocate immaterial resources mostly to concrete people who need help or compassion, while actors allocate material goods to people in need whom the actor hardly knows.

Actors sometimes meet the following dilemma: shall I do volunteer work or donate money? In allocation terms: the dilemma is whether the actor chooses to deliver service or to allocate money. The attitude of observers would probably be that a rich man offering money will not receive a lot of love or respect, while the same man offering time and energy to help will receive much love and respect. People appreciate a poor person offering money more than the same person's service. Why is that, and can this difference in appreciation be explained by the allocation theory of moral behavior? Appreciation for the rich person donating money will only be high if the amount of money donated is high in comparison with their wealth. When, in other words, the actor considerably reduces the inequality between self and recipient. Offering a small amount will not substantially reduce the inequality, and consequently the rich person has to justify the behavioral decision. Observers accept the justifications more if the rich person does something extraordinary and bridges the gap between self and recipient more than the observers might expect. The same argument can be given for the poor person donating money instead of giving support: donating a small amount of money bridges the gap between the actor and recipient. Thus, I argue that when allocating plentiful resources, actors must allocate large amounts in order to receive much love and respect. Only then does the actor reduce the inequality sufficiently.

## Elements of Moral Behavior

Whether moral behavior concerns the operation of a trait of character (Aristotle 1987), a virtue (Hurka 2001; Swanton 2003), an obligation (Kant 1785a), or justification (Scanlon 1998), these ideas form only one element of moral behavior. Other important elements of moral behavior concern expression of moral behavior, its latitude, and its strength. These other elements play a vital role in deciding whether behavior is moral, just, or not. The problem is that operation of the justice motive—and morality—is often difficult to assess. Even the actor is often not sure whether he/she acts in a just way. In general, people often do not know why they acted in the way they did. A parent may ask himself/herself why he/she gave so much attention to the youngest child compared to the attention given to the other children. Supervisors may be unsure whether promoting one of their subordinates was correct compared to what others received. Actors, in other words, are often unsure whether they act in accordance with morality or the justice motive. In addition, if actors are unsure about the moral basis of their acts, how sure is the recipients' and observers' knowledge of the actor's motives? Because the actor's explanation of their motives is often unknown or seen as not sufficient to judge whether the actor allocated resources justly, recipients and observers have to rely on additional knowledge of the allocation event. Some authors, for instance, stress the recipient's well-being as an indication of the actor's moral behavior. Others emphasize the recipient's deservingness as an indication of the actor's just allocation. For instance, did God act justly, having a benevolent attitude toward Abel's offer but not to Cain's offer? Swanton (2003), therefore, distinguishes several modes (ways of expression) of moral behavior, such as love and respect. And from the amount of love and respect shown by recipient and observer one can infer the moral quality of the actor's behavior. Furthermore, a basic issue in the study of moral behavior concerns the latitude of the behavior. Is the behavior (symbolically) directed to close relatives, as is the case with family love, or is the behavior directed to all human beings, as is the case with universal love? Is the actor prepared to rescue a drowning person he dislikes or who is clearly a foreigner? An additional issue concerns the strength of the moral response. Is jumping into the water to rescue a person or "only" shouting for help the correct moral response?

These three issues of moral behavior will now be discussed: modes of moral behavior, the latitude, and the strength of moral behavior.

### *Modes of Moral Behavior*

At the basis of moral behavior stands acceptance of the actor's justifications in terms of love and respect: Actor, act so that the justifications you give for your allocation decision (deviation from equality) receive the most love and respect. If love and respect are modes of moral behavior, as Swanton (2003) states, the question is how they relate to moral behavior, separately and in combination.

Some scholars assume that moral behavior and respect are closely linked. Kant (1988), for instance, in the second formulation of the categorical imperative, states in the Formula of Humanity as an end in itself: "So act that you use humanity, whether in your own person or in the person of any other, always at the same time as an end, never merely as a means." What does it mean when Kant states: "So act?" In itself, it is a simple two-word phrase but it contains a complexity that Kant elaborated in the Groundwork for the first time. To elucidate moral behavior, Kant gives the example of a man who seriously wants to die because he is overwhelmed with his own sorrow, but feels it his duty not to do so. According to Kant, this man acts out of duty and his decision has high moral worth. It is as if the man conquers his desire to die and lives on purely out of duty. Where does the mental state of what Kant labels duty come from? Is it counteracting the selfish desire, in this case the desire to die, or does it come from the man's deliberation—in a purely detached way—that living on is what he has to do? In both cases, duty has to do with reasons: there must be reasons to deviate from the selfish path and go in another direction. In the first case, the reason is to go against the desire and in the second case, reasons are otherwise. In the second proposition, Kant states this idea as follows: "An action that is done from duty doesn't get its moral value from the purpose that's to be achieved through it but from the maxim that it involves, giving the reason why the person acts thus" (Kant 1785b: 9). In other words, to conquer the desire (to die) as such has no purpose (it is not done in order to feel better) but directs the behavior (follow not the desire) away from the selfish impulse. Kant gives the reason(s) for the behavior to conquer the desire in the third proposition: "To have a duty is to be required to act in a certain way out of respect for the law" (10). Thus, following the law is the reason for doing one's duty. In other words, respect for the law inspires men to conquer their desires.

Kant's conclusion that doing one's duty adds moral worth to one's actions is not restricted to Kant, as an observer, alone. What Kant means is that any person who has respect for the moral law will conclude that the man's decision to stay alive adds moral worth. Thus also the man himself will come to this conclusion. And although the man will not be motivated to acquire the highest moral worth, the side effect is that he becomes aware of his high moral position when doing his duty. The man, therefore, receives respect from himself as well as from others for his decision to stay alive. And not only respect: Doing ones duty, following the law, induces love as well (Swanton 2003).

The example, Kant's explanation, and its implications can be phrased in allocation terms. In Kant's case, the man with the profound desire to die but who stays alive out of duty is an actor who has discretionary power to allocate the resource service (doing something to the person or body) to himself. Taking the decision to stay alive maintains equality between self and other. This decision needs no justification. It is only in this way that the man who has taken the decision to stay alive will have the love and respect that he deserves. It is not that the man strives for love and respect, but it will be his part when taking this decision. Following his desire (and deciding to end his life) makes him a less moral person, for himself as well as for others: the man creates a huge inequality between self and others. The actor has to justify this decision and the justification will be scrutinized by both actor and observers. If they receive the justification with love and respect, his decision has moral worth.

How, then, can we view Kant's maxim to treat the other as an end in itself and not as a means to an end? It is every person's duty to act like that, and the maxim is phrased as a categorical imperative that concerns not the material part of the action, nor its consequences, but the form and the principle out of which the action arises; the essential good of an action is the inclination, irrespective of the result (Kant 2005). Inclinations are difficult to observe, but their manifestations are not. One of the manifestations is the love and respect shown by others. If all people show the actor love and respect for the allocation decision, it approaches the limit of a moral law stated as a categorical imperative. The categorical imperative forms the ultimate limit approached closer and closer by increasing public consent, but that people never reach. One can compare the metaphysics of morality with the definition of a limit in mathematics.

But does reception of the love and respect of others not introduce a teleological element into the theory propagated here? This is indeed the case in so far as actors are sure of others' evaluation of their justifications. But that is often not the case. The public's evaluation is like a whimsical wind that blows from every direction. To count, beforehand, on the public's favor is a dangerous affair. Actors cannot be sure of the public's valence with respect to the given justifications. Actors follow their tendencies and hope to get approval through doing so.

One could say that taking the perspective of the other has not improved our knowledge of the moral implications of allocation decisions. That seems true, but we have gained in that now we know what the discussion focuses on, that is on the acceptance or rejection of arguments. But what measuring rule decides which argument is morally superior to other arguments? Scanlon would argue that the well-being of the drowning person is at stake and that this argument forms a necessary condition for help. That means that well-being is the determining factor of the decision to help. There are two problems with the argument that another's well-being is the determining factor for moral behavior. The first problem is that it is difficult to decide how exactly to assess another's well-being, as stated before, and the second problem is that assessing another's well-being shows a one-sided, paternalistic view that is inconsistent with the actor–recipient relationship propagated here.

Although in Kant's view the moral law is the object of respect, in the Groundwork he asserts that persons can be objects of respect as well (Klimchuk 2003). According to Klimchuk, one may have respect for persons because they: (1) are part of humanity; (2) have an earned capacity; and (3) limit their self-esteem by the dignity of humanity in another person. Thus, according to Kant, doing one's duty, or following the moral law, deems respect and love. In other words, the man's decision to stay alive maintains equality and coincides with the maxim: follow the moral law. This will result in the highest love and respect from self and others.

Would it mean that committing suicide is not permissible? No, it is permissible, but the actor creates an inequality and he should subject the justification to public evaluation.

One may rephrase Kant's maxim, therefore, as follows:

**Maxim 4**: Actors allocate resources equally. Unequal allocation is only permissible if the justifications given for the allocation outcome receive love and respect from self, recipients, and observers.

An actor tries to earn love and respect for the reasons he communicates in order to allocate resources as justly as possible. In the first place, the actor applies justifications that he assumes to result in the highest amount of love and respect for self and others. The reasons given for a particular allocation outcome are such that they boost the actor's self-esteem. The actor's self-love and self-respect should be gratified by the reasons given for the allocation decision. Actors must stand for their allocation decision for other reasons than self-esteem as well. If actors wish their justifications to be accepted, recipients as well as observers should be convinced that the allocation decision comes from the actor's deep-felt motivation. But the amount of love and respect that the justifications accompany should also be received from the recipients and observers. And these amounts of love and respect should be highest for self, recipients, and observers. For example, the President of Zimbabwe, Robert Mugabe, allocates all kinds of resources (money, land) unequally between his followers and other civilians—the followers receive far more of these resources than other civilians do. Mugabe justifies his allocation decisions by stressing the important role of his followers in the liberation of his country from English domination. And he accuses many of the other civilians of high treason. Both justifications give Mugabe an argument for treating the other civilians as enemies and thus badly. The justifications are manifestations of a lack of love and respect for a great number of people in Zimbabwe. The only love and respect the justifications show are for his family, friends, and followers. So, the love and respect received from self and followers exceeds by far the love and respect received from all other civilians. Love and respect received are highest from followers but lowest from other civilians. The unequal allocation of respect and love is an indication of the low moral quality of his allocation decisions. Is it then not permissible to allocate resources unequally? No, but the justifications should be such that they receive more love and respect from others. For instance, it is permissible to give followers the farms owned by the white population. But this should be done only under the condition that the new farmers produce the same amount of food as previously. That was not the case. The farms deteriorated and people suffered from the lack of food. The people of Zimbabwe were worse off than before.

An equal and high allocation of love and respect from self and all others forms the basis of moral behavior. The motivation to interact with others is instigated by exchanging or allocating resources and is primarily based on fear reduction and the operation of the egoistic motive and the altruistic motive (see Chapter 1). The issue is not about giving or receiving love or respect, but how love and respect are applied to justify allocation decisions resulting in being a moral person or not. One must not forget that our animal instincts are still operating and that regulating these instincts has evidently been profitable for our species. Evolutionarily, the human species has learned to control these impulses, so that human beings automatically or consciously regulate them. In regulating one's own innate impulses, like being too egoistic or too altruistic, a balance between the two impulses can be reached resulting in just or moral behavior.

Swanton (2003) posits that non-teleological as well as teleological considerations must be part of a theory of moral behavior. That is, that a virtuous life as an actor, allocating resources equally, is a sufficient condition for being a virtuous person. This action need not be based on its serving ends but on their quality of splendor, excellence, or admiration. Critics of this idea say that expression of non-teleological considerations cannot serve as examples for others on how to become virtuous. However, creating equality between self and other is the way to become virtuous.

Hurka (2001) states that the values pleasure, knowledge, and achievement are intrinsically good, whether actors like them or not. And that loving these values, that is, desiring to obtain these values, is also intrinsically good. In both versions of virtue ethics, love as well as respect is a mode to accomplish something.

### *Latitude of Moral Behavior*

The explanations given for God's behavior in denying Cain's offering reflect the different ideas that exist in the literature about morality. Some authors (Aristotle, Augustine, and Plato, for instance) state that moral behavior is the expression of good character. Not all people have the virtue and those that have it do not all possess it to the same degree. In *The Nicomachean Ethics*, Aristotle includes justice as one of the four cardinal virtues. To live in accordance with these virtues is necessary to gain the highest happiness. In this view, an actor who is trying to allocate resources as justly as possible between recipients does this not for the sake of justice but to attain a higher level of happiness. Justice is practiced as a means to attain something else. Moreover, justice is a personal characteristic that some people possess in higher amounts than others. For those people, acting justly brings happiness. This eudemonic vision, to obtain happiness for oneself by behaving justly, courageously, and so forth, has a certain amount of selfishness in it. At least, it is a manifestation of the motivation to maintain ones self-regard. In addition, the Greek polis exempted women and slaves from achieving justice and happiness. In other words, for Aristotle, the latitude of becoming a moral person is restricted to a certain group of people. The polis allocated status unequally, leading to experiences of fear.

The relative ethics of Aristotle can be found in the works of Augustine. In his view, people belong to the city of God or to the city of Men. In the city of God people obey God and live in accordance with his laws and rules, while in the city of Men people live according to their own wishes and desires. The question of how people could enter the city of God is not based on merit but on the mercy God gave to some. Those who do not get God's mercy cannot enter the city of God. According to Augustine, we are not allowed to ask the question why God gives mercy to some and not to others: "according to a deeply hidden but just policy" (Augustinus 1983, Book XV, 6: 681). However, God's policy is not as deeply hidden as Augustine stated. The number of places for people to occupy in the City of God is restricted. God has already decided that the angels who have not fallen could enter the City, complemented with a certain number of people, holy people. And God decided, without any justification, which persons could enter the City. For Schopenhauer (1981), this God was a cruel and not a just God.

I would describe the idea of a restricted moral community, and the creation of inequality expressed by the early scholars, in a different way. The Biblical story of Cain and Abel is a good example of it. As already mentioned earlier in this chapter, God showed respect for Abel's offer and showed no respect for Cain's offer. But Cain and Abel were not the only people involved in the allocation event. There were two others as well: Adam and Eve, the parents of Cain and Abel. In other words, God's decision not only affected Cain and Abel but also their parents. They were the observers in the allocation event. And just as Aristotle exempted women and slaves from the moral community, God exempted Adam and Eve from it. If God was a high moral authority He would have taken the perspective of the parents into consideration. The question, therefore, is whether God would have received love and respect from Cain's parents in condemning Cain's behavior and respecting Abel's? Would God's justification that Cain had a bad character convince Adam and Eve? That is not likely if they saw that Cain gave his offering to God. Might they not have reasoned that he who offers out of duty, against his own desire, and strives for equality with Abel adds moral worth? Moreover, would Abel not be unpleasantly embarrassed when God respected his offer but not Cain's? So, God took only his desires into consideration when disrespecting Cain's offer and not those of the others involved.

It is important for an accurate judgment about an actor's moral behavior which persons he includes in the moral community. In the case of Cain and Abel it was rather simple to define the size of the moral community, but other communities are more difficult to define. The following example of an allocation event will elucidate this point. A teacher favors one of two brothers. The brothers do not differ in performance or sociability, but the teacher has a preference for one brother and not for the other. In front of all the other pupils, the teacher constantly denies the performance of one of the brothers while he treats the other brother with the highest respect. The teacher may defend his policy by stressing the good character of one of the brothers, but would that justification be convincing for the other pupils? And what would the parents of the two brothers and the parents of the other pupils think of the teacher's behavior? Is it necessary that the teacher should consider all the people mentioned here, or can the teacher restrict the community to the one brother and leave all others out? To solve this issue one can think of the existence of spheres in the moral community. There is the sphere of the two brothers, the sphere of the parents of the two brothers, the sphere of the other pupils, and the sphere of the parents of the other pupils. An additional sphere consists of the larger public of citizens, experts, and other teachers. The sphere of the brothers is the most interior sphere, followed by that of the parents of the brothers, the sphere of the pupils, the sphere of the parents of the other pupils, and the sphere of the larger public. The more a sphere extends to the outside, and the more impartial they are, the less strongly the actor—in general—needs to take the perspective of that sphere into account. But the evaluation of the outer spheres is crucial in determining the moral worth of the justifications.

People involved in an allocation event, self, recipients, and observers, will initially have no clear judgment about the actor's allocation behavior. In the example of the teacher, favoring one of the brothers, the brothers will probably discuss the teacher's behavior between them and eventually come to an agreement about the (in)appropriateness of the teacher's decision and justifications. However, it is also possible that the brothers will disagree with regard to the teacher's behavior: The behavior is favorable for one brother and not for the other. The brothers' agreement while they have different interests in the case increases the possibility of a correct judgment. Other principles are impartiality (Leventhal 1980; Tyler and Lind 1992), and veil of ignorance (Rawls 1971). The position of the other pupils is either impartial or not. If they agree with the brothers' rejection or acceptance of the teacher's justifications, the judgment wins in strength. The agreement will not be reached without discussion. Some pupils may initially disagree, or not have a clear judgment. Good reasons for rejection may alter their attitude. Disagreement may endure and that makes the judgment less strong.

In the process of favoring one brother and disfavoring the other, the teacher learns how others judge the behavior. Should that have effect on the teacher? Yes, it should, and the more so the more the judgments correspond with each other.

Initially, the teacher clearly followed the desire to favor one of the brothers. Because the difference in treatment is so evident, the teacher should have known that it was wrong. The teacher uses justifications to veil the differences; following the discussion, the teacher learns from all spheres that the behavior is wrong. Initially, the teacher gives reasons for it. However, when people criticize the behavior more the teacher's mind will change with the conviction that the behavior should change. Does the change in behavior have moral worth? Not for this occasion, but when the teacher has learned from it and, in future events, takes the perspective of others into account, then it may add moral worth to the behavior. An actor, for instance, who has the tendency to favor one of her pupils but conquers her desire out of the moral rule, emerged in the community, does her duty. She treats her pupils as equals. Her behavior adds moral worth.

In the discussion of the bonuses of bankers that started during the financial crisis in 2008, bankers gave reasons in favor of high bonuses and reasons against high bonuses. It was clear in the discussion that people in general evaluated high bonuses as unjust and that they should be limited. The rule was accepted, although some banks continued to give high bonuses. Some bankers, however, felt the duty to act according to this new rule and paid part of their bonus back to the bank. It is possible that some bankers did it out of cool calculation to receive a positive opinion, but others were probably affected by the new insights the moral rule induced.

### *Strength of Moral Behavior*

The public often judges actors' protests against bad practices as courageous. Well known are the whistleblowers who protest against waste of money and goods by members of large or bureaucratic organizations. These protests are courageous when one considers the aggressive reactions of the target organization, such as efforts to blacken the whistleblower's good name. Some people portray the whistleblower as a traitor, a person who fouls their own nest. The actor who, under such conditions, continues to protest against bad practices is strong, of high moral standards, although the targeted company will probably judge the protester otherwise. Why is the whistleblower of strong moral standards?

The whistleblower has to decide whether he/she will share their knowledge of bad practice with others. In other words, the whistleblower has to decide to allocate the resource information with all people or that he/she shares the information with the company: an equal allocation of the resource information or an unequal allocation. An equal allocation of information is preferred in that the actor need not discriminate between recipients. But sharing the information about bad practice puts the actor's career in jeopardy. The consequences of the whistleblower's act may be severe for him or her. It has happened that whistleblowers have to sell their house in order to pay a lawyer. If the targeted company defends itself effectively, whistleblowers lose their job and their reputation, and other companies may be very reluctant to hire them. In other words, whistleblowers often take a high risk with their protest. They act against their self-interest and that is something that generally indicates a high morality.

The question whether one can ask such a sacrifice of an actor is answered negatively by Scanlon (1998: 224). In his view, the actor cannot reject the principle of helping another who is in great pain when a small or moderate sacrifice of the actor can reduce or remedy the pain. In such a situation, the actor ought to help. Scanlon defines two principles, the Rescue Principle for severe cases and the Helpfulness Principle for cases when the other is not in desperate need. These principles "[require] us to take others' interests into account when we can very easily do so" (225).

The moral claim the whistleblower is facing, however, falls outside the limits defined by the Rescue and Helpfulness Principles: the whistleblower's sacrifice is higher than moderate, one cannot ask that much.

But the assessment of the amount of sacrifice and the weight of self-interest damage is rather subjective and dependent on the assessment point in time. The whistleblower's self-interest has been damaged, but assessment at a later point in time may show another picture: the whistleblower may get help to find another job. It is therefore unsure whether the criterion of the whistleblower's well-being or welfare is a sufficient one to evaluate the amount of sacrifice. Or whether the well-being or welfare of eventual others is a sufficient criterion to decide if a claim can be put on an actor's degree of sacrifice for helping others. In the same vein, the welfare of the worst-off is an unsure criterion for the moral quality of helping behavior as well. This issue will be described in Chapter 4.

An actor is sometimes unprepared when confronted with others who are in need. How far ought the actor to go in helping those in need? Can we ask the actor in all circumstances to offer help even at the expense of their own interests? Further than Scanlon's Rescue and Helpfulness Principles indicate? Yes, we can ask that much. On the one hand, actors owe much to others: their status, skills, education, and knowledge are for a large part the result of others' contributions. The actor is a dwarf on the shoulder of giants. On the other hand, the actor who shows courageous behavior can count on the appraisal of many others outside the circle of recipients. Observers praise the actor for this behavior by honoring the actor with the Nobel Prize for Peace and other prizes. It is therefore not too much to ask actors to behave in a sacrificial way.

Observers play the important role in many services of giving praise. Sportsmen and artists are praised for their performance, and observers expect large sacrifices from these actors: they ought to behave according to those expectations. For excellent behavior, actors must often wait for praise, sometimes for longer than initially foreseen. But some sportsmen, though trying hard and sacrificing a lot, do not succeed: they are not praised, but instead receive pity or scorn.

Of course, there is a difference between a heroic act to save others and success in sport. For the hero the praise is a by-product of the behavior, while for the sportsman the praise is the intended outcome. But for both actors there comes a moment of choice—whether to engage in action or not. One should distinguish an action like one in which the behavior or decision of a company is criticized but with the ultimate intention of serving oneself. Dutch people who invested in shares with borrowed money protested against an omission in the signing-up procedure when they experienced financial loss after the collapse of the stock market. The disadvantaged people started a lawsuit in which they showed that the signing-up procedure was illegal because husband and wife had to sign the contract rather than just one of the partners. Although the protest is morally correct, the people who previously experienced a financial gain did not protest against the legally incorrect signing-up procedure. In this case, in which protest served self-interest well, one may speak of a weak morality.

## Concluding Remarks

The present chapter has outlined the allocation theory of morality (as part of a theory of justice) in which equal allocation of resources is an intrinsically good act, fear reduction is the driving force, and egoistic and altruistic tendencies direct allocation behavior. People not only desire to get more positive-valued resources—they desire to allocate positive-valued resources as equal as possible between self and other (minimax principle, advocated by Rawls 1971). Equality is used here as an axiomatic and approxiomatic quality: complete equality will never be reached. There is some circumstantial evidence for this axiom. Equal allocation of positive-valued resources is a good related to fundamental processes in the social and physical world. One of the three main laws of physical phenomena is the increase of chaos in physical systems. Physical systems are subject to the law of entropy. Social systems are subject to social entropy as well. A democracy is more chaotic than a dictatorship: A dictatorship changing into a democracy is more likely than a democracy ending in a dictatorship. An unequal division of a resource in which one person receives all and others far less changes into a system of approximated equality: the entropy of an approximated equal division is larger than of an egoistic or an altruistic division of resources. For social systems, entropy is assessed by the entropy equation developed by Shannon and Weaver (1949)—see Vermunt (1981).

Actor, recipient(s), and observers evaluate the moral quality of allocation outcomes in terms of love and respect. The higher the attributed love and respect for the allocation outcome, the more the actor (or their behavior) will be evaluated as moral. The model presented here is a hybrid one: it contains teleological (using justifications to get acts accepted, to reduce fear) as well as non-teleological aspects (equality as a good in itself).

Equal allocation of resources reduces fear most. Equal allocation satisfies actors' egoistic tendency and promotes their altruistic tendency. Equal allocation needs no justification, but unequal allocation does. The reasons given for an actor's unequal allocation are subject to the judgments of actor, recipient, and observers. The outcome of the discussion—in terms of given love and respect—is determinative of the moral quality of the actor (or their behavior).

Maintaining the egoistic and promoting the altruistic tendency (and sometimes maintaining the altruistic tendency and promoting the egoistic one) is a less strong view of morality than previous ones in which counteracting the egoistic tendency is claimed (Augustinus 1983; Hobbes 1983, 1985; Kant 1785a; Taylor 1938). Counteracting the egoistic tendency is like abstaining from something desirable in order to do something else. Such an act demands much from actors and is often detrimental for their social "mass," their self-esteem. People's self-esteem is to a certain degree determined by possessions, that is, their money and goods. Donating relatively large amounts of material resources may affect self-esteem, while relatively small amounts do not. Moreover, doing good to others need not be restricted to allocation of material resources but can be extended to allocation of immaterial resources, like service. Maintaining the egoistic tendency and promoting the altruistic tendency compares with physical exercise to increase muscle strength. To increase an actor's arm muscle, strength exercises must be concentrated on that part of the body, but one can choose exercises so that other muscles do not decrease in strength.

In addition, my view of the operation of the two tendencies is different from other views. Aristotle (1987) claimed a sort of mean operation of egoistic and altruistic tendency: not too much of the one and not too much of the other tendency. Plato (1987) and Machiavelli (1997, 2007) opted for a balance between the two tendencies: if one of the tendencies starts to dominate the other, it should be balanced by strengthening the other tendency. Others claim the beneficial operation of teleological (others' well-being, achievements; Hurka 2001) and non-teleological values (living a good life as an example to be followed by others; Swanton 2003) to conquer the tendencies.

Allocation behavior needs a community of people to evaluate an actor's justifications for unequal outcomes. A precondition for moral behavior is the existence of a community in which free discussion can take place between members about the appropriateness of justifications for unequal resource allocation outcomes. The result of these discussion rounds can be guidelines for future evaluation of justifications. These guidelines may become part of the community's culture: as informal rules or formal rules. An informal rule is that one keeps one's promise, and these precipitate in fairy tales and other written and oral traditions. Formal rules precipitate as rules to regulate behavior, as in sports games; or as rules of hospitality, as criminal and civil laws, and as rights like human rights. Compliance with these rules and regulations is proof of a moral community of which an actor is part, and not of the actor's high moral quality. However, there can be occasions in which compliance with the law shows high moral quality when acting causes personal suffering, as in the case of the whistleblower.

Members' opinions about allocation behavior can change over time and discussion about appropriate behavior may arise anew. In a dynamic community discussion about justifications is a frequently occurring phenomenon that may cause unrest and insecurity, but is necessary in order to accommodate the community to new situations. External (climate change) influences, technical innovations, economic and social crises can pop up and disrupt the way members view allocation outcomes and their justifications.

This chapter has described moral behavior in terms of allocation outcomes of all types of resources. That was necessary in order to emphasize the moral quality of allocation behavior. A community needs more than only evaluating allocation behavior. A community cannot exist long when important resources are not allocated centrally, because improving community members' welfare and well-being with their different interests cannot be achieved without central allocation of resources. The next chapter will focus on this aspect of resource allocation.

**References**

Aristotle. 1987. *The Nicomachean Ethics*. Translation and Introduction by Sir David Ross. Revised by J.L. Ackrill and J.O. Urmson. Oxford: Oxford University Press.

Augustinus, A. 1983. *De stad van God* (The City of God). Baarn: Ambo.

Barnes-Holmes, Y., McHugh, L., and Barnes-Holmes, D. 2004. Perspective-taking and theory of mind: A relational frame account. *The Behavior Analyst Today*, 5, 15–25.

Baron, M.W. 2002. Love and Respect in the Doctrine of Virtue, in *Kant's Metaphysics of Morals: Interpretative Essays*, edited by M. Timmons. Oxford: Oxford University Press, 391–407.

Baron, M.W. 2005. Justifications and excuses. *Ohio State Journal of Criminal Law*, 2, 387–406.

Codol, J.-P. 1987. Comparability and incomparability between oneself and others: Means of differentiation and comparison reference points. *European Bulletin of Cognitive Psychology*, 7, 87–105.

Deutsch, M. and Krauss, R.M. 1965. *Theories of Social Psychology*. New York: Basic Books.

Dijkhuis, H. 1999. *Kaïns kinderen. Over Kaïn en de oorsprong van het kwaad* (Cain's Children: About Cain and the Origin of Evil). Amsterdam: Boom.

Foa, U.G. And Foa, E.B. 1974. *Societal Structures of the Mind*. Springfield, IL: Charles C. Thomas Publisher.

Folger, R. 1986. Rethinking equity theory: A referent cognitions model, in *Social Justice in Social Relations*, edited by Bierhoff, H., Cohen, R., and Greenberg, J. New York: Plenum Press, 145–62.

Haidt, J., and Graham, J. 2007. When morality opposes justice: Conservatives have moral intuitions that Liberals may not recognize. *Social Justice Research*, 20, 1, 98–116.

Hauser, M. 2009. Evolving a moral instinct. Leiden University: Tinbergen lecture.

Hinman, L.M. 2001. *Immanuel Kant and the Ethics of Respect*. Chicago: University of Chicago.

Hobbes, Th. 1983. *De Cive*. Edited by Howard Warrender. Oxford: The Clarendon Press.

Hobbes, Th. 1985. *Leviathan*. Edited by C.B. Macpherson. London: Penguin Group.

Hofstede, G. 1980. *Culture's consequences*. London: Sage Publications.

Hurka, Th. 2001. *Virtue, Vice, and Value*. Oxford: Oxford University Press.

Jassso, G. 2007. Studying justice: Measurement, estimation, and analysis of the actual reward and the just reward, in *Distributive and Procedural Justice*, edited by Törnblom, K., and Vermunt, R. Aldershot: Ashgate Publishing Company, 225–54.

Kant, I. 1785a. *Fundamental Principles of the Metaphysic of Morals*. Translated by T.K. Abbott. Online edition, available at http://www2.hn.psu.edu/faculty/jmanis/kant/Metaphysic-Morals.pdf [accessed 22 November 2013].

Kant, I. 1785b. *Groundwork for the Metaphysic of Morals*. Translated and amended by Jonathan Bennett; Online version 2008, available at http://www.earlymoderntexts.com/kgw.html [accessed 22 November 2013].

Kant, I. 1900. *Dreams of a Spirit-Seer*. Translated by E. Goerwitz, edited by F. Sewall. London: Swan Sonnenschein and Co.

Kant, I. 1998. *Critique of Pure Reason*. Whitefish: Kessinger Publishing.

Klimchuk, D. 2003. Three accounts of respect for persons in Kant's ethics. *Kantian Review*, 7, 38–61.

Lerner, M.J. 1980. *The Belief in a Just World: A Fundamental Delusion*. New York: Plenum Publishing Company.

Leventhal, G. 1980. What should be done with equity theory? New approaches to the study of fairness in social relationships, in *Social Exchange: Advances in Theory and Research*, edited by Gergen, K., Greenberg, M., and Willis, R. New York: Plenum Press, 27/55.

Lewin, K. 1964. *Field Theory in Social Science*. New York: Harper.

Machiavelli, N. 1997. *Discorsie, gedachten over Staat en Politiek*. Amsterdam: Ambo.

Machiavelli, N. 2007. *De heerser*. Kerkdriel: Librero.

Maslow, A. 1954. *Motivation and Personality*. New York: Harper.

Mill, J.S. 1987. *Utilitarianism and Other Essays*. Edited by Alan Ryan. London: Penguin Books.

Plato. 1987. *Plato, schrijver*. Teksten gekozen en vertaald door Gerard Koolschijn. Amsterdam: Uitgeverij Bert Bakker.

Rawls, J. 1971. *A theory of justice*. MA: Harvard University Press

Scanlon, T.M. 1998. *What we Owe to Each Other*. Cambridge, MA: Harvard University Press.

Scanlon, T.M. 2008. *Moral Dimensions*. Cambridge, MA: Harvard University Press.

Schopenhauer, A. 1981. *De wereld een hel* (The world a hell), translation Heleen Pott. Amsterdam: Uitgeverij Wereldbibliotheek.

Schopenhauer, A. 2001. *De wereld als wil en voorstelling*. Vertaald door Hans Driesen. 3de druk. Amsterdam: Uitgeverij Wereldbibliotheek.

Shannon, C.E., and Weaver, W. 1949. *The Mathematical Theory of Communication*. Urbana: University of Illinois Press.

Swanton, Ch. 2003. *Virtue Ethics: A Pluralistic View*. Oxford: Oxford University Press.

Taylor, A.E. 1938. The ethical doctrine of Hobbes. *Philosophy*, 13(52), 406–24.

Twersky, A. 1977. Features of similarity. *Psychological Review*, 84, 32–52.

Tyler, T.R., and Lind, E.A. 1992. A relational model of authority in groups, in *Advances in Experimental Social Psychology*, edited by Zanna, M. CA: Academic Press, 115/191

Van Dijk, E., De Kwaadsteniet, E., and Koning, L. 2012. About behaving (un)ethical: Self-interest, deception and fairness, in *Behavioral Business Ethics: Shaping an Emerging Field*, edited by De Cremer, D., and Tnebrunsel, A. New York: Psychology Press, 105–21.

Vermunt, R. 1981. *Sociale Orientatie: Theorievorming en onderzoek* (Social Orientation: Theory and Research). Leiden: Dissertatie.

Vermunt, R. 2002. The justice motive in perspective, in *The Justice Motive in Social Life: Essays in honor of Melvin Lerner*, edited by Ross, M., and Miller, D. New York: Cambridge University Press, 31–46.

Vermunt, R., and Extra, J. 1993. Point of reference, prototypicality, and categorization, in *Studies on the Self and Social Cognition*, edited by M. Pichevin, M. Hurtig, and M. Piolat. Singapore: World Scientific, 106–14.

Verplaetse, J. 2008. *Het moreel instinct* (The Moral Instinct). Amsterdam: Uitgeverij Nieuwezijds.

# Chapter 4
# Resource Allocation and Justice in Society

## Introduction

Reduction of anxiety or fear, by allocating resources, guides the activation of the egoistic and altruistic motive. Chapter 3 discussed the allocation behavior of *individual actors* independent of other individual actors. This chapter will introduce the *group context* and explain allocation behavior and justice issues when individual actors are in interdependent relationship with each other. The group context demands tuning in and coordinating the allocation behaviors of group members.

In all communities and societies, formal and informal institutions—or leaders—allocate scarce resources. In primitive communities, the group of hunters decides to whom and how to divide the catch. Some anthropologists state that skill determines leadership and often find individual leadership in hunter–gatherer communities. However, that picture is only part of the daily routine in those communities. Specifically, when hunting large game, a group of hunters is more effective than one skilled hunter. In this context, researchers observe that the whole group of hunters rather than just one of them determines the allocation of food. For instance, excavations in Pincevent, France, showed that the group of hunters and not an individual hunter dominated the community (see Chapter 1). The activities of the hunters have to be coordinated, and the allocation of meat necessitates some tuning in. In societies with a more elaborate social structure, institutions such as governmental, semi-governmental, and non-governmental organizations (e.g., companies) are set up to (re)allocate scarce resources.

However, in order for these bodies to (re)allocate scarce resources, there must be basic agreement among the citizens of the principles that govern resource allocation. It is reasonable to assume that these principles only lead to effective functioning of society if the citizens accept them. The development of new principles and their adaptation is a continuous process. Chapter 2 showed that basic rules of justice change during times of environmental and technological change. New principles arise and a process of adaptation to the new principles starts. This process can sometimes go smoothly, but in most cases it will involve violent actions. In such situations of societal upheaval, citizens look forward to arriving at a more peaceful and just society where everyone gets what he or she deserves. In today's Western societies, certainties about income, status, service, and information are challenged. It is fair to assume that citizens at the beginning of the twenty-first century probably see themselves as members of a society that is in great turmoil economically and culturally, as well as with regard to the basic structure of society. What kind of future society do citizens of present Western societies have in mind, and what is the best method to tap these ideas?

One of the methods to tap ideas of people about allocation of scarce resources is to use a metaphor. The metaphor I will use is the one in which people are gathered in a waiting room and are confronted with an emergency. I will show that this metaphor offers a better representation of present-day society than former metaphors, like the state of nature (Hobbes 1985), or the original position (Rawls 1971), as expressions of the social contract idea (Rousseau 1978). More important, however, is that application of the waiting room metaphor leads inevitably to the conclusion that citizens: (1) should be benevolent in their allocations; and (2) prefer a small inequality in one resource to complete equality in that resource, but should be compensated by a small inequality in another resource (complex inequality, Walzer 1983).

## The Original Position and its Consequences

Allocation behavior in a group context implies origination and operation of group structure, group culture, and personality (see Parsons 1954; Elias 1969) and their effects on this behavior. When in a group of people each member endowed with resources (money, goods, information, status, services and love; Foa and Foa 1974) strives to reach a goal, a hierarchy as well as a set of rules for mutual interaction and distribution of resources develops. Individual talents (Nozick 1974) may become the starting point for a certain hierarchy in which the more talented occupy the more influential positions. A division of labor arises in order to provide the group with essential resources to survive. It is remarkable in hunter-gatherer groups that the group of hunters that bring in about 10 percent of the food has a more influential position in the group than the women, children, and older people who bring in about 90 percent of the food. Clearly, a set of values and attitudes developed in the group that makes the meat providers the most influential persons in the group. Some would argue that meat is hard to find, and providing scarce resources is valued more highly than providing less scarce resources. According to Nozick, the most talented thus receive the highest positions, and that is fair. However, for Rawls (1971), the basic question remains why the less talented will agree with this institutional arrangement. He asserts that in order to reach some form of social cooperation, group members, who will certainly differ in their conceptions of scarce resource allocation, that is, differ in their conception of justice, must have similar ideas about the basic principles of justice. In other words, if group members have no knowledge about "(their future) place in society, their class position or social status, nor does anyone know their fortune in the distribution of natural assets and abilities, their intelligence, strength, and the like" (12), they choose their principles of just allocation behind a veil of ignorance. People's mimetic desires (Achterhuis 1988) or their mimetic dislikes (e.g., discrimination) are activated. In such a hypothetical situation,

Rawls argues, rational and reasonable group members will agree on the following two basic principles: (1) equality in the assignment of basic rights and duties; and (2) social and economic inequalities of wealth and authority are just only if they result in compensating benefits for everyone (Rawls 1971: 14–15). Because the less fortunate in the hunter-gatherer community gain from eating meat, and thus improve their well-being, they accept the hunters' authority and even their relative wealth.

For rational and reasonable people, the hypothetical situation described as the original position (Rawls 1971) reflects their decision environment well. Rational is usually defined as taking the most effective means to given ends, while reasonable means that the interests of others are taken into account in trying to reach those ends. However, a fundamental propensity of people is that they are anxious as well as rational and reasonable—anxious about fundamental issues in life, such as identity, what to do, mortality, life prospects for themselves and their offspring, future wealth. Rational as well as reasonable people are anxious about the ends to define, and/or the means to reach those ends.

Anxiety is just as fundamental for people in the original position as rationality and reasonableness. If, as Rawls argues, people in the original position do not know their special psychological propensities, and have no knowledge about their state of anxiety, and have no clue about their social identity (Freeman 2003: 11), they will probably have no knowledge about their rationality or reasonableness either. More important, the absence of knowledge about other participants, about their own psychological propensities and identity, is a situation in which the rational and reasonable person is thrown back on their own. The prospect for loss of identity goes together with anxiety. Short-term triggers like life transitions and significant life changes cause anxiety. Being in the original position and making rational and reasonable choices for justice principles in a situation in which one has no knowledge about desires and identity marks a significant life change. Anxiety, as existentialists like Kierkegaard would argue, is just as fundamental for subjects in the original position as rationality (see also Crosta 2013).

Moreover, Nietzsche (1996) has objected to the abstract approach to morality and asks for a subjective approach in which a subject's rationality is not the only decision instrument, but that subject's experiences with the world should be included as well. In interactions with the animate and inanimate world, a subject builds up a unique constellation of experiences. Acts are the way in which knowledge about the world is built up, and form the subject's history. Nietzsche does not derive morality from basic principles: morality is the consequence of our acting in a world in which some dominate others and determine the kind of morality that is applied. Nietzsche called it *Übermensch*: the strong individual who operates on their own strength and not the strength derived from social position, or religion. In some way, each subject is *Übermensch*. A subject is a subject because they are endowed with resources. Each subject, with their unique history, has a unique constellation of resources that they can allocate. A subject's history, to which belongs the struggle to survive, is marked by a continuous revaluation of resources: Some resources become more salient than others, and individuals who by chance are endowed with characteristics that make them more suited in the struggle to survive dominate group life and strengthen the value of some resources and, consequently, their social position. Interpreting Nietzsche with regard to people in the original position results in an observation—although the people are behind a veil of ignorance—of differences between people. So, the hypothetical situation of the veil of ignorance wipes out some of the differences, but not all: the valuation of resources is not influenced. Moreover, the veil of ignorance deprives the individual of an important instrument: predicting the consequences of their own actions and thus of their allocation behavior. The veil of ignorance deprives the individual of their most important instrument for survival in this world: cognition. An individual in the original position, deprived from their social roots and from their cognitive instrument, that in the struggle for life has become a mighty weapon, is not behind a veil, but is like sitting in a dark pit.

The presence of anxiety in the original position is a fundamental social psychological issue. Terror Management Theory (TMT; Pyszscynski, Greenberg, and Solomon 1999) states that human beings are aware of the finiteness of life and that thoughts about it make people anxious. People's worldview and thus their perception of their position in society can avert their thoughts from this finiteness and create a sort of infinite life. Religion, for example, promises an eternal life after death. If, as is assumed for people in the original position, they are deprived of their worldview, people become anxious because the cultural fence does not protect them from thoughts about death. It is very likely that people, thrown in a dark pit, become anxious. Anxiety is so overwhelming that it strongly colors actions.

Some utilitarians have proposed a thin veil of ignorance including knowledge of everyone's desires but not of their social identity. As argued in the preceding paragraphs, however, depriving people of their social identity makes them anxious as well. In addition, knowledge about their desires and wants may enter into their deliberations about the arrangement of a just society (Freeman 2003).

Research shows that anxious people suffer from loss of control and experience confusion; they have a blank mind and tunnel vision (Crosta 2013). These cognitive impairments and emotions may hamper rationality and reasonableness, and hence decisions as to what is best for them and others. Anxiousness hampers people's capacity to define ends, and the means to attain those ends. In other words, anxiety hampers rational choice. The following section makes clear what can happen to anxious people in the original position.

## The Waiting Room: How it Begins

The situation is one in which some individuals are waiting in a public room to be transported to different addresses by different means of transportation: bus, train, or taxi. Other individuals seek shelter from the rain, others are there to meet friends, or to ask for information. People walk around, read the posters on the walls, and check arrival and departure times of trains and busses. Some people stand in small groups, talking to each other, others eat food they have bought in the small shops nearby. People on benches try to sleep, others are in a hurry to catch a train or bus. It looks like a small community. The room has six walls in a hexagonal configuration, as Figure 4.1 shows.

Each wall has a window close to the ceiling with a door beneath that functions as an entrance as well as exit. Thus, there are six doors and six windows through which people can see the sky. The room is a small cosmos on its own with connections to the outside world. People have their own goals and worries. It is a public place and people restrict their behavior in order to get along well with each other. From the speakers in the waiting room a bell rings and a voice tells the people not to worry but that the electronic system to open and close the doors is not functioning well. The waiting room people ask what is going on, talk to others, try to get information, become less at ease.

People in the waiting room have no idea of each other's specific goals, motivations, or other personal characteristics. They have general knowledge about people's propensities: to get out of the room. People are disinterested in others, but realize that they have opposing views. They have no idea whether their kind of action will be favorable or unfavorable to them because they do not know what is going to happen (see Figure 4.2).

The primary good the people in the waiting room "possess" is the space they each occupy, although that space is not their own: it is a public good. The people there may have the conviction that they possess the space, that it is a good in the terms of Foa and Foa (1974). Therefore, people increase, allocate, or exchange space. A person may give "his" space to another person. According to Rawls (1971), people in the original position will opt for justice as fairness and distribute space equally when they gather to find the best spatial position.

The question is how the people will react when the situation worsens a little—light smoke hangs below the ceiling—and whether these rational, reasonable, and anxious people organize themselves to cope with the new situation. In all likelihood, the people in the room will try out several coping strategies, like fight, flight, or immobilize. A flight strategy may be to go to one of the doors and try to open it. When this effort has no success, a fight strategy may be pursued by some people, while others may propose a more or less cooperative strategy. When the information is well understood, after some time, that one of the doors will open in the near future a discussion may start as to how to cope as a crowd with this challenge. How do people decide in this anarchy about a way to organize themselves and others when one of the doors opens? Some philosophers suggest that the state of nature or the original position looks like filling out a questionnaire: people answer, independent of others and in complete freedom, questions about the distribution of civil liberties and primary goods among themselves and their successors in a future situation. But as the behavior of people in the hypothetical situation of the waiting room shows, in the state of nature and in the original

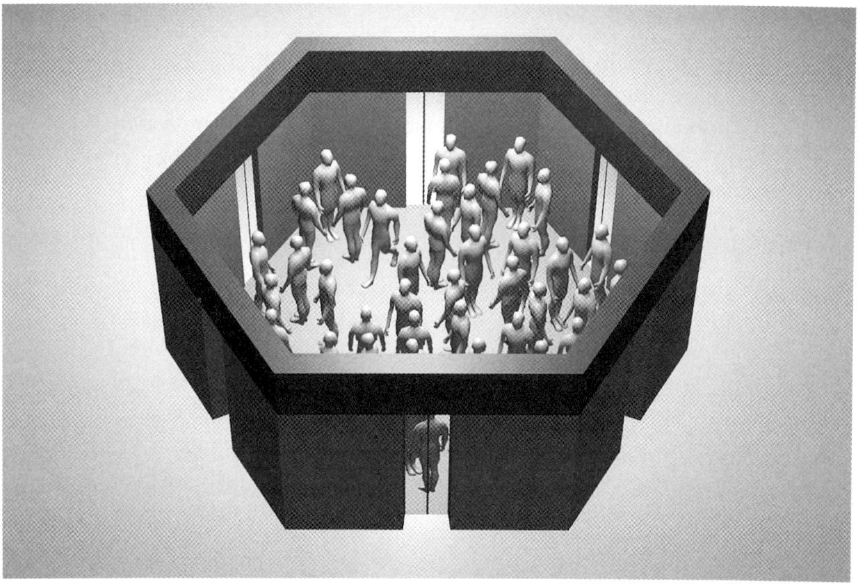

**Figure 4.1 Hypothetical spatial positions of all persons in the waiting room prior to smoke release**

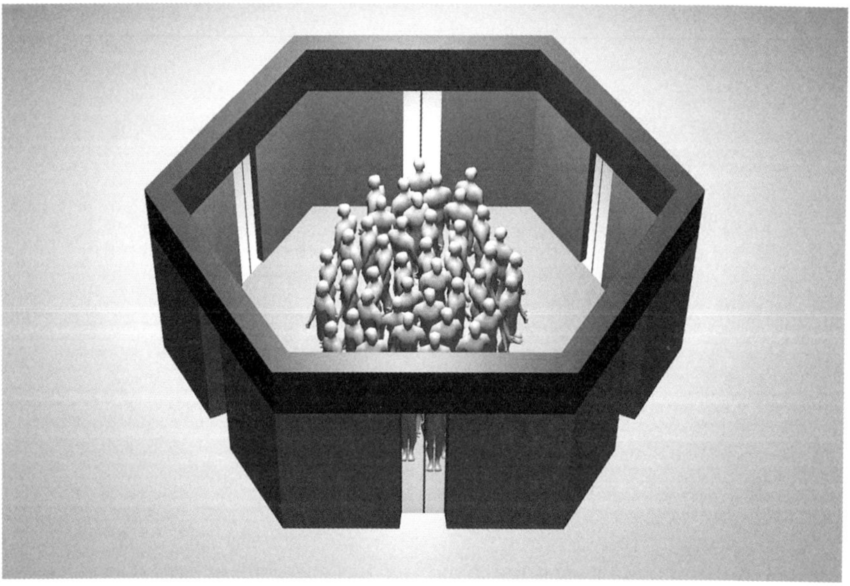

**Figure 4.2 Hypothetical spatial positions of the people in the waiting room after smoke release seeking an equal distance from each of the doors**

position independence and freedom are absent. People are anxious about their present situation as well as about their position in the future situation. They are emotionally upset, they influence each other and try to convince others to take their side in order to reduce their anxiety. But actions will not, or will only to a certain degree, result in anxiety reduction because the people are ignorant as to which door will open.

Part of the anxiety is inherent on being on this earth, in a hostile world where the other is the enemy (*l'enfer c'est l'autre*), while part of the anxiety arises from being in a crowd with people who also want to get out. The degree of anxiety reduction depends on the success of the group members in seeing the others as individual persons with the same goal. When this humanizing process succeeds, anxiety will be less. Both alternative conditions are possible because people influence each other. The ability to perceive these processes is part of the general psychological knowledge people have. In this potentially explosive situation, the people in the waiting room have to find ways to get out as safely as possible.

In such a position, people will not easily give up their rights and undertake to do duties. Some people will take a special position which they think will give them the best opportunity to get out when a door opens. But when all people think this way a crowd will form, decreasing the chances for everyone to get out.

Following Rawls, the people in the room will opt for a position in the middle of the room at an equal distance from each of the doors, because they think that is best for them and for others. However, very soon people realize that equal division of space—equidistant from the doors—is not feasible, because everyone wants to occupy the same position and a war of all against all will become likely. This situation is comparable to Hardin's fable of "the tragedy of the commons" (Hardin 1968). In the community, herdsmen let their sheep graze on the land that is property of all residents, the common. Next to this public property, each farmer has their own property where sheep can graze. It is profitable for each herdsman to graze their sheep as often as possible on the common: they can extend their flock. If only one herdsman does that, the common is not exhausted. But if every herdsman acts in this way the common land does not recuperate in time and the herdsmen lose the use of it. The system only stays intact if the herdsmen restrict their use of the common. Although this idea is often criticized for its lack of precision in defining common property and of historical accuracy (see, e.g., Ostrom et al. 1999), the fable is an instructive tool to show the destructive elements of human interaction. Would the people in the village—behind a veil of ignorance—opt for a moderate use of the common? If they do not know their future position in the village, why would they choose moderate use? They will probably not.

Seeking the middle of the room—equidistant from the doors—as a solution for future action is out of the question. Anxiousness in the crowd occupying the middle of the room motivates people to seek other solutions. People thus will not choose an equal division but an unequal division of space with regard to the distance from the doors. The reason for this is as follows, where I confine the situation to one where two doors are present of which only one will open. The people are ignorant as to which door will open. A person may choose to go to one of the doors, or he/she can choose a position equidistant from the two doors, as is represented in the following example given by Rawls (1971: 153). Let us assume that there are two states of the world for person A: door 1 and door 2. Person A has two options: to choose a position close to door 1 and far from door 2, or a position equidistant from the two doors. Option 1, close to door 1, results in zero injuries when choosing door 1 and four injuries when choosing door 2. Option 2 results in two injuries choosing door 1 and three injuries when choosing door 2.

Let us assume that person A chooses door 1. If door 1 opens then person A leaves unharmed, but if door 2 opens then person A will sustain serious injury (four injuries) trying to get out. Decision 2 implies person A chooses a position at an equal distance from the two doors, and if one of the two doors opens person A will receive a moderate amount of injuries (two or three injuries). Person A has not the faintest idea which state of the world will be activated, and in that case, according to Rawls (1971; see also Freeman 2003), person A will choose decision 2. However, if everyone in the room chooses decision 2 then a crowd will form and nobody will get out of the room because the crowd will block the exit. The people, however, are ignorant as to whether or not this spatial position is favorable when one of the doors opens. Dividing themselves between the two doors decreases the crowd by half.

Dividing the total group into (two) smaller groups decreases the anxiety that arises when people experience a large group. Moreover, the crowd contains fewer people when they choose to position themselves around each of the doors and the group splits itself into two halves. The small group passes more quickly through the open door than the whole group, and thus the chances are better (fewer injuries) for the people in the group at the other door to leave safely. It might thus be to each person's advantage to choose the extreme alternative, contrary to the maximin rule. In other words, people prefer a larger inequality to a smaller inequality because they judge it as better for themselves. The ultimate consequence of Rawls' thinking is that people opt for an unequal allocation of resources instead of an equal one when they are in a situation behind the veil of ignorance and devoid of any identity.

### *Primary Goods and Civil Liberties*

The question now is how people will divide basic liberties and primary goods among themselves behind the veil of ignorance. Rawls suggests six basic liberties: there is the liberty of judging as one thinks best; speaking one's mind; associating with others; holding private property; casting a vote; and putting oneself forward for office (Rawls 1971: 61). Foa and Foa define status as follows: it indicates an evaluative judgment that conveys prestige, regard, or esteem. Thus, what Rawls suggests is that actor allocates the scarce resource status (judging as one thinks best, speaking one's mind—status in relation to information, associating with others, casting a vote, putting oneself forward for office, the right of holding private property—status in relation to money and goods) equally between group members. Each person has equal status with regard to civil liberties. In the second (difference) principle, Rawls permits a certain inequality between members with regard to the material goods, but only as the inequality favors the worst-off group members.

The issue is that civil liberties have properties that the resource status and other resources do not have. Civil liberties are dichotomous entities while the resource status is a continuous entity. One has the opportunity to speak one's mind, or one does not. An actor gives the recipient the opportunity to speak their mind, or not. Of course, one can argue that the recipient receives less opportunity to speak one's mind. For instance, that certain words or groundless accusations may not be used. However, this restricted freedom of speech will be viewed by many as not having freedom of speech.

In my view, actors giving recipients the opportunity to speak their mind means that actors allocate status. However, the more status an actor allocates, the more status the recipient receives, showing status as a continuous quality. To fit civil liberties in the resource status one should accept that civil liberties form a scale from low to high, as status does.

The dichotomous character of civil liberties is one of the main causes of their equal allocation among people. One cannot accept, for instance, that some people have the opportunity to cast a vote and some do not. Arrangements like the constitution of a nation or its application in terms of laws have to defend the equal division of civil liberties among people. However, this does not mean that the day-to-day allocation of resources among people always maintains equality. People like to have the same amounts of civil liberties as others, but for themselves a bit more than for others. Moreover, I assume that anxious people behind the veil of ignorance opt for unequal division of civil liberties: people overestimate their chances of receiving the best possible position later.

An additional distinction between civil liberties and material resources means that we evaluate differences in civil liberties differently than differences in material resources. For instance, people accept large differences in income while they do not accept even small differences in civil liberties. One reason for this difference is that people earn income, while they receive status from others. Income relates to a certain extent to one's own actions—is achieved—while status is ascribed, in the constitution, for instance. Moreover, income is, to a certain extent, under the actor's control, while status is only to a lesser extent. It is said that income is the result of an actor's potentialities—high income is the result of the actor's high efforts and thus is accepted. Although plausible and generally accepted, this vision is only partially evident, in that the efforts of other actors, of luck, and of situational factors play a crucial role in having income. Each actor's income is as dependent on the efforts of others as on their own efforts. The earnings are not allocated according to each person's efforts, but are one-sided towards the lucky person. Income, therefore, merits the same position as status: people receive it from others to a high degree. This reasoning leaves two options open: the first is to accept only small differences in income, and the second is to accept larger income differences *only* in exchange for large responsibilities for the high-income actors.

## The Waiting Room: How it Ends

### *Before the Door Opens*

People in a high state of anxiety often overestimate the positive and underestimate the negative consequences of their choices. For instance, they will underestimate the chances of choosing the wrong door. Consequently, they will adhere to the belief that their evaluation of the situation and their plan of action are better than those of the other people in the room. In other words, rational, reasonable, and anxious people are convinced that an unequal allocation of space is more just than an equal division of space because they think they deserve it. Even in the situation of ignorance about which door will open.

They will be most interested in how to get the best position when the door opens. Tunnel vision and reduced operation of cognitive abilities make anxious people less vulnerable to what others have to say, what they do, and what their (space) rights are after the disaster. Are they then inclined to give themselves more rights and freedoms than they give other people in the room after the door opens? That is likely, as stated before, and the stress situation in the waiting room is not the optimal condition for asking people how to divide space. Not because there is little time—in the hypothetical situation of the waiting room, time for deliberation is not an issue—but because the cognitive and emotional state of the people hampers rational deliberation. Decision-making under stress—and people in the room are anxious and thus under pressure—does not follow the path of rational choice and reason. Compared to a more relaxed situation, people will be strongly inclined to make a decision without taking into account all possible arguments. Moreover, in an emergency situation people have other things on their mind than deliberating arguments pro and contra (un)equal division space. People are concerned and their minds are busy with thoughts and emotions regarding a safe exit from the room. They are concerned with finding the best spatial position when one of the doors opens. And as psychological research has shown, people under cognitive overload and who are emotionally upset often opt for a quick answer to the question of how to divide space between self and others in the waiting room while not knowing which door will open (Hardy-Vallee 2007).

The people in the waiting room are interested in getting the best position possible. They strive for the optimal spatial position so that when one of the doors opens they have the shortest distance to the door. Let us assume that all the people agree with the spatial arrangement in the room when one of the doors opens. Does agreement also imply that all people in the room stick to this agreement when one of the doors opens? The dispersion of people through the room has the advantage that it avoids a crowd when one of the doors opens (see Figure 4.3).

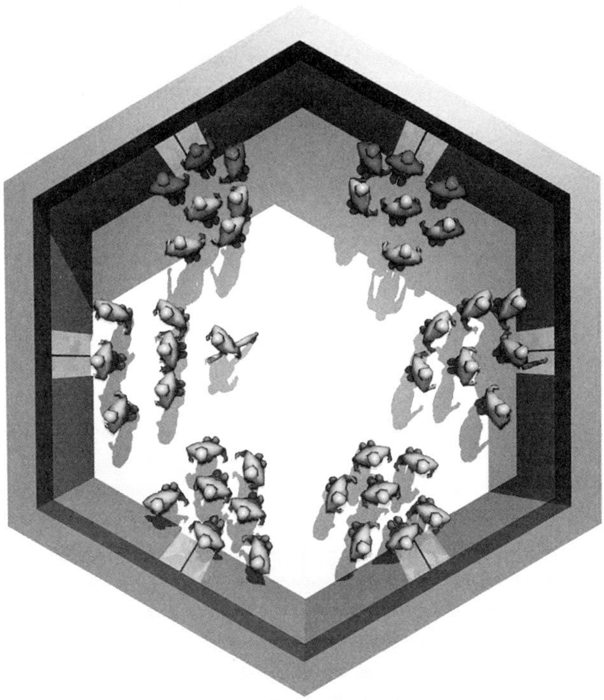

**Figure 4.3 Hypothetical structural arrangement for the people in the waiting room**

People need time to cross the room to the open door, and the time the crossing takes will give people closer to the open door the chance to leave the waiting room unharmed. This arrangement of the people gathering around each of the six doors may be accepted, but the question remains as to whether people will stick to the arrangement when one of the doors opens. The people close to the open door will be the first to leave the room. The question is whether the people around the other doors are disciplined enough to accept the most successful order of leaving the room. For instance, the order may be that the groups at the two adjacent doors go first. However, because the distance from these doors to the open door is equal, the two groups of people have to wait for each other. The same disciplined behavior is necessary for the people in front of the other doors. If anxiety is high, such discipline will be difficult—it is more likely that people will follow their own impulses. Some people let others go first, while other people will be strongly motivated to be first in line. People in the waiting room, deciding about which spatial position to take before the door opens, reason according to general psychological insights that some are faster runners than others. It is like the people in Rawls' original position who reason that some people are worse off with regard to primary goods than others. Unequal allocation of primary goods is the result of the operation of the equity principle: those who work hard or have a higher capacity may earn more. The worst-off people receive more primary goods, which is the result of the operation of the need principle. These principles apply for the allocation of space as well.

### *After the Door Opens*

When the door opens, the troubles for the people in the room are not over. Uncertainty about which of the doors will open is lower, but the problem of how to get out unharmed is not over. Other people, despite their anxiety, will seek a good position to a lesser degree. After these trials, people start to realize the impossibility of finding on their own a way to get out as safely as possible. They are still anxious, but also rational and reasonable. Some people pick up the idea of contributing to find a solution. And when one of these ideas is adopted by part of the crowd it may contribute to a solution for an optimal structure. One person, independently, may thus arise who will lead the crowd through the next phase. Under circumstances of low levels of anxiety, the people in the room would probably not accept a "leader" to whom they would hand over some of their rights. But anxious people are more inclined to do so.

One solution could be that the group closest to the open door goes first, then the people close to the adjacent door, and so forth. In fact, rational, reasonable, and anxious people in the room choose inequality in spatial position rather than equality. They expect to stand by the correct door, and also expect that if they have chosen the wrong door they still have a chance to get out.

The next issue that the group of people has to solve is the spatial arrangement of the people in the small groups. From the flight–fight reaction during the panic situation at the beginning, the crowd, endowed with general psychological knowledge, separates the more fanatical and passionate people in the group from the less so. The question is whether the fanatical people will be situated at the front or at the back of the small groups. The second alternative assumes that the fanatical people will be so fast in reaching the door that they push away the less fanatical people. The consequence is that a crowd is formed that blocks the door. Because the fanatical people—or the most talented—will not feel disposed to give the less fanatical people enough room to reach the door, a crowd will form. Therefore, it will be better to give the fanatical people an advantaged position so that they can proceed in accordance with their impulses. Does that mean that their behavior is unrestricted? No, because when the fanatical people run too fast to the open door, they will meet the slowest from the earlier small group. So, in order not to form a crowd that diminishes everyone's chances to get out unharmed, the fanatical people will find no acceptable justifications for acting according to their impulses. Realizing this, they will decrease their pace a little in order to increase both their chances and those of everyone else of getting out unharmed. The less fanatical or disadvantaged people, who cannot walk that fast, have no acceptable justifications for being slow and holding up others. Realizing this, they will do their best to reduce the chances of the fanatical people catching up to them and thus increase their chances of getting out unharmed. This is the social contract both the advantaged and the less advantaged in the room have to endorse in order to increase their chances of getting out unharmed.

Rational, reasonable, and anxious people behind the veil of ignorance will choose unequal divisions of primary goods and civil liberties. However, out of self-interest as well as out of interest for others, people reduce inequality. People opt for inequality, but only for small inequalities. A little difference from others with regard to civil liberties and primary goods satisfies their rationality and reasonableness, and reduces their anxiety. However, these inequalities must be justified. Large inequalities should be justified more and are permissible only if people accept the justifications given with love and respect.

## Waiting Room Solutions

Chapter 3 described the position of an actor independent of the behaviors of other actors. In explaining an actor's moral behavior, this independent relationship between actors is insufficient because the presence of other actors is a condition that may affect the actor's allocation behavior. For instance, in the Drug scenario from the previous chapter, one actor is the physician who delivers the drug, but the person in Room A is also an actor: the person with the organs suitable for the people in Room B. Both people make moral decisions independent of each other. In most allocation events, however, actors are dependent on each other to a greater or lesser degree. In the state of nature (Hobbes 1985), where there is no controlling power, mimetic desire (Girard 1978) motivates people to get what the other has, resulting in a war of all against all. The mimetic desire arises because people are influenced by the land or goods of another, which they desire. To prevent the war of all against all, people should freely deliver some of their power to a central agency that then protects their property (Hobbes 1985). The inequality in material goods remains the same as in the state of nature. But the origination of a controlling power is not the only way to solve the issue of fear of mutual destruction. Rational, reasonable, and free men in the original position would, according to Rawls (1971), choose justice principles in which the basic liberties are allocated equally among all and in which inequality is permissible only when it is to the advantage of the least well-to-do.

From the foregoing analysis of the behavior of rational, reasonable, and anxious actors in the waiting room, I infer that actors will choose small unequal distributions of civil liberties and inequality with regard to material goods. As will be remembered, the fast runners in the waiting room receive the best position in order to prevent a crowd in front of the doors. But if the faster runners run too fast they will catch up with the slow runners from the former run. The fast runners, therefore, have to restrict their speed to avoid a crowd. According to Kant and Rawls, the fast runners reduce their speed if they see it as their duty to do so: Only rational and reasonable runners will carry out their duty and reduce their speed. However, as stated before, people in the waiting room confronted with an emergency are not only rational and reasonable: they are anxious as well. In this case, the runners will not stick to their contract.

If the runners have no intention of reducing their speed, and thus bring danger to the people in the waiting room, they have to justify their behavior. They can try to convince others that their fast behavior will be good for all: by their leaving the room quickly they make space for others. However, if others do not accept the justification, a chaotic situation arises, because the slow runners will not get out of the way. The subgroup prevents a chaotic situation by letting the fast runners keep their speed and encouraging them to help the slow runners. However, that is only possible if the slow runners do their utmost to walk as fast as possible.

If this does not work, the only workable and efficient solution is the emergence of a leader to create order from the chaos. The leader encourages the fast runners to help the slower runners to get out of the room, and encourages the slow runners to be as fast as possible. The leader, or ruler, convince the fast runner to keep their pace and at the same time to help the slower runners. The ruler convinces the slow runner to be as fast as possible so that the fast runner is able to help them better. What kind of leader or ruler best suits the people in the waiting room?

## The Waiting Room Revisited

### *The Community of Equals*

The people in the waiting room are there for several reasons. They hear that there is a small inconvenience in that the electronic door systems are defective. People feel a bit uneasy, and closer to each other in that they are all in the same position. If in such a situation of uncertainty leadership is needed, what kind of leadership is most appropriate?

#### *Aristotle seeking eudemonia*

Aristotle distinguishes between intellectual excellence and moral excellence. Intellectual excellence shows itself when making choices for action: Actors do not deliberate about ends but about means. To acquire information (the ends), the actor deliberates about the means to get it. In allocating resources justly (the ends), the actor must decide about the means to complete it. For instance, the actor should decide who will be the recipients, and how much each recipient will get. According to Aristotle, making these kinds of decisions is like solving a geometrical problem.

Aristotle describes moral excellence or virtue as "a state of character concerned with choice, lying in a mean, i.e. the mean relative to us, this being determined by a rational principle, i.e. by that principle by which the man of practical wisdom would determine it" (Aristotle 1987: 39). Aristotle distinguishes between excess of something, deficiency, and mean. A virtue is the mean of something. With regard to goods, Aristotle distinguishes between giving and taking, of which he labels the mean as liberality, the excess prodigality, and the deficiency meanness. The prodigal exceeds in giving and falls short in taking, while the mean man exceeds in taking and falls short in giving. With regard to honor, he views honor as virtue and dishonor as vice, the mean is known as proper pride, excess is named empty vanity, and deficiency is named undue humility. As with goods, in my view, one can also differentiate between giving honor and taking honor. Excess is that one takes too much honor for one's own action or status position and gives little to others, or deficiency that gives too much honor to others and too little honor to oneself.

Aristotle's idea of the geometrical mean thus applies for several allocated resource types. However, an excess or shortage is, under certain conditions, just or morally permissible as well: if the allocation decision can be justified acceptably. Present-day bankers receive an excess in income. The excess bonus was accepted as long as all the stakeholders of the bank agreed on it. When the acceptance rate reduced to nearly zero, it became morally less permissible or even impermissible for bankers to accept a high income. What becomes apparent is that rules to which people should conform develop in a societal context and can change over time. Refraining from higher income requests is not a question of virtue. Virtue, according to Aristotle, is a state of character of which some actors have the right amount (mean) and others do not. Character is a faculty that can be trained. Men are responsible for virtuous acts as well as vicious acts. Moreover, some actors are more inclined to commit wrong actions than other actors. Some actions, however, do not admit of a mean: adultery, theft, and murder are bad in themselves: in the mean, or in excess, or in deficiency.

*The ruling class, according to Plato*

One of the first philosophers to explicit discuss the leader's motivation in governing others is Plato. In *Politeia* he had Socrates answer questions by Trasymacho, Glauco, and Adimantus. Tracymacho starts with the observation that actors who behave according to rules of justice and integrity are always worse off than actors who behave unjustly but combine it with a good reputation. The question is why actors should behave justly. Socrates' answer focuses on the importance of an actor's personality. Being a just person means that the person lives in balance with their desires. According to Socrates, the human psyche consists of three elements. Each human being has three types of needs or desires: desire for eating, desire for drinking, and sexual desire or passion; Plato derives others from these three desires, such as the desire to attain high status or to become rich. These three horses pull the wagon; they set the person into motion. The horses have to be guided and the way actors are able to manage the horses gives insight into the actors' moral quality. In other words, actors who are able to control their desires will become morally high persons and those who cannot control their desires will not.

Justice as a core value or core virtue is not something that relates to our acts toward the social environment but to the inner core of our personality. An activity is described as morally right only if it contributes to the maintenance and perfection of the psyche. Plato views morality as an instance of a healthy psychic state, as an optimal muscle tone is for a healthy physical state. In as much as actors strive to attain good physical health, so they will strive for good psychic health as well. So, the question why actors would behave morally well is now answered: to attain good psychic health.

Thus, in Plato's vision a highly moral person is one who combines the manifestation of self-regard as well as consideration of people of other classes—their needs and desires. It might be concluded, therefore, that Plato, in fact, views a moral person as one who seeks a balance between selfish and altruistic motivation; that is, that actors exert self-regulation in order to control "the inner animal nature into a civilized human being" (Vohs and Baumeister 2004: 1).

Plato's and Aristotle's thoughts about morality and justice presuppose a societal order in which there is total agreement between its classes about what is right and wrong. As Nietzsche has already analyzed, what people conceive as right and wrong are the beliefs of the ruling class. The traits, the values they appreciate most are those which contribute most to the reduction of danger or fear for conflict. The resulting allocation of resources in the Greek polis is confined to the noble men in the community. Women and slaves are left out of this schema; the ruling class has not sought consensus on the main moral issues between all classes. Nietzsche would label such a morality "*Herrenmoral*." However, in the rather quiet community of waiting room people—with a small external threat—a self-controlling, virtuous leader is the right person to take the lead (Hirshi 2004).

### *The Waiting Room as Battlefield*

All at once, smoke is coming in through the walls and ceiling. Everyone in the room detects the smoke. People become anxious, and focus on the will to survive. Each person in the room concentrates on what is necessary to get out as quickly as possible. Because it is unknown which door will open, people have to make a decision under uncertainty. Some people run around, some run to the doors, push others away, and even fight with others. Other people will try to attain the best position possible for when one of the doors will open. That can be a position in the middle of the room at equal distance from each of the doors. However, if everyone in the room mimics this behavior, the advantage is undone, and a fight of all against all will start. The fight is in vain because each person is ignorant of which of the doors will open. After the initial struggle, some or many people in the room will realize this fact and they may start to search for idea of how to handle this challenge. Who are the people who start to think of a solution?

*Hobbes' ruler*

Hobbes gives another way to exert influence. To prevent a war of all against all, to escape a situation of war that is the consequence of the natural desires of men, and thus to secure their own life, people give up their rights. Hobbes (1983) states it as follows: "that the right of all men, to all things, ought not to be retain'd, but that some rights ought to be transferr'd, or relinquisht: for if every one should retain his rights to all things, it must necessarily follow, that some by right invade; and others, by the same right, might defend themselves against them ... therefore War would follow" (Chapter II, Article III). That, according to Hobbes, is against reason and against natural law. People make a social contract, through which they hand over their natural rights to a beneficiary or third party, who is neutral, and they promise to obey the third party. It is as if someone says to another: "I authorize this person or this assembly, and give up my rights to guide myself to him, under the condition that you too will give up your rights to him, and in the same way authorize all his acts." If this happens we call this mass, now united in one person, a state. The state has most power or, some would say, absolute power, but has it only if the state cares for the subjects' well-being. Hobbes breaks with the medieval and thus classical idea that the classes in society should live in harmony with each other. Hobbes' ruler faces individuals who have given up some of their rights but who still possess their mimetic desires: that, is the desire to have what others have (Girard 1978). In Article VI of Chapter I of *De Cive*, Hobbes says is as follows: "But the most frequent reason why men desire to hurt each other ariseth hence, that many men at the same time have an Appetite to the same thing." This desire is, according to Hobbes, what other persons fear.

Achterhuis (1988) suggests that this desire is the only reason for economic scarcity. He derives the desire from Girard's idea of the mimetic desire. Girard investigates the mimetic desire in the works of such diverse authors as Cervantes, Goethe, Dostoyevsky, and Proust. Girard's analysis focuses on the mimetic desire in relation to love: the actor only desires another person when he or she observes that a second actor (his or her rival) loves the other person. In Goethe's *Die Leiden des jungen Werthers* (1774), Werther starts to love Lotte when he discovers that she already has a lover. Swann, in Proust's *In Search of Lost Time*, gets a great passion for Odette when he observes on his nightly walks to her house that she receives other lovers as well (the observation, however, was the product of his fantasy). In their love for Odette, both Swann and the other lovers are equals. In other words, Swann compares himself with others who are in the same relationship with Odette and desires to have what these lovers "possess": Odette's attention or love. So, equality breads passion and jealousy, asserts Achterhuis. Maybe that is the case for love, but the question is whether equality also triggers comparison processes for other material and immaterial resources (Foa and Foa 1974). For instance, researchers found that people do not compare themselves with people of an equal status but with people from somewhat higher status. People do compare themselves with people with higher, but not too much higher, abilities, and not with people with the same level of abilities. The motivation to compare oneself with someone higher triggers the imagination of already being like that higher other. A person compares himself with equals as well. That is not out of fear, but because one is uncertain about one's own opinion and would like to check with an equal other. If the equal other has the same opinion one feels more certain about it. Seen in this way, it might be that Werther was uncertain about his feelings toward Lotte, and seeing that another person loves Lotte as well and thus has the same attitude toward Lotte might have strengthened Werther about the correctness of his love (or opinion, attitude).

Moreover, love, opinion, abilities, and status are immaterial resources to allocate. For these resources, equality might be more or less a trigger for comparison processes. However, that still is no mimetic desire. In addition, to infer the mimetic desire for material resources (scarcity) from mimetic desire for immaterial resources, as Achterhuis (1988) did, looks to me too big a step.

There is another important point to make with regard to the mimetic desire and the fear it causes. The perception that others love Odette as well implies that there is some consensus about what is desirable. Few people, sometimes many people, even the public at large, share the consensus. There must be consensus about the value of the desired object. Would an actor desire an object another person possesses that is without value to others? That is unlikely. One might state, therefore, that the mimetic desire is only functional if there is consensus about the public value of the object or person. And consensus means the operation of some sort of society. An actor's perception of the mimetic desire of another, which causes fear, only has significance in a community of people, thus in a society.

How should Hobbes' ruler have to act in this situation where people constantly compare themselves with others? In *Behemot*, Hobbes (1990) describes the difficult situation of Charles I, who starts a war against the Scots but lacked the resources for it. Parliament was very reluctant to grant him resources and rebelled. One of the reasons Hobbes gives in Dialogue 1 is that some English people wanted to have what other people had, specifically the perceived richness and independence of the people of the Low Countries.

Hobbes' ruler has absolute power, because the citizens have handed over their rights to him, whether the ruler is a leader of all people (democracy), of some people (aristocracy), or of one person (monarchy). However, a just ruler sometimes forebears the exercise of his right and the reason for that is consideration of the citizens who are busy about their private interests (Hobbes 1983: Chapter VI, Note 3). In addition, Yoksas (2009) argues that in later writings Hobbes puts limits on what a ruler may do, and that Hobbes suggests prevention of the exercise of authority unjustly. Hobbes' later writings suggest that what determines an effective monarchy from an ineffective one depends on a system where the ruler governs jointly with Parliament (Hobbes 1990). In *Leviathan*, Hobbes (1985) describes equity as a duty of the ruler toward his people rather than a duty the people have toward each other. In *Leviathan*, Hobbes states that equity is part of the ruler's duty to ensure the safety and well-being of the people: that is, to administer justice equally to all subjects regardless of station (status, richness, might). In Chapter 15 of *Leviathan*, Hobbes defines equity as the equal distribution to each man of that which reason ascribes to him, which may or may not entail an equal distribution amongst individuals in general. Equity must be—in Hobbes' writings—differentiated from justice: justice is something for the citizens and magistrates, but equity is something for the ruler. It is a ruler's concern and not that of the average citizen. Equity is more than ordinary law: it transcends law. Yoksas concludes that Hobbes' notion of equity recognizes that citizens are all equals under the ruler's laws, but also recognizes that the ruler has a special burden: to maintain both the appearance of fairness and fairness itself. In other words, Hobbes suggests that rulers should care about the consequences of their acts and decisions. In the case of Charles I, who was beheaded in 1649, Hobbes supports the king but criticizes him in his handling of the Scottish Rebellion. In this rebellion, the Scottish gentry reacted furiously against an English bishop's acclamation of a new law that was detrimental for the Scottish Church. Charles I underestimated this reaction and had to activate—after ten years—Parliament to ask for funds to raise war against the Scots. The Parliamentarians regarded the decision as a token of disrespect and thus as unfair.

The situation at this point in time is a representation of the original position (Rawls 1971). The only difference between Rawls' original position and the waiting room is that the people in the room are very anxious: they scream, and shout, and cry.

### *The People in the Waiting Room as Enemies*

If the people in the waiting room come to terms with the situation, they realize that for all of them to stand in the middle of the room offers no solution. A benevolent leader like Hobbes' ruler splits up the group into six, and positions each subgroup adjacent to a door. It is not individuals but subgroups who confront each other, and this constellation is less chaotic. However, now, not one but six leaders are necessary. When one of the doors opens, the nearest subgroup has the advantage, and antagonism between subgroups arises.

#### *The ruler according to Machiavelli*

Machiavelli puts forward another class of ethical ideas about the state. In his view, rulers are ethically correct if the results of their actions are in accordance with the common good. In other words, rulers may act selfishly and attain more power, if that promotes the common good.

According to Plato, the ideal state is the one in which the relationships between the most important classes are in equilibrium. This view tolerates no deviations from equilibrium or changing relationships between the classes, because they are not then reflections of the eternal and steady form. According to Machiavelli (1997), the world is not a place where nothing is changing. In his vision, everything is constantly moving and conflicts between classes are common practice. The question now is how a ruler in the flux of moving relationships and conflicts can make the best decisions for the people he/she is ruling. In other words, how can a ruler behave ethically in this turmoil? If the founder of a state has sufficient wisdom not to think of their own interests but of the interests of the community, they have to strive for absolute power. When settled, the ruler can give up power partly and allocate it to other categories of people, such as the aristocracy and citizens. For Machiavelli, a Platonic society where the ruling class dominates is only a structure in transition.

Machiavelli states that one of the most important things to allocate is power. The way the ruler allocates power depends on the aims the ruler has in mind about the form of government he wants. For creating a monarchy, the ruler should strive for inequality of power between the aristocracy and the people, while for creating a republic an equal division of power is best. In allocating land, Machiavelli relies on Roman practice (Livy 1997). When the Romans conquered a city or area, they divided it so that colonists could work the soil and protect the new borders. Rome divided the area evenly among the colonists. Rulers who want to keep the land under their control should do the same thing, and allocate the soil evenly among the colonists. Rulers who want to attain a large empire should provide political rights to strangers who have been conquered. Rome, in contrast to Athens and Sparta, became so powerful, according to Machiavelli, because Rome assigned rights to strangers and could consequently command a large army.

For Machiavelli, justifications of decisions regarding the property of men, their women, and life are necessary to keep up their reputation. The prince (Machiavelli 1946) should make ample use of justifications. Machiavelli goes even further. Every reason given for an allocation decision is ethically correct if it serves the health of the state or city. An incriminating act should find its argument in the results; the end result is the justification of a decision, and if the result is good than the justification will be good. It is in the interests of the ruler to present allocation decisions as being to the recipients' merit. As an example of this principle, Machiavelli learned from Livy about a decision of the senate (aristocracy) that the republic should pay soldiers for their costs. Until then, the soldiers had to compensate costs out of their own pocket. The senate viewed this as undesirable, and presented the compensation as a favor. The people of Rome valued this decision highly, although their representatives, the tribunes, warned them that they paid for it with higher taxes. In other words, by justifying allocation decisions in the proper way, people can be persuaded to see the decision as just and to accept it. In other words, Machiavelli applies justifications to reach consensus.

The question is how ethically a ruler should behave toward their people. According to Machiavelli, rulers should treat their people as equals. The example Machiavelli gives is that of the army commander Valerius (Machiavelli 1997) who treated his soldiers graciously and the soldiers rated him highly. Another type of commander or ruler Machiavelli highly respected is the ruler who is highly disciplined and lives in accordance with the laws. Manlius is the example Machiavelli gives. Manlius was a powerful person who gave his orders with much vehemence. These two things go together. Manlius, as consul, was harsh, acted according to the laws and let his son be executed after he acted unlawfully but courageously (Livy 1997: 537). For this decision, Manlius received the respect of his soldiers and of the people, resulting in obedience to and acceptance of his orders.

A ruler who has the intention of serving the interests of the citizens, has, firstly, to act in such a way that dispels envy. People often mistrust rulers, thinking that rulers who like to act for the common good are actually doing it for their own good. Rulers, therefore, have to give good reasons for their decisions. Rulers can do this best by taking decisions that a neutral person would take; a person who has proven to act for the common good.

What is remarkable in Machiavelli's thinking is that actions and decisions taken to serve the common interest are ethically good. In his view, an ethically good ruler need not coincide with ethically correct decisions. This vision of a good ruler stands in sharp contrast to Plato's vision of a good ruler, and to the medieval writers like Augustine—an ethically good ruler or philosopher/king can only take ethically good decisions. Machiavelli is far more realistic, but it does not mean that his vision lacks the ultimate knowledge about what is the best government for the people. However, as Wolin (1961) states, Machiavelli found these classical and medieval ideas politically insufficient. Of the papacy, Machiavelli says: "These are the only princes who have states and do not defend them, subjects and do not govern them; yet their states are never taken away from them as a result of not being defended" (Machiavelli 1946: 60–61). Machiavelli's predecessors relied on natural law and discarded the importance of power. Therefore, Wolin views Machiavelli as the first truly political thinker. In fact, what makes Machiavelli a true political thinker is the focus on analyses of the government of his time on the distribution of power and other resources. I define power as having relative excess of resources. The greater the excess on the more resources, the more power a person has. An ethically good ruler is one who uses that power for the common interest. Machiavelli connects the ethicality of governing a state or city with the allocation of power, with the use of justifications in allocating or reallocating resources, like offices, land, taxes, and wealth. But if justifications can be used to get people to accept actions that may be good for the common interest but cause suffering and deaths for many opponents, how can these actions be defended morally? According to Machiavelli, a society is not a static, physical body in which the parts relate to each other and lead from one center. In such a static view of society, a conflict is a disease, which one can dispel by cutting out the diseased part, after which the original state of the body is regained. A society, however, is not something static, but is in constant flux, where factions fight battles to gain or regain influence. In such a changing political landscape, the only way to work for the common good is to use violence, but then in such a way that the use is in proportion to the severity of the conflict. An actor in such a situation cannot avoid inflicting injury on someone. As Wolin put it, "He must act while hemmed in by vested interests and expectations, privileges and rights, ambitions and hopes, all demanding preferential access to a limited number of goods" (Wolin 1961: 221).

In other words, political ethics is nothing more than to work for the common good by trying to reallocate scarce resources by the controlled application of force. Therefore, a successful prince must be courageous and thus be part lion. But he must also be deceptive and thus be part fox.

Machiavelli reasons that he who uses violence (power) economically for the common good is a successful and ethical ruler. The subgroups in the waiting room are each other's enemies and subgroup leaders may use violence to defend their own position.

*People Making Room*

The moment one of the doors opens, a rush starts. This rush must be coordinated so that each subgroup waits until the subgroup before them has left the room, thus freeing the space in front of the door. Distance to the door is the norm for coming into action. Subgroup leaders have an important task to perform to calm the subgroup members and to let them conform to the norm.

*Hume's moral philosopher*

For Hume (1957), morals comprise more than rules for social behavior, "they include virtues and valuable dispositions in the persons themselves, in their minds and characters" (xvii). It comprises moral distinctions, virtues, and vices, valued personal qualities, and rules of conduct (see Aristotle 1987). Individuals learn and experience these valued dispositions or personal qualities through education. It is, contrary to Hobbes, not only individual reason and the state of nature that guides behavior, but also the knowledge and experience of existing societal norms. This concerns not knowledge about facts but knowledge about the value of a person's character and actions as well. This knowledge derives not from reason but from sentiments. A virtuous or high moral character is defined as: "a quality of the mind agreeable to or approved by everyone who considers or contemplates it" (Hume 1957: Section VIII, note to the heading). Hume concentrates on two virtues: benevolence and justice (later he added fidelity). When talking about justice, the issue of public utility is nearby. Individuals have a duty to ask what their actions mean to society or to the world: specifically for peace and order among humankind. So, actions must be useful to civil society. This implies that actions that favor humanity overrule actions in favor of self. Hume states that this usefulness also applies between societies, and in this way acknowledges the importance of a type of world government. Virtues must be evaluated in terms of the common interest and utility they bring forth. Specifically, Hume regards the utility of human action not so much in terms of subjective happiness but more in terms of objective humanity: the human quality of men and their life. The question of why human beings have an interest in humanity is answered by Hume in that human beings experience it as a principle in human nature, a sort of human sympathy that makes human beings sensitive to social utility. Hume argues that moral values and practices cannot be deduced from the principle of self-love but require a reference to sympathy and a concern for others. However, Hume admits that degree of self-love is a ground of moral action. Hume states that a person can value morally and approve qualities belonging to another person that are only useful to that person (Hume 1957: xiii). And the person is the judging person him/herself as well: thus, utility for the person him/herself may be grounds for moral behavior, introducing a degree of self-love into the theory of morals.

Hume (1957) states that reason has no initiating role in moral behavior. It cannot determine goals for action, nor can it determine preferences or values. Goals and values originate from sentiments or feelings, that is, the sanctioning of virtuous behavior that comes forth from the common principle of human quality or humanity. How is reason then related to sentiments? Reason, according to Hume, gives weight to and affects the morality of action. Reason gives intelligence of the facts of the situation and the consequences of any action. Knowing the consequences of a benevolent act like almsgiving, "we (may) retract our first sentiment and adjust anew the boundaries of moral good and evil" (Hume 1957: Section II, 13). In the case of the virtue justice, Hume states that reasoning gives the person a clue about the utility of "that virtue" (Hume 1957: Section III, 8).

Another case concerns propriety of things. In the state of nature, men cannot claim something as their own: things are common. When the city receives its propriety, citizens will have theirs. The citizen has no propriety where the ruler has no right.

To keep the anxious people in the waiting room in the six subgroups, Hume's ruler has compassion with his/her "own" subgroup people as well as with the people in the other subgroups. Hume's ruler keeps the subgroup intact and justifies it by emphasizing the utility of the arrangement.

### *Summary*

Philosophers describe rulers from different perspectives and endow them with different qualities. The God from Genesis seems to be a ruler who has no compassion for "sinners" or their family. Not only does he create a climate that led to the killing of Abel, God did not consider the consequences of the murder for the safety and well-being of Adam and Eve, Cain's parents, and later of Seth. Cain walks around freely. In as much as he was motivated to kill Abel, why would he not be motivated to kill his parents and his younger brother? God might be viewed as a rather egoistic ruler who has no consideration with the needs and interests of the people directly involved (see also Chapter 3).

The ruler suggested by Aristotle is also a one-sided ruler. This ruler is a virtuous person who stands on the right side of the power line (Nietzsche 1996). Concerns for the position of women and slaves are absent. The ruler seems not to care about the safety and well-being of all people. Plato's philosopher/king controls his desires and cares for the common good of the people, apart from slaves and women.

This picture of a ruler is quite different from the picture Machiavelli shows us. Machiavelli's ruler is a true defender of the safety and well-being of all citizens. He shows us a ruler who, to be effective, should support the diversity of the people qua status, race, and gender. People should complement each others' abilities and opinions in order to guarantee their safety and well-being as best as possible. In doing so, rulers use all the means they have. No ethical or other considerations may hinder their task of protecting the people. In fact, they may use all justifications in wielding power in order to convince people of the correctness of their decisions. In other words, Machiavelli's rulers should be unethical, that is, harm other people, if that brings their goals nearer.

Hobbes' sovereign is a mixture of the virtuous ruler of Aristotle and the welfare-promoting prince of Machiavelli. They are absolute in the use of power to care for the safety and well-being of their citizens, but they are also considerate with regard to their needs and interests. In other words, in deciding about action, Hobbes' ruler should apply good reasons to justify it. Something Charles I did not do, creating turmoil and insecurity, and ending on the scaffold. Is, therefore, Hobbes' ruler not the just ruler I am looking for? Maybe, but Hobbes' ruler, however attractive he might be, is not fully described. There are questions left open, such as the origin of his rights. According to Hobbes, the ruler derives these rights from God. In the light of the foregoing analysis about God's decisions, it is doubtful whether this reference is the most optimal. How can we, therefore base Hobbes' ruler more firmly in the waiting room situation?

Machiavelli's ruler is one who protects citizens under conditions of great turmoil—the (possible) attacks of other city-states on Florence. Machiavelli is considerate with regard to the needs and interests of the citizens. However, Machiavelli's rulers miss the quality of being considerate about the acceptance of the justifications they give for their actions. The given justifications are not only valid through their inherent quality but also through their acceptance by others. The question is whether Hobbes' rulers would have the consent of the poor people for their justifications—probably not. Leviathan leaves the inequality of the state of nature intact in the civil society. Hume's rulers are considerate about others' passions and, therefore, will certainly take care that people accept their justifications. What kind of ruler(s) or leader(s) would support or coach the people in the waiting room best? The answer to that question depends on the allocation motivations and behavior of the people in the waiting room. The next section describes what these motivations and behavior are.

## The Economics of Benevolence in the Waiting Room

A person in the waiting room may choose to let others go first, so that he/she has more chance of getting out, but in the group this individual action only affects the overall state of affairs if more people follow. If the fast-running people offer the others some time to leave the room, many people may come out unharmed.

Moreover, the slow-running people should do their best to let the fast persons go first, or run as fast as possible while the fast runners help them push forward, or—as a last resort—carry them. To elucidate the idea of offering others the opportunity to leave the room I will start the analysis with two people, one person who is capable of getting out on his/her own and saving his/her life, and another person who is less capable and needs some help to get out of the waiting room. Neither person knows the other, so they do not share the same experiences. According to the theory of group behavior, two persons form the smallest possible group. Let us assume that one person has more resources than the other. He is the faster runner and offers some help to the slower runner in order to get the other out of the room unharmed. If the talented realizes that he cannot run too fast and that the other follows, the task is not that heavy. In that sense, the more talented is at that moment a leader, although the number of members of the group is only one. The talented person has no obligation to help the other. However, in helping others to get out of the room he also helps himself. Offering service or money to another increases the other's welfare and/or well-being. I label the talented person, person *i*. Then

$$U_i = U_i\,(Z_1, \ldots, Z_m),$$

where $U_i$ is the utility function of the *i*th person and $Z_1, \ldots, Z_m$ are the basic wants and commodities (Becker 1974). These commodities are produced with the market goods ($x_j$), quantities of his own time ($t_j$), $E^i$ is *i*'s education, and $N^k_j$ are the needs of other people affecting *i*'s output of his commodities, for instance, an appeal to offer resources. *I*'s utility can be expressed in terms of the relative satisfaction the person has when acting according to rules of fairness and justice. $Z_i$, therefore, can be conceived of as the experience of fairness derived from his actions.

In other words,

$$Z_j = f^i_j\,(x_j, t_j, E^i, N^1_j, \ldots, N^r_j),$$

where $x_j$ are quantities of different market goods, $t_j$ are quantities of his own time, $E^i$ stands for his education, experience, etc., and $N^1_j$ to $N^r_j$ are characteristics of other persons, for instance the status position of other persons. My idea is that *I* can change another's status position by his efforts. For instance by helping the other directly, saying comforting words, or by calling an ambulance. However, helping another is at the expense of one or more of *i*'s resource(s). Thus *i* has to make a choice between helping self or helping other.

Helping self or other, or a combination of helping self and other, can be expressed as follows—a single commodity (justice) produced with a single good (status), and a single characteristic of other (status–need–position of other). Then, maximizing utility is equivalent to maximizing the output of the commodity justice:

$$U_i = Z(s, S),$$

where $s$ is the good called own status position, and $S$ is the status position of the other as people in general would see it under standard conditions.

Adapting Becker (1974), $S$ can be written as

$$S = O_i + h,$$

where $h$ measures the effect of $i$'s efforts, and $O_i$ the perceived status of $S$ when $i$ makes no effort. Person $i$ has a time budget: when $i$ helps himself it is at the expense of helping the other, and vice versa. The time constraint can be expressed as

$$p_s s + p_s h = T_i,$$

where $T_i$ is his time budget, $p_S h$ is the amount of time he spends on $S$, $p_s$ is the price of a unit of time, $p_s s$ is the amount of time $i$ spends on himself, and $p_s$ the price of a unit of time. As Becker (1974) did, substituting $S - O_i$ for $h$ in the last equation results in

$$p_s s + p_S S = T_i + p_S O_i.$$

The right-hand side gives $i$'s time budget and the budget of spending time on the other, and is called his subjective time. The left-hand side of the equation shows how his subjective time is spent: partly on his own status position, and partly on the other's status position.

According to Becker (1974), the equilibrium condition is

$$\partial U_i/\partial s \;/\; \partial U_i/\partial S = p_s/p_S.$$

That is, that equilibrium is expressed as the price of a unit of time spent on working on the status position of self compared to the price of a unit of time spent on working on the status position of the other. A fair allocation of the resource "service" is reached if $p_s/p_S$ is 1, that is if that actor values his time spend on self is equal to that of the time spend on another, resulting in spending time on self as on the other.

Although elements of the present analysis of group behavior are derived from Becker's analysis, I have made several adaptations to the model. One of the main differences between the analyses is that Becker focuses on the effects of the social environment on a person's behavior to maximize utility. For instance, Becker assumes that the social environment is homogeneous in the attitudes toward the person. But as social psychologists have found time after time, others' attitudes differ strongly. So, if utility is derived from others' opinions, but these opinions differ, how can utility be maximized? For instance, if giving to charity is highly valued by part of the social environment but not by the other part, utility maximization is hard to accomplish.

Moreover, in the formula $U_i = Z(x, S)$, producing $x$ as well as $S$ is directed at increasing one's own commodities (distinction). A person offers some money in order to become more distinct. In the Nobel lecture in 1992, Becker argues that his approach is "a method of analysis, not an assumption about particular motivations" (Becker 1992: 385). But if people are trying to increase their distinction is that not the outcome of the operation of a (selfish) motivation? And because in Becker's analysis $Z$ is maximized by producing a single monetary good as well as working on others' opinions, a distinction between favoring self or favoring others need not to be made; neither the issue of the operation of motives. The basic tenet of $i$'s behavior is to increase own income, and this goal may be reached by a gift to the other. More in line with my ideas about allocation behavior in a group context is Kolm's (2006) analysis of gift giving. Kolm states that gift giving is aimed at increasing the other's utility: $U_i = u_i\,(u_{-i}, x_i)$. Gift giving is, in Becker's view, allocation of resources to increase own (actor's) utility, and in Kolm's view to increase the other's (recipient's) utility. In my view, as worked out here, justice is attained when the actor increases his/her own as well as the recipient's utility, or the utility of the pair.

The above analysis is carried out with service to self and other as resource. The actor spends time on self and spends time on other. It is easy to see that this analysis can also be carried out using the resource money. However, in the situation of the waiting room, service to self or other is more relevant than money, although people can buy service. I state that reducing inequality qua spatial position is best for getting the people out of the room as safely as possible. The question is, how do the people in the room achieve reduction of inequality while they have different talents and spatial position?

Recapitulating, the people find themselves in a situation they neither sought nor were forced into by others. It happened to them, and they have to adapt to the new situation. The people—rational, reasonable, and anxious beings—have to propose an arrangement that results in the unharmed exit of as many as possible when one of the doors opens, and they have to decide about the allocation of material (space) as well as immaterial resources (health, well-being) for that future situation. Proposing a certain arrangement is feasible because it is rational (it increases the perceived chances for each person to get out unharmed), it is reasonable (others are part of the schema), and it reduces anxiety (a structured group is less threatening than a crowd). To split up the crowd into small groups adjacent to the doors results in an inequality of spatial position when one of the doors opens. The second inequality arises within each of the small groups when they move in the direction of the one open door. The arrangement the people in the room have selected is to give the fast runners some room while backing the slower runners. In the waiting room emergency, running fast is a favorable talent for its owner. This talent is only favorable if the group splits itself up into smaller groups. In the case where people are standing in the middle of the room, bodily strength is probably more favorable than speed. However, bodily strength also plays a role in the split-up group. The strong but slow runners are able to prevent the fast runners from reaching the door. The arrangement of the smaller groups at each door, however, favors the fast runners more than the strong people. Give the talented (1) an advantageous position and (2) remind them that others have talents to frustrate them. What I propose here is reduction of inequality, in that fast runners reduce their speed and strong slow runners reduce their strength. Only in this way will the more advantaged fast runners support the slow runners to reach the door. Service to other balances service to self. Recognizing strength as a resource increases the fast runners' acceptance of less inequality. Walzer (1983) states that talents are distributed randomly among actors of a population and promotes complex equality by stating that institutions should prevent concentration of resources—like information, status, material goods, and offices—in the hands of a relatively small group of people.

*Equality in Groups*

Working out the idea of complex—and simple—equality, I propose the following: Let us assume that there three people with certain amounts of resources. Each person has a certain amount of Goods, has some degree of Status, and can provide a certain amount of Service. These amounts are shown in matrix [O] (O for origin). Based on all kinds of reasoning, another matrix ([F], for final) is made for the desired end state, indicating the amounts of resources the three people should have. The purpose of this exercise is to find the transition matrix [T] indicating the motivation the three people should exert in order to achieve the desired end state given their original resource positions. This approach has the unique feature that theoretically interesting end states can be formulated and the motivations or efforts people should deploy to change their start position into the desired end state can be examined.

The combination of the motivational forces is dependent on the purpose of allocation behavior. If the purpose is to change the start position of each person with regard to the resources they have, than the final resource distribution should contain the amounts of the desired resources for each person. If it is to attain simple equality (Walzer 1983), than the final matrix will contain cells with the same score. This means that each person receives the same amount of Goods, Status, and Service to allocate as each of the other recipients. For instance, each cell contains the score $x$, indicating that each actor has the same average amount of Goods, Status, and Service as the other persons.

What are the results of this exercise? By defining a random initial matrix [O] and a designed final matrix [F], it is possible to define a so-called transition matrix [T] in which, for each person, the amount of what they have to offer to others and/or receive from others can be calculated as indicated by linear equation (1) below. From the magnitude of the cell entries, the underlying allocation drive can be inferred.

(1) $[O] \times [T] = [F]$,

where matrix [O] has the following content:

[O]: $3(a_1, a_2, a_3) \times 3(\text{Gds, Stat, Serv})$

| Resources | | Gds | Stat | Serv |
|---|---|---|---|---|
| Actors | $a_1$ | 5 | 4 | 2 |
| | $a_2$ | 4 | 4 | 2 |
| | $a_3$ | 3 | 2 | 6 |

[O] is the original matrix, [F] the final one, and [T] the transition matrix. In [O], the entry 5 means that actor $a_1$ has 5 units of the resource Goods, for the resource Status $a_1$ has the score 4, and for Service the score 2.

[T] can be calculated by multiplying the left and the right part of equation (1) with $[O]^{-1}$, where $[O]^{-1}$ is the inverse of [O], as in equation (2):

(2) $[O]^{-1} \times [O] \times [T] = [O]^{-1} \times [F]$.

Because $[O]^{-1} \times [O]$ equals [I], the identity matrix, it follows that

(3) $[I] \times [T] = [O]^{-1} \times [F]$,

where $[I] \times [T]$ equals [T], resulting in

(4) $[T] = [O]^{-1} \times [F]$.

The inverse matrix $[O]^{-1}$: $3(a_1, a_2, a_3) \times 3(\text{Gds, Stat, Serv})$ has the following content:

| Resources | | Gds | Stat | Serv |
|---|---|---|---|---|
| Actors | $a_1$ | 1 | -1 | 0 |
| | $a_2$ | -0.09 | 1.2 | -0.1 |
| | $a_3$ | -0.02 | 0.01 | 0.2 |

Let us now denote the final matrix [F]: $3(\text{Gds, Stat, Serv}) \times 3(a_1, a_2, a_3)$ as:

| Recipients | | $a_1$ | $a_2$ | $a_3$ |
|---|---|---|---|---|
| Resources | Gds | 4 | 4 | 4 |
| | Stat | 3.3 | 3.4 | 3.3 |
| | Serv | 3.3 | 3.3 | 3.4 |

The final matrix [F] has resources as rows and recipients as columns. The matrix denotes the amount of resources recipients $a_1$, $a_2$, and $a_3$ get as the result of the reallocation process. [F]'s cells show that each actor receives the same amount of each of the resources Goods, Status, and Service; their score differs between resources. In other words, there is complex equality (Walzer 1983). The average amount of each resource for all recipients is the same as in the start matrix [O], but the means are different for the different resources. To attain a state in which each of the recipients receives the resources as shown in [F], the transition matrix in which the entries denote the amounts of giving and receiving, [T] has the following content, as derived from equation (4):

Matrix [$T_{ce}$]: $3(a_1, a_2, a_3) \times 3(a_1, a_2, a_3)$

| Recipients | | $a_1$ | $a_2$ | $a_3$ |
|---|---|---|---|---|
| Actors | $a_1$ | 0.7 | 0.6 | 0.7 |
| | $a_2$ | 0.03 | 0.15 | 0.02 |
| | $a_3$ | 0.19 | 0.2 | 0.21 |

The higher the score in the cells of matrix [$T_{ce}$] the more actors are willing to allocate (part of) their resources to others. So, to end up in a state of complex equality, that is that all recipients have the same score within a resource but different between resources, $a_1$ has to be willing to allocate resources (Goods and Status) to $a_2$ and to $a_3$ as strongly as what $a_1$ allocates to self. Actor $a_2$ has to be willing to a small degree to allocate resources to others, while $a_3$ has to be willing to allocate a relatively large resource to $a_1$ but hardly anything to $a_2$. The greatest sacrifice is offered by actor $a_1$ and the least by actor $a_2$. Does that mean that actor $a_1$ acts from a stronger justice motive than actor $a_2$? I think that this is not necessarily so. However, to arrive at the desired end state—the positions of the actors on each of the resources in [F]—$a_1$ has to decide whether he will join in with the others to accomplish the desired state. And when they do it, the decision is instigated by the justice motive: to offer others some of their resources without neglecting their own position on the resources. Actor $a_3$ has to sacrifice a little of his resources to actor $a_1$ and a little to $a_2$. For $a_3$, the sacrifice is about the same as for $a_1$, so he still has to apply the operation of the justice motive. Actor $a_2$'s decision is the least susceptible to the operation of the justice motive. Actor $a_2$ has to decide whether he will accept that the reallocation will bring him relative advantage compared to his fellow group members.

Complex equality means that recipients have the same position on each of the resources but differ between resources, as is presented in the following matrix [F]:

[F]: 3(Gds, Stat, Serv) × 3($a_1$, $a_2$, $a_3$)

| Recipients | | $a_1$ | $a_2$ | $a_3$ |
|---|---|---|---|---|
| Resources | Gds | 0.25 | 0.25 | 0.25 |
| | Stat | 0.3 | 0.3 | 0.3 |
| | Serv | 0.45 | 0.45 | 0.45 |

Entries in matrix [F] here are the percentages each recipient has on each of the resources, totaling for each recipient to 100 percent. The total amount of all resources of all recipients is the same as in the starting matrix. However, the distribution of the resources over the recipients is different from the one in the initial matrix. In the final matrix, the recipients have fewer Goods than in the initial matrix, a little less Status, while the position of the recipients on Service is increased. Is that a realistic scenario? It means that—in a society—people lose income but get better opportunity for education. In the group of three actors, they spend Goods and lose a bit on Status, but gain on Service.

Multiplying $[O]^{-1}$ by [F] results in the following transition matrix [T] in which the entries denote the motivational forces.

[$T_{ce}$]: 3($a_1$, $a_2$, $a_3$) × 3($a_1$, $a_2$, $a_3$)

| Recipients | | $a_i$ |
|---|---|---|
| Actors | $a_1$ | 0.67 |
| | $a_2$ | -0.15 |
| | $a_3$ | 0.48 |

Actor $a_1$ has to be the most willing to reallocate resources in order to get a complex equality resource distribution, specifically Status to $a_2$; $a_2$ needs to be the least willing to contribute to others; while $a_3$ has to be willing to reallocate Goods to $a_2$ and a little to $a_1$, and receives some Service from $a_1$.

How can one relate the matrix data to the processes that take place in the waiting room? With regard to Goods, actor $a_1$ is the most advantaged of the group of actors. In the waiting room scenario, $a_1$ belongs to the group of fast runners. And as we know from the metaphor, the fast runners have to reduce their speed in order not to overrun the slow runners in reaching the open door or to support the slow runners. With decreased inequality, the chances of getting out unharmed for as many persons as possible become better. In other words, actor $a_1$ has to offer Service to the other group members, and that is what one can see in matrix [$T_{ce}$], showing the transitions necessary to reach less inequality.

## Conclusions

### *Allocation of Resources*

The waiting room metaphor shows that rational and reasonable people in an anxious state choose for unequal allocation of rights (freedoms) and duties, and for unequal allocation of primary goods. People behind the veil of ignorance find themselves in a dark pit. From there, people find it hard to imagine a fair arrangement of equals. However, in the ongoing process of getting themselves and other people out of the room, benevolence turns out to be favorable for self and others. The resulting behavior decreases inequality to the benefit of all. Research shows that small inequality is more favorable for people and societies than large inequality. People in more equal societies show less anxiety than people in unequal and rich societies. In their study, Wilkinson and Picket (2009) claim that for physical health, mental health, drug abuse, education, imprisonment, obesity, social mobility, trust and community life, violence, teenage pregnancies, and child well-being, unequal, rich countries are worse off than more equal countries.

Although the threat one faces is less than the threat one imagines, anxiety affects actual allocation decisions as well. A negative economic outlook temporarily increases anxiety favoring unequal allocation of civil liberties and attempts to increase income differences. Rational, reasonable, and anxious people easily strengthen their motivation to increase their own social and economic position—make rational choices—at the expense of others' economic and social positions—they become less reasonable.

The situation of these individuals is a good approximation of present-day citizens of Western societies asked to design a future society for themselves and/or their children. People are not sure at all whether their children will have a better life than they have at this moment: They have, in other words, no clue of their future status, income, social bonds, and cultural activities. However, to maintain the hope for a better life for themselves and their children people are inclined to give up civil liberties and/or to exclude certain groups of citizens from these liberties. Anxiety about their future status and identity makes people vulnerable to threats and they more easily give up the equal division of rights, duties, and freedoms. In Switzerland, in a referendum in November 2010, the population voted for more severe legal punishment for transgressions by immigrants than by other citizens.

Does the "blind"—behind the veil of ignorance—choice for unequal division of primary goods, rights, and duties mean the end of the moral community, a community where people are equal and help each other when need is there? That is not necessarily the case. As we have seen from the waiting room metaphor, fast runners get the foremost position in the small groups before one of the doors opens. This is only possible if the strong slow runners agree with the division of spatial position. What they ask of the fast runners is that they decrease their running speed when trying to reach the open door, and that the slow runners do their best to run as fast as possible. Both groups, the advantaged and the less advantaged, have to agree the positional set-up and—even more important—stick to their speed: the fast runners slow down and the slow ones run fast. In their own interests, as well as in the interests of the whole group, the small groups should behave as expected. In other words, the advantaged as well as the less advantaged group members should curb their egoistic tendency and promote their altruistic tendency to make way for justice-motivated behavior. In terms of the economics of benevolence model, the advantaged group allows the less advantaged group more time to arrive at the open door, or gives them a hand. The economic model of benevolence for the less advantaged group shows that they run as fast as possible in order to level their speed with the advantaged group as far as possible. By doing so, people, the fast runners as well as the slow runners, help themself as well as others. The actual situation of the waiting room rectifies people's original position preference for unequal resource allocation. However, benevolence only works if the people are not anxious.

### *Ruler's Behavior*

Each individual in the waiting room will get out as safely as possible. To reach that goal a successful way is to follow a procedure in which the total group is divided into smaller groups, with each small group situated around one of the doors. A second procedure positions the fast runners in each small group first and the slow runners thereafter. Of course, there are probably more ways to get the group of people out unharmed. The fundamental issue is not the content of the procedure, but the fact that a procedure is clearly necessary to get out of the room as safely as possible. The question is how the group arrives at and carries out the procedural decisions. One serious possibility is that one person—man or woman—stands up and proposes the procedure. If the person has authority in the eyes of the others, they may accept the proposal of splitting up the group and create the special structure of the small groups. And the proposer needs full authority, because most people in the room realize that it is likely that not everyone will get out unharmed. There is a (small) chance that some will go under while attempting to get to the exit. An authority has the best chances of convincing others of the plan if he/she is consistent and persistent in proposing and working out the plan. Moreover, under conditions of fear and anxiety people are more inclined to listen to an authority, and deliberation of the best way of getting out takes time, and time is not amply available in the waiting room (see the examples of rulers earlier in this chapter). But how will the people in the room decide whether the ruler is the most capable person to guide them? What cues do the people in the room use to decide on the most appropriate ruler? One cue is the person's appearance, and another is their expertise. Appearance is rather easy, while expertise is more difficult to perceive. Sloterdijk (2011) claims that the body of the athlete—in the Greek mythology he is a god-athlete—exemplifies perfectly and convincingly the manifestation of authority (34). According to Sloterdijk, athletes strive to excel themselves and achieve excellence by discipline, training, and practicing, and constantly repeating it. Sloterdijk is critical about the cynical way humankind acts in the light of the severe consequences of climate change. He observes no serious reaction to counteract the inevitability of the upcoming catastrophe. He gives in his book a wake-up call to change our way of life, each individual as well as humanity: *Du muß dein Leben änderen*. In doing so, each of us becomes a god-athlete who deals effectively with the crisis. In my view, some of these god-athletes are more god than other persons, and become leaders for the others. The god-athletes function well in the waiting room: they are an example as well as an authority for the other people in the room.

The dual process model of information processing assumes that people generally process information in two ways. One way is the peripheral and the other way is the central way of processing information. The most important feature of peripheral information processing is that the listener to the message focuses on additional cues in the information process. The listener is more focused, for instance, on the person of the messenger, their appearance or status, than on the content of the message. Central information processing focuses on the content of the message and the arguments given in favor or not in favor of a certain stance regarding the subject matter. Peripheral information processing occurs when the receiver of the message is under some pressure, or is not motivated to listen to the message carefully. This may be the case when a person is in a high state of anxiety, as the people in the waiting room are when the smoke appears. The people in the waiting room, therefore, look for additional cues in the proposer: Is the proposer someone of acceptable status? If the people in the room accept the status of the proposer, the focus shifts from their appearance to the content of the message.

People infer the status of the proposer from the fact that the person is the first one to make a proposal for a procedure, is determined, gives good reasons for the proposal, and shows consideration for everyone, and these cues offer enough clues to make a choice for this person. People who are rational, reasonable, and anxious are inclined to choose for a dedicated proposer: rational, in that the proposal may be in the interests of each person in the room; reasonable, in that the proposal may be in the interests of all the persons in the room; anxious, in that a dedicated proposer may reduce each person's anxiety most.

The proposer has a difficult task to convince the other people in the room of the adequacy of their proposal. He/she has to convince the strong people not to take by force the middle position equidistant from each of the doors. He/she has to convince the slow runners to take a position behind the fast runners in the small groups and to run as fast as possible; and he/she has to convince the fast runners to reduce their speed when one of the doors opens, and the slow runners to run as fast as possible. A powerful argument for convincing people of a certain plan of action is to give good reasons for it (see also Chapter 3 for the role of justifications). However, anxious people hardly listen to arguments, reasons, and justifications. The proposer, therefore, must give arguments as clear and concrete actions, and not in elaborated reasoning. Clear action sequences convince people of the adequacy of the proposal. Moreover, they reduce anxiety because people doing something are diverted from their anxious thoughts and emotions, and they do not need to reflect on a lengthy account of the arguments.

A ruler in the waiting room situation must be determined and considerate. In other words, he must be a combination of a Machiavellian ruler and a Humian ruler. Machiavellian rulers are necessary because people have to carry out their decisions, because they reduce their anxiety, and protect them, and because the subgroups are antagonistic. Humian rulers are necessary because they are able to show that the decisions favor the rulers as well as the other people in the room.

One ruler, however, will not be enough. Each subgroup has a unique constellation of talents and personalities. It has a unique atmosphere that is different from the other subgroups. Each subgroup needs a ruler at the subgroup level to manage it and to emphasize the uniqueness of the subgroup. The ruler at the lower level must stick to the general ruler's decisions. Only in this way will the whole group leave the room as safely as possible. A "Machiahumian" ruler is necessary on several levels.

Contemporary Western societies need these rulers as well. Rulers at all organizational levels of society are necessary to let society run smoothly. Mayors of small and big towns must have Machiahumian qualities.

Institutions are not the best governing bodies to lead communities (see also Bell 2002). Parliament, for instance, consists of factions making few attempts to unite the people, but more often to divide them. They are a mirror of the society they have to rule. Institutions are battlefields unable to take adequate decisions. They can function well as political bodies to control the rulers' decisions.

## Discussion

When the people in the waiting room realize that they are trapped (anxious) they make attempts to get out of the room as quickly as possible. It is likely that everyone will run to the doors, to find that they are closed. After the message has been given that in due course one of the doors will open, the people in the room may start to find the best place. But because everyone starts to run to the best place, a crowd arises that blocks the aspirations of all the people to get out. It is then, probably, that people start to realize that they need a more adequate reaction to the emergency. And it might, then, be that people will listen to a proposal from someone in the crowd. Anxious people, confronted with a situation in which their lives or social identity are at stake, or their status in the group is threatened, will act first and reason afterwards. They follow their autonomous responses to save themselves from loss of life, identity, or status. After the first panic reaction fades people may start to realize that a somewhat readjusted reaction serves their own interests better. This readjustment requires that people make room for others as well. So, it is unlikely that people in this situation first think and then do something, but they first do something and then start to ponder about alternative courses of action. In an emergency situation, people may first choose to take the best spatial position, but will inevitably realize that making room for others is a good action to do and may be good for them as well (see also the paragraph earlier in this chapter about the economics of benevolence).

It would be unrealistic to assume that everyone in the waiting room will accept the proposal to split up the group into smaller groups. Some people in the group may insist that they will keep the central position in the room, equidistant from the doors, being sure that they will get out unharmed. If the group of dissenters is small, their actions may be integrated into the overall plan. For instance, they start to run to the open door after the second or third group has reached the door. But the fate of the group becomes worse if the dissenter's group is built up of people with certain qualities. For instance, if the strongest people position themselves in the middle of the room assuming that when one of the doors opens they can get out safely by force. The small but strong group will reduce the chances of all group members getting out unharmed. And if all other group members realize their deteriorating chances of getting out unharmed, they may start a fight against the small group of strong people. This would end in a disaster for all present in the waiting room. This conflict or potential conflict can only be overcome if the small group of strong people gives in, or if all find an acceptable compromise.

Even if the people in the room accept the proposal, the question remains whether all will stick to it when one of the doors opens. Hobbes (1990) and Rawls (1971) claim that people will stick to their contract. However, they introduced rational and reasonable, but not anxious, people in their philosophical inquiry. Anxious people easily lose self-control and start running prematurely, destroying the running scheme. Absence of any group feeling enhances the drive to escape. There are six antagonistic subgroups striving for the best position. The god-athlete must try to achieve a superordinate goal (Sherif and Sherif 1953), for instance by introducing a short ritual: a sports ritual (Sloterdijk 2011), such as a short collective exercise. To overcome chaos it might be proposed that an appeal is made to other members of each of the small groups who are less anxious and have more self-control to help the more anxious to overcome their tendency to run prematurely.

## References

Achterhuis, H. 1988. *Het rijk van de schaarste: van Thomas Hobbes tot Michel Foucault* (The Empire of Scarcity: From Thomas Hobbes to Michel Foucault). Baarn: Ambo.

Aristotle. 1987. *The Nicomachean Ethics*. Translation and Introduction by Sir David Ross. Revised by J.L. Ackrill and J.O. Urmson. Oxford: Oxford University Press.

Baumeister, R.F. and Vohs, K.D. 2004. *Handbook of Self-Regulation: Research, Theory, and Applications*. New York: The Guilford Press.

Becker, G.S. 1974. A theory of social interactions. *Journal of Political Economy*, 82(6), 1063–93.

Becker, G.S. 1992. *The economic way of looking at life*. Nobel Lecture, December.

Bell, S. 2002. Economic Governance and Institutional Dynamics. Melbourne: Oxford University Press.

Crosta, P. 2013. What is Anxiety? A Guide to Anxiety. *Medical News Today*. Available at http://www.medicalnewstoday.com/info/anxiety/ [accessed 23 November 2013].

Elias, N. 1969. *Über den Prozess der Zivilization*. Bern: Francke Verlag.

Foa, U.G., and Foa, E.B. 1974. *Societal Structures of the Mind*. Springfield, IL: Charles C. Thomas Publisher.

Freeman, S. 2003. Introduction. In S. Freeman (ed.), *Rawls*. Cambridge: Cambridge University Press.

Girard, R. 1978. *Des choses caches depuis la foundation du monde*. Paris: Grasset and Fasquelle.

Hardin, G. 1968. The tragedy of the commons. *Science*, 162(3859), 1243–8.

Hardy-Vallée, B. 2007. Decision-making: A neuroeconomic perspective. *Philosophy Compass*, 2(6), 939–53.

Hirschi, T. 2004. Self-Control and Crime, in *Handbook of Self-Regulation: Research, Theory, and Applications*, edited by R.F. Baumeister, and K.D. Vohs. New York: The Guilford Press, 537–52.

Hobbes, Th. 1990. *Behemot; Or the Long Parliament*. 3rd edition, edited by Ferdinand Tönnies. Chicago, IL: University of Chicago Press.

Hobbes, Th. 1983. *De Cive*. Edited by Howard Warrender. Oxford: The Clarendon Press.

Hobbes, Th. 1985. *Leviathan*. Edited by C.B. Macpherson. London: Penguin Group.

Hume, D. 1957. *An Inquiry Concerning the Principles of Morals*. Edited by C.W. Hendel. New York: The Bobbs-Merrill Company.

Kolm, S.-Ch. 2006. Introduction to the Economics of Giving, Altruism and Reciprocity, in *Handbook of the Economics of Giving, Altruism, and Reciprocity*, edited by S.-Ch. Kolm and J. Mercier Ythier. Amsterdam: Elsevier, 1–122.

Livy, T. 1997. *Sons of Mars. The History of Rome I–X*. Amsterdam: Atheneum.

Machiavelli, N. 1946. *The Prince*, trans. A.H. Gilbert. Putney: Hendricks House.

Machiavelli, N. 1997. *Discorsie, gedachten over Staat en Politiek*, trans. P. van Heck. Amsterdam: Ambo.

Nietzsche, F. 1996. *On the Genealogy of Morals*, translated and edited by Douglas Smith. Oxford: Oxford World's Classics.

Nozick, R. 1974. *Anarchy, State and Utopia*. New York: Basic Books.

Ostrom, E., Burger, J., Field, C.B., Norgaard, R.B., and Policansky, D. 1999. Revisiting the commons: Local lessons, global challenges. *Science*, 284(9), 278–82.

Parsons, T. 1951. *The Social System*. Glencoe, Ill: Free Press.

Pyszczynski, T., Greenberg, J., and Solomon, S. 1999. A dual process model of defense against conscious and unconscious death-related thoughts: An extension of terror management theory. *Psychological Review*, 106, 835–45.

Rawls, J. 1971. *A Theory of Justice*. London: Oxford University Press.

Rousseau, J.-J. 1978. *Het maatschappelijk contract* (The social contract). Utrecht: Het Spectrum.

Sherif, M., and Sherif, C. 1953. *Groups in harmony and tension: An integration of studies on intergroup relations*. New York: Octagon.

Sloterdijk, P. 2011. *Je moet je leven veranderen* (You have to change your life). Amsterdam: Boom.

Vohs, K.D., and Baumeister, R.F. 2004. Understanding Self-Regulation, in *Handbook of Self-Regulation: Research, Theory, and Applications*, edited by R.F. Baumeister and K.D. Vohs. New York: The Guilford Press, 1–9.

Walzer, M. 1983. *Spheres of Justice*. London: Basic Books.

Wilkinson, R.G., and Pickett, K. 2009. *The Spirit Level: Why More Equal Societies Almost Always Do Better*. London: Allen Lane.

Wolin, S. 1961. *Politics and vision: Continuity and innovation in Western political thought*. London: Allen & Unwin.

Yoksas, A. 2009. *Equity in the thought of Thomas Hobbes*. Paper presented at the 67 Annual Meeting of the Midwest Political Science Association, April 2–5.

# PART III
# Justice-Related Mental States

# Chapter 5
# The Psychology of Just Resource Allocation. Part I: Emotions and Cognitions

## Introduction

Justice motivation is in conflict with the egoistic tendency as well as with the altruistic one, and it is essential to curb both in order to employ justice. Of course, the self is nearer to the acting person than the other is, and fulfilling one's own needs is often more satisfying. In certain periods of time, in certain cultures and situations, curbing the egoistic tendency is a more strenuous task than curbing the altruistic one. Moreover, the more the self is cognitively accessible while making allocation decisions the more effort will be needed to counteract the egoistic tendency as, for instance, in Actor–Recipient allocations as compared to Actor–Recipient–Recipient allocations (the actor divides a resource among two or more recipients; see Chapter 3). Many philosophers have designed principles and laws to overcome the egoistic tendency. Counteracting the egoistic tendency is labeled by some philosophers (e.g., Kant 1778; see, however, Nietzsche 2003) duty, by others it is labeled virtue (e.g., Plato), while for Hobbes (1985; Taylor 1938) the egoistic tendency should be counteracted by a strong authority. It is curious that no philosophical systems have been developed that counteract the altruistic tendency.

This chapter confines its description of allocation behavior to events of conflict between the egoistic and the altruistic tendencies, and justice considerations, focusing on the justice domain which lies at the left and right hemisphere of the oval in Figure P.1 of this volume. It is the part of the justice domain where egoistic and altruistic tendencies easily pop up, for instance as a result of cultural and/or situational pressure. The actor has to make an effort, cognitively, emotionally, and behaviorally, to regulate the egoistic and altruistic tendencies.

The issues I would like to focus on in this chapter are the salience of the justice motive, how an actor deals with the eventual conflict between justice considerations and egoistic/altruistic tendencies, how an actor solves the conflict, and how the conflict can be made visible.

### *The Psychology of Allocation Behavior*

The allocation event, in which an actor allocates resources between himself/herself and another, or between two or more others, is viewed in this book as the core of human interaction. The preceding chapters have discussed the motivational basis of allocation behavior (Chapter 1), the social impact on just allocation behavior

(Chapter 2), the development of a moral theory based on allocation principles (Chapter 3), and some ideas for a theory of justice (Chapter 4). Although Chapter 1 discussed the motivational basis of allocation behavior, cognitive and emotional processes and their physiological correlates were—intentionally—not included in that discussion.

One can imagine that allocation behavior is not only affected by the moving force that instigates it (Chapter 1), but also by the type of resources to be allocated (Prologue; Chapter 3), the rules that are developed, like the equality rule or the equity rule (Chapter 2), but also by emotions, like guilt, that may accompany allocation decisions—see Cropanzano et al. (2011) for a thorough and expert account of the relationship between justice and emotions. To illustrate this point, let us take the example of the man standing at a railway switch (Hauser 2009). If the man does nothing, a train will continue on the main track and collide with five people. If the man operates the switch the train will continue on a side track where a large man can stop the train but only at the expense of his own life, saving five lives. Chapter 3 discussed the morality of the railway switch man's action: giving service to one party (saving five persons) or the other party (saving one person). The question as to what the man at the switch feels, how he will come to decide what course of action he will pursue, how he will oversee the consequences of his act, and whether he can live with these consequences have not been discussed. The man at the switch is certainly motivated to consider action or to actually act, he is emotionally aroused and will use his cognitive abilities to find a solution to the dilemma. One issue might be the man's preoccupation with what to tell other people about his decision to operate the switch or not. The man may reason that saving five people is better from a moral point of view than saving one person. But the man may keep feelings of guilt because he could not save the life of the fat man. Or he may feel angry about being "maneuvered" into that position. Another example concerns the feelings of the people in the waiting room, as described in Chapter 4. They are motivated to reach one of the doors, feel panic rising and estimate their chances to get out safely. But at the same time they are anxious, frustrated about the other people's presence as obstructions for their own strivings, as well as worried about other the people's fate. So, it is not only a question of helping self and/or helping another, but emotions and cognition are also essential in each allocation event.

Fortunately, many allocation decisions are not of the dramatic type described above. In standard allocation events, dividing resources goes more or less automatically. If someone rings the doorbell and asks for a gift for a well-known charity organization—and it is not for the first time—the answer can be short: yes or no, without much deliberation or emotion. Nevertheless, the actor has to think over what to do and has positive or negative feelings about the gift and/or the organization, but motivation is not pulling hard, the emotions are not intense, and the cognitive effort is moderate. But even in this standard allocation event, it is important to delineate the factors—motivation, emotion, cognition—affecting the allocation decision.

A theory that encompasses the behavior of individuals in social interaction as well as their collective behavior is viewed in this book as a theory about sequences of allocation events: an actor can be an individual, or an institution, or an organization. Chapters 1 and 2 have treated humans as if they were interchangeable, as if each human being would be motivated to allocate a resource to the same degree as each other human being. One could compare the generalized subject described in these chapters with the concept of "average citizen" in sociological thinking and research. The purpose of these types of analysis is to facilitate, for instance, comparisons between life in a city and life in a rural environment. The allocation behavior of a specific town dweller or farmer will likely differ from each other, for instance with regard to religion. Town dwellers are less religious than rural dwellers, and for the groups as a whole their attitudes about, for instance, criminality will differ in general. In addition, city dwellers—and farmers—differ from each other, and then it is fruitful to study carefully the personalities of the town dwellers in order to study differences in (allocation) behavior or attitude. Chapters 3 and 4, in which the moral, respectively the cooperative, component of allocation behavior is described, have given an account of an individual subject's behavior or the behavior of a collective subject as if these subjects were not persons of flesh and blood. Ethicality as well as cooperation, which forms the bases of the theory, is studied in terms of what it means to be ethical or cooperative and to develop criteria that distinguish ethical behavior from unethical behavior: the philosophical approach. An abstract description of moral and cooperative behavior supports the development of a theory of allocation behavior, but fails to account for a full applicability of the theory. Moreover, one could argue, as did chapters 3 and 4, that the abstracted subject confronted with a moral issue experiences anxiety. Is that anxiety not an instance of the psychological characteristic of the subject? No, because that anxiety is of an abstract or metaphysical nature: the philosophical analysis tries to grasp the intuitive meaning of anxiety and to reason out the criteria for when the subject is anxious or not. For instance, it is the fear of the subject whose existence is in constant danger due to the presence of others (Sartre), or because of the meaninglessness of existence (Camus). But, certainly, that anxiety or fear can be empirically studied, and psychological research of anxiety or fear may help our philosophical intuitions about fear and vice versa—see, e.g., Scholl's discussion of object persistency in psychology and philosophy (Scholl 2007).

This chapter will go into the motivational, cognitive, and emotional bases of allocation behavior and into the theoretical relationship between the motivation, cognition, and emotion of an individual's behavior.

## The Model

An actor allocating a resource between self and recipient or between recipients mutually starts to think about the final outcome of the process: how much of the resource to offer to the recipient and how much to keep for himself or herself.

Whatever amounts the actor allocates, if asked, the actor will explain that he/she allocated the resource fairly or justly. He/she will not say that he/she has offered the recipient an unfair amount of resources.

Moreover, every language on earth has a word for or a notion of justice, not only the Western countries of the present day, but also hunter-gatherer communities that live in remote areas in Africa, South America, and New Guinea (see, however, Kidder and Muller 1991). Every person on earth has a sense of justice and injustice as is exemplified in the operation of the justice motive (Lerner 1980). People do honestly believe that the world is a just place where everyone gets what he or she deserves.

Besides, research has shown the operation of a kind of justice centre in the brain: Knoch et al. (2006) reported that disrupting the right prefrontal cortex diminished fairness responses. The researchers let experimental subjects play an economic game, while undergoing a functional Magnetic Resonance Imaging (fMRI) scan of the brain. In an fMRI machine, neural activity is measured by magnetic fluctuations of the hemoglobin that is used by active neurons. In a former fMRI study of individuals who had to decide whether to accept or reject unfair offers, it was shown that two main brain areas were involved: the anterior insula and the right and left dorso-lateral prefrontal cortex (DLPFC). The DLPFC is assumed to be involved in the inhibition of pre-potent responses, that is that these parts of the brain are involved in the control of impulsive reactions. And this is exactly what happens to recipients in a UBG: In first instance, individuals are inclined to satisfy their self-interested needs. Control of this impulse by the DLPFC—it is an unfair offer—overrides the primary impulse. If that assumption is valid then impairing the DLPFC by low-frequency repetitive trans-cranial magnetic stimulation (rTMS), which will inhibit the control function of the DLPFC and thus strengthen the self-interest motive, will result in acceptance of more unfair offers. Subjects that underwent rTMS in the right DLPFC, but not in the left DLPFC, accepted more unequal and thus more unfavorable offers than the other subjects. One could say that the brain contains one or more areas where not only the interests of self but also others' needs and position are taken into account, which is defined here as justice.

Another indication of the evolutionary importance of justice is the presence of spindle cells or Von Economo neurons in the human brain (Allman et al. 2005). The spindle cell is four times larger than other brain cells and appears in two brain regions, the frontal and temporal cortex, that are essential for engaging in social interactions and in intuitive sensing of another person's state of mind. The cells probably play an important role in processes in which people feel compassion with the fate of others. It is therefore plausible to assume that the spindle cells are important in fairness evaluations. For instance, in equity theory it is assumed that individuals weigh the inputs and outcomes for self with those of others. The Von Economo neurons may be relevant in the justice evaluation process in that they make people more sensitive to the fate of others. It seems that parts of the brain are specifically suited for evaluating the correctness of allocations.

In addition, research among young male and female children of about 2.5 years old, male and female chimpanzees between 3 and 30 years old, and orangutans between 3 and 10 years old showed that children and apes had the same level of skills of physical cognition such as the ability to locate food, but that children had advanced skills with regard to social cognition like vicarious learning, communication, and theory of mind (Hermann et al. 2007). Specifically, the more advanced skills related to theory of mind are important because these skills open up possibilities for being sensitive for the fate and position of others.

Taking these considerations into account the following allocation behavior model is developed.

*Psychological Model of Resource Allocation Behavior*

ASSUMPTION

- There is an innate drive to allocate resources fairly, that is, allocate resources taking into account one's own *and* others' positions reasonably; "reasonably" may be defined as lying between equal division and golden ratio division ($\varphi = 1.618$; in allocating 100 units of a resource—money, goods, service, love, status, or information—the actor will receive 61.8 and the recipient 38.2). 1.618 may be seen as the upper limit of what is judged as fair.

HYPOTHESES

- As a consequence of several factors—approaching positive emotions or avoiding negative emotions (anxiety) related to egoism/altruism motivation—individuals modulate the drive.
- To arrive—still—at a perceived fair allocation of resources, individuals activate (mobilize) cognitive resources (justifications).
- Activation (mobilization) is assessed by physiological and behavioral indexes.
- Personality factors (e.g., egoism/altruism preference) and social context (e.g., business versus family) affect activation (mobilization) of cognitive resources.

### Modulation of the Drive

Based on these notions, the assumption is that people have a primary urge to take into account the interests of others combined with self-interest and thus to allocate resources fairly. Contrary to what Knoch et al. (2006) assume, it is the justice motive that dominates the allocation process, while the egoistic and altruistic motivations try to override it. Later in this chapter it will become clear that my assumption is theoretically tenable in the light of empirical evidence. This basic assumption is the starting point of my (social) psychological model of justice. The justice model will explain why people, intending to do just allocations, fail to create a social environment that is just.

The Prologue and Chapter 1 discussed the relationship between egoistic, altruistic, and justice motivations, and stated that the justice motivation is a combination of egoistic and altruistic motivations. The point to make here is to explain: (1) that the combination of the two motivations does not signify that these separate motivations have disappeared; and (2) what kind of combination is being discussed. First, the assumption is that the egoistic and altruistic motivations are still operative, and through societal changes, as described in Chapter 2, sometimes gain in salience. A major societal change was the transition from hunting and gathering to agricultural ways of acquiring food. What I have argued is that as a result of the agrarian revolution and the subsequent sedentary life of the population, possession of resources like goods (houses, furniture) became more popular and producing, exchanging, and allocating them became important activities in everyday life. While the operation of an egoistic and altruistic motivation was significant for survival in the hunter-gatherer communities, in the settled communities the operation of the motives became a force for innovation, but also a burden. People gathered and allocated goods with probably the same vigor as the hunter-gatherers gathered food, but the survival value of the goods was less dominant. It is as if an old apparatus that was used for thousands of years for survival purposes (to find food in the presence of enemies) now became used for other purposes, like demonstrating one's status. One may compare the egoistic and altruistic motives then and in modern times with the bodily condition of people in hunter-gatherer communities and of people now. Because food was often eaten uncooked, the intestines and the appendix broke down the difficult-to-digest parts of the food. Now that food is cooked or otherwise made more edible, the appendix is not needed anymore. But the presence of the appendix can sometimes become a burden in that it causes infection and then needs to be removed.

### *Motivation in the Social Context*

It is because of the changing, man-made, conditions in which people live that the egoistic and altruistic tendencies differ in strength. At the beginning of the twenty-first century, for instance, the slogan of becoming rich is openly propagated by government, media (e.g., announcements for participation in the lottery), and other institutions. Many people strive to improve their economic condition and do that with the utmost vigor, which seems to lead to the unbounded operation of the egoistic motive. So, in this period of history, it seems that the unleashing of egoism has partly a detrimental effect on the way people live together, but also on the wish to produce and innovate, and that the altruistic motivation is becoming less prominent and less stimulated by cultural and social forces, as is the egoistic motivation. However, there were times when the altruistic motivation was stimulated more than the egoistic tendency. It is often suggested that after the revolution in France, in 1789, the demand for equality, cooperation, and helping others was stronger than it is now. One might thus conclude that social conditions shape the salience of the operation of both the egoistic and altruistic motivations. In periods were the egoistic drive is stimulated, parents are more motivated to equip their children as best they can, and offer them social and economic tools so that they can survive as best as possible (see Chapter 2). Through classical and instrumental learning, children develop approach behaviors for goal attainment; they learn to develop positive emotions as well as the appropriate cognitions. For instance, a child who will not stand up enough for himself or herself on their own may be taught how to do that. If the child shows the behavior of standing up for himself or herself, the parents reward the child (instrumental learning) which results in positive emotions (e.g., the child is happy). After sufficient reinforcements, the child will have the positive emotions when he/she displays the behavior. In this way, the parents strengthen an already present drive, the drive to survive. Parents may teach their children to deploy the justice drive as well. They reward behavior that is aimed at fostering others without disregard for self, for instance, by allocating candies equally between self and others. The parents' reward strengthens the child's positive moral emotion (e.g., the child is proud, that is, feels noble) and the already present justice drive. Depending on the direction of social influence, the child develops both drives, the one stronger, the other weaker. In social psychology and behavioral economics, these drives are known under the labels of proselfs and prosocials (Van Lange 2000), although it is unclear whether prosocials execute the justice drive or the altruism drive, or a combination of both drives.

All individuals are endowed with a basic anxiety due to being on this earth and due to the presence of others, and through a learning approach some of them are rewarded by outperforming others and to take the benefits for themselves. They also learn to become averse to giving in and letting others benefit as well. With this orientation, proselfs reduce their basic anxiety. This proself orientation becomes operational in future allocation events. Other individuals learn through approach conditioning to trust others, and that giving in and letting others benefit reduces their basic anxiety. In this way, prosocials reduce their feelings of guilt or shame as well.

When a child, conditioned in this way, is confronted with a social event in which he/she cannot fully satisfy the egoistic/altruistic drive or the justice drive, the stimulus situation may become threatening. Negative self-preservation emotions like fear and anger, or negative moral emotions like guilt and shame, may arise. In a culture in which the proself orientation is stimulated, parents will teach their children, and these children their children, to use proself behavior rather than prosocial. Would that imply that the prosocial orientation will disappear after two generations?

*Motivation and Emotion*

This observation of the salience of the egoistic motivation leads to the conclusion that satisfying the egoistic tendency can be viewed as an appetite (a positive emotion) and blocking of the egoistic tendency as a defense (a negative emotion), while satisfaction of the altruistic motivation lags behind. It does not mean that people do not show altruistic behavior. People show it in the appropriate conditions. But at this time, the beginning of the twenty-first century, the standard condition is one in which the egoistic motivation is triggered most.

The relationship between egoistic and altruistic motivation can be viewed in terms of the biphasic activation of appetitive and defensive motivation (Cacioppo and Berntson, 1994). In this model, activation of the egoistic motivation can be reciprocal or co-active with altruistic motivation, or both motivations can be activated independently of each other. Reciprocation implies that the more the egoistic motivation is activated the less the altruistic motivation is activated, and vice versa. Co-activation implies that both motivations are activated to the same degree, while independent activation implies activation of the one while the other motivation is not activated. Co-activation of both the egoistic and altruistic motivation seems unlikely, while reciprocal or independent activation is likely. Can one describe the relationship between egoistic/altruistic motivation on the one hand and justice motivation on the other in terms of the biphasic activation, as could be done between egoistic and altruistic motivation? That is, is there a reciprocal/independent relationship?

As already indicated, culture in some historical periods triggers the egoistic motivation in allocation processes more than in other periods. A soon as the egoistic motivation is activated by cultural norms and economic developments, the egoistic motivation becomes more dominant than the altruistic motivation in shaping allocation behavior. In those times, for events in which all types of resources are allocated, the egoistic drive is thus activated faster than the altruistic motivation. The obsolete but still operating egoistic tendency will conquer the justice tendency. Both tendencies (or drives or motivations) are appetitive tendencies and biphasic activation is not directly applicable as a model. As described by Bradley (2000), biphasic activation is an appropriate model if it concerns the activation of an appetitive motivation and a defensive motivation. So, I have to redefine one of the motivations to fit the biphasic activation model.

Activation of one appetitive motivation at the expense of the other implies that one gains the possession of a desired resource but loses the possession of another desired resource. When a person allocates money fairly, he will lose money compared to allocating money egoistically. Losing money is the defensive motivation and people will try to avoid losses, while behaving fairly is the appetitive motivation. People are anxious not to lose too much of both—they are loss averse (Tversky and Kahneman 1991) and try to keep the loss as small as possible. Losses are twice as powerful psychologically as gains (see also Cacioppo and Berntson 1994). These effects have been shown in studies in which the resources to allocate were money or goods; whether losses in other types of resources are twice as powerful, as in the case of money/goods, is questionable.

*Gains, losses and fairness*

In order to be fair on the one hand and not to lose money on the other hand, a person wriggles cognitively and emotionally in such a way that he gains the most of both or gains the most of one and keeps the other at the same level. In this case, the fear of losing money is the defensive motivation while being fair is the appetitive motivation. Because losses—specifically with regard to money—are regarded as twice as powerful as gains, psychologically speaking, the motive of being just (gains) will have to conquer the eventual loss of money.

An actor dividing resources between self and another is often confronted with the question of how to reconcile the two motivations. Loss of money is certainly not attractive; neither is loss of respect (by behaving unfairly): The actor tries to be judged by self and others as a moral person and will at the same time try not to lose too much money. The amount of money the actor will retain will be less than in the condition in which he/she allocates egoistically. In other words, being fair and just will have a damping effect on an actor's rummaging behavior. But the egoistic motivation will still be a strong force and pushes the actor to keep more. Therefore, actors will engage in emotional and cognitive activity to defend their allocation behavior in which they try to lose as little as possible. Actors engage in emotional activity by emphasizing adherence to justice, and this exposes positive feelings for justice. Support for this reasoning is found in the results of the study of Nelissen et al. (2011). They reasoned and found that actors contemplating (positive) offers are driven by fear and guilt, where fear is more related to the perceived consequences of having one's offer rejected, and guilt is more related to concerns for others' outcomes.

Moreover, cognitive activity will also be triggered, revealing itself in the (exaggerated) use of justifications. The more actors use justifications, the more they will try to conceal deviation from a fair allocation and the more actors show their adherence to justice. Indirect evidence for the relationship between unfairness and use of justifications is found in the study by Shalvi et al. (2011). These authors investigated the relationship between availability of justifying information and lying. Participants lied more in order to attain a desirable outcome when justifying information was available. In my words, self-justification availability increased the participant's intention to promote inequality of information between self and other (lying). Using justification made the act of lying less unethical. Figure 5.1 depicts the relationship between an actor's allocation injustice and actions to restore justice.

The horizontal axis represents the justice dimension, with values between negative injustice and positive injustice (unjust allocation toward other, just, unjust toward self). The vertical axis shows the actor's efforts to restore justice: the higher up the axis, the more effort the actor exerts. Effort is expressed in terms of the justifications used, but also in emotional reactions, stress, and attempts to convince others. The figure shows a curvilinear relationship between

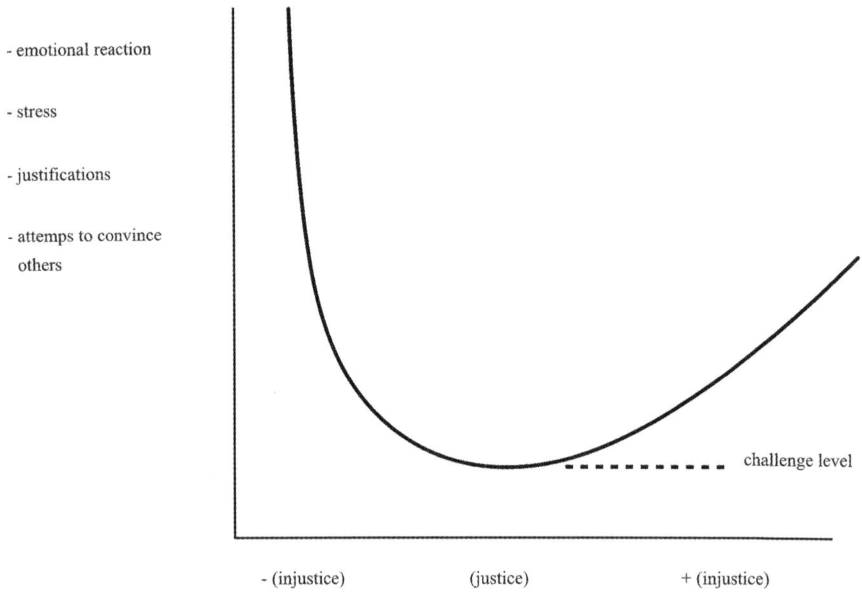


**Figure 5.1 Assumed relationship between an individual's allocation (in)justice and actions to restore justice**

justice–injustice and the amount of emotional and cognitive activity to restore justice. The curve is skewed: actions to restore justice have to be stronger with respect to the egoistic drive than to the altruistic one. I predict, therefore, that the more an actor distributes resources to self as compared to offering them to others, the stronger will be the attempts to satisfy the justice drive. In addition, the more an actor distributes resources to others as compared to self, the stronger will be the attempts to restore justice; the effort is less than in the case of the egoistic drive. The next section elaborates the psychological model of allocation decisions in neurophysiological terms. This approach makes it possible to test the hypotheses of the model.

## The Struggle for Fair Allocation: A Neuropsychological View

Children learn from parents and teachers the behaviors the tutors think fit for their pupils. Through classical and instrumental learning, pupils learn the appropriate behaviors. Parents reward their children when they allocate resources fairly between themselves and other children, or they teach their children that allocating a large part of the resource to self is most satisfying. It may be that parents reward their children for allocating money evenly between self and others, while they teach them to defend their status position at all costs—children learn to divide material resources evenly, but status unevenly. Later, when the grown-up child engages in allocation events, relevant memory systems are activated to guide behavior.

Classical conditioning research shows that the *temporal difference learning* model is a good approximation of how brain networks process information from an arbitrary initially affectively neutral stimulus (CS) and an unconditioned stimulus (US) having appetitive or aversive qualities. In classical conditioning, a CS is presented together with an US. The experimenter presents food (US) to a hungry dog who salivates (behavior), and at the same time a bell rings (CS) after which the dog receives the food, but sometimes not. Repetition of the sequence shows saliva production when the bell rings even when food is absent. The CS has received affective value for the dog because of its predictive relevance. Behavior is linked to the conditioned stimulus without the presence of the unconditioned stimulus. This temporal sequence repeats itself but sometimes only one of the stimuli—sometimes the CS—is presented and the reward is omitted, as is normal in daily life. The bell rings but the dog receives no food. The dog expects food after the bell rings, and when he receives no food a difference between what he expected and what he received occurs: the prediction error. Learning is equivalent to reducing the prediction error. The expected value of the CS converges to the value of the reward, and if this occurs further learning will not take place. Every time the sequence appears, fully or not, the brain produces prediction error signals: observed from the wavelike activity of dopamine neurons in human subjects (O'Doherty et al. 2003) and primates (Schultz 1998). O'Doherty (2009) produced a time series analysis specifying the model-predicted prediction error signals. The time series data were then regressed against fMRI data from the subject. The resulting high correlation between the haemodynamic response, observed in the ventral striatum and the orbitofrontal cortex, and the time series data confirmed the prediction error hypothesis.

### *A Short Anatomy of the Prefrontal Cortex (PFC)*

It is generally accepted that the PFC consists of three interconnected regions with more or less separate functions (Wolters and Raffone 2008). First, the ventromedial and orbitofrontal regions represent and process reward and affective information, participating in emotionally and motivationally driven behavior; these regions have reciprocal connections with the amygdala and the temporal lobe. Second, the medial regions of the PFC consist mainly of the anterior cingulate cortex involved in error monitoring and in detecting conflicts between competing stimuli and responses, like discrepancies between expected and actual resources. Third, the lateral and anterior PFC areas involved in all the executive functions needed for organized goal-directed behavior, such as allocation behavior. These PFC areas have strong reciprocal links with the parietal and temporal areas, the hippocampal formation, and with the rest of PFC. The PFC guides and controls internal states and intentions, suppresses automatic processes, and is active when shifts in action–outcome chains need to be made quickly. According to Wolters and Raffone, the PFC allows an internalization of the action, outcome, and evaluation loop, so that without an external source, information is maintained in an active state by recurrent connections between the PFC and the rest of the cortex. The PFC activates or inhibits motor programs—for instance, allocating more to self than to another. The crucial role of the prefrontal cortex in high-level cognition is also suggested because it is a late evolutionary development that co-occurred with the development of language and complex social environments. So it is in the PFC that intentional moral decisions about concepts like fairness, loyalty, respect, and reciprocity are made. The lateral and anterior PFC areas are involved in all executive functions needed for organized goal-directed behavior, and for maintaining information in an active format, even in the face of interfering input (e.g., like maintaining a task set or instruction). These PFC areas have strong reciprocal links with many areas in the parietal and temporal cortices (giving it access to perceptual information and allowing control over selective attention by top-down signaling), the hippocampal formation (giving it access to episodic memory), the medial PFC areas (giving access to emotional evaluations) and primary and secondary motor areas (allowing control over the initiation of actions).

*Cognitive and Emotional Conflicts*

Repetition of the CS/US sequence draws traces in the cortex, resulting in a drive to carry out the appropriate behavior after activation of the appropriate brain parts. Encoding and retrieval of information about an allocation event is an emotion-laden cognitive process in which emotion networks are connected to "objective" cognitive states. The cognitive states are better retrieved from memory if they are connected to emotional states than to neutral states (Smith et al. 2004). Reward learning goes together with emotions like happiness or pleasure (self-preservation emotions) as well as compassion and pride (moral emotions). Children who have learned to find pleasure in satisfying the moral emotions will be inclined in subsequent allocation events to neglect the egoistic/altruistic tendencies and adhere more to justice.

Reward learning follows the previously described pattern. However, can one adequately describe avoidance learning, the tendency to avoid harmful or noxious stimuli, with the same pattern? Because avoidance learning does not fit the principles of instrumental conditioning—children only have to experience pain once to avoid it in the future without repeated exposure—it is difficult to find prediction error models to describe the process. But avoiding noxious stimuli is a reward, and is subject to reward learning. This assumption is of great importance for justice studies as individuals learn to avoid negative states like fear or guilt or shame.

Classical and operant learning strengthen the built-in emotional state structures and networks in the brain by approach and avoidance learning. If these structures and networks are strengthened in childhood, they affect future allocation decision-making. The memory systems involved in classical and instrumental learning are, next to the hypocampus and ventral striatum, situated in the prefrontal cortex. In other words, the memory systems are situated in separate brain structures, which have mutual connections and interact with each other (Gharemani and Poldrack 2009). The prefrontal cortex and the amygdala are also seats of self-preservation and moral emotions.

*Egoistic versus just motivation*

Actors, allocating resources between self and others, often experience a conflict between different learning outcomes. In mixed-motive games, individuals have to decide about a course of action under uncertainty. The decision to choose an action is dependent on the decision another takes. In a prisoners' dilemma, a participant has two choices, to cooperate or to deflect. Cooperation might be attractive, but if the other deflects then the participant receives nothing while the other receives all. The best strategy is to deflect. Proselfs choose this strategy more than prosocials. Using fMRI scans during decision-making, researchers were able to detect activity in the relevant brain parts. Emonds, Declerck, Vandervliet, Boone, and Parizer (2011) found that proselfs show activity in the dorso-lateral region of the prefrontal cortex, while prosocials show activity in the lateral orbitofrontal cortex. Both proselfs and prosocials showed activity in other brain areas as well. Proselfs showed activity in the temporo-parietal junction and precuneus, areas interconnected with the amygdala and related to expression of negative emotions like fear. Prosocials showed activity in the superior temporal sulcus (STS) and the inferior parietal lobule (IPL), areas interconnected with the amygdala and related to negative emotions like guilt and shame.

Researchers further assume that the ventromedial prefrontal cortex holds linkages between the facts of a given situation—in our case an allocation event—and the emotion previously linked to it during classical or operant conditioning. The ventromedial prefrontal cortex itself does not contain the representation of the situation or the emotion connected to it, but establishes a linkage between cortical and subcortical structures that contain the facts and the emotions previously connected to the facts (Bechara et al. 2000). I assume that the facts of an allocation event are represented in cortical areas of the brain like the dorso-lateral prefrontal cortex or the lateral orbitofrontal cortex. Emotions are represented in cortical and subcortical substructures like the amygdala, and its interconnected parts, the STS and IPL, and the temporo-parietal junction and precuneus. The representation of an allocation event, according to Bechara et al., contains a set of response options and the short-term and long-term outcomes of each option. Prosocials choosing the deflect option experience shame: the short-term outcome of this response option. To reduce the aversive state of shame, prosocials open the learned response option of justification: "I chose this response option to prevent the other receiving all and I nothing."

Participants in the Emonds et al. (2011) study certainly experienced a conflict between fear of loss of resource (egoism) and guilt of being unfair (fairness motivated), but also pride in being fair (justice motivated) and happiness at receiving more (egoism motivated). Proselfs chose the cooperative strategy in the cooperative game, but deflected in the prisoners' dilemma game. In other words, when they are certain of a positive outcome, proselfs chose a cooperative strategy. Van Dijk et al. (2012) found that, in a public good dilemma, proselfs showed no anger when the public good was provided despite the fact that the participants' contribution did not reach the appropriate level, while prosocials became angry. According to the authors, the results show that proselfs choose for equality for instrumental reasons—the public good is provided—and seem to care less about fairness, that is, the appropriate contribution. I conclude that when proselfs experience low fear of loss they engage in a cooperative strategy resulting in a fair decision: the proself chooses the option in which the other receives the same amount of a monetary reward as the participant.

*Altruistic versus just motivation*

The same reasoning applies to describe a conflict between the altruistic and justice motives. In this case, the positive self-preservation emotion would be contentment with feelings of pleasure, calmness, serenity, or peacefulness, versus the positive moral emotions like pride. Or it could be a conflict between avoiding the negative self-preservation emotion of sadness and avoiding the negative moral emotions like guilt or shame. The following real life story is an example of this conflict. A 68-year-old couple struggles with the physical condition of the husband. He has to take medication to reduce rejection of an implanted liver. Later on, the husband develops Parkinson's disease, which not only increases the amount of medication but also creates problems with regard to the coordinated intake of medication. There are times when he can move reasonably well, but all of a sudden he can slide back into a state of illness; the frequency of this recurrence increases gradually. And now the beginnings of dementia have set in. His physical condition is a burden for him but also for his wife. It is impossible for her to leave him alone and go out for more than a short time. She is always busy dressing him in the morning or undressing him at bedtime and helping him with the medication. She helps him to go to the toilet. She has hardly any time of her own. She teaches adults about architecture and the history of old buildings, but has to give it up to care for her husband. A couple of months ago she decided to let him spend two mornings a week in a care center. For her it was a relief, but she feels guilty about it because her husband does not see why this is necessary. Now she has told us to extend the period in the care center by one day, but she has a difficult time doing this because she feels guilty about it. To suppress feelings of guilt, she emphasizes that this decision makes her more able to support him.

What I see here is a conflict between the altruistic motive and the justice motive. Of course, one cannot ask too much from the husband in his position, but a more balanced division of the burden seems morally defensible and just. She admits rationally that a more balanced division is better, but emotionally she finds it difficult to accept. She justifies her altruistic behavior by referring to his deplorable physical state. She has compassion and pity for her husband. She not only has to convince her husband about her behavior but also her children, friends, and neighbors. Some of these people comment on her altruistic behavior, emphasizing that it will not be good for her psychological and physical health. Others, like her husband (and children), agree with her present decision and have difficulty in accepting a more balanced care regime. She tries to deal with the disagreement by gradually increasing the care center days, and discussing it with all the relevant people. In the altruistic case, it seems that to reach a more just allocation of resources (e.g., care), the recipient (in this case the more vulnerable party) has to give in. This outcome stands in contrast with the egoistic case, in which the actor has to give in to reach a more just allocation of resources.

*Egoistic versus altruistic motivation*

Batson et al. (1997, 1999) asked participants to assign to themselves and another (who was not present) two different tasks: a desirable and an undesirable one. The participants learned that the other did not know they were allowed to assign the tasks, but believed that it was done by chance. The participants assigned the desirable task to themselves 80 percent of the time. Batson et al. concluded that the participants' actions failed to fit their moral principles. The task, however, forces the participant to be egoist or altruist: assign the desirable task to self or to the other. The definition of justice and morality I promote here is that there is a balance between self-interest and other-interest. So, strictly speaking, Batson et al. did not investigate fairness. The dilemma was not one between fairness and egoism or between fairness and altruism, but between egoism and altruism.

*Motivational conflict and emotion*

Interaction between networks of different brain areas with regard to retrieval of emotion-related allocation information that has been acquired through learning may show avoidance reactions when the pathways (nodes) of two relevant positive emotions or two relevant negative emotions are activated. Bower (1981)—see also Labar (2009)—assumed that an (allocation) event activates certain mood states (a general emotional state) that are associated with the specific emotion(s) elicited by the event. An allocation event in which a resource is allocated between self and another may activate a fear-conditioned response: fear of loss. With regard to the positive emotions happiness and pride, fear of loss of happiness (a self-preservation emotion) concurs with fear of loss of pride (guilt, a moral emotion). The more both emotions are of the same strength during an allocation decision process, the larger will be the prediction error signal. And the greater the difference in strength, the smaller the prediction error signal. The phasic form of the signal is observed from the wavelike activity of dopamine neurons in human subjects (O'Doherty et al. 2003). The resultant aversive reaction in the amygdala initiates sympathetic as well as parasympathetic activity (Bradley 2000). The stronger the emotion information in a network (nodes), the more that emotion will affect the amygdala's output to the peripheral nervous system (Labar 2009).

This and other studies assessing emotions during or after resource allocation decisions show that more than one emotion operates. And the question for one emotion having a lower level than another is that the experimenter has given a good reason for the low level. The experimenter has explained that the participant in an economic game (UBG; Nelissen et al. 2011) receives 90 percent of the resource when the recipient refuses the offer. This information reduces the fear of rejection but increases feelings of guilt. In my view, in a situation in which an actor has to divide a sum of money he/she hovers between fear and guilt. Fear of rejection is often stronger than guilt feelings; the tendency to offer self more and the other less is stronger than the reverse tendency. But viewing self as an unjust person is a threatening experience as well, and ends in making justifications for offering self more while still being evaluated as a just person. To tap the effects of justification in the Nelissen et al. (2011) experiment is to inform the participant that he/she will receive 50 percent of the resource if the recipient refuses the offer. Knowing that the recipient refuses an offer when the actor offers the recipient less than 40 percent of the resource, the actor has some leeway to offer the recipient between 40 and 60 percent. Offering the recipient 40 percent satisfies the actor's egoistic tendency to a moderately high level, and also keeps feelings of guilt at a moderate level: the actor feels moderate fear as well as moderate guilt. To let the balance sway in a direction more appropriate for the actor, the actor uses reasons for the allocation decision. For instance, the actor may come up with the idea that he/she has the responsibility for the division of the resource and thus deserves more than the recipient, who "only" has to sit and wait for the decision to be taken.

My assumption is that under no-fear allocation conditions, the moral emotions exert a stronger effect on the amygdala's operation than the self-preservation emotions. The drive to pursue happiness (and reduce fear) and to allocate unfairly decreases feelings of pride or compassion and increases feelings of shame. Negative emotions result often in stress.

### *Stress*

Demands from the environment, as exemplified in the reward strategies of parents and other tutors, leave traces in relevant brain areas and may conflict with each other in new allocation events. The conflict between fear of loss of happiness and fear of loss of pride is a stressor and may cause stress (Vermunt et al. 2007; see also Chapter 8 of this volume). It results in elevated heart rate and blood pressure and produces these effects with minimal motor demands and maximal mental effort. Several authors describe the complex psycho-physiological processes as follows—for a more detailed discussion of the HPA system, see Dickerson and Kemeny (2004), or Lovallo and Thomas (2000). The hypothalamic-pituitary-adrenal (HPA) axis is a complex set of direct influences and feedback interactions between the hypothalamus, the pituitary gland (a pea-shaped structure located below the hypothalamus), and the adrenal (or suprarenal) glands (small, conical organs on top of the kidneys). The interactions between these organs constitute the HPA axis, a major part of the neuroendocrine system that controls reactions to stress and regulates many body processes. Anatomical connections between brain areas such as the amygdala, hippocampus, and hypothalamus facilitate activation of the HPA axis. Sensory information arriving at the lateral aspect of the amygdala is processed and conveyed to the central nucleus, which projects to several parts of the brain involved in responses to fear. At the hypothalamus, fear-signaling impulses activate both the sympathetic nervous system and the modulating systems of the HPA axis. Activation of this neuroendocrine system by stress or fear-induced activity in the amygdala causes the release of various neurotransmitters and neurohormones—dopamine (DA), norepinephrine (NE), glucocorticoids—in large parts of the brain where they strongly modulate the ongoing neural activity and affect thinking and behavior. This system has an important survival function, alerting brain and body of danger and possible action, but high levels of DA and NE may impair higher cognitive and executive functions in the prefrontal cortex (e.g., Shansky and Lipps 2013).

Psychological stress starts with events initiated by the cerebral cortex, where input is evaluated. Experience of being treated unfairly (see Vermunt et al. 2007) or treating others unfairly results in psychological stress. Full percepts are established in the prefrontal cortex. The next phase in the process of psychological stress is linking the percept to bodily responses that result from the emotional coloring of the evaluative process, taking place in the amygdala, a structure that is necessary for the formation of aversive associations. The cortical-amygdaloid circuit is a critical link in the initiation of emotionally based evaluations of events. It is also possible that the hypocampus plays a role in this process. According to Lovallo and Thomas (2000), the next step in connecting events to physiological responses is mediated by the hypothalamus. The hypothalamus modulates the reticular formation that coordinates the activities of the vital organs, like heart and lungs. The hypothalamus achieves these coordinated tasks by releasing corticotropin releasing factor (CRF) into the appropriate parts of the pituitary gland, causing the release of adrenocorticotropin hormone (ACTH) and β-endorphin into general circulation. ACTH is transported to the adrenal glands (above the kidneys) where it leads to the secretion of cortisol (Lovallo and Thomas 2000). In the event that justifications are perceived as effective by the actor, the stress response is reduced and the conflict will be viewed as a challenge. Stress level will increase when the justifications turn out not to be effective.

### *Justifications*

Children learn to strive for self-preservation (self-enhancement) as well as for integrity or fairness. If parents stress integrity but children have pursued self-enhancement in a certain allocation event they may try to convince their parents that the decision was right by telling them the reasons for it. A positive response from the parents to the given reasons for the decision strengthens the relationship between emotion pathways and cognition pathways. The child may repeat the reasons in a future event, so that they become part of the cognitive repertory. The reward for actors (children) in the use of reasons for taking a certain allocation decision is that their behavioral repertory becomes more extended and adaptation to events more effective. After all, in times in which pursuing individual self-enhancement is raised to the highest goal in life, confining oneself too rigidly to moral values may be self-destructive. An effective use of reasons or justifications helps an actor to pursue moral values as well as pursuing self-enhancement. Reasons or justifications are amply used for this goal, and society has, over the course of time, provided individuals with a sufficient number of justifications (see Chapter 2). These activities are not primarily intended to deceive others but to preserve an actor's moral integrity.

*Justification content*

When cultural influences exert a strong force on the attainment of happiness, fear of loss of happiness may compete with the fear of loss of pride (respect). Individuals are driven to satisfy their happiness as well as their pride, and thus have to find a solution which does satisfy both. Happiness as well as pride, or avoiding fear as well as avoiding guilt or shame, can be attained when the cognitive content that has been connected to the emotional state(s) can be retrieved directly. The appropriate cognitive content has been learned but has to be checked in this specific context with regard to its acceptance by others. Normally, when justifications are used that have been provided by the community, they are accepted and thus can be used effectively. Other justifications may be subject to changes due to societal and cultural developments. As described in Chapter 2, being rewarded for the amount of effort a person has invested, and not for status as had been the normal practice, was introduced during the period of the Industrial Revolution and the ideological reaction to it. In the beginning, this type of reward was not generally accepted, but struggle, negotiations, and protest culminated in the gradual acceptance of an equitable payment. The general acceptance of it made the application in terms of a justification in comparable circumstances possible.

The content of justifications can be differentiated according to the target that is involved in the allocation event. The target can be: (i) the position of the actor (e.g., "I deserve it"); (ii) the position of the recipient (e.g., "He has no right to complain"); and/or (iii) the relationship between the actor and the recipient (e.g., "I worked harder than he did"; "I worked as hard as she did").

Justifications used by an actor are subject to cognitive distortions (see Adams 1965. An actor may have the strong belief that they worked harder than the recipient and therefore claims a higher reward. Consequently, the actor allocates more to self than to the recipient. But the recipient may think otherwise and a stalemate arises that has to be solved, for instance, by calling in a third party (observer).

*Justification and emotion*

The crucial theoretical question for the egoism–justice-difference hypothesis is whether the use of justification will alter the balance between the felt emotions fear and guilt. Let us assume that an actor is given the opportunity to think or ruminate about justifications, or is not given the opportunity. The first condition—thinking about justifications—is one that seems automatically to take place. Participants easily come up with a justification about the difference between their own role and the recipient's role in the game (see Van Dijk and Vermunt 2000). In order to examine the effects of justification on felt emotions it is necessary to curb the "automatic" emergence of justifications. A way to accomplish restriction of the emergence of justifications is to enhance competing cognitive activity and thus to keep the brain busy. Increasing the cognitive load hampers cognitive activity in adjacent brain centers and thus may curb the emergence of justifications. Cognitive load can be increased in different ways. Skitka et al. (2002) created a 60-minute tape of synthesized flute tones at varying pitches. Each pitch was assigned a random number of repetitions from two to eight, and the order of pitches was similarly determined using a random number generator. A tone sounded on the tape every five seconds. Cognitive load was manipulated by having participants track the number of tones that sounded before a pitch change (the high-cognitive-load condition) versus not doing the tracking task (the low-cognitive-load condition; Skitka et al. 2002).

An experiment to investigate the effects of justification on resource allocation emotion could be set up as follows. The participant plays a Dictator Game in which the actor makes an offer. The rule of the game is that the recipient can only accept the offer; the recipient is not allowed to refuse the offer. As indicated before, offers made to the recipient of between 40 and 60 percent will in almost all cases be accepted. We ask the actor to allocate in such a way that he will receive 80 percent and the recipient 20 percent (high result), or reversed, with 20 percent for the actor and 80 percent for the recipient (low result). That is, even in a DG, the offer is unfair: unfair for the recipient or, respectively, for the actor. So, in fact, the actor has initial ownership of the sum of money, but is asked to allocate far more to the recipient versus far less to the recipient. In the low result condition it is reasonable to assume that the actor fears loss of money, while in the high result condition the actor will feel guilty. During the short process of the actor's rumination on the decision to take, the actor will attempt to find a justification for the decision. The most plausible justification is that the actor will feel excused for the behavior because the experimenter is forcing the actor to make the decision. By justifying, the actor will feel only a little fear of loss as well as a little guilt. How short the rumination period is affects whether the actor is able cognitively to come up with this justification. What will happen if the actor is not able, or is less able, to produce the justification? With regard to the emotions, the justification is less able to dampen fear and guilt, resulting in higher activation of both emotions. To restrict the justification activity, the actor will be given an additional task during the decision-making period. In the restricted justification condition, the actor hears a 60-minute tape of synthesized flute tones at varying pitches (Skitka et al. 2002). In the high-cognitive-load condition the participants are asked to track the number of tones that sound before a pitch change, while in the low-cognitive-load condition the participants only listen to the tones and do not perform the tracking task.

Above, I have designed a 2 (Result: high versus low) × 2 (Cognitive-load: high versus low) experiment with fear and guilt as the emotions to assess. I predict that fear and guilt will be experienced more when the participant is too cognitively restricted to come up with justifications. To test this hypothesis, the setting will be one in which the participants have electrodes on their head to assess brain activity, as well as electrodes to assess additional activities like heart rate, blood pressure, and so forth. The physiological measurements can bring more clarity into the regions involved in the cognitive and emotional operation of brain networks. The peripheral assessment of the emotions is carried out by looking at the differential effects on the additional system when fear and guilt are activated. In this way, the hypothesis that hindering the justification process produces more feelings of guilt (or fear) than not hindering it can be tested.

Assessing the central nervous system as well as peripheral nervous system activation is planned in order to infer conclusions about cognitive and emotional processes with more certainty than applying only one of the two kinds of assessment. The problem is that using additional assessment together with fMRI is not feasible because the magnetic forces of the fMRI apparatus disrupt assessment of additional activity by electrodes. My solution is to use a cap with fixed electrodes instead of fMRI. Interpretation of data based on only one type of assessment has the drawback that cognitive activities cannot be distinguished from each other. For instance, Greene and Paxton (2009) showed that neural activity associated with honest and dishonest moral decisions covered the same brain area in an fMRI picture. With assessment of peripheral nervous system activity (for instance, shame assessment), fMRI assessment data could be complemented.

### *Attempts to Convince Others: Persuasive Communication*

The more an actor attempts to justify an allocation decision the more it can be viewed as indication of a conflict between allocation motives, and the more the actor will try to convince others of the justice of the allocation decision. Convincing others is part of persuasive communication. Persuasion is the process of guiding people toward the adoption of an idea, attitude, or action by rational, heuristic, and symbolic (though not only logical) means. It is a problem-solving strategy, and relies on "appeals" rather than force. In terms of allocation behavior, persuasion can be viewed as allocation of information to recipient(s) and observers. Information can refer to the content of the message or to the person who communicates the message (actor). An emphasis on content presupposes that the recipient or observer process the information intensively. Recipient and observer are motivated to weigh the arguments in favor or against a certain stance and base their attitudes on it. An emphasis on the actor presupposes that the recipient and observer process the information peripherally and arrive at a certain attitude or position based on the perceived favorability of the sender. In other words, allocate information content to recipients and observers whom one assumes will process information centrally, and allocate information to recipients and observers whom one assumes process information peripherally. For instance, when recipients and observers view the information as threatening it may be more effective for acceptance of the message to emphasize the vulnerable position of the actor. For other recipients and observers it might be more effective for attitude change to emphasize the content of the message.

If the actor does not succeed in convincing self, recipient, and/or observers, the actor may experience stress, because the demands from the environment ("your behavior is unfair") surpass the actor's own fairness evaluation of the behavior.

## Detection of the Operation of the Justice Motive

Assuming the salience of the justice motive in allocation decisions, a conflict may arise when this motive concurs with the egoistic or altruistic motivation. As described in the previous section, an actor uses justifications when he fails to provide a just allocation. The use of justifications reduces stress and makes the allocation acceptable. If an actor is asked whether the allocation was just he/she will answer "yes." However, for an observer it is often quite clear that the allocation decision was unfair and resulted in an unequal division of resources. How is the observer able to get behind the intricate processes that led to this answer? People will agree and say that justice is in the eye of the beholder, and that the actor thinks differently about it than the observer. Is it not possible, then, that actor and observer can come to terms about the fairness of the allocation decision? Yes, I think that this is possible and that physiological assessments play a crucial role in it. In the short time that an actor decides to deviate from a fair allocation—a prosocial decides to deflect the actor experiences distress which is traceable in the central and peripheral nervous system. Justifications reduce the distress. However, the short struggle between motivations and the approach/avoidance of positive, respectively negative, emotions is detectable by physiological measures.

The operation of the peripheral nervous system in human beings has its counterpart in sub-cortical, particularly limbic structures (Bradley 2000). The parasympathetic and sympathetic branches of the autonomic nervous system are important in the study of motivation. The branches have a different anatomy and functionality. The sympathetic nervous system has postganglionic fibers, which are quite lengthy and which branch and divide as they make their way to specific target organs: a single sympathetic fiber activates a number of different effectors enabling the body to make a cascade of responses: heart rate, blood pressure, electrodermal reactions, increase in respiration rate and depth. The postganglionic fibers in the parasympathetic branch are short and target a specific effector. The biphasic model of emotion mentioned earlier can also be applied to the operation and functioning of the sympathetic and parasympathetic branches of the autonomic nervous system. The systems can be independently active, reciprocally controlled, or co-active (Bradley 2000). Bradley, therefore, proposes independent measures of both the operation of the sympathetic as well as the parasympathetic autonomic systems. For instance, the effect of sympathetic stimulation of the heart results in increased heart rate and increases the force of contraction, while parasympathetic stimulation results in decreased heart rate and force of contraction. Eye pupils dilate with sympathetic stimulation and constrict with parasympathetic stimulation (see Bradley 2000).

The conflict between motivational states initiates one or more emotions. For instance, actors motivated to satisfy the egoistic motive by keeping all for themselves may experience fear of revenge or retaliation, or may become angry because they feel constrained to act in this way. Or actors may become embarrassed or ashamed when realizing that they keep all for themselves and leave little or nothing for others. Or actors may become anxious when realizing that the separation between them and others has become too wide as a consequence of their allocation decision. Combinations of emotions are also possible, for example actors who feel angry but also anxious: actors who would like to take all for themselves but feel restricted by the justice motive, and become angry. By carrying out the decision, actors become less angry but will keep their level of anxiety.

A conflict between the altruistic motive and the justice motive may arise as well. This conflict will not have the intensity of the egoistic/justice conflict, but will still result in an emotional state of some kind. It is said that deciding altruistically brings with it a state of positive emotion (see, e.g., Batson et al. 1997. However, in my view it will produce a negative emotion when it collides with the justice motive. An actor may feel depressed or sad when realizing that his/her own welfare or well-being is to be sacrificed to help other.

The peripheral nervous system, and also the central nervous system, has connections with the affective network. It is generally accepted that the dorso-lateral prefrontal cortex (DLPFC), the orbitofrontal cortex, the amygdala (with STS, IPL), and the cortex cingularis anterior are part of the affective network. The amygdala plays an important role in the mediation and control of major affective activities like friendship, love, and affection, on the expression of mood, and, mainly, on fear, rage, and aggression. The amygdala, being the center for identification of danger, is fundamental for self-preservation. When triggered, it gives rise to fear and anxiety, bringing the animal into a state of alertness, getting ready for fight or flight (Amaral et al. 1992). Humans with marked lesions of the amygdala lose the affective meaning of the perception of outside information, like the sight of a well-known person. The subject knows, exactly, who the person is, but is not capable of deciding whether he or she likes or dislikes the person. The amygdala has connections with the orbitofrontal cortex, which plays a role in the expression of emotions (see Krolak-Salmon et al. 2004; Rolls 2004). Berlin et al. (2005) showed that people with lesions in the orbitofrontal cortex had higher levels of anger compared to healthy people. The orbitofrontal cortex has pathways to the amygdala, of which the central nucleus controls cardiovascular responses like heart rate and blood pressure, and respiration. The amygdala and other cortex structures send signals to the peripheral nervous system through the HPA axis, as described previously.

For several emotions, the following describes the operation of the peripheral nervous system as well as the central nervous system. In a review article, Kreibig (2010) described the emotional effects on physiological responses in the additional nervous system in 134 publications. Assessment of these emotions during the allocation decision process unveils something of the struggle between operation of the justice motive and egoistic and altruistic motivations.

### *The Negative Self-preservation and Moral Emotions*

#### *Fear (a negative self-preservation emotion)*

Fear of retaliation by the recipient induced by egoistic allocation may reach moderate to high levels. In general, fear is induced in the laboratory by showing participants a film, or sound, by personalized recall, or by manipulating real-life events. The fear levels in these conditions are lower than for phobias, in which fear may become extremely high. Studies show broad sympathetic activation such as cardiac acceleration, vasoconstriction, and increased electrodermal activity (increased skin conductance response) (Kreibig 2010: 404).

#### *Anger (a negative self-preservation emotion)*

Autonomic nervous system (ANS) reactions to anger differ whether the anger is directed at another or at oneself. I assume that the conflict between egoism and a justice-motivated decision is directed at self, and is labeled by Kriebig as "anger in." The self-directed anger results in increased heart rate, stroke volume, and cardiac output. (In cardiovascular physiology, stroke volume (SV) is the volume of blood pumped from one ventricle of the heart with each beat. SV is calculated using measurements of ventricle volumes from an echocardiogram and subtracting the volume of blood in the ventricle at the end of a beat—called end-systolic volume—from the volume of blood just prior to the beat—called end-diastolic volume. The term stroke volume can apply to each of the two ventricles of the heart, although it usually refers to the left ventricle. The stroke volumes for each ventricle are generally equal, both being approximately 70 ml in a healthy 70 kg man.) One must, however, keep in mind that in the studies reviewed anger is generated by voluntary subjects watching a film or being harassed by the experimenter. These situations are different from ones in which the actor has to divide a resource between self and other. But the resulting anger elicits the above-mentioned peripheral nervous system activities. If the cascade of additional nervous system activities can be demonstrated in a study in which an actor has to divide a resource, we may cautiously infer that a conflict between motives stands at the basis of the physiological response. If "anger in" is the result of the conflict of the operation of the egoistic and justice motive, anger may arise, as assessed by increased heart rate, stroke volume, and cardiac output with unchanged diastolic and systolic blood pressure and decreased total additional resistance pattern.

*Shame or guilt (a negative moral emotion)*
The conflict between motives may also result in other emotions, specifically shame. It is certainly conceivable that an unjust allocation creates a larger psychological distance between actor and recipient. And that the actor feels embarrassed by it. Tumbull (2003), for instance, states that when actors evaluate their behavior as unacceptable or as less acceptable they may experience a higher or lower degree of traumatization at the interpersonal level that may cause stress.

Studies inducing shame report increased heart rate, accompanied by decreased pre-ejection period, and increased total peripheral resistance, increased systolic blood pressure and diastolic blood pressure, decreased heart rate variability, and increased skin conductance level. At the central level, the orbitofrontal cortex operates when decisions have to be made and supports behavior that is potentially rewarding from behavior that is potentially punishing. For instance, patients with orbitofrontal damage are not embarrassed by their inappropriate behavior and actually report increased pride after behaving inappropriately (Beer et al. 2006).

*Sadness (a negative self-preservation emotion)*
Sadness is often associated with the experience of loss or the anticipation of a loss. For instance, observing a film in which someone experiences the loss of a dear person elicits reactions of sadness. In an allocation event in which an actor offers everything to another a sense of loss may arise, although the positive emotion (pride, happiness) of helping the other may arise as well. The feelings of sadness will be smaller than the feelings of happiness for the other. It is not fear of loss in this case. Sadness reveals a pattern of sympathetic–parasympathetic co-activation. Cry-sadness is differentiated in the literature from non-cry-sadness. Non-cry-sadness, which I associate most with feelings of loss in an allocation event, is characterized by a general withdrawal of sympathetic activity (e.g., no increased heart rate, no sweating). What distinguishes sadness from other emotions is the decrease in electrodermal activity in almost all of the studies.

*The Positive Self-preservation and Moral Emotions*

*Pride (a positive moral emotion)*
Laboratory induction of pride has used film clips, personalized recall, or real-life manipulations of experimenter praise. These studies report decreased heart rate and unchanged heart rate variability (normal sinus respiration rate interval difference), increased skin conductance level, and a small increase in heart rate together with unchanged pre-injection period, cardiac output, and total peripheral resistance (Kreibig 2010: 407). Because of the small number of studies focusing on pride, these results must be treated with caution.

*Happiness (a self-preservation positive emotion)*
The autonomic response pattern of happiness is characterized by increased cardiac activity due to vagal withdrawal, vasodilation, increased electrodermal activity, and increased respiratory activity. This response pattern points to a differentiated sympathetic activation state of decreased α- and β-adrenergically mediated influences, while at the same time cholinergically mediated effects are increased. Happiness shares with various negative emotions a central cardiac activation component due to vagal withdrawal, whereas it is distinguished from these by additional vasodilation (Kriebig 2010: 406).

*Contentment (a self-preservation positive emotion)*
Studies on psychophysiological effects of contentment or pleasure have particularly relied on film clips displaying nature scenes, standardized imagery (e.g., wood fire, book reading, soft music) or personalized recall. Taken together, decreased cardiovascular, respiratory, and electrodermal activation is suggestive of decreased α-, β-adrenergically, and cholinergically mediated sympathetic activation and mild cardiac vagal activation. Compared to the physiological response to amusement, the physiological response to contentment appears to have a stronger sympathetically deactivating component, whereas both share cardiac vagal activation (Kriebig 2010: 406).

### *The Reality of Economic Dilemmas*

The egoism–justice-competition and altruism–justice-competition hypotheses both claim that human beings are driven by justice emotions and considerations, and that these emotions and considerations have to compete with obsolete emotions and considerations of egoism and altruism. Although these hypotheses will not be tested in this book, there are less rigorous ways of testing, such as showing the plausibility of the hypotheses. A hypothesis is said to be plausible if the hypothesis is able (1) to explain existing data and eventual contradictions in them, and (2) to conduct a realistic experiment that in the future may be carried out.

To work out the first criterion I will review some data derived from studies on economic games. Economic games like the Ultimatum Bargaining Game (UBG) and Dictator Game (DG) have been developed to find out how and in what conditions individuals divide money or other commodities between self and recipient (see also Chapter 2). In addition, economic games are used to describe and test an individual's motivation to cooperate or not, as in the prisoners' dilemma games (see also Mellers et al. 2010).

In a UBG, an actor is asked to divide a sum of money between self and a recipient. When the recipient accepts the offer, the money is divided accordingly. Economists predict that in a UBG the actor will offer the recipient the smallest amount of the commodity. This reasoning is derived from the assumption that if the recipient refuses the offer they (as well as the actor) will receive nothing. And, so reason economists, a little bit of a commodity is always better than nothing, so the recipient will accept the actor's offer. Findings from numerous studies focused on UBG have demonstrated that these assumptions do not work. Recipients refuse offers that in their eyes are not acceptable. The question I would like to raise is how actors divide money in economic games. Do they allocate money or other commodities according to strictly economic assumptions? The answer is that most of the actors do not allocate money according to economic principles of self interest. Most individuals allocate money in such a way that the recipient is offered about 40 percent of the money and the actor keeps about 60 percent of it. Of course, there are outliers who allocate very small amounts to the recipient, but also outliers who give more than they keep for themselves.

It is interesting to look at the frequencies of different amounts of money that are offered. In a study by Van Dijk and Vermunt (2000) on UBG and DG, actors divided money and in the UBG most offers are in the 50–54 category, indicating that they tend to allocate rather equally. However, not all offers are in the 50–54 category: One actor scored in the 20–24 category, indicating that this actor offered only 20 percent of the money to the recipient, while one actor offered 80 percent of the money to the recipient. Very remarkable is the difference between the symmetric and asymmetric information conditions. In the symmetric information condition, the actor has been told that the total number of chips (each chip representing a value of 10 cents) to be allocated is known to the recipient. In the asymmetric condition, the actor is informed that the recipient does not know whether the number of chips is 100 or 60. So, if the actor offers 30 chips to the recipient and the recipient thinks that 60 chips is the total number to be allocated, the recipient evaluates 30 chips as fair, but it is not fair because the actor has 100 chips to allocate, and thus keeps 70. But even in the asymmetric information condition, 12 actors offered 50 chips.

Opponents of the fair allocation hypothesis interpret these findings differently. They view these data as supporting the self-interest hypothesis: Only 12 actors in the asymmetric information condition as compared to 16 actors in the symmetric information condition allocated the chips evenly. Moreover, seven actors in the asymmetric information condition as compared to no actors in the symmetric information condition allocated 30 chips. In other words, actors in the asymmetric information condition make use of the recipient's ignorance about the total number of chips to serve self-interest: The actors act unfairly in this condition but appear to be fair. This is an interesting issue. Why would an actor be motivated to appear fair? Why not be motivated to appear efficient? Appearing fair is the expression in these circumstances of the urge to do justice, moderated by the drive to be good to self. In other words, actors are driven by fairness considerations to be fair or to appear fair.

Even more compelling conclusions about justice motivation can be derived from the results of participants' allocation behavior in the Dictator game (DG). As will be remembered, in the DG, the actor need not worry about the recipient's reaction to the offer, in that the recipient can only accept it. Fear of retaliation in DG is absent, in contrast to UBG. Although in DG most offers are in the vicinity of the 50 percent category, actors offer less than in UBG. Economists explain these differences in terms of the self-interest motivation of the actors. But is that all that there is to say about allocation behavior in DG? The difference between a DG and a UBG can be described in terms of the dependency relationship in each game. In a DG, the recipient is more dependent on the actor with regard to the offer than in a UBG. That opens an avenue of possibilities for the actor to reward himself or herself, but it also increases his responsibility to the recipient. And this responsibility is an indication of the actor's concern about the recipient's position. This concern can best be shown by making the recipient even more dependent on actor. In the second experiment of the Van Dijk and Vermunt (2000) study, the authors accomplished the increased dependency, and thus the actor's concern, by inducing the recipient's ignorance about the total number of chips to be divided: the actor is informed that the recipient is ignorant about the total number of chips to be divided, 60 or 100. As compared with the recipient's knowledge about the number of chips to be divided (100), the ignorant recipient in the DG is greatly dependent on the actor's allocation decision. The results show that actors do take care of the recipient in this dependent situation and allocate relatively large numbers of chips to the recipient: the overwhelming majority of actors offer the recipient a fifty–fifty division of chips in the symmetric as well as in the asymmetric conditions. The actors did not misuse their favorable position towards the recipient to allocate more chips to themselves than to the other. These data show once more the operation of the justice motive.

## Conclusions

This Chapter has described and explained the psychology of allocation behavior. Individuals allocating resources experience a dilemma between doing good to self and doing good to another. The solution proposed is that individuals try to balance the two motives, resulting in a fair allocation of resources. Egoism and altruism are conceived as two extremes in a two-dimensional area in which the medium position is taken by justice considerations. Allocation behavior is a battlefield between the operation of the egoistic and justice tendencies and altruistic and justice tendencies. The problematic issue of what a motivation is, is solved by looking at motivation as a drive to acquire a positive emotion or to avoid a negative emotion. The emotion is either a self-preservation emotion related to own happiness or a moral emotion related to others' needs. Cognition and emotion play a crucial role in allocation behavior: cognition can compensate for the negative effects when a positive moral emotion is not easily acquired through the operation or activation of a positive self-preservation emotion. For instance, actors will become proud by offering a recipient a needed gift, but their feelings of contentment in spending the money for their own satisfaction is stronger. To still feel proud of themselves, actors justify their behavior by reminding of the last time they made a gift. Cognition can also compensate for the negative effects in the case where avoiding a negative moral emotion interferes with avoiding a negative self-preservation emotion. For instance, actors will not feel guilty about withholding a gift to a needy recipient, but their fear of loss of money is stronger. To avoid feelings of guilt, actors justify themselves by trivializing the recipient's needy position.

I have propagated and defended the view that in most situations of modern and relatively safe life the urge for self-preservation is reduced. This does not mean that self-preservation has no role in daily life, but its value is often exaggerated. The extreme form of self-preservation—the propagation of becoming rich or living a life directed at satisfying the senses—is obsolete in modern society. Many parents, however, raise their children to live a life that is directed at fulfilling the senses, resulting in a world or society in which fulfilling the senses is the highest good. Activating moral emotions is, in this picture, emphasized to a lesser extent. Does this mean that people only try to satisfy their self-preservation motives? Yes, but it does not mean that people offer less to others. It means only that gifts are offered not per se to satisfy positive moral emotions but also to satisfy positive self-preservation emotions. It feels good to offer gifts to needy people if that is accompanied by TV shows and other huge public media spectacles. Is that a bad thing? No, but in daily life many allocation events are not accompanied by mass spectacles, satisfaction of self-preservation emotions is absent, and the question is how people will decide in those kinds of situations. Then the presence of a moral compass is necessary. But this compass is not well developed.

In the course of human history, the forebears of primates evolved into hominins, and hominins evolved into *Homo*. An important feature of this evolution is the gradual development of moral emotions, that is, that hominins learned to punish free-riders and to take care of others who were not direct kin. This transition left traces in the evolving brain. It created networks in which moral emotions were encapsulated. This phylogenetically evolved network, however, should be enhanced ontogenetically in each human being by training.

## References

Adams, J.S. 1965. Inequity in social exchange, in *Advances in Experimental Social Psychology*, edited by Berkowitz, L. New York: Academic Press, 267–99.

Allman, J.M., Watson, K.K., Tetreault, N.A., and Hakeem, A.Y. 2005. Intuition and autism: A possible role of Von Economo neurons. *Trends in Cognitive Sciences*, 9, 367–73.

Amaral, D.G., Price, J.L., Pitkanen, A., and Carmichael, S.T. 1992. Anatomical Organization of the Primate Amygdaloid Complex, in *The Amygdala: Neurobiological Aspects of Emotion, Memory, and Mental Dysfunction*, edited by J.P. Aggleton. New York: Wiley-Liss, 1–66.

Batson, C.D., and Thompson, E.R. 2001. Why don't moral people act morally? Motivational considerations. *Current Directions in Psychological Science*, 10, 54–7.

Batson, C.D., Kobrynowicz, D., Dinnerstein, J.L., Kampf, H.C., and Wilson, A.D. 1997. In a very different voice: Unmasking moral hypocrisy. *Journal of Personality and Social Psychology*, 72, 1335–48.

Batson, C.D., Thompson, E.R., Seuferling, G., Whitney, H., and Strongman, J. 1999. Moral hypocrisy: Appearing moral to oneself without being so. *Journal of Personality and Social Psychology*, 77, 525–37.

Bechara, A., Damasio, H., and Damasio, A.R. 2000. Emotion, decision making and the orbitofrontal cortex. *Cerebral Cortex*, 10, 295–307.

Beer, J.S., John, O.P., Scabini, D., and Knight, R.T. 2006. Orbitofrontal cortex, and social behavior: Integrating self-monitoring and emotion-cognition interactions. *Journal of Cognitive Neuroscience*, 18, 6, 871–9.

Berlin, H.E., Rolls, E.T, and Iversen, S.D. 2005. Borderline personality disorder, impulsivity, and orbital frontal cortex. *American Journal of Psychiatry*, 162, 2360–73.

Bower, G.H. 1981. Mood and memory. *American Psychologist*, 36, 129–48.

Bradley, M.M. 2000. Emotion and Motivation, in *Handbook of Psychophysiology*, 2nd edn, edited by J.T. Cacioppo, L.G. Tassinary, and G.G. Berentson. Cambridge: Cambridge University Press, 602–42.

Cacioppo, J.J., and Berntson, G.G. 1994. Relationships between attitudes and evaluative space: A critical review, with emphasis on the separability of positive and negative substrates. *Psychological Bulletin*, 115, 401–23.

Cropanzano, R., Stein, J.H., and Nadisic, Th. 2011. *Social Justice and the Experience of Emotion*. New York: Routledge.

Dickerson, S., and Kemeny, M. 2004. Acute stressors and cortisol responses: A theoretical integration and synthesis of laboratory research. *Psychological Bulletin*, 130, 3, 355–91.

Emonds, G., Declerck, C., Boone, Ch., Vandervliet, E., and Parizel, P. 2011. Comparing the neural basis of decision making in social dilemmas of people with different social value orientations, a fMRI study. *Journal of Neuroscience, Psychology, and Economics*, 4, 11–24.

Gharemani, D.G., and Poldrack, R.A. 2009. Neuroimaging and Interactive Memory Systems, in *Neuroimaging of Human Memory: Linking Cognitive Processes to Neural Systems*, edited by F. Rösler, Ch. Ranganat, B. Röder, and R. Kluwe. Oxford: Oxford University Press, 77–89.

Greene, J.D., and Paxton, J.M. 2009. Patterns of neural activity associated with honest and dishonest moral decisions. *Proceedings of the National Academy of Sciences*, 106(30), 12506–11.

Hauser, M. 2009. *Evolving a moral instinct*. Leiden University: Tnbergen Lecture.

Hermann, E., Call, J., Hernandez-Lloreda, M.V., Hare, B., and Tomasello, M. 2007. Humans have evolved specialized skills of social cognition: The cultural intelligence hypothesis. *Science*, 317, 1360–66.

Hobbes, Th. 1985. *Leviathan*. (Edited by C. Macpherson). London: Pinguin.

Kidder, L., and Muller, S. 1991. What is "fair"in Japan, in *Social Justice in Human Relations, Volume 2*, edited by Steensma, H., and Vermunt, R. New York: Plenum Press, 139–54.

Knoch, D., Pascual-Leone, A., Meyer, K., Treyer, V., and Fehr, E. 2006. Diminishing reciprocal fairness by disrupting the right prefrontal cortex. *Science*, 314(5800), 829–32.

Kreibig, S.D. 2010. Autonomic nervous system activity in emotion: A review. *Biological Psychology*, 84(3), 394–421.

Krolak-Salmon, P., Hénaff, A.-M., Vighetto, A., Bertrand, O., and Mauguière, F. 2004. Early amygdala reaction to fear spreading in occipital, temporal, and frontal cortex. *Neuron*, 42, 4, 665–76.

Labar, K.S. 2009. Imaging Emotional Influences on Learning and Memory, in *Neuroimaging of Human Memory: Linking Cognitive Processes to Neural Systems*, edited by F. Rösler, Ch. Ranganat, B. Röder, and R. Kluwe. Oxford: Oxford University Press, 331–48.

Lerner, M. 1980. *The belief in a just world: A fundamental delusion*. New York: Plenum Press.

Lovallo, W., and Thomas, T. 2000. Stress hormonoes in psychophysiological research: Emotional, behavioral, and cognitive implications, in Handbook of Psychophysiology, edited Cacioppo, J., Tassinary, L., and Berntson, G. Cambridge: Cambridge University Press, 342–67.

Mellers, B.A., Haselhuhn, M., Tetlock, P., Silva, J., and Isen, A. 2010. Predicting behavior in economic games by looking through the eyes of the players. *Journal of Experimental Psychology: General*, 139, 743–55.

Nietsche, F.W. 2003. *The Genealogy of Morals*. (Translated by H.B. Samuel). New York: Courier Dover Publications.

Nelissen, R.M.A., Leliveld, M.C., Van Dijk, E., and Zeelenberg, M. 2011. Fear and guilt in proposers: Using emotions to explain offers in ultimatum bargaining. *European Journal of Social Psychology*, 41, 1, 78–85.

O'Doherty, J. 2009. Reinforcement Learning Mechanisms in the Human Brain: Insights from Model-Based fMRI, in *Neuroimaging of Human Memory: Linking Cognitive Processes to Neural Systems*, edited by F. Rösler, Ch. Ranganat, B. Röder, and R. Kluwe. Oxford: Oxford University Press, 45–65.

O'Doherty, J., Dayan, P., Friston, K., Critchley, H., and Dolan, R.J. 2003. Temporal difference models and reward-related learning in the human brain. *Neuron*, 38, 329–37.

Rolls, E.T. 2004. The functions of the orbitofrontal cortex. *Brain and Cognition*, 55, 11–29.

Scholl, B.J. 2007. Object persistency in philosophy and psychology. *Mind and Language*, 22(5), 563–91.

Schultz, W. 1998. Predictive reward signal of dopamine neurons. *Journal of Neurophysiology*, 80, 1–27.

Shalvi, S., Dana, J., Handgraaf, M.J.J., and De Dreu, C.K.W. 2011. Justified ethicality: Observing desired counterfactuals modifies ethical perceptions and behavior. *Organizational Behavior and Human Decision Processes*, 115, 181–90.

Shansky R.M. and Lipps, J 2013. Stress induced cognitive dysfunction: Hormone–neurotransmitter interactions in the prefrontal cortex. *Frontiers in Human Neuroscience*, 7, 1–6.

Skitka, L.J., Mullen, E., Griffin, TH., Hutchinson, S., and Chamberlain, B. 2002. Dispositions, scripts, or motivated correction: Understanding ideological differences in explanations for social problems. *Journal of Personality and Social Psychology*, 83, 2, 470–87.

Smith, A.P.R., Henson, R.N.A., Dolan, R.J., and Rugg, M.D. 2004. fMRI correlates of the episodic retrieval of emotional contexts. *NeuroImage*, 22, 868–78.

Taylor, A.E. 1938. The ethical doctrine of Hobbes. *Philosophy*, 13(52), 406–24.

Tumbull, D. 2003. Shame, an acute stress response to interpersonal traumatization. *Psychiatry*, 66(1), 53–64.

Tversky, A., and Kahneman, D. 1991. Loss aversion in riskless choice: A reference dependent model. *Quarterly Journal of Economics*, 106, 1039–61.

Van Dijk, E., de Kwaadsteniet, E.W., and Koning, L. 2012. About Behaving (Un)Ethically: Self-Interest, Deception and Fairness, in *Behavioral Business Ethics*, edited by D.D. de Cremer and A.E. Tenbrunsel. New York: Routledge, 105–23.

Van Dijk, E., and Vermunt, R. 2000. Sometimes it pays to be powerless: Strategy and fairness in social decision making. *Journal of Experimental Social Psychology*, 36, 1–25.

Van Lange, P.A.M. 2000. Beyond Self-Interest: A Set of Propositions Relevant to Interpersonal Orientations, in *European Review of Social Psychology*, edited by W. Stroebe, and M. Hewstone. New York: Wiley, 297–331.

Vermunt, R., Peeters, Y., and Berggren, K. 2007. How fair treatment affects saliva cortisol release in stressed low and high type-A behavior participants. *Scandinavian Journal of Psychology*, 48, 547–55.

Wolters, G., and Raffone, A 2008. Coherence and recurrency: Maintenance, control and integration in working memory. *Cognitive Processes*, 9, 1–17.

# Chapter 6
# The Psychology of Just Resource Allocation. Part II: Relationships

## Introduction

Actors allocating resources to recipients are not isolated from each other. Not only do actors have a relationship with recipients, but also with other actors as well as observers. The mutual relationship between actors and between actors and recipients shapes the allocation process. If two actors have a good relationship with each other, they will probably develop or have the same opinion about how to divide resources. A boss planning to advise a subordinate on a task may take into account how other bosses would tackle the issue. In meetings with the boss, colleagues suggest that advising is only allowed in exceptional cases because of the possible envy it raises in co-workers. An actor may think this over before giving advice. It is likely that actors compare their allocation beliefs and behaviors and tune them in with those of other relevant actors.

The relationship between actor and recipient, as well as between actors, can be described in terms of two dimensions: a horizontal dimension indicating whether a relationship is close or distant and a vertical dimension indicating whether a relationship is equal or unequal, that is, whether it is a relationship between equals or unequals. Distance will be defined here as the ease with which resources are allocated. In close relationships valued resources are easily allocated to other, while in distant relationships this is far more difficult. Equality is defined here in terms of the difference in the amount and type of relevant resources between actor and recipient—Foa and Foa (1974: 134) label this "power." In a married couple, the man and wife do not differ much in the allocated resource love. Parent and child do differ much in the amount of service they provide to each other. Thus, the relationship between the married couple is close and equal; the relationship between bosses is equal and rather distant; between parents and children, the relationship is close and rather unequal.

According to Lerner (1981), the relationship between actor and recipient is of crucial importance for the type of rule that is applied to allocate resources. Lerner states that in close relationships in which the actor identifies strongly with the recipient, partners allocate resources according to the recipient's needs. Parents offer attention or food to their children whenever and however much they need it. The relationship between a boss and a subordinate is, according to Lerner, a unit-relationship: they have the same goal—production of a good—and perform tasks to reach this goal. Allocation of resources—salary or bonus—is dependent on the contribution (effort, ideas) each worker delivers to make the article (e.g., a bicycle). In a non-unit relationship, actors see each other as different, requiring self-promoting strategies to win. Allocation of resources in a non-unit relationship is guided by egoistic tendencies and competition in which winner takes all. In other words, the non-unit relationship is characterized by large distance and inequality.

Distance and equality can be described in objective terms as in the case between a rich man and a poor one. These two men are unequal with regard to the resource money and they are distant from each other when one compares the sites where each lives: the poor man in the slums of a large city, while the rich man has his residence in a nice, healthy environment. With this objective difference between both men, the rich man will not easily allocate resources to the poor man, for instance by lending the poor man some money. But objectivity is only one way to describe the relationship between actor and recipient. People who are objectively close to each other may perceive each other as distant and unequal. Siblings, for instance, who are close, may perceive the other as not belonging to the close circle of the family but to an adversary group. Taylor and Norris (2000) studied sibling relationships and conflict in the transfer of the parents' farm. Some siblings evaluated others as having low family warmth and were not satisfied about the procedure and outcome of the farm transfer.

This and other evidence (Törnblom and Vermunt 2007) show that the relationship between actor and recipient is crucial in allocation processes. This chapter will further expand on the effects of the relationship between actor and recipient on allocation behavior, and specifically on allocation motives in situations that are perceived by actors as potentially threatening: the outgroup recipient. I will show that actors' allocation decisions change drastically following only small differences in the relationship with the recipient. Outgroup recipients form another threat for justice-motivated actors, next to their egoistic and altruistic drives. This chapter will also describe the allocation behavior of actors belonging to the same category—the actor views recipients as equal individuals. The allocation behavior of these actors contrasts sharply with that of actors who view themselves as different from the recipient or who feel threatened by the recipient because they belong to another category or because they experience that the recipient is able to retaliate.

## Normal and Abrupt Transitions in Allocation Behavior

Changes in the distance and equality dimensions of the actor–recipient relationship correlate with changes in resource allocation. In the close and unequal quadrant of the two-dimensional relationship between parent and child it is found that the amount of need and the amount of care correlate. There is a linear and smoothly increasing regression line between the two variables: the more one variable increases, the more the other does.

Adams (1965) summarizes the unit relationship and describes inputs (contribution) and outcomes (reward) by the so-called equity formula: $O_i/I_i = r_A$ in which $r_A$ is a constant for all participants *I*, $O_i$ is *i*'s reward (outcome), and $I_i$ is *i*'s effort. The formula implies that an increase in *i*'s contribution is followed by an increase in reward and the increases in inputs and outcomes are related linearly or monotonically. So, if person *i* increases their effort it will be followed by an increase in reward. To pin down the equity formula (Harris 1983) some hurdles had to be taken. For instance, how to deal with negative inputs. Harris showed that the same $r_A$ could be the result of different combinations of inputs and outcomes, specifically when some of the inputs are negative. Let us assume that person $i_1$ delivers a contribution of say −2 and receives an outcome of +2, while person $i_2$ contributes +2 and receives an outcome of −2. For both people the $r_A$ has the same value (−2/+2 = −1, and +2/−2 = −1). Despite some of the hurdles, empirical evidence shows the strength of equity theory as the basis of the equity formula in cases where inputs are positive or negative. Vermunt and Van Kreveld (1981) asked a sample of respondents to indicate desirable payments for several aspects of work: Quality of work (e.g., responsibility, quality of work delivered), Effort (number of hours worked, much work to do), and Environment (dirty work, dangerous work). The respondents were first asked to read the following story: "We describe in the following pages several work events. In each event two employees are doing the work, employee A and employee B. In each work event A's work forms the standard. And in each event B differs from A in one respect…"

A performs a standard job in each event, while B performs more or less than A, as exemplified in the following four situations:

1. B does much more, say 50 percent, than A (VAR4);
2. B does a bit more, say 10 percent, than A (VAR3);
3. B does a bit less, say 10 percent, than A (VAR2);
4. B does much less, say 50 percent, than A (VAR1).

Worker A always receives the same net payment, €100, for four hours of work. The question to the respondents is always how much B should be paid. To arrive at desirable payments the authors devised several calculation rules. One of the rules is derived from the equity formula (Adams 1965). That is, for each of the financial rewards given by each of the respondents for the four inputs of B (as compared to A) the equity of the financial reward is calculated with the following rule:

$$(\mathrm{ABS}(\mathrm{VAR1}-50)/50 + \mathrm{ABS}(\mathrm{VAR2}-90)/90 + \mathrm{ABS}(\mathrm{VAR3}-110)/110 + \mathrm{ABS}(\mathrm{VAR4}-150)/150))/4. \quad (1)$$

In formula (1), the absolute value (without +/− sign) is calculated for each payment (financial reward VAR*i*) the respondent gives to B corrected by the input values of B, summed, and divided by four. The higher the score, the more the rewards deviate from equitable rewards.

Working out the relationship for each of the three aspects of work—Effort, Work Quality, and Environment—between desirable payment and work contribution shows a linear trend. There are small deviations with regard to the under-performance as compared to over-performance of worker B compared with worker A for Effort and Environment, but these deviations fall within the acceptable range of linearity. The linearity test reveals that the three relationships of B's input (Effort, Work Quality, and Environment) with B's reward are linear with significant levels of the $F$-values, $p \leq .05$.

From the results of this study, I conclude that people are able and willing to financially reward workers in proportion to their inputs for important aspects of their work. Translated to the types of allocation behavior advocated in this book, these results fit allocation behavior in which an actor divides resources (money) among recipients. Of course, it is a small study and the results cannot be directly related to other types of allocation behavior like allocating resources between self and other(s). But as I have shown from the results of the questionnaire study, workers who perform a job that is rather familiar to the respondents (equal) and belong to the same culture (distance) as the respondents can count on proportionality of rewards for their work.

Given the linear correlation between inputs and outcomes in judgments about payments for the work of two recipients, it would be crucial for testing the allocation behavior model whether the linearity prevails when an actor allocates resources between self and another. The modified Ultimatum game is an excellent way to show how actors allocate resources between self and other and how an actor's offer is dependent on the relationship between actor and recipient. Suleiman (1996) investigated, in an Ultimatum game setting, the actor's offer for several levels of a discount factor $\delta$ (see Figure 6.1[1]). In this so-called modified Ultimatum game, the actor allocates a resource $R$ between himself and a recipient. For any offer, $[R-x, x]$ being the actor's and recipient's shares, respectively, the recipient can either accept the offer or reject it. If the offer is accepted, it is realized. But if the recipient rejects the offer the actor will receive $(R-x) * \delta$, and the recipient will receive $x * \delta$. Delta ($\delta$) is the discount factor with ($0 \leq \delta \leq 1$). It is interesting to note that when $\delta = 0$, the modified Ultimatum game becomes the standard

1 To make the graph, mean offers for all values of delta in both studies must be known. However, for the Suleiman study I have mean offers for deltas of 0, 0.2, 0.5, 0.8, 1, and for the Handgraaf et al. study I have mean offers for deltas of 0, 0.1, 0.9, 1. To estimate the mean offers for deltas 0.1 and 0.9 for the Suleiman study I have taken the mean of the mean offers of the adjacent deltas. I applied the same procedure for the missing mean offers in the Handgraaf study. This procedure seemed to me the best approximation, although the assumed linearity of the mean offers for the deltas need not be the case. Moreover, the offers between the Suleiman study and the Handgraaf et al. study differ in the type of currency: in the Suleiman study participants allocated NIS (New Israeli Shekel, about \$13), and in the Handgraaf study chips were allocated with a value of \$0.05 per chip. I have converted both NIS and chips into dollars.

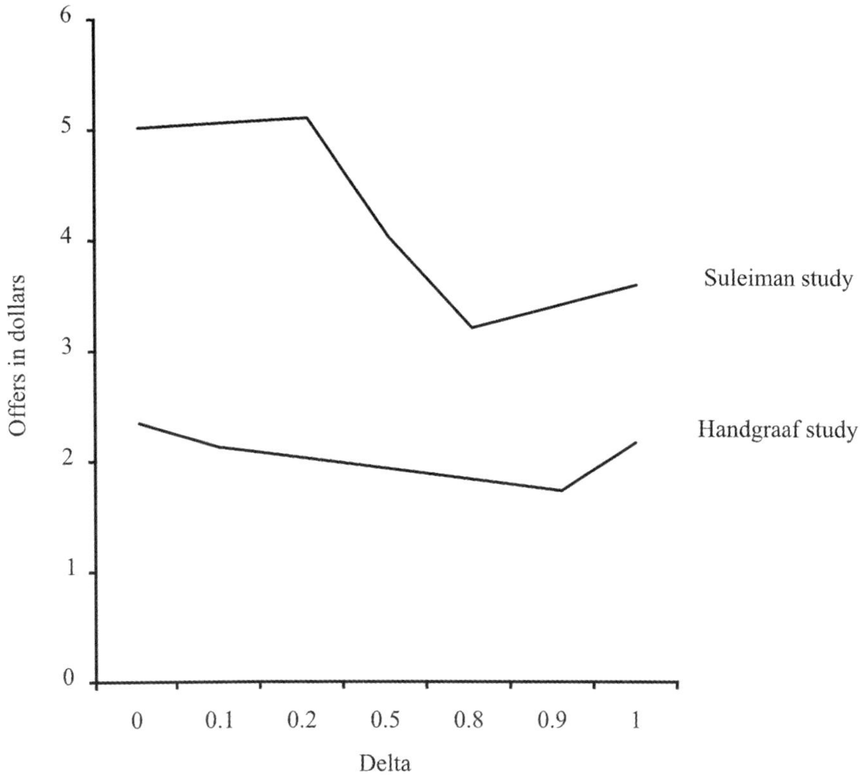


**Figure 6.1 Mean offers as a function of delta**

Ultimatum game in which both players receive nothing if the recipient rejects the offer. And when $\delta = 1$, the modified game becomes the standard Dictator game in which both players receive what the actor has proposed irrespective of the recipient's acceptance or rejection. Suleiman (1996) played the modified game for several levels of $\delta$ and showed that the mean offer is an inverse linear function of $\delta$: The lower the value of $\delta$, and thus the more the recipient has a say in what the actor (and recipient) receives, the higher the actor's offer to the recipient is.

Notwithstanding the anomalies at both ends of the graph, Suleiman evaluates the results as supporting the linear trend he predicted. Van Dijk and Vermunt (2000) and Handgraaf et al. (2008; see Figure 6.1), however, evaluated the violations not as random fluctuations of a rather linear pattern but as a fundamental feature of the actor–recipient power relationship. They argue that the actor evaluates the allocation event differently depending on whether the recipient has a little power or no power at all. As Handgraaf et al. reasoned, having absolute power over the other elicits a sense of responsibility towards the recipient, while when the actor observes that the recipient has some—however little—power, strategic considerations are triggered. The possibility of even a small opportunity for the recipient to retaliate—reject the offer so that the actor gets less or nothing—elicits a threat response in the actor resulting in a higher offer for the recipient.

Suleiman (1996) assumes that $\delta = 0$ and $\delta = 1$ form the end points of the delta scale. In the case of $\delta = 1$, the modified Ultimatum game is identical to the Dictator game. But as Van Dijk and Vermunt (2000) have shown, the Dictator game (DG) can be made even more extreme—they added an element that made recipients even more powerless. Recipients now not only had no say about accepting or not the actor's offer—and the actor knew this—but recipients did not even know the value of the chips that the actor used in the allocation, while the actor knew that his chips had a higher value than the recipient's chips (the asymmetric information condition). I conclude that $\delta$ was not 1 in this study, but more than 1. It is interesting to note that in the context of the total powerlessness of the recipient, the actor's offer of chips was higher in DG than in UBG, the ultimatum bargaining game, contrary to expectation.

In the same vein, a comparable argument can be made for the other end point of the delta scale. $\delta = 0$ does not necessarily form the extreme of the scale—a negative $\delta$ is also conceivable. $\delta = 0$ stands for the situation that if the recipient refuses the actor's offer then both players receive nothing. I will argue that there is a delta minus condition in which the recipient's refusal of the offer results in the actor getting nothing while the recipient receives, say, 10 percent, or another percentage of the offer. In that case, the recipient's influence over the actor is even larger than in the standard Ultimatum game. In conclusion, the delta range between 0 and 1, as conceived of by Suleiman, forms only part of the entire power spectrum of the relationship between actor and recipient.

The study in which an actor is asked to allocate resources (money) to recipient B given the inputs of both recipient A and recipient B (Vermunt and Van Kreveld 1981) and the studies in which an actor is asked to allocate money to self and recipient (Van Dijk and Vermunt 2000; Handgraaf et al. 2008; Suleiman 1996) show some similarities, but also important differences. One feature in which both studies are similar is the type of allocated resource: money. A second feature is the implicit or explicit comparison that the actor makes to allocate the resource. In the comparable payment study, the actor makes an explicit comparison between A an B to allocate the resource. The respondent is even asked to make the comparison. In the modified Ultimatum game study, a comparison is made as well, but is more implicit. The actors compare their (power) position with that of the recipients and allocate resources according to the perceived power difference between them. In both studies, the actor applies a criterion—or justification—on which to base the allocation decision. In the comparable payment study the criterion is the input of B as compared to that of A, and in the modified Ultimatum game study the criterion is the perceived power difference between actor and recipient. In both cases, the allocation process shows a linear relationship between the criterion and the final payment. The greater the input of B compared to A, the more payment, and the more the actors perceive their power position as greater than the recipients', the more the actors keep for themselves.

The important difference between both studies is that in the comparable payment study the actors make a comparison between two recipients, while in the modified Ultimatum game study the actors allocate between themselves and the recipients. This turns out to be a fundamental difference. It is assumed that the actors experience fear of retaliation from the recipient if they offer a bid that the recipients might evaluate as too low, as too unjust. Under this threat, the actors compare as accurately as possible their power position with that of the recipients and decide how much of the resource to offer. Fear of retaliation is most certainly not present in respondents of the comparable payment study.

The crucial difference between both studies is the degree of threat. In the case of the comparable payment study, threat is absent and does not in any conceivable way interfere with the actors' judgment of their own position in relation to recipient B's position. In the modified Ultimatum game study, fear of retaliation causes a threat, resulting in higher offers. The threat motivates the actor to focus on self. However, the absence of threat in the extended DG (Van Dijk and Vermunt 2000) motivates the actor to focus on the recipient and propose higher offers instead of lower. It is as if the presence/absence of threat blocks certain cognitive/emotional processes or makes these processes inaccessible while opening up other cognitive/ emotional processes.

With the Van Dijk and Vermunt (2000) and the Handgraaf et al. studies (2008), one part of the Suleiman curve (Figure 6.1) has been specified: the tail of the curve at the right-hand end. But the top-left tail of the curve has not been discussed, although the deviation from the linear trend is nearly as strong as in the other case. The data depicted in Figure 6.1 show that the actor's allocation decision is different when $\delta$ moves from $\delta = 0.2$ to $\delta = 0$. Mean offers fall from $R = 17.03$ to $R = 16.7$, showing a reverse direction for the top-left tail as compared to the bottom-right tail. A curve-fitting analysis on Suleiman's data with delta as independent variable and mean offer as dependent variable shows a linear as well as a cubic trend, with the cubic trend far stronger than the linear trend. However, the Handgraaf et al. study did not find the inverse S-curve from the Suleiman study. Instead, Handgraaf et al. found no decrease in offer for $\delta = 0$ as compared to $\delta = 0.1$.

To be consistent in reasoning, the actors' behavior at the top-left tail of the Suleiman curve should be explained in terms of responsibility and strategic considerations, as was done for the behavior at the bottom-right tail of the curve. But applying the strategic argument for the top-left tail would imply a larger offer at the $\delta = 0$ point than the offer at the $\delta = 0.2$ point, in that at the $\delta = 0$ point the actor's power is less than at the $\delta = 0.2$ point. But a significantly lower bid is offered at the $\delta = 0$ point than at the $\delta = 0.2$ point. Is it the decreased responsibility that can explain the actors' behavior? As long as the Suleiman data have not been replicated, it is difficult to answer this question. From the Van Dijk and Vermunt as well as from the Handgraaf et al. studies, I infer that an actor's allocation behavior changes drastically and abruptly when δ moves from very low to zero, and is accompanied by feelings of threat or no threat at all.

## Intra-Group and Inter-Group Relations in Allocation Behavior

The foregoing section has shown that small changes in the so-called control factors δ (the normal factor) and threat (the splitting factor) can initiate drastic changes in allocation behavior. This section will show that the interplay between other factors may also result in drastic changes in allocation behavior. The factors I have in mind are crucial for human interaction—and even more salient, perhaps; these factors have played an essential role in the development of the human species (see chapters 1 and 2). These two chapters argued that hominins living in groups at the fringes of grassland and forest could only survive if they stuck together as a (family) group (the ingroup) and protected their own group from other group(s)—the outgroup—in the fight for food. As stated in Chapter 2, based on theoretical and simulation studies, differentiation between ingroup and outgroup has been part and parcel of hominin and *Homo* development. I argued that the evolution from the hunter-gatherer's way of subsistence to an agricultural way of subsistence sparked the beginning of a new group of people—farmers—developing new practices and habits. These newcomers had to integrate into the world of the traditional hunter-gatherers. The differentiation between newcomers and settled plays a central role in modern human interaction as well. But the context with respect to human personality, culture, and society has been changed drastically since hominins walked on earth two million years ago, respectively 15,000 years ago. The human personality has undergone changes related to the volume and complexity of the brain; culture has become more complex in that many languages arose, many different cultural expressions were created, and many ethical systems and religions developed. Human groups dispersed over the earth and the differences between human groups became more diversified. In the beginning the groups could live in relative isolation, but as powerful groups started to conquer other groups, despite all animosity, groups became more and more dependent on each other. This interdependence makes the ingroup–outgroup relationship complex, because though groups may compete with each other over some resources, they have to cooperate in order to acquire some of the resources or to receive more of other resources. Oil distribution is a good example to make the idea of interdependence clearer. Some Arabic countries have huge amounts of oil, and in fact they could allocate oil resources to whomever they please to deliver it. Or they may stop allocating oil. But stopping delivering oil will harm the country itself in that the Arabic countries are—even now—not able to feed their own people. In this respect, the country is dependent on the countries to which they deliver oil. Moreover, Arabic countries have a type of religion that is different from that of many of the countries to which they deliver oil. Over many years, conflicts between groups based on the Koran, the Bible, and the Torah have flared up and died away. This interdependence decreases the power the country could have been wielding in conditions of independence in resource allocation. It is as if the Arabic countries and Western countries play an Ultimatum Bargaining Game rather than a Dictator Game to illustrate their interdependence.

The study of groups in social psychology started early in the 1930s. The Sherifs (Mustapha Sherif and Caroline Sherif) observed extensively groups of children at summer camps to gather knowledge about how groups operate in isolation as well as in the presence of other groups (Sherif and Sherif 1953). Based on theoretical considerations about stages of intergroup conflict, the Sherifs let children carry out tasks in several compositions. In the first stage, children engaged in activities on a camp-wide basis (see also Turner 1981). In the second stage the children were divided in two groups. It was arranged, for example, that good friends were assigned to different groups. The separated groups evolved status and role differentiations. The third stage was devoted to competition between the two groups. In this stage overt hostility emerged between the groups, both during and outside the contest. In the final stage the groups engaged in collaborating activities to reach goals that each of the groups separately could not attain, but only when they worked together. Encounters between members of both groups reduced antipathy. These and other studies showed that intergroup competition tends to strengthen social relationships within groups and disrupt them between groups. Further studies showed that intergroup cooperation and competition as such do not in themselves reduce or enhance intergroup antipathy and hostility, but that these conditions of intergroup relations reduce or enhance the salience of we–they distinctions. Similar reasoning can be applied to attitude similarity or dissimilarity: Attitude similarity reduces the "we–they" distinction and reduces antipathy between members of groups. The distinction between "we" and "they"—or the categorization of people into "we" (those people whom I find belong to my group) and "they" (the people belonging to the other group)—is crucial for allocation attitudes and decisions.

### *Immaterial Resource Allocation*

The studies cited above (Vermunt and Van Kreveld 1981; Handgraaf et al. 2008; Suleiman 1996) focused on allocation of material resources (money, or chips representing money). The question arises whether comparable results would be found when immaterial resources are also allocated, because this would increase trust in the findings described above. Sole et al. (1975) conducted an interesting study investigating the relationship between attitude similarity on a relevant issue and helping behavior; in terms of allocation behavior, helping behavior can be subsumed under the resource "service": Services involve activities that affect the body or belongings of a person and that often constitute labor for another. The authors manipulated the degree of attitude similarity between a subject and a stranger: 0, 25, 50, 75, and 100 percent attitude similarity. The research question was to study the amount of help given to the stranger as a function of the degree of attitude similarity between subject and stranger. As can be inferred from the data, helping dramatically increased for total attitude similarity as compared to helping when helper and victim differed only slightly in attitude on an important issue.

According to Sole et al., "The dramatic step-wise pattern of these data leads us to feel that the subjects divided their world and granted help to those strangers who were included in what can be described as their 'we-group'" (1975: 8).

From a social identity point of view, the Sole et al. data show that we-feelings are derived from attitude similarity. But as Tajfel postulated, we-feelings can be derived from the categorization process itself: Give half of a group of friends a red cap and the other half a blue cap and they will show less helping behavior to the other group. The we-feelings they had when part of the entire group are reduced after they were categorized in two subgroups. According to Tajfel (1978), the reason for intergroup differentiation lies in the need to provide social meaning through social identity to the intergroup situation (86). People strive for positively valued psychological distinctiveness to achieve an adequate social identity (95). Social identity is generally defined as that part of a persons' identity that is derived from their membership of groups or categories. To arrive at an adequate social identity people apply different strategies: They create new forms of distinctiveness, or exaggerate existing forms of distinctiveness. The motivation for this cognitive enterprise is that the current social identity is not adequate and does not fulfill the member's need to differentiate self from relevant others and to affiliate self with relevant others. In other words, the person's social identity is threatened. Reaction to the threat is the attempt to regain an adequate social identity by achieving intergroup distinctiveness, which may result—by the process of social comparison—in derogating members of the other group, as in outgroup derogation, or in favoring one's own group disproportionately, as in ingroup favoritism. Relating the social identity approach to the findings of the Sole et al. results, attitude similarity is a way to express a person's belongingness to the category of "alike" people which one will be eager to help, contrary to people with whom one differs in attitude and who are viewed as outgroup, resulting in more resistance to helping.

Several studies have confirmed Tajfel's assumptions about the effects of mere categorization on allocation behavior (Tajfel et al. 1971; Tajfel 1974). Applying a minimal group setting, Tajfel and his co-workers were able to show that school pupils, who knew each other well, and who were split up into two subgroups on irrelevant criteria, created a reward difference between members of their own subgroup and members of the other group. They allocated money so that maximum difference between own and other subgroup members was preferred to maximum joint payoff, as well as to maximum ingroup payoff. In other words, participants were motivated to reward in such a way that maximum distinctiveness was created between their own subgroup and the outgroup, even at the expense of their own subgroup payoff. These results show clearly that adding a simple and irrelevant criterion (preference for Kandinsky or Klee; Tajfel et al. 1971) created a mindset that overruled the supposedly present mild reward preference for one pupil as compared to another pupil, for instance, because of a stronger liking for the one than for the other pupil.

Supposedly, because in hardly any studies on intergroup behavior has a baseline payoff condition been set up in which a participant rewards pupil Henry and pupil John without any further reference. One exception is the study by Vanbeselaere (1987). In this study, participants performed a perceptual ability task in which they had to decide which of two lines is the longer. After this task, participants estimated the performance of individuals and the performance of members of their own group and another group. Based on the work of Deschamps and Doise (1978), Vanbeselaere added a second category to the already introduced green and red groups: preference for seashore slide versus preference for forest slide. This created four groups of participants: green/seashore group, green/forest group, red/seashore group, and red/forest group. According to Deschamps and Doise, introduction of a common category (green) to the categorization based on preference for a slide (seashore/forest) decreases the effects of the original categorization (slide preference), resulting in less prejudice and discrimination. Figure 6.2 presents Vanbeselaere's performance estimation data for the no-categorization conditions, the one-category conditions, and the crossed-categories conditions. In the no-categorization conditions, participants estimated their own performance as well as the performance of the four other persons. As can be inferred from Figure 6.2, in general, participants estimated their own performance lower than the performance of others, although this difference did not reach statistical significance. The estimated performance of own and other group—greens versus reds, and seashore versus forest—is extremely different: the performance estimates of own group are far higher than performance estimates of the other group. The differences in performance estimates decreased strongly after adding a second category.

Deschamps and Doise's (1978) categorization explanation of the results deviates from the social identity explanation of Tajfel et al. (1971). Deschamps and Doise argue that adding a common aspect (green) to the already presented separation (preference for seashore versus preference for forest) creates a cognitive "conflict between the accentuation both of differences and similarities inside each of the categories and between the opposing categories … leading to a decrease in the extent of categorical differentiation" (Deschamps and Doise 1978: 145). Contrary to the social identity approach from Tajfel et al., in which social identity is optimal when one is a member of a valued group that is differentiated from other relevant groups, Deschamps and Doise argue that positive social identity can also be achieved by being complementary to others. People are bound together in some way and do not see others as "not I." Deschamps and Doise refer to real social situations in which mixed or crossed categorizations are more common than the artificially simple categorizations created in the laboratory. Their argument is correct, but does not invalidate Tajfel's arguments. Moreover, Tajfel and others will not disagree with it. The reason is that people, living in a complex social reality in which categories are crossed, create a dichotomous social reality in which only two groups exist: their group and the other group. If people were

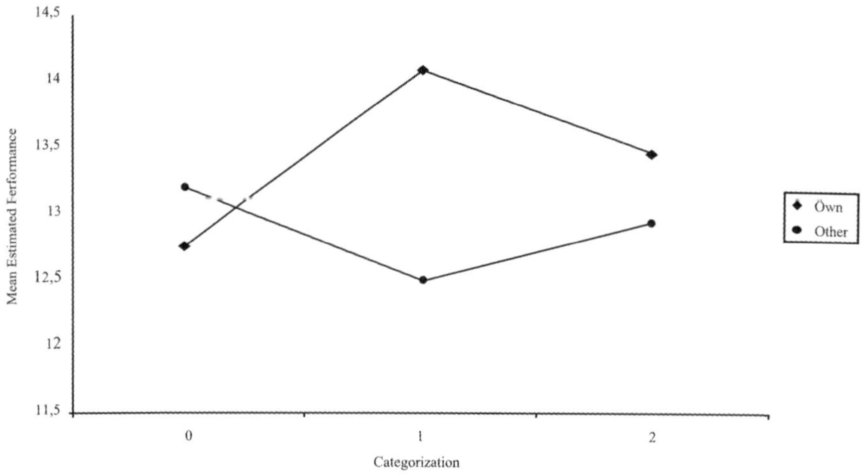


**Figure 6.2 Performance evaluation of own group, other group, and of individuals for different categorization levels**

cognitively and emotionally able to realize that their social world is complex and that category membership is always mixed, then differentiation between social groups would be small. But, clearly, people have a need to confirm that their group is highly valued, and each imagined or real attack on this valued position threatens their social identity. To restore their social identity, people create a dichotomy and differentiate between their own and the other group.

The foregoing reasoning is shown in Figure 6.2. Reading the figure from right to left, there is a small difference in performance estimates for own and other group in a social environment in which people's need for an optimal social identity is satisfied with the evaluation of the groups present. If the social environment changes—the status position of a relevant other group rises, for instance—then members' social identity may be threatened resulting in cognitive and emotional processes to regain an optimal social identity. In these circumstances, threatened members may go over to outgroup derogation and ingroup favoritism. Later research has modified the findings of Vanbeselaere (1987), but has not fundamentally changed them. For instance, Crisp (2006) has found that ingroup favoritism was most strong for high identifiers and weak for low identifiers.

Most important in Figure 6.2, however, is the transition from performance estimates of individuals—self versus other person—and those of group members: own group versus other group. A dramatic change in performance estimates occurs when no-categorization (estimates for individuals) estimates are compared to categorical estimates. The only explanation that is plausible in this context is that in the categorical estimates people use the intergroup context to boost their social esteem (social identity) by giving undeserved higher performance ratings to own group as compared to the no-category estimates.

Performance estimates can be subsumed under the heading of allocation of information (Foa and Foa 1974). Information includes advice, opinions, instruction, or enlightenment. Individuals acquire this knowledge through the cognitive process of guessing. One might also claim that it is an opinion. From intergroup studies, I infer that allocation of information changes drastically when social identity threat influences the allocation process, as compared to no threat. I predict that changes on one social dimension (δ on money allocation, attitude similarity on helping behavior, number of categories in performance estimates) combined with small changes on a second dimension (threat or no threat) result in behavior that differs drastically from an actor's preceding one (offering more money instead of less money, helping more instead of less, and estimating performance lower instead of higher). These behaviors stand in sharp contrast to the behaviors of individuals at other positions on the first social dimension. The extensions ($\delta < 0$, $\delta > 1$; 75 or 100 percent attitude similarity; no category versus categorization) of the different spectra (δ, attitude similarity, number of categories) is important for the purpose I would like to attain: to view the dramatic shift in financial offers, in helping, and in performance estimation as a catastrophe.

## Allocation as Catastrophe

Another way to look at the results of the Suleiman study and the Handgraaf et al. study is to view the dramatic change in offers when the recipient has some influence on the actor's decision to allocate money, or no influence at all, as a catastrophe (see Flay 1978). Catastrophe theory distinguishes factors—motivations, attitudes—that, when active, result in behavior. The gradual increase or decrease in the levels of the factors correlates with increase/decrease of behavioral reactions. Figure 6.1 shows that the less severe the effects of a recipient's refusal, the lower the proposals. A dramatic change in the direction of the behavior suddenly appears when one of the factors reaches a certain level, while the other factor continues to increase or decrease. In the studies cited earlier, the actor proposes lower offers the less the recipient's decision affects the actor's outcome (the amount of money the actor receives). However, as one can see in Figure 6.1, the actor gives more while the recipient's influence decreases drastically. In other words, although the recipient's influence gradually decreases, resulting in lower offers, all of a sudden the actor proposes relatively higher offers instead of lower ones. The factor that probably causes the dramatic shift in offers is perceived threat. When an actor perceives a recipient's influence as gradually decreasing, the actor may still be anxious of the recipient's ability to retaliate. However, when the actor perceives the recipient's influence as no longer threatening, the actor's own position and thus the actor's own outcome becomes less salient. As Van Dijk and Vermunt (2000) stated, one does not harm a fragile old woman because she is not a threat to a strong young man. Although she can still influence the young man's behavior, she is not a threat to him. Handgraaf et al. (2008) assume that two motives rule an actor's behavior. One motive is a strategic one, ruling the actor's bid in such a way that the actor will get the most out of the game while the recipient still has more or less influence. The other motive is the responsibility motivation, stating that the actor feels responsible for the recipient's fate and offers more money. The issue here is that the responsibility motive seems to be absent in the case when the actor views the recipient as a threat, while strategic motivation is absent when the recipient is not experienced as a threat by the actor. In other words, the authors need two types of motivation to describe and explain the actor's behavior. The description and explanation of an actor's behavior is clearer and simpler if one replaces the two motivations by one other behavioral dimension: direction of allocation. Direction changes as the control factor and splitting factor reach certain levels. The control factor is delta: the amount the actor will *receive* after the recipient's refusal of the proposed offer. This factor increases gradually, from small amounts of the resource that the actor will receive after the recipient's refusal to relatively large amounts. The splitting factor is the perceived threat. When the perceived threat reaches a certain low level while delta is still increasing, the resulting behavior—the proposed offer—is directed at *rewarding other* and not on *rewarding self*. The behavior changes from a *self-directed* (strategic) allocation to an *other-directed* (responsibility) allocation. Direction of allocation is one factor with two levels, self and other, instead of two factors, responsibility and strategic considerations. Moreover, the two levels of direction contrast with each other. Concluding, an actor's behavior is instigated by the continuous operation of two factors: the control factor, the actor's power over the recipient (delta); and perceived threat of the recipient's refusal of the offer. Catastrophe theory describes, explains, and accurately predicts (abrupt) changes in the behavior of materials as well as social phenomena. The theory gives an insight into allocation behavior and the influence of intergroup relations on this behavior.

In order to apply catastrophe theory (see Poston and Stewart 1978 for a mathematical description of it) to describe and explain behavior that—in our case—radically changes in direction, the behavior must fulfill five conditions (see Flay 1978). One condition is that the behavior is bimodal for some values of the control factor: rewarding directed at self versus rewarding directed at another. It is assumed that at some levels of the control factor the actor is primarily rewarding self, while a small increase or decrease in the control factor—due to the operation of the splitting factor—changes abruptly the actor's direction of reward: other instead of self. The second condition is that abrupt, catastrophic, changes are observed between one mode of behavior and another. Theoretically, it is possible to observe rewarding self and rewarding other, for instance through eyeball tracking. The third condition is that hysteresis is present: When one goes from more to less (actor's) power, the onset of perceived threat is at a different level of delta than when one goes from less to more power. Delta is 0.8 or smaller when one goes from less to more power and 1.0 or higher when one goes from more to less power. It may be concluded from the delta factor that only one level of delta ($\delta = 1.0$) gives rise to no threat. However, research from Suleiman (1996) and Van

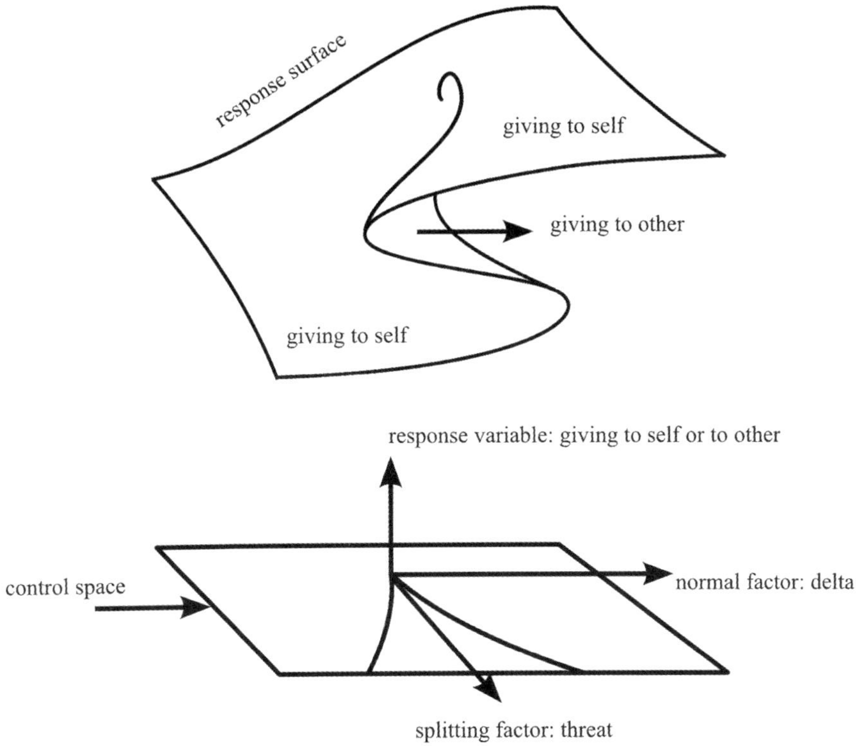


**Figure 6.3 Interaction of the two factors "delta" (amount of influence: normal factor) and "threat" (splitting factor) on direction of allocation behavior**

Dijk and Vermunt (2000) shows that this concerns perceived threat level. This means that less threat is present in principle at all levels of delta, but is most likely when delta is larger than $\delta = 0.5$. The value of $\delta = 0.5$ is chosen because it is the lower boundary of what an actor probably judges as comfortable to receive when the recipient refuses the offer. Each value of delta higher than $\delta = 0.5$ will give an actor more than 50 percent of the offer. The fourth condition is that there is an inaccessible zone of behavior for some values of the control factors. It is impossible to focus on rewarding another when the threat is active. The fifth condition is met as well. That condition says that the possibility of divergent behavior is implied.

In the game behavior case, the divergent behavior is to focus on rewarding the other. Threat, as one of the control factors, is defined here as the splitting factor, while delta is defined as the normal factor. Figure 6.3 shows the interplay between the two control factors and their effects. In the cube of Figure 6.3, two planes in the six-plane cube are important: the ground plane and the top plane. The ground plane is called the control space where the factors that steer the behavior—the response variable—are depicted. The normal factor and the splitting factor interact with each other. The top plane forms the behavior response surface: it depicts the behavior that is the result of the two interacting factors on the ground plane. The top plane is not a two-dimensional plane with length and width like the ground plane. It is a three-dimensional plane with a lower surface and upper surface and curve in between the two surfaces. The bifurcation set is the projection of the top plane curve on the ground plane: a left bifurcation line and a right one, starting from the origin that corresponds to the singularity of the top plane. The line indicates the boundary between interaction of the two factors resulting in normal behavior (outside the two lines) and divergent behavior (in between the two lines). Starting at a random position on the ground plane on the left side of the left bifurcation line, the position represents a certain level of each of the factors. Going from left to right in a diagonal direction on the ground plane changes the level of both factors. With this movement there is a corresponding linear change in position on the lower surface of the top plane. In the case of allocation it means that when threat decreases offers become lower, and is primarily directed at increasing own monetary value. Until one reaches the curve; then the behavior changes dramatically, although as one can see on the ground plane the change in the two factors is very small: from outside the bifurcation line to the inside of it. Instead of making an offer that is primarily directed at increasing own monetary value, the offer becomes primarily directed at increasing the other's monetary value.

As one can see in Figure 6.3, the dramatic change in behavior is only visible when the threat level is moderate. The cusp opens itself at the foreground of the cube and not at the background. At the background, the threat level is high and it seems that in the background the linear trend is still intact. If the resource delivered is not money but, for instance, negative service—like torture—it does not matter whether the recipient has some (information) power, the threat level is so high that the recipient's information—and thus power—will motivate the actor to more torture.

Another feature of the cusp catastrophe is the onset of the catastrophe when one arrives at the cusp from the lower surface or when one arrives from the upper surface. Coming from the lower surface the catastrophe starts at a higher level of the control factor than when one comes from the upper surface. The downward abrupt change starts at another level of the control factor than the upward abrupt change. Is this feature of a catastrophe present in the modified Ultimatum bargaining game? An actor who is confronted with a recipient who gets more and more power over the allocation outcome will probably direct the focus from self to recipient at rather high levels of delta ($\delta > 1$). Conversely, the actor will refocus from other to self when delta is not that high ($0.2 > \delta < 1$). The other behaviors described in this chapter—helping and performance estimates—can also be explained in terms of catastrophe.

I conclude from the foregoing analysis of game behavior (rewarding self versus rewarding other), helping (less helping versus more helping), and performance estimates (favoring self versus favoring other) that catastrophe theory gives extra insight into an actor's allocation behavior at different levels of the actor–recipient power relationship.

## Identity Threat

In the modified Ultimatum bargaining game (Handgraaf et al. 2008; Suleiman 1996), the attitude similarity study (Sole et al. 1975), and the performance estimate experiment (Vanbeselaere 1987), I state that actors experience threat when respectively confronted with a potentially retaliating recipient, with a member of another group based on categorization, or attitude dissimilarity. Actors who experience a threatened identity allocate resources in a completely different way than actors who experience no threat. Differences in behavior seem to occur abruptly as described by catastrophe theory, and not smoothly and gradually as described by linear models. The abruptness versus smoothness of the differences in behavior I infer from the results of experiments in which participants received different treatments. Some of the participants received information, for instance, about a potentially retaliating recipient, while another group of participants received information about a powerless recipient: a so-called between-subjects design. And it turned out that the behavior of the two groups of participants is completely different. From these differences I interpret the participants' behavior in terms of change, abrupt or smooth. Participants in the different conditions of the experiment are assigned randomly to each of these conditions. So, there is no reason to assume that participants in one condition differ from participants in another condition. Therefore, it is safe to assume that if participants—after being exposed to the treatment of one condition—receive another treatment, they will experience the treatment of that condition and react to it in nearly the same way as an independent group of randomly chosen participants. However, it is still an inference based on a between-subjects design and not a direct proof as would be possible using a within-subjects design. In a within-subjects design, a participant is exposed to a treatment and subsequently to another treatment. In a within-subjects design, participants are their own reference group and changes can be assessed between the first treatment and the second one. In addition, changes in reaction can be attributed with confidence to differences in treatment on the same participant. In the case, for instance, of the performance estimates of the Vanbeselaere (1987) study, participants would first be exposed to the inter-individual treatment, than to the intergroup treatment and finally to the cross-categorization treatment. Because of the often unknown effects of one treatment on the other, researchers prefer a between-subjects design.

What it is absolutely necessary to know is an assessment for a single individual of the type of change in reaction to a treatment: abrupt or smooth. More specifically, is it possible to assess an individual's change in reaction to a threatening situation following a non-threatening situation? With catastrophe theory researchers are able to predict abrupt changes on a social psychological level. However, a physiological analysis to assess the threat level and (abrupt) shifts in threat level should follow this social-psychological approach. Only in this way can the theory about the justice motive and its intergroup challenges be tested fully. Because the degree of threat of a situation affects an individual's emotions and cognitions (allocation decisions), a model that describes these effects would satisfy well. One such model is LeDoux's (2002) emotional processing model, and another is the appraisal model (Lazarus 1999).

*The Brain Train*

The previous part of this chapter has argued that changes in reaction to a stimulus often occur abruptly. The abrupt nature of the change is due to the operation of two factors, a control factor and a splitting factor. Initially, the behavior resulting from the operation of the two factors varies smoothly with an increase or decrease of both factors. Only when one of the factors—the splitting factor—reaches a certain value does the smoothness of the relationship between the two factors on the one hand and the resulting behavior on the other hand change abruptly, sometimes in a direction opposite to the previous behavior. The splitting factor that I assume to be the most plausible and real in affecting allocation behavior is perceived threat (social identity threat or self-identity threat). The perception that an individual is a member of another group elicits fear resulting in a defensive reaction to protect one's social identity, culminating in downgrading another group and/or upgrading one's own group in an exaggerated way. How do the body and the brain respond to fear, the emotion that is activated by threat? As outlined in Chapter 5, in the laboratory context, studies show broad sympathetic activation such as cardiac acceleration, vasoconstriction, and increased electro-dermal activity. Studies found increased heart rate, increased skin conductance response, increased skin conductance level.

In the lab, guinea pigs, like humans and rats, become fear conditioned by turning a meaningless stimulus, like a tone pip, into a fear-arousing event by presenting a few occurrences of the pip at the same time as an aversive stimulus, like a mild shock to the skin (GABA inhibition; LeDoux 2002: 214). A meaningless stimulus like a tone pip activates neurons in the lateral nucleus of the amygdala (see also chapters 5 and 8 of this volume) but the release of glutamate inhibits the signal of eliciting a response. If the tone pip is associated with an aversive stimulus then the incoming signal is amplified in the lateral nucleus and reaches the basic nucleus, where emotional reactions are initiated. A study by Phelps, O'Connor, Cunningham, Funayama, Gatenby, Gore, and Banaji (2000) showed increased amygdala activation when participants compared faces of white Americans and black Americans. After the fMRI scan, participants filled out the Implicit Association Test (IAT; Greenwald et al. 1998), the Modern Racism Scale (McConahay 1986) and—a week later—undertook the eyeblink startle response on the same black and white faces. The IAT indirectly measures race bias at the presence of an indirect or uncontrollable behavioral response that exhibits a preference for one group over the other; the Modern Racism Scale measures conscious self-reported beliefs and attitudes toward black Americans; the eyeblink startle reflex is also a measure of indirect racial bias, potentiated by aversive stimuli and related to amygdala activation. Amygdala activation correlated with unconscious IAT data and, less strongly with the eyeblink startle response, but not with scores on the Modern Racism Test. The results show the activation of the amygdala processing culture-generated aversive stimuli. In a second experiment, Phelps et al. demonstrated the role of an additional characteristic combined with the black–white categorization used in the first experiment. The additional characteristic was whether the black and white faces were from well known or unknown people. The addition of the second characteristic resulted in less activation of the aymgdala and the activation did not correlate with the IAT and eyeblink startle response.

It is interesting to remark that the addition of the second characteristic can be viewed as adding a second category to an initial category, as has been done frequently in intergroup perception research (see Deschamps and Doise 1978; Vanbeselaere 1987; Crisp 2006). In this so-called crossed categorization, Phelps et al. showed decreased amygdala activation, indicating lower levels of fear in white participants perceiving black faces. Introduction of a second characteristic diminishes the aversive nature of the stimulus resulting in decreased activation. This result confirms the Deschamps and Doise and Vanbeselaere results: cross-categorization reduces intergroup discrimination. However, as in the first experiment of Phelps et al., the amygdala activation did not correlate with scores on the Modern Racism Scale. But it can be assumed that using a less obtrusive measurement of racism, like performance evaluation (Vanbeselaere 1987), the correlation would be found. Another issue decreasing the value of the Phelps et al. study as evidence for the effects of crossed categorization is that Turner (1981) and others have argued that the Deschamps and Doise study did not assess the strength of the second as compared to the first categorization: the age category may be less strong or stronger than the gender category. This critique is applicable to the Phelps study as well. Familiarity as a dimension diminishes amygdala activation less, because familiarity still reminds participants too much of the black–white label. Adding an independent category label to evaluate black–white faces will probably result in even less amygdala activation.

According to Phelps et al. (2000) and LeDoux (2002), the absence of a relation between amygdala activation and responses on the self-report assessment of the Modern Racism Scale is evidence of the superiority of the processing approach to the appraisal approach. The processing approach to emotion sidesteps subjective experience and allows the study of unconscious emotional functions. The appraisal approach treats emotions as appraisals, as thoughts about a given situation (LeDoux 2002: 209). And, according to LeDoux, this appraisal is tapped by unreliable self-reports, giving rise to a credibility problem. In my view, however, it cannot be denied that a stimulus has first to be evaluated before action can take place. A stimulus that is evaluated as benign or neutral will not elicit a bodily response, in contrast to an aversive one. A threatening stimulus evokes a response and activates the amygdala's lateral nucleus. But the stimulus must be experienced as aversive. Whether this process is labeled a conscious or unconscious one depends on the definition of consciousness. Consciousness has been defined by scholars as: subjectivity; awareness; the ability to experience or to feel; wakefulness; having a sense of selfhood; or the executive control system of the mind. LeDoux defines consciousness clearly in terms of subjectivity and ability to experience. But an aspect of consciousness that is part of the concept is that consciousness comprises the executive control system of the mind. And this executive system may operate subconsciously or preconsciously. This aspect of consciousness stands far from aspects like subjectivity and experience, but is still a conscious process.

Moreover, a method to assess cognitive activity, like self-report, cannot serve as evidence of the existence of the credibility gap. The Modern Racism Scale is a direct self-report assessment of racial attitudes, while an indirect self-report assessment can be applied as well. For instance, by asking participants to allocate money to black stimulus individuals as compared to white stimulus individuals (Tajfel et al. 1971).

In addition, a study by Gonzales et al. (2004) showed the effects of a medial prefrontal cortex lesion on amygdala activation in rats, indicating the role of cortex function on emotion processing. The lesion resulted in low amygdala activation. The authors conclude that "from an ethological view, this study showed that the integrity of the MPFC is required for displaying adaptive strategies against predator threats" (Gonzales et al. 2004: 161). In other words, a kind of consciousness is involved in processing emotion-laden stimulus information, also according to the processing approach to emotion. I conclude from these arguments and findings that the processing approach and the appraisal approach do not differ substantially from each other in describing and explaining emotions.

## Allocation Justice and Threat: Some Conclusions

### *Actor–Recipient Allocation*

Just allocation of resources to other individuals as well as to members of other groups is challenged by fear of those individuals as well as the presence of other groups. Individuals who are capable of retaliation are treated with caution and mistrusted, while members of groups perceived as threatening are derogated and discriminated. Is there evidence for the threat explanation of allocation behavior as I have outlined above? Moreover, what do these findings tell us about allocation behavior?

I found mixed evidence of the threat explanation of allocation behavior. My explanation was that participants in the UBG and DG have consideration for the recipient if the threat was low, and were more focused on their own (financial) position when threat was increasing. If, in those types of game, the threat is high, amygdala activitation should be high as well. A study from Emonds, Declerck, Boone, Vandervliet, and Parizel (2009) showed no amygdala activation of participants playing a prisoners' dilemma game. It is too early to conclude that these findings are conclusive for absence of fear: the researchers focused on the difference in decision-making between proselfs and prosocials. No difference in amygdala activation between the groups was revealed in fMRI scans. Moreover, it is not completely clear how sensitive—1.5 Tesla with voxel size 3×3×4 mm—their instrument is. Their results showed that brain areas near the amygdala, IPL, and STS were activated. It might be that more sensitive instruments can better differentiate between the regions of interest.

Amygdala activation was assessed in studies in which the participant was a member of another group or category (Cunningham et al. 2004). White participants confronted with pictures of black faces showed heightened activation, 30 ms after exposure, of only the amygdala and not the frontal cortical structures. However, 525 ms after exposure, the control and regulation structures of the frontal cortex were also activated.

Chapter 5 stated that humans have a profound preference for being fair and just, but that other motivational forces (egoistic, altruistic) often keep human beings from fair allocation decisions. I have argued that even when people allocate resources unfairly they do their best to look fair and to convince others of their fairness—fair intentions or fair outcomes. And why would actors perform costly persuasion activities if they are not convinced that others—recipients and observers—will evaluate their allocation decisions in terms of fairness? Numerous research results show that recipients and observers evaluate allocation decisions in terms of fairness, showing the ubiquity of fairness.

But other psychological forces than egoistic and altruistic motivation are found that can block the operation of fairness-motivated allocation behavior. In a recent study, Van den Bos et al. (2011) decreased participants' opportunity for observing others' evaluation of their behavior. Referring to the work of Asch (1956) and Milgram (1963), the authors reasoned that when the pressure of the social environment is absent, people will be more willing to behave in accordance with their own moral or prosocial values. And, indeed, people being encouraged to behave freely showed more distress when confronted with an advantageous but unfair reward than inhibited persons. Clearly, social pressure induces feelings of fear, and inhibition of these feelings drives people to act more fairly. As argued earlier in this chapter, perceived threat and the activation of fear responses decreases activation of the fairness response. If the fear response, resulting from perceived threat, is absent, individuals are more prone to take the perspective of the other into account when allocating resources. And taking the perspective of the other is a crucial element in taking fair allocation decisions. Absence of fear increases individuals' willingness to help others, to inform others appropriately, and to decrease ingroup favoritism, outgroup derogation, and unfair resource allocation.[2]

In the game studies participants experienced fear of loss of material resources (money), while in the intergroup studies participants experienced fear of loss of immaterial resources (status, identity). A basic question is whether fear of loss of material resources is experienced differently from fear of loss of immaterial resources. To investigate this question, I rely on data from brain studies. Fear of loss of material resources leads to relatively low amygdala activitation (Emonds et al. 2009; but keep in mind the restrictions given above), while fear of loss of status (identity) correlates with increased amygdala activation. I conclude that for intergroup encounters fear is imminent and that for economic encounters fear is likely to be imminent. Fair behavior in those threatening encounters is challenged. Skarlicki and Kulik (2005) stated that the circle of moral regard is easily applied to ingroup people, and De Cremer and Van Hiel (2006) found that people care more about the observer's fair treatment when they have a positive relationship with them. These findings might refer to an absence of threat experience with ingroup encounters and the presence of threat in outgroup encounters. The findings correspond well with the tenets of the relational model of justice experiences (Tyler and Lind 1992).

### *Recipient–Recipient Allocation*

Thus far, this chapter has focused on self–other allocations in which an actor allocates resources to recipients as categorized individuals. In order to investigate group phenomena like discrimination I treat the recipient not as one entity—a group or collective—but divide that group into partitions, individuals, or subgroups. The vital question then becomes how the actor allocates resources mutually among the different individuals or subgroups. To answer this question, behaviors such as discrimination, but also prejudice and ingroup favoritism, should be translated in terms of allocation behavior. Philosophers define discrimination as disadvantageous treatment or consideration (Horta 2010). This definition is somewhat obscure in that disadvantage can occur without discriminating against someone. For instance, a worker's bonus is reduced as a result of low production. The reduction is disadvantageous for the worker, but can hardly be called discriminatory, because the disadvantage is based on the generally accepted relationship between bonus and production. The boss is discriminating if he gives a male co-worker a higher bonus which is not based on higher production while he cuts the bonus of a higher-producing female co-worker. Thus, a treatment is discriminating if a difference between individuals is made on irrelevant grounds. Horta's definition is not only concerned with treatment but also with considerations. The boss also discriminates if he shows less respect for female workers than for male workers.

2 Perceived threat can also occur when individuals become uncertain about observing or interpreting elements of their social or physical environment.

Low respect can be expressed in terms of denigrating remarks or gestures. In contrast with the allocation of a material resource—a bonus—showing respect or disrespect for a person is less dependent on social comparison. Clearly, there are more generally accepted standards of what disrespectful treatment is than is the case when allocating a financial bonus. In addition, it is easier to find justifications for not allocating a bonus than for disrespectful treatment: low production is an acceptable reason for not allocating the bonus. There are hardly any generally accepted justifications for rude or disrespectful treatment.

Prejudice is most often used to refer to preconceived judgments toward people or a person because of race, social class, ethnicity, age, disability, obesity, religion, sexual orientation, or other personal characteristics. Prejudice concerns the expression of attitudes or opinions about a person in which the information contained in the attitude or opinion is not verified. Because the co-worker is a senior, the boss judges their work quality as insufficient based on a general judgment about older people. The information the boss has about the senior worker is negative and based on an idea of older workers in general. I, therefore, argue that the boss allocates negative information about the worker unfairly.

### *The Abruptness of the Threat Reaction*

The perception that someone belongs to another group may be evaluated as a threatening event. The perception is an aversive stimulus that induces fear resulting in a fight, flight, or freeze reaction (Lazarus 1999; Mobbs, Marchant, Hassabis, Seymour, Tan, Gray, Petrovic, Dolan, and Frith 2009; Vermunt, Peeters and Berggren 2007). These reactions to threat are not restricted to the human species. Animals and other species react to threat with an immediate fight or flight response. Our physiological make-up has, in the course of (animal) and human development, been constructed in such a way that reactions occur directly without cognitive interference. The amygdala and the limbic system take precedence in guiding actions to threats. The prefrontal structures have little or no participation in those reactions (Cunningham et al. 2004). The way human beings are equipped makes the fight, flight, or freeze reaction immediately result in an abrupt change from previous behavior. Running animals freeze, animals sitting still start to flee, and quiet animals start to fight. These changes occur in a split second and it is difficult to foresee which reaction, fight, freeze, or flight, will prevail.

Because of the above-described fundamental role of threat, previous behavior does not accurately predict individual responses. Increments in one factor (power) predict, for instance, lower bids in an Ultimatum bargaining game: a linear relationship. This goes on until a certain level of another factor (threat) is reached. Then a small increment of the power (delta) factor combined with a slight increase in threat leads to a completely different behavior: a catastrophe starts.

I conclude that perception of threat instigates an immediate reaction, the content of which differs strongly depending on a small increment (or decrement) of one of the factors. The speed of the change as well as the absence of frontal cortical activation makes the role of justifications small. Human beings learned justifications through approach and avoidance learning (O'Doherty 2004) represented in subcortical (ventral striatum; see also Everitt et al. 1989) regions and in cortical (control) substructures (bilateral orbitofrontal cortex, medial and ventromedial prefrontal cortex); in situations of threat, these cortical substructures are not activated.

## References

Adams, J.S. 1965. Inequity in social exchange, in *Advances in Experimental Social Psychology*, edited by Berkowitz, L. New York: Academic Press, 267–99.

Asch, S.E. 1956. Studies of independence and conformity: A minority of one against a unanimous majority. *Psychological Monographs*, 70(416).

Crisp, R.J. 2006. Commitment and Categorization in Common Ingroup Contexts, in *Multiple Social Categorization: Processes, Models and Applications*, edited by R. Crisp and M. Hewstone. New York: Psychology Press, 90–111.

Cunningham, W.A., Johnson, M.K., Raye, C.L., Gatenby, J.C., Gore, J.C., and Banaji, M.R. 2004. Separable neural components in the processing of black and white faces. *Psychological Science*, 15(12), 806–13.

De Cremer, D., and Van Hiel, A. 2006. Effects of another person's fair treatment on one's own emotions and behaviors: The moderating role of how much the other cares for you. *Organizational Behavior and Human Decision Processes*, 100, 231–49.

Deschamps, J.-C., and Doise, W. 1978. Crossed Category Memberships in Intergroup Relations, in *Differentiation Between Social Groups: Studies in the Social Psychology of Intergroup Relations*, edited by H. Tajfel. London: Academic Press, 141–68.

Emonds, G., Declerck, C., Boone, Ch.,Vandervliet, E., and Parizel, P. 2011. Comparing the neural basis of decision making in social dilemmas of people with different social value orientations, a fMRI study. *Journal of Neuroscience, Psychology, and Economics*, 4, 11–24.

Everitt, B.J., Cador, M., and Robbins, T.M. 1989. Interactions between amygdala and ventral striatum in stimulus-reward associations: Studies using a second-order schedule of sexual reinforcement. *Neuroscience*, 30, 1, 30–75.

Flay, B.R. 1978. Catastrophe theory in social psychology: Some applications to attitudes and social behavior. *Behavioral Science*, 23, 335–50.

Foa, U.G., and Foa, E.B. 1974. *Societal Structures of the Mind.* Springfield, IL: Charles C. Thomas Publisher.

Gonzales, L.E., Quinonez, B., Rangel, A., Pino, S., and Hernandez, L. 2004. Tonic and phasic alteration in amygdala 5-HT, glutamate and GABA transmission after prefrontal cortex damage in rats. *Brain Research*, 1005, 154–63.

Greenwald, A.G., McGhee, J.L., and Schwartz, J.L. 1998. Measuring individual differences in social cognition: The Implicit Association Test. *Journal of Personality and Social Psychology*, 74, 1464–80.

Handgraaf, M.J.J., Van Dijk, E., Vermunt, R.C., Wilke, H.A.M., and De Dreu, C.K.W. 2008. Less power or powerless? Egocentric empathy gaps and the irony of having little versus no Power in social decision making. Journal of Personality and Social Psychology, 95, 1136–49.

Harris, R.J. 1983. Pinning down the Equity Formula, in *Equity Theory. Psychological and Sociological Perspectives*, edited by D.M. Messick, and K.S. Cook. New York: Praeger Publishers, 207–41.

Horta, O. 2010. Discrimination in terms of moral exclusion. *Theoria: Swedish Journal of Philosophy*, 76, 346–64.

Lazarus, R.S. 1999. *Stress and Emotion: A New Synthesis*. New York: Springer Publishing Company.

LeDoux, J. 2002. *The Synaptic Self. How Our Brain Become Who We Are*. New York: Viking Penguin.

Lerner, S.C. 1981. Adapting to Scarcity and Change (I): Stating the Problem, in *The Justice Motive in Social Behavior: Adapting to Times of Scarcity and Change*, edited by M.J. Lerner, and S.C. Lerner. New York: Plenum, 11–35.

McConahay, J.P. 1986. Modern Racism, Ambivalence, and the Modern Racism Scale, in *Prejudice, Discrimination, and Racism*, edited by J.F. Dovidio and S.L. Gaertner. Orlando: Academic Press, 91–125.

Milgram, S. 1963. Behavioral study of obedience. *Journal of Abnormal and Social Psychology*, 67, 371–8.

Mobbs, D., Marchant, J., Hassabis, D., Seymour, B., Tan, G., Gray, M., Petrovic, P., Dolan, R., and Frith, Ch. 2009. From threat to fear: The neural organization of defensive fear systems in humans. *Journal of Neuroscience*, 29, 12236–43.

O'Doherty, J. 2009. Reinforcement learning mechanisms in the human brain: insights from model-based fMRI, in *Neuroimanging of human memory: linking cognitive processes to neural systems*, edited by Rösler, F., Ranganat, Ch., Röder, B., and Kluwe, R. Oxford: Oxford University Press, 45–65.

Phelps, E., O' Conner, K., Cunningham, W., Funayama, E., Gatenby, J., Gore, J., and Banaji, M. 2000. *Journal of Cognitive Neuroscience*, 12, 729–38.

Poston, T., and Stewart, J. 1978. *Catastrophe Theory and Its Applications*. Belmont, CA: Fearon-Pitman.

Sherif, M., and Sherif, C. 1953. *Groups in harmony and tension: An integration of studies on intergroup relations*. New York: Octagon.

Skarlicki, D.P., and Kulik, C. 2005. Third-Party Reactions to Employee Mistreatment: A Justice Perspective, in *Research in Organizational Behavior*, edited by B. Staw and R. Kramer. Greenwich, CT: JAI Press, 183–230.

Sole, K., Marton, J., and Hornstein, H.A. 1975. Opinion similarity and helping: Three field experiments investigating the bases of promotive tension. *Journal of Experimental Social Psychology*, 11, 1–13.

Suleiman, R. 1996. Expectations and fairness in a modified Ultimatum game. *Journal of Economic Psychology*, 17, 531–54.

Tajfel, H. 1974. Social identity and intergroup behaviour. *Social Science in Formation*, 13, 65–93.

Tajfel, H. (ed.) 1978. *Differentiation between social groups. Studies in the social psychology of intergroup relations*. London: Academic Press.

Tajfel, H., Billig, M., Bundy, R., and Flament, C. 1971. Social categorization and intergroup behavior. *European Journal of Social Psychology*, 1, 149–78.

Taylor, J.E., and Norris, J.E. 2000. Sibling relationships, fairness, and conflict over the transfer of the farm. *Family Relationships*, 49, 277–83.

Törnblom, K.Y., and Vermunt, R. (eds). 2007. *Distributive and Procedural Justice. Research and Social Applications*. Burlington: Ashgate Publishing Company.

Turner, J.C. 1981. The Experimental Social Psychology of Intergroup Behavior, in *Intergroup Behavior*, edited by J.C. Turner, and H. Giles. Oxford: Basil Blackwell, 66–102.

Tyler, T.R., and Lind, E.A. 1992. A Relational Model of Authority in Groups, in *Advances in Experimental Social Psychology*, edited by M. Zanna. New York: Academic Press, 115–91.

Vanbeselaere, N. 1987. The effects of dichotomous and crossed categorizations upon intergroup discrimination. *European Journal of Social Psychology*, 17, 143–56.

Van den Bos, K., Van Lange, P.A.M., Lind, E.A., Venhoeven, L.A., Beudeker, D.A., Cramwinkel, F.M., Smulders, L., and Van der Laan, J. 2011. On the benign qualities of behavioral inhibition: Because of the prosocial nature of people, behavioral inhibition can weaken pleasure with getting more than you deserve. *Journal of Personality and Social Psychology*, 101(4), 791–811.

Van Dijk, E., and Vermunt, R. 2000. Strategy and fairness in social decision making: Sometimes it pays to be powerless. *Journal of Experimental Social Psychology*, 36, 1–25.

Vermunt, R., Peeters, Y., and Berggren, K. 2007. How fair treatment affects saliva cortisol release in stressed low and high type-A behavior participants. *Scandinavian Journal of Psychology*, 48, 547–55.

Vermunt, R., and Van Kreveld, D. 1981. Comparable payments? The influence of several comparison criteria on desirable rewards. *Gedrag*, 9, 3, 125–43.

# PART IV
# Reactions to Unfair Decisions

# Chapter 7

# Reactions to Unfair Allocation Behavior. Part I: Role of Recipient and Observer

## Introduction

Chapters 1 to 6 have described the role of the actor in allocation events. In such events, an actor allocates resources to recipients or among recipients, while the event is scrutinized by observers. The next two chapters will shift the focus from actors to recipients and observers, and investigate how they react to the outcomes of the actor's allocation decisions. The reaction of recipients and observers to allocation outcomes forms the onset of a new allocation event. In this new event, the recipient-actor and/or observer-actor activates motivations, emotions, and cognitions to engage in a next allocation event. The difference between the new event and the old one—as described in the previous chapters—is the salience of characteristics of the preceding allocation event, such as its allocation outcome. Hence the labeling of recipient as recipient-actor and of observer as observer-actor. So, every time the terms recipient and observer appear in this chapter, I mean recipient-actor and observer-actor.

From the previous chapters I conclude that actors do their best to allocate resources fairly, but in trying to do so they are confronted with psychological forces that interfere with the initial motivation to act fairly. I have differentiated the egoistic motives (guided by self-preservation emotions) and altruistic motives (guided by compassion), as well as perceptions of threat, making fair allocations a challenge for the actor.

Because of the crucial relevance of allocation events in people's lives, outcomes of allocation decisions are scrutinized with great interest by recipients and observers. The recipient's interest is drawn because they are directly affected by the outcomes, as well as the way these outcomes are accomplished, while the observers are interested in allocation outcomes because these outcomes and the way they are accomplished may affect their worldview. Recipients and observers are especially focused on allocation outcomes that they evaluate as unfair, resulting in feelings of anger, distress, or fear, mental states they would like to avoid or to remedy. How recipient and observer succeed in coping with it is the subject of this chapter and the next.

As Van den Bos et al. (2008) found, unfairness alerts recipients of things to come that may be less advantageous for them. The disadvantage is a possible deteriorated position in the group (Lind and Tyler 1988), a deteriorated relationship with the actor (Tyler and Lind 1992), a blow to self-esteem (Koper et al. 1993), or increased stress (Vermunt et al. 2007). As can be inferred from the results of these and numerous other studies, disadvantageous unfair outcomes and procedures exert more influence on subsequent reactions than advantageous unfair outcomes and procedures, showing the relative dominance of the egoistic motive to the altruistic motive in the recipient's reactions (see also chapters 1 and 2).

Unfair allocations activate the observer's emotional and cognitive mechanisms in that they are often motivated to keep a worldview in which everyone gets what they deserve. An unfair outcome disrupts this positive worldview, activating emotional and cognitive mechanisms to discard the unfairness in order to consolidate the positive worldview. But other types of reaction to unfairness are possible as the literature shows, like weak attempts to punish the perpetrator (Modde 2002).

It is not only observers who come into action to attempt to punish the actor. Recipients have a whole range of responses to thwart actors. The justice literature is full of results showing the detrimental effects of unfair treatment. For instance, Skarlicki and Folger (1997) found in a real-life study among workers that unfair treatment by the boss leads to destructive behavior from the subordinates, like theft or destroying equipment and materials. The estimated yearly costs of such actions by subordinates as a reaction to unfair treatment by their companies are estimated in Europe at 40 billion euro. Unfair treatment, therefore, is worth extensive discussion, not only for the psychological damage it causes but also for its economic costs.

The following sections will first describe and explain recipients' reactions to fair and unfair treatment, confining themselves to the reactions of individual recipients and not of recipients as a group. The concluding part of this chapter will go into group reactions to unfair treatment, and will also focus on observers' reactions to unfair treatment of the recipient.

## Recipients' Reactions

Recipients' reactions to fair and unfair allocation outcomes are preceded by an overall assessment of the event: the assessment includes evaluation of the actor, the outcome, how the actor derived the allocated outcome, and the type of resource allocated. A recipient's reaction concentrates on the total fairness of the event, the fairness of the actor's motives and behavior, the fairness of the final outcome of the allocation decision, the fairness of the rules the actor used to arrive at the final outcome, and evaluation of the type of resource allocated. Fairness theories concern fairness evaluations of and reactions to the actor's motives and are usually labeled retributive fairness; fairness evaluations of and reactions to the final outcome are subsumed under distributive fairness; while fairness evaluations of and reactions to the applied rules are labeled procedural fairness. Resource theory is concerned with the appropriateness of resources in a given allocation event:

people react to the inappropriateness of resources mainly in terms of frustration and anger rather than in terms of unfairness.

The four theories have in common that a feeling of injustice—or frustration, in the case of resource theory—is generated by the perceived discrepancy between the expected and actual received resource (Törnblom and Vermunt 2007; Vermunt et al. 1996). For instance, person A expects to be rewarded with a certain amount of a resource, and if person A gets less/more than expected (i.e., based on what they think they deserve) than the perceived difference between expected and actual outcome generates feelings of unfairness. And if a person receives a resource (information) but expected to receive another resource (love), this person will feel frustration because the need for love is not satisfied.

### *Perceived Discrepancy between Actual and Expected Outcome*

According to Törnblom and Vermunt (2007), three types of theories—distributive justice theories, procedural justice theories, and resource theory—have in common that a discrepancy between actual and expected outcome causes psychological tension or stress (Vermunt and Steensma 2005), instigating reactions to lower the tension. "All three theories posit an ideal ('ought') goal state toward which people are assumed to strive. An ideal goal state is achieved when a person's actual situation matches the ideal. If the two do not match, the person will perceive the situation as discrepant, resulting in psychological/emotional and behavioral responses" (Törnblom and Vermunt 2007: 314). Retributive justice theory posits that actors behave according to some rule of character, and when the actor deviates from the rule he will be punished.

#### *Distributive justice*

Equity theory, as a special case of distributive justice theories, identifies the discrepancy as the perceived difference between the ratio of a person's investment (contribution, input) and reward as compared with the ratio of another comparable person (Adams 1965). Distributions based on equality and need are made irrespective of the delivered inputs, and the mismatch is between the received allocation outcome and the expected one, based on deservingness (Deutsch 1985). Taking a person's inputs into account as a type of resource brings equity within the realm of allocations that are based on equality and need. After all, taking inputs or investments into account means for recipients that they are viewed as respectful persons about whom all relevant information (input) is applied to decide on the allocation of a resource (e.g., promotion; the ratios of both recipients are equal). In addition, equity is also conceived of as justified deviation from equality: For instance, the recipient has the right education (status information), and works hard (service information). In this case, the actor decides not only about allocation of one resource (service to actor, hard work) but on information about other resources delivered to the actor as well. For instance, the actor informs recipients that they have performed less than other recipients. And the actor's decision about allocation of specific information is essential for recipients' experience of a discrepancy. Thus, the actor gives reasons for deviating from equality, and if these reasons are accepted by the recipients then they feel justly treated. Because of the complicated allocation decision—not one but two resources are allocated: promotion (status) and reason (information)—it is plausible that researchers have searched for a more parsimonious description of the allocation event in which two or more resources are allocated. Adams' equity formula is a good way out of complexity. But the essential message of the equity formula is that the recipient needs to be convinced that all relevant information is taken into account to decide about the allocation outcome or reward.

From a justice point of view, equity may be regarded as a justified deviation of equality. One could argue that every person should be rewarded equally. But, as stated in Chapter 2, in part as a consequence of experiences of the Protestant Ethic and the Industrial Revolution, individual differences (i.e., in contribution) became salient and hence the need for differential reward. Because differential reward deviates from equality, justifications were introduced to make differential reward morally acceptable (see also Chapter 3). In due time, reward systems were developed to account for different types and quantities of individual investments and contributions, and in the course of time and with much struggle these systems became generally accepted and applied. The next part of the chapter will treat equity as a special case of one basic principle of allocation: equality. Deviation from equality can also be justified by referring to the need position of the recipient: one person is more in need of resources than the other person.

*Procedural justice*

For the procedural justice theories, discrepancy is defined as a mismatch between the actually applied procedural rule and the rule considered just (e.g., Lerner 1975, 1977; Lerner and Whitehead 1980; Folger 1987; Vermunt et al. 1996), and the larger the discrepancy the more unfair the procedure will be evaluated. Thus, discrepancy is viewed as procedurally unjust and conceptualized as a perceived mismatch between the expected and applied procedural principles (Törnblom and Vermunt 2007).

*Retributive justice*

For the retributive justice theories, discrepancy is conceived as a mismatch between appropriate behavior and actual behavior. What is defined as appropriate behavior is behavior that brings honor to the group. Behavior that deviates from appropriate behavior is viewed as dishonoring the group (Cloward and Ohlin 1964; Davis 1983).

*Resource theory*

Foa and Foa (1974) defined discrepancy in a way that is different from the three above-mentioned justice theories. In fact, Foa and Foa's resource theory is not a theory trying to describe and explain justice feelings and evaluations. It is a theory which allows behavior to be analyzed in terms of giving and receiving. Within the context of resource theory, *interpersonal behavior* is conceived as "a channel for resource transmission," and *resource* is defined as "any commodity—material or symbolic—which is transmitted through interpersonal behavior" (Foa and Foa 1974: 36).

The six resource classes can be differentiated on the basis of three fundamental resources (see the Prologue). Money and Goods have Currency as a fundamental resource, Service and Love have in common that they need Time to exchange the resource, and Information and Status have in common that Bits of information form the basis of the resource. Most convenient in resource allocation is that the same fundamental resource is exchanged. A money–money exchange is more easily calculated than a money–goods exchange, and these exchanges are far easier to calculate than money–time or money–bits exchanges. People prefer, therefore, money–money exchange to money–time or money–bits exchange, and vice versa. This assumption is associated with one of the core ideas of social resource theory: "the more distal the resource of reciprocation/retaliation the larger the amount necessary for establishing equity" (Foa and Foa 1974: 265).

The major concern of social resource theory is about allocation of types of resources, and discrepancy is defined as the difference between the expected resource type and the actual received resource type. In the case of justice theories, discrepancy is defined as the difference between the expected (deserved) amount of a resource and the actual received amount of that same resource (Törnblom and Vermunt 2012). This last idea is well formulated by Jasso (1978, 1990). In her view, the justice evaluation of a distributed good is a function of the actual received reward minus the just reward. If the actual reward is equal to the just reward then recipients feel they are being rewarded fairly; when the actual reward deviates from the just reward then the recipient feels unfairly rewarded.

### *Rules and Resource Class*

Equity theory is mainly concerned with allocation of material resources and the principles that guide the amounts of the allocated resource. These principles can be subsumed under the heading of resource classes as well: the most important resource for guiding the distribution of material resources is information: an actor should use all relevant information to justify the allocation outcome (promotion, financial bonus, demotion, salary cut).

According to Törnblom and Vermunt, procedural rules can be viewed as expressions of behaviors related to resource classes, and they can therefore be treated as resources that can be allocated. First, let us examine if and how the notion of similar form between procedural/interactional justice rules and resource classes makes sense. The most striking observation is the apparent similarity between interactional justice rules and the *status* and, perhaps, *love* resource classes. Interactional rules refer to both *what* is said and *how* it is said. They prescribe interpersonally sensitive behaviors and express concerns that behavior should be based on criteria such as respect, truthfulness, propriety of questions, explanation for (especially negative) decisions, and two-way communication (Törnblom and Vermunt 2007; see also Bies and Moag 1986; Gilliland 1993). These behaviors are most likely to be interpreted as expressions or signs of one's regard and (though probably to a lesser extent) affection for the object person. Thus, interactional justice rules appear to have the same form as status and love resource classes. Still other procedural rules can be understood as instances of status as well: process control or voice, decision control, ethicality, consistency across persons, and representativeness (see Thibaut and Walker 1975; Leventhal 1976, 1980).

A small group of procedural rules may be interpreted as ways of conveying more "person-detached" resources. These rules are isomorphic with information (advice, opinion, instruction, or enlightenment): bias suppression, accuracy, correctability, and predictability of information (Törnblom and Vermunt 2007: 321, 322). Money and goods can still be a representation of a procedural rule: to soften the blow of demotion, a supervisor informs the subordinate during a dinner.

Retributive justice theory is concerned with punishment following crime, and that the punishment should be in proportion to the severity of the crime. The side-effect of retributive justice may be that the aggrieved party is satisfied. Discussion arose about what can be viewed as a proportional punishment: punishment should be proportionate to the harm caused. Another conception of retributive justice is that punishment should be proportional to the unfair advantage gained by the wrongdoer (Davis 1983). In some cultures, revenge for the loss of honor of a member of the family (nearly always a woman) is a form of retributive justice. The wrongdoer is punished and often killed by stoning to preserve the group's honor. In this case, loss of status by a member's behavior is restored by removing the perpetrator; in doing so, this restores the family's status.

In an allocation event, the recipient reacts to the perceived allocation outcome by: (1) identifying the received outcome in terms of the resource class(es) under which the outcome can be subsumed; (2) experiencing an eventual discrepancy between the expected resource and the actual received resource (see also Brockner and Weisenfeld 1996). A more elaborate proposal for isomorphism between distributive, procedural, and retributive rules or principles and resource classes is given in Figure 7.1.

Resource allocation according to the equality rule means that decisions to allocate resources do not take inputs, and thus other resources, into account: each recipient receives the same quantity of a resource irrespective of the delivered inputs. For some scholars, equality stands for the highest grade of justice. The reasoning is that each person is of equal worth to every other person because all are human beings and each human being is equal before the law. Equality of opportunity to apply for office is—in theory—such a rule. Being equal before the law is exemplified, for instance, in the claim of freedom of speech. Human beings are not only members of a world community from which they derive their rights and duties; they are also engaged in social and economic activities in which their capacities and contributions to the world community are of vital significance.

| **Justice rules** | | **Resource type** |
|---|---|---|
| Distribution: | need | Service |
| | equity | Information |
| | equality | Status |
| Procedure: | bias suppression, accuracy, truthfulness, justification | Information |
| | voice, correctability, justification, propriety of questions, consistency over time and persons | Status |
| Retribution: | proportionality | Status |

**Figure 7.1 Congruence between justice rules applied in resource allocation evaluation and resource type**

People are also employers, or employees, fathers, or mothers, parent and child, lovers. And in those capacities their contributions do matter and they will evaluate the resources they receive in terms of the contributions they deliver or the need state in which they are situated.

## *Physiological, Psychological, and Behavioral Reactions to Perceived Discrepancy*

### *Neuro-physiological components of discrepancy*

In neuropsychological terms, "money" or other resource activates substructures in the prefrontal cortex (PFC) relating information from the visual cortex with information retrieved from memory. I assume that information about "money" is represented in perception, action, and perception-of-action loops. The money received is compared with the expected money, and the recipient makes actions to receive the money. However, when expected and received money differ in amount or type, another loop is activated with an important drive from subcortex structures and the PFC to handle the situation—a new script is activated. Assessment of a discrepancy is accomplished in the same bundle of loops. In the case of different fundamental resources, different loops are needed to compare the expected and received resources. From this assumption, interesting hypotheses can be formulated with regard to the recipient's reactions to the actor's unfairness or the inappropriateness of the resource allocation. Reactions in terms of the same resource class are preferred, need relatively small effort, and leave the smallest traces of feelings of unfairness or frustration.

When recipients experience a discrepancy between, for instance, the salary promised by an actor and the actual salary, two pieces of information are compared with each other. The promised salary and the actual salary are pieces of information retrieved from memory, respectively from the visual cortex. These pieces of information may show a discrepancy, which means that the expected outcome from memory and the actual outcome from the visual cortex do not fit. So-called predictive coding models propose that this process of cognitive inference "proceeds as an iterative matching process of top-down predictions against bottom-up evidence along the visual cortical hierarchy" (Egner et al. 2010: 16601). One could say that the top-down prediction in the case of, for instance, salary comparison, is based on memory retrieval of information. And the bottom-up evidence is derived from the visual cortex. It is further assumed that one group of units in the cortical hierarchy encodes conditional probabilities of a stimulus (expectation), and another group of units encodes the mismatch between prediction and bottom-up evidence. In their study, Egner et al. (2010) used faces and houses appearing in expected and unexpected orders to investigate neural activity in the fusiform face area (FFA), an area that is specifically sensitive to visual information about faces. By repeated presentations, Egner et al. connected an unconditioned stimulus—a green frame—with a conditioned stimulus: faces. The repetitions led to low prediction errors during face presentation. After some repetitions a face was replaced by the picture of a house. It was shown that neuron firing in the FFA increased when the picture of a house was presented in the green frame and not the "familiar" face. I conclude from these findings that a discrepancy is detected between two signals, causing increased neuron firing in the FFA. In the case of information presentation—a bonus is promised—as a top-down process, it will not be the FFA area that will be the region of interest but likely the medial PFC involved in error monitoring and detecting conflict between competing stimuli and responses (Wolters and Raffone 2008).

*Physiological reactions to perceived discrepancy*

Summerfield et al. (2006) showed that when bottom-up evidence of new information (e.g., about salary) does not fit the already present information, a mismatch will be signaled. As discussed in the foregoing paragraph and in Chapter 5, the perceived discrepancy may be accompanied by increased neuron firing in the medial PFC. The PFC and amygdala exchange signals with each other. The amygdala exchanges signals with other brain regions like the hypocampus and pituitary gland to trigger these brain structures to release hormones to several parts of the body. These signals can lead to the release of cortisol as a stress hormone, or the signals can lead to the motor cortex for initiating action. When a discrepancy is detected in information that is viewed as vital to the person, physiological reactions may be strong. Particularly when learning and consolidation of information in memory is accompanied by strong emotions, neural activity during the detection of discrepancy is increased. Signals from the amygdala to other brain parts will also be strong, resulting in strong reactions.

*Psychological reactions to perceived discrepancy*

Based on assumptions within cognitive consistency theories (Festinger 1957; Deutsch and Krauss 1965), the perception and subsequent feelings of discrepancy create tension resulting in dissatisfaction, anger, and guilt (Homans 1958; Adams 1965). In the case of unjust salary, there is a mismatch between the amount of resource received and expected. The magnitude of the tension is assumed to be proportional to the magnitude of the mismatch as experienced by the recipient, and is assumed to result in a proportional strength of motivation to eliminate or reduce the discrepancy. In sum, discrepancy as perceived injustice leads to experienced psychological tension which, in turn, generates negative feelings like anger and/or guilt, as well as motivation to accomplish psychological balance by restoring justice.

In procedural justice theories, a discrepancy between the just and the applied principle or procedure (i.e., consistency in making decisions about salary) is assumed to be experienced as an injustice. An unjust procedure triggers several cognitive, emotional, and attitudinal reactions such as anger, resentment, and distress.

In resource theory, the greater the discrepancy between the actual and the appropriate resources allocated, the greater the assumed resulting psychological tension. Foa and Foa (1974: 221) concludes that people are "frustrated" when they are deprived of an expected resource. Thus, the person deprived of some resource (when the expected resource type and actual resource type are discrepant) will be frustrated and motivated to accomplish psychological balance.

According to retributive justice theory, psychological reactions to an experienced discrepancy between appropriate behavior and inappropriate behavior generate tension and feelings of revenge. Appropriate behavior is often derived from religious or ideological beliefs and, therefore, are often deep rooted (see also moral mandate, Skitka and Houston 2001, or moral intuitions, Haidt and Graham 2007) and severely experienced. Inappropriate behavior not only endangers the respect of the person(s) involved, but also of the family, tribe, or religious or ideological collective.

### *The Nature of Behavioral Responses to Discrepancy*

When people are treated unjustly or are frustrated in receiving resources, they react to the injustice or frustration in several ways. Allocation events consist of several elements, and each element or combination of elements can be the focus of the recipient's attention. Attention can be focused on the final outcome of the allocation process, on the way the allocation decision is taken, on the type of resource distributed, on the personality of the allocating actor, or on the relationship between recipient and actor (Törnblom and Vermunt 1999).

*Allocated outcome*

Adams (1965) proposed six different response alternatives for unfairly treated recipients: Recipients can alter (1) inputs and/or (2) outcomes; (3) they can cognitively distort inputs and outcomes; (4) they may leave the situation; (5) act on the other, or even (6) change their object of comparison. So, Adams proposes that when recipients do not accept an actor's justifications for deviating from equal division they not only experience aversive feelings (injustice, moral indignation, anger, guilt, and the like), but they also tend to act (cognitively or behaviorally) consistent with those feelings in order to restore justice.

*Procedural rules*

In the case of behavioral reactions to unjust treatment, procedural justice research has provided convincing evidence that procedural injustice may cause a wide array of behavioral reactions, including theft, arson, absence from work, destruction of equipment, violence, disloyalty, and gossip, to mention a few (see Modde and Vermunt 2007).

*Resource type*

Resource theory states that when people are deprived of expected resources they become frustrated. Frustration may result in retaliation attempts, which is the major way in which people deal with being denied an expected positive resource or receiving an unexpected negative resource (Donnenworth and Foa 1974). According to theory and relevant research, the victim prefers retaliation by taking away from the source of deprivation a resource similar to the one that the victim was deprived of, or by reciprocating a negative resource similar to the one received. The more dissimilar the resources, the more residual frustration and hostility remain subsequent to retaliation, which in turn might remain over time, add to other frustrations, and result in future flare-ups of hostility. Foa and Foa (1974) suggested that people may retaliate in three different ways to reduce or eliminate frustration. In *direct retaliation* (the most effective revenge) the victim retaliates directly against the source of frustration; retaliation against a third party is called *displacement* (an ineffective way of reducing frustration); and in vicarious retaliation (which appears to increase rather than decrease frustration): someone other than the victim retaliates against the source of frustration.

*Person of the actor*

Retributive justice theories state that revenge will often take the form of punishing the wrongdoer (Darley and Pittman 2003). The wrongdoer has violated a social norm, often leading to moral outrage in the community members. The violation disrupts the fabric of community rules, and the wrongdoer should be punished in order to deter others from violating the rules. Social norms can be part of a society as a whole, but also of specific groups or collectives. A criminal gang can develop norms, and when members violate the norms they are punished severely. Some religious groups also exert severe punishment when norms—religious norms—are violated. Revenge out of honor is accepted in some religious groups in order to defend the respect of the family, and is directed toward the wrongdoer.

*Recipient–actor relationship*

The relationship between recipient and actor can be one of mutual trust and dignity, or of mistrust and indignity. To restore justice or to overcome frustration recipients may engage in actions to lower an actor's status or to increase their own status. Gossip, for instance, is often applied to change the status difference or balance between actor and recipient (see Mikula and Schwinger 1978).

*The strength of the behavioral reaction to discrepancy*

Reactions, thus, are preferred when they are congruent with the discrepancy of the focal resource: reaction in kind. Resource theory states that reactions are in accordance with the degree of the experienced discrepancy and with the type of resource under which the reaction is subsumed. The further away the resource is from the focal resource—based on difference in fundamental quantity—the stronger the reaction has to be to reduce the injustice and frustration of the experienced discrepancy.

### *Injustice and Frustration*

Why do people feel injustice in the one case and frustration in the other? As will be remembered, I have defined the discrepancy triggering emotions of frustration as one between two types of resources: the resource type expected and the resource type actually received. Someone in need of food who receives a pat on the shoulder is frustrated because their basic need for food is not fulfilled. When this type of discrepancy is detected—as described above—self-preservation motives are triggered which initiate actions of self-protection—in some cases, self-protection will take the form of aggression (Foa and Foa 1974). The amount of frustration runs parallel with the type of resource that is applied in replacement of the resource necessary to fulfill the need. An actor's pat on the shoulder (status) instead of the expected food is further away from need fulfillment than receiving money—the next neighbor of food in the circumplex structure designed by Foa and Foa (1974). The frustration in receiving a pat on the shoulder while being hungry will be greater than in the case of receiving money. The needy person can buy food with the money provided, while a pat on the shoulder does not contribute to fulfill this need

The case where a person is rewarded with the "wrong" resource—the pat on the shoulder while hungry—may also result in feelings of injustice. Comparing their own situation with that of another recipient, quantity differences in allocated resources trigger feelings of injustice. If one determines that the difference between self and other is not deserved, then this can result in feelings of injustice. In this case, the person is doubly punished: frustrated by not having the actual need fulfilled *and* unfairly treated by the undeserved suffering: the pat on the shoulder

| | Right resource | Wrong resource |
|---|---|---|
| Right quantity | Satisfied + Just | Frustrated + Just |
| Wrong quantity | Satisfied + Unjust | Frustrated + Unjust |

**Figure 7.2 Combination of self preservation and moral emotions as a function of resource content and quantity**

is less than another received and less than the person finds appropriate. Other combinations of frustration and justice feelings are possible as well: a person may receive the correct resource for need fulfillment, but receives too little of it. This is the standard situation that is investigated most in social justice research, whether it concerns research in the realm of distributive justice, procedural justice, or retributive justice (Greenberg and Cohen 1982). Another important combination of frustration and justice feelings is if a person receives the right amounts but of the wrong resource (if that is possible to measure). An example is the child who did not receive the present they asked for, but received one that is just as expensive and liked just as much. The combination that is experienced as most positive with regard to self-preservation as well as moral emotions is when a person receives the right resource in the right quantity; that person is satisfied and feels justly treated. Figure 7.2 depicts the four combinations.

*Allocation Event as a "Gestalt"*

As said before, in the final outcome of an allocation event the resource type and how the allocation decision was carried out are part of the overall assessment of the appropriateness of the allocation decision. This implies that two crucial emotions are involved when the allocation decision is not taken appropriately: frustration and injustice (see Figure 7.2). Recipients will experience both emotions when confronted with inappropriate allocation decisions, but in varying degrees. Frustration will be experienced because goal behavior is blocked and self-preservation emotions are activated. But injustice will also be experienced because the amount of actual received resource is not in accordance with the amount of expected resource, and moral emotions are activated. Whether the recipient will experience frustration or injustice is dependent on the content of the perceived discrepancy: quality or quantity. If the discrepancy is perceived between the actual and expected type of resource, frustration is most likely to occur. And if the discrepancy is between the amounts of the same resource, injustice is likely to occur.

It is not only emotions that are triggered by experiencing discrepancy between expected and received amount and type of resource in an allocation event: experiences of discrepancy with regard to one resource trigger cognitions on other elements as well (Folger 1977, 1987; Folger et al. 1979). The discrepancy experience may trigger cognitions about the reasons for the experienced discrepancy, as well as cognitions about the way the allocation decision that led to the discrepancy was carried out. Moreover, the discrepancy triggers cognitions about the actor who took the allocation decision. Because the allocation event is seen as a unity, as a "Gestalt," a script, learned from former confrontations with allocation decisions, recipients have these elements of the event cognitively within their mental set. According to consistency theories, to reduce tension between the relevant elements, the recipient searches for ways to reduce tension. And according to resource theory, the elements that are closest to the focal resource (for which the discrepancy is experienced) will be triggered first, followed by other relevant elements. And as a consequence, actions to reduce tension will follow the same course. In addition, the stronger the discrepancies that are experienced, the stronger will be reaction to reduce tension and thus to restore justice and satisfaction.

### *Integration of Justice Theories and Resource Theory*

An overall assessment of the fairness of an event requires information about the outcomes (distributive justice) as well as the processes by which the outcomes were produced (procedural justice) and the type of resource allocated (resource theory). Provided this information is available, we need to know how these forms of justice judgments combine to enable an assessment of how just or how frustrating an allocation event is in its totality. Moreover, as any given allocation event involves different kinds of resources (e.g., money, respect, information, goods, etc.), we need information not only about the impact of their valences (in addition to the resulting outcome valence of the allocation event) on justice judgments (see Törnblom and Vermunt 1999; Fararo and Skvoretz 1993); we also need to know whether and how the qualitative nature of the resource may affect justice conceptions and behaviors.

Based on these considerations, I will attempt to integrate the three relevant theoretical approaches: distributive justice theories, procedural justice theories, and resource theory. Törnblom and Vermunt (1999, 2007) have already made attempts to integrate distributive and procedural justice theories, procedural justice theories and resource theory, and distributive justice theories and resource theory. Now the time has come to integrate all three theories. Figure 7.3[1] depicts the relationship between the three theories. The three circles indicate the operational area of the three different theories. Each of the three theories has a unique area, but also an area in common with another theory and with both other theories. For instance, distributive justice (DJ) theories have an area in common with resource theory (RT), indicated by DJ ∩ RT, and procedural justice theories also have an area in common with resource theory, indicated by PJ ∩ RT. Törnblom and Vermunt (2007, 2012) developed hypotheses based on resource theory assumptions about the type and intensity of reaction to distributive unfairness and procedural

1 ∩ (intersection) in set theoretical terms means that both areas show overlap

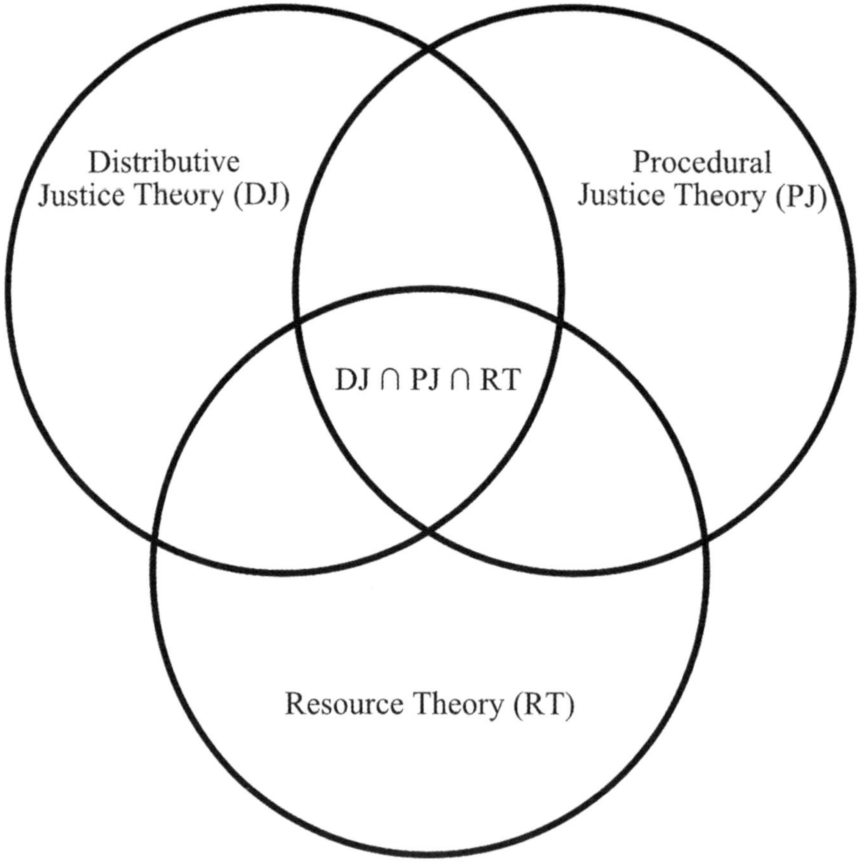


**Figure 7.3 The relationship between distributive justice theory, procedural justice theory, and resource theory**

*Source:* Adapted from Törnblom and Vermunt 2012.

unfairness. The commonality of distributive justice theories and procedural justice theories, denoted by DJ ∩ PJ, is a core activity of justice researchers as well (see Greenberg and Colquitt 2005). In Figure 7.3, the area denoted by DJ ∩ PJ ∩ RT has not, as yet, been explored. This area represents the parts the three theories have in common.

With just the insights given by Törnblom and Vermunt (2007), integration of the three theories will hardly be possible: discrepancies with regard to outcomes for an allocated resource have to be combined with discrepancies with regard to procedures, another resource, both of which are often representations of a different resource. For social resource theory this combination is not optimal in that two different types of resource are involved. According to Foa and Foa (1974), people reciprocate in kind, which means that people prefer allocation outcomes and procedures of the same resource. Justice theories, however, suggest that recipients compare amounts of resources: a fair procedure (accurate procedure, Information) can to a large extent compensate for an unfair outcome (not getting a deserved bonus, Money; Folger et al. 1979; Van den Bos et al. 1997). Moreover, Van den Bos et al. (1998) showed that information about the fairness of a procedure (or outcome) is used as a proxy for estimating the fairness of the outcome (or procedure). Justice theories do not bother about the type of resource involved. One way to solve this issue is to look more carefully at the content of the six resources conceptualized by Foa and Foa. The six resource classes defined by Foa and Foa are positioned on a circle. This structure implies that some resource classes are adjacent to each other while others are not or even opposite from each other. Adjacent resource classes have more in common than further away or opposite resource classes. So, money has more in common with goods than with the resource class love. The status resource class has more in common with the information resource class than with goods. The positions of the six resource classes is shown below:

Love

Status Service

Information Goods

Money

Moreover, hypotheses in which the effects of the three components (outcome, procedure, resource type) on fairness judgments are predicted will be possible only if distribution, procedure, and resource type are not only described in terms of amounts, as in the fairness theories, but also in terms of the expected and received types of resources.

Table 7.1 shows the relationships between type and amount of resource. I make a differentiation between the focal resource (outcome) to which the recipient's attention is drawn and the additional resource (procedure) that may compensate, justify, or mitigate the unfairness and/or frustration experienced with the focal resource. The recipient may experience a discrepancy between the expected type of the focal resource (efr) and the received type of the focal resource (rfr), i.e., efr $\neq$ rfr versus efr = rfr. The recipient also may experience a discrepancy between the expected amount of the focal resource (efra) and the received amount of the focal resource (rfra); efra $\neq$ rfra versus efra = rfra. The same reasoning applies for the additional resource: The recipient experiences that the expected type of the additional resource (ear) is the same as or different from the received type of the additional resource (rar): ear $\neq$ rar versus ear = rar. The recipient also experiences whether the expected amount of the additional resource (eara) is the same as or different from the expected amount of the received additional resource (rara);

eara ≠ rara versus eara = rara. That part of Table 7.1 is shown in which the type of focal and additional resource are not the same (fr ≠ ar): the most interesting part visualizing the combination of justice theories and resource theory. Moreover, Table 7.1 depicts the usual combination of outcomes and procedures applied in distributive and procedural justice research.

In an allocation event, the recipient often has information about the outcome, the applied procedure, and resource type, and experiences discrepancies between the expected and received types and amounts of a resource. The evaluation process starts with the experience of a discrepancy on a *focal resource*: the recipient gets less (more) than expected (not expected) of a resource, allocated by an actor who delivered it by an expected (not expected) *additional resource*. For instance, employees received an unfair small financial bonus (Money), while they expected sufficient support (Service) from their superior, and the superior made the bonus decision without expected discussion (Status: cell 8 of Table 7.1). The employees' overall evaluation of the allocation event will be negative and they will experience feelings of frustration and unfairness. The employees are now in a state of stress and will be strongly motivated to reduce the stress.

**Table 7.1 Equal and unequal amounts and types of resources**

| | **efr = rfr** | | **efr ≠ rfr** | |
|---|---|---|---|---|
| | efra = rfra | efra ≠ rfra | efra = rfra | efra ≠ rfra |
| **fr ≠ ar** | | | | |
| eara = rara | 1 | 2 | 3 | 4 |
| ear = rar | | | | |
| eara ≠ rara | 5 | 6 | 7 | 8 |
| **ear vs rar** | | | | |
| eara = rara | 9 | 10 | 11 | 12 |
| ear ≠ rar | | | | |
| eara ≠ rara | 13 | 14 | 15 | 16 |

The 16 cells in Table 7.1 contain fairness evaluations as well as experiences of happiness/frustration, type and intensity of behavioral responses, and residual frustration and feelings of unfairness when the experienced discrepancy is not solved completely. Cell 1, for example, represents an allocation event in which recipient receives the expected kind and amount of a focal resource, delivered by an expected type and amount of the additional resource. The actor gives the financial bonus (money) the recipient expected, in a respectful way (status), and both in the right amounts. The recipient feels happy and fairly treated, and will not engage in any action to alter the situation. Cell 2 describes a rather similar allocation event. The only difference between cell 1 and cell 2 is that the received amount of the focal resource does not match the amount the recipient expected: the recipient does not receive sufficient bonus. The recipient feels happy at receiving the right type of the focal and additional resources, but has feelings of unfairness because of the discrepancy between the expected and received focal resource amount. Applying fairness/resource theory, the recipient will try to restore the unfairness. In the case of financial bonus, the recipient prefers actor's action to increase the bonus. In other words, the recipient prefers correction of the unfair bonus, thus prefers a procedure that is aimed at compensating the bonus (correctability rule; Leventhal, 1980). If this attempt does not lead to an appropriate bonus, the recipient is left with a residual amount of feelings of unfairness which may lead to stress and depression. The recipient in cell 5 feels happy about the amount and type of financial bonus received but experiences that the way the bonus is conveyed is not what they expected. The recipient feels happy and fair but they experience the given reasons for the bonus insufficient: the recipient feels traces of uneasiness related to unfairness, The recipient may let it go or takes steps toward the actor to ask for more details (accuracy rule; Leventhal 1980). Mark that the additional resource information (accuracy criterion) becomes the focal resource. Cell 6 tells another story. The recipient feels unfairly rewarded as well as unfairly treated—the amounts of both the focal resource as well as of the additional resource do not match with expectations. The recipient is angry about the actor's behavior, and his/her feelings of unfairness are therefore higher than one expects from the "double" resource discrepancy. I assume that in cell 6 the unfairness feelings are strong: "I deserve the bonus and my boss uses the wrong arguments to withhold me the bonus". The recipient prefers to convince the actor to restore the wrong arguments used to withhold the bonus (correctability, accuracy). The recipient asks for good reasons for withholding the bonus. In this way the recipient tries to correct the unfair bonus. If the actor is not inclined to correct the given arguments for the unfair felled bonus the recipient keeps a high degree of anger.

With the resources Love and Service, it is a different matter. It is difficult to disentangle the focal and additional resource: The love given is part and parcel with the way the love is given (Törnblom and Vermunt 2007). An actor cannot give love or service in an inappropriate way; if so, the love is infected. The recipient finds it difficult to weigh both unfairness experiences because they have no point of reference: Does the amount of love increase if the actor conveys the love more warmly? It is conceivable that happiness with the love is lower in cell 6 than in the other cells of the first quadrant, although the right type of resource is allocated. It is not only feelings of unfairness that appear, but also frustration: is the actor allocating something else?

Based on the model, hypotheses can be made about: (1) the injustice and/ or frustration felt; (2) the most preferred action the recipient can take to restore justice and/or to remove the obstacles that block goal attainment; (3) the strength of the action; and (4) the amount of residual injustice, frustration, and/or stress after action. Let us start with a simplified allocation event in which the recipient receives the right type of resources but with a difference in the amounts expected and received.

Because the right type of resource is allocated, the recipient's feelings of frustration about not reaching the goal—getting the bonus—are negligible in all cells 1, 2, 5, and 6 of the top-left quadrant of Table 7.1. The recipient experiences feelings of injustice in varying amounts in cells 2, 5, and 6. Recipients in cell 1 experience no injustice because the received amount of the right resource is equal to the expected amount of the right resource. In the sociological and economic distributive fairness research tradition, people's evaluation of their salary is a subject of investigation. They are asked to indicate how satisfied they are with their salary, and how fair they evaluate it to be. These types of questions generate data that can be subsumed under the content of cells 1 and 2. Jasso (1978) developed a formula relating the just reward evaluation with the actual received reward to predict people's satisfaction with, for instance, their income. Procedural fairness researchers, mainly psychologists, investigate the impact of the fairness of the rules and procedures that actors apply in allocating a resource. The procedural fairness studies started with research Thibaut and Walker (1975) carried out in courts to investigate suspects' reactions to their treatment by the judges. The results showed, among many other things, the suspects' satisfaction when the judges were kind to them. Later on, justice researchers conducted studies to investigate the effects of fair/unfair procedures on the fairness of outcomes. In the above-mentioned Thibaut and Walker study, it turned out that suspects judged the verdict as more fair when they got the opportunity to inform the judge about their case than in cases where the suspects did not get this opportunity. Thibaut and Walker explained these results in terms of self-interest: in explaining their case, suspects increase the chances that the judge will be mild in the verdict. Lind et al. (1990) however, found that fair procedures (voice) had a positive influence on the fairness of the verdict, even when voice was given after the final decision was made. Lind et al. reasoned that the judge's attention being given to the suspects increased their status, which was strongly reduced through being suspects of criminal behavior. It is interesting to note that in those cases the type of resource of outcome and procedure are similar: status loss and status gain.

Developing the fairness/resource theory, I hypothesize that experience of an unfair focal resource (outcome) combined with a fair additional resource (procedure) that is close to the focal resource, will be preferred more, will elicit less strong attempts to restore fairness and leaves less tension, than a further away additional resource will do (see also Törnblom and Vermunt 2007). In other words, an additional resource promoting compensation (money for money, service for service: 'compensation' is used here more strictly than usual) changes outcomes most effectively (Adams 1965), and is the strategy that the recipient prefers most. In the case where an actor gives false information, the recipient prefers to get the truth out of the actor (compensation). If compensation does not work, the recipient can try other strategies as well. After an unfair allocation of information (lying), the recipient prefers that actor offers excuses or justifications (information for information; "I was confused when I told you that", respectively "The matter was too complex") than de-appreciating the importance of the information ("The topic was not important enough to worry about"; status is situated next to information in the circle). Love (interactional justice; Bies and Moag 1986) often softens the blow of an unfair action (mitigation: "although I did not tell the truth, I still like you"; love is further away from information), but is preferred least. Changing the object of comparison, or cognitive distortion of outcomes and inputs (Adams 1965), mitigates the unfairness as well (see also Vermunt 2002; Vermunt and Steensma 2001).

Information is often used to justify actions or allocation decisions: The actor gives reasons for the allocation decision: *justification*. Further, I differentiate *appreciation* of components of the allocation event: the recipient tries to lower the actor's status or decision and thus works on their own self-esteem (Vermunt and Steensma 2001), or deprecates the value of the focal resource. Compensation and justification are strategies primarily aimed at the actor as causing agent (see also Adams 1965) and are, therefore, most preferred, while appreciation and mitigation are strategies primarily aimed at the recipient as agent and are less preferred. I assume, further, that the recipient prefers these strategies to strategies aimed at violating norms and rules like reducing effort (Adams 1965), taking longer breaks, or taking more destructive actions like arson or theft. However, if "legal" actions have no success, the recipient may be tempted to go over to norm-violating behavior. Relevant in this respect is the study by Skarlicki and Folger (1997) who found norm-violating behavior to perceived injustice by mistreated employees toward their employer.

I emphasize here that the recipient's reaction to unfairness elicits a fairness loop, as described in chapters 3 and 5. Those chapters raised the issue of how a person (actor) behaves when confronted with a moral dilemma or problem. I made clear that the actor's motivations, emotions, and cognitions play a key role in handling the situation. Now that actors have a history, with a salient preceding allocation event, how will they act? The four strategies the recipients (the actor in the next allocation event) apply can be positioned in a two-dimensional plane spanned by axes defined as the degree to which self-preservation emotions (high, low) are fulfilled by the recipients' action and/or moral emotions (high, low). The emotions trigger the motivation to restore justice and/or reduce frustration. Compensation is positioned high on both dimensions because recipients get back (self-preservation) what they thought they deserved (moral). Compensation fulfills the self-preservation emotions as well as the moral emotions, and is preferred most. Justification is preferred next: justification is positioned high on the moral emotion dimension but (moderately) low on the self-preservation emotion dimension. Appreciation is positioned moderately high on the self-preservation emotion dimension and moderately high on the moral emotion dimension, while mitigation is positioned low on the moral emotion dimension and moderately low on the self-preservation emotion dimension.

The main difference between mitigation and justification is that mitigation triggers mainly emotional responses while justification triggers mainly cognitive responses. As outlined previously (Chapter 3), giving reasons for an allocation decision is an important component to labeling a decision "moral" (the decisive criterion is that the reasons are accepted by group members). Thus, from a moral point of view, justification is a more important ingredient of moral reasoning than mitigation. The last strategy is aimed more at protecting self. These arguments may lead to the following hypotheses:

*Hypothesis 1a*

Recipients confronted with an unfair focal resource allocation and a fair additional resource experience less unfairness when the additional resource matches the focal resource then when not.

Hypothesis 1a specifies recipient's reactions to an unfair outcome combined with a fair procedure (the fair process effect). Notwithstanding the reduction of unfairness by applying a fair procedure, residual feelings of unfairness still exists and the more so when the applied procedure not matches with the outcome. Recipients' most preferred reaction to unfair resource distribution is to increase the resource outcome, and in this way restore justice. Information about recipients' performance as a basis for unfair outcome distribution may lead to an increase in their performance or to a decrease. The precise action depends on the way the actor has allocated the resource information and/or financial outcome/reward. A recipient's experience that the actor treats the recipient with disrespect will not result in improved performance. When recipients have experienced respect from an actor they will be more inclined to improve their performance (status increase for status increase). So, the nature of the reaction to injustice depends on the characteristics of the entire allocation event that the recipient has in mind.

The most preferred reaction to status loss is to increase own status or to decrease the status of the actor. This may result in showing disrespect for the actor, for instance by directly, face to face, taking a denigrating stance towards the actor. When status differences are large, it may be risky to denigrate the actor, recipients go over to a less risky strategy: the recipient may spread negative information about the actor, or make depreciating remarks about them. A last resort action would be to take goods or money from the actor; a last resort action in that the resource money is far away from the resource status and will not reduce effectively feelings of unfairness and frustration (Modde and Vermunt 2007).

*Hypothesis 1a1*

Recipients confronted with an unfair focal resource allocation with a fair additional resource make stronger attempts to restore justice, whether by compensation, justification, appreciation or mitigation, when the additional resource matches the focal resource then when not.

If recipients strive for compensation for the unfair focal resource—where the actor has intentionally decided to lower the focal resource amount and the recipient finds this unjust—they must make strong attempts to restore the former level of the focal resource. Recipients will probably have far less hard a task to get a friendly word from the actor. Asking for the reasons for the reduced amount of the focal resource makes actors more vulnerable and costs recipients time and energy to get actors to give the reasons.

*Hypothesis 1a2*
The residual negative feelings of receiving an unfair focal resource are smallest when carried out with a fair additional resource that matches most the focal resource: thus negative residual feelings are smallest for compensation and strongest for mitigation.

According to Foa (1971), people tend to reciprocate and retaliate in kind. It is less likely that they will react via behaviors that are not congruent with the behaviors that caused the tension. Moreover, Foa and Foa (1974) suggested that retaliation or reciprocation is most effective (with the least tension remaining) via behaviors subsumed under the same resource: trying to get your stolen money back is preferred to getting the opportunity to voice your opinion about it. However, the fair process effect shows that an unfair financial bonus is evaluated as less unfair when the accompanying procedure (voice) is evaluated as fair than as unfair (Folger et al. 1979). Applying Foa and Foa's ideas to the content of focal (outcome) and additional resource (procedure) leads to the hypothesis that the fair process effect will be more effective—reduces unfairness most—if both the focal and additional resource are of the same type than if they are different.

*Hypothesis 1a3*
Given an unfair focal resource, reduction of tension will be better accomplished by a fair additional resource allocation if the additional resource is of the same type as the focal resource than of a different type.

If the received salary cut is experienced as unfair, financial compensation in terms of a one-time bonus will reduce tension more than receiving voice. Even if the given voice is experienced as fair, the remaining tension will be greater by receiving voice than when financial compensation is offered (Hypothesis 2b).

*Hypothesis 1a4*
Remaining tension—after reduction attempts—will be smaller if the focal and additional resource are of the same type than of a different type.

Not all hypotheses generated according to the model presented in Table 7.1 are described here; I have concentrated on cells 2 and 5 of Table 7.1. In cell 6 of the table, the recipient experiences unfairness in the focal as well as the additional resource. When a recipient experiences unfairness in both modes of resources (focal as well as additional), I assume that the unfairness in the additional resource has to be undone before the unfairness in the focal resource can be properly evaluated. I assume that the recipient prefers a change in the applied additional resource. Changing the additional resource means that the recipient first of all seeks compensation for the applied procedure. For instance, when an actor does not use all available information to make the focal resource allocation (e.g., demotion), the recipient first tries to influence the actor to use all the available information. If the recipient does not succeed in finding compensation, the recipient tries to convince the actor to give good reasons for not using all the information. Next in line are appreciation and mitigation attempts. Compensation and, to a somewhat lesser extent, justification, if realized, bring a proper evaluation of the focal resource unfairness closer. When an actor uses all relevant information and the amount of the focal resource is still less than the recipient thinks they deserve, the fair additional resource increases the fairness evaluation of the focal resource allocation (the fair process effect; Folger et al. 1979).

*Hypothesis 2a*
When a recipient is confronted with focal as well as additional resource unfairness, the recipient prefers working on the actor to change the amount of the additional resource than changing the focal resource.

*Hypothesis 2b*
A recipient prefers compensation to justification, appreciation, or mitigation to restore additional resource fairness.

*The scarcity argument*
The top-right quadrant of Table 7.1, with cell numbers 3, 4, 7, and 8, represents receiving a focal resource the recipient did not expect; in cell 3, the amounts of focal and additional resources are received as expected; in cell 4, the amount of the focal resource is not received as expected while the amount of the additional resource is received as expected. In these four cells the combined effects of unfairness and frustration are described, and they form the essence of the fairness/resource theory.

I will explain the allocation process in cell 4. Let us assume that a group of rioters in a courtroom await the judge's verdict. Each group member is accused of violence during a football match. Their actions caused no injuries, but material damage was relatively large. The group of hooligans expect a financial punishment—a fine. Their general opinion is that they deserve a mild fine: the circumstances were such that a group supporting the opposite team challenged them time after time. Instead, the judge decides differently: they receive a task fine (Service) instead of a financial fine (Money). Some of the group members evaluate the magnitude of the unexpected fine as fair (cell 3), while other group members evaluate the magnitude of the unexpected fine as unfair (cell 4). Both groups evaluate the opportunity the judge gave them to present their case as fair. The group members have demanding jobs, are able to pay a fine, but have a hard time performing the task. They are all frustrated and the members who evaluate the fine as inappropriate despite the given voice reason that the judge did not listen to them, and had not given them due consideration (Tyler and Lind 1992). Outside the courtroom they shout, and some of them promise not to leave it at that and proceed to a higher court. They seek compensation. The group members are frustrated with regard to the focal resource, while they feel unfairly treated in that they think that the judge did not listen well to them. It is frustrating for the rioters: For them, time is a scarce resource while money is less scarce. For a beggar, the verdict would be much easier to accept. The beggar has enough time but no money. The frustration is not primarily due to the difference in expected and received resource type but in the scarceness of the resource. The rioters and the beggar prefer the loss of a less scarce resource to the loss of a scarce resource. Scarceness is expressed in amounts: The task fine represents the scarce resource time and is viewed by the rioters as an unfair verdict. I assume that feelings of unfairness (moral emotion, see Chapter 5) have precedence over feelings of frustration (self-preservation emotion). In the terms of Skarlicki and Folger (1997), the given legal case is an example of a three-way interaction between distributive justice, procedural justice, and interactional justice. In the case, distributive unfairness is experienced with the undeserved verdict, procedural fairness is experienced in the received voice, and interactional unfairness is experienced in that the judge gave no due consideration. The example presented of the rioters' case gives rise to the formulation of a four-way interaction between type and amount of target resource, and additional resources of status (voice and consideration). For the sake of argument, I propose the following hypotheses.

*Hypothesis 3.1*
Loss of a scarce focal resource results in more frustration than loss of a less scarce focal resource.

*Hypothesis 3.2*
A discrepancy between amount of an expected and received focal resource which is scarce is evaluated as more unfair than a discrepancy between amount of an expected and received focal resource which is less scarce.

*Hypothesis 3.2a*
A discrepancy between amount of an expected and received additional resource will be evaluated as less fair when the focal resource is scarce in comparison to a less scarce focal resource.

*Hypothesis 3.2b*
Attempts to restore justice will be stronger for an unfair and scarce focal resource than for an unfair and less scarce focal resource.

*Hypothesis 3.2b1*
Compensation as a restoring strategy will be preferred to other strategies in that it reduces feelings of unfairness as well as of frustration.

*Hypothesis 3.2c*
Unsuccessful attempts to restore justice leave more residual feelings of unfairness in the case of a scarce resource as compared to a less scarce resource.

Not seeking compensation leaves the rioters with a residue of frustration, but if the judge gives good reasons for deviating from the rioter's preference, justice is restored. But in the case of justification, frustration is still present, although justice restoration positively influences the rioters' mood and improves the relationship with the court. It is even possible that the residue of frustration is devalued.

## Observers' Reactions

Most people, at least once in their lifetime, have observed how others allocate resources (love, service) mutually. Sometimes these allocation events are positive, like a child watching his/her parents exchange glances showing their affection. Other events have negative valence, like bystanders watching men attacking a passer-by. In the justice literature there is much attention for the observation process of allocation events. As already stated, an allocation event consists of an actor, a recipient, the resource types allocated, the outcomes, and the procedures, and also consists of people who observe the event. Observers sometimes focus on actors and their allocation decision, on recipients, or on the total event. It depends on the theoretical approach advocated as to which element of the event is focal. According to the relational model of authority (Tyler and Lind 1992), the observers' attention is focused on the actor's behavior to infer their relationship with the actor. If the actor is fair towards the recipient, an observer may infer that the actor will also be fair to him/her should the observer become a recipient. In studies on lay-offs, it was shown that the treatment of the victims of the lay-off had a strong impact on the behavior of those who were not affected. The observers had more trust in the authority and accepted more the lay-off decision when they perceived that their colleagues were treated fairly.

Observers sometimes only have information about a recipient's behavioral outcomes in events in which no specific actor can be distinguished. The only information the observer has is about the recipient's fate. Often, the recipient is an innocent victim of crime and the observer constructs a judgment about the causes of the victim's fate. According to Lerner (1980), observers are often inclined to seek a causal connection between a recipient's fate and their behavior. People who believe that the world is a just place where all people get what they deserve tend to attribute a victim's fate to their bad or improper behavior: In a just world, bad behavior is followed by bad consequences. People who have only observed the victim's bad consequences infer that this must have been caused by bad behavior.

An observer even derogates an innocent victim in order to maintain the belief in a just world (Montada and Lerner 1998).

Belief in a just world may also be a factor that explains why some people do not help victims of crime. The Kitty Genovese case showed that more than 30 observers watching the attack on Kitty Genovese did not react properly. Some of the observers thought that she deserved the treatment and did not intervene, or intervened very late. Of course, the literature has come up with other explanations for the observers' reluctance to react properly. One is that observers do not react because they think that others will do. The term coined for not behaving properly in such instances is "diffusion of responsibility." In the Kitty Genovese case, observers watched the entire allocation event in which a perpetrator attacked a victim. In this situation, the actor, the recipient, and the actor's action—the killing of Kitty Genovese—were all visible to the observers. The thought that other observers would react caused the observers' inaction.

In many other allocation events the consequences of an actor's behavior are not lethal, and eventual differences between recipient and observer reactions to the actor's behavior can be compared. Unfortunately, studies comparing recipient and observer reactions to an actor's actions are scarce, though there are some exceptions: one is the study Jacqueline Modde (2002) carried out as part of her dissertation. In her study, participants were treated differently in an experiment consisting of two parts At the beginning of the experiment participants were informed that they could earn some extra money, dependent on test performance, on top of the standard earnings based on participating in the experiment. In the first part, participants had to make a test and the experimenter told half of the participants that he would look at all four elements of the test as was announced earlier in the experiment (fair treatment). The experimenter told the other participants that he would only look at the results of two elements of the test, breaching a promise (unfair treatment). Observers were unobtrusively brought into a position where they could hear the two experimenters talk to each other about the procedure to follow. Before the participants were given their test score they were asked to evaluate the test procedure so far. Participants (recipients as well as observers) were given a questionnaire in which they could evaluate the experimenters, indicate their own affect, indicate their intention to protest against the (eventual) breach of procedure, and answer a self-esteem measure. In the second part of the experiment the participants got the opportunity to calculate the amount of money they had earned and (anonymously) to take the amount from a pouch in which several coins were placed. Because of time constraints the experimenter was not able to count the total value of the coins.

From the findings of the first part of the experiment, thus before they received their test score, the participants reported more negative affect in their role as recipient than in their role as observer. Intention to protest was not different between recipient and observer. Self-esteem was lower for recipients of the unfair treatment than for observers of the unfair treatment, indicating the loss of status due to the disrespectful treatment. Recipients of the unfair procedure took more money from the pouch than observers did. A conclusion from the results is that observers react more mildly to an actor's unfair behavior, partly due to lower involvement with the unfairness than recipients, and partly due to the effect of the belief in a just world: if the actor is being unfair, the recipient must also be responsible for it.

*Discrepancy between Observed and Expected Behavior*

Individuals have learned which types of behavior are appropriate in an allocation event and which are not. Being rewarded for appropriate behavior and punished for inappropriate behavior gives the child the instruments to behave appropriately and to evaluate their own and others' behavior according to these instruments. These instruments may be norms, values, or behavioral goals. Individuals differ in the level of enhancement of these instruments. Moreover, instruments can be derived from learning in the groups to which an individual adheres, in the collectives to which one belongs. The instruments acquired from the different environments may differ in content, so that the individual may be confronted with cognitive and/or moral dilemmas.

The instruments are not acquired in isolation, but in a social context. The context can be the family, school, social group, work or other social environments like being in a restaurant or while traveling (in public or private transportation). The instruments are connected to chains of actions, of which most are carried out automatically (see also Bargh et al. 1996). These so-called scripts are stored in memory, together with what is or is not appropriate in the situation (the perception, action, and perception-of-action loop: Wolters and Raffone 2008). It is inappropriate to have dinner in a restaurant and not to pay for it. The restaurant script prescribes what is appropriate in that situation and what is not.

With learned scripts in mind, individuals evaluate how others behave according to the rules and norms of the script. Allocation events have a script-like nature. The only difference is that allocation scripts are universal because allocation of resources is a general phenomenon. A restaurant script has features relating to allocation processes in common with all other scripts. With the scripts in mind, individuals evaluate, for instance, the experiment script in Modde's study. Observers of an interaction between actor and recipient expect that the actor—experimenter—will behave respectfully toward the recipient. There are also norms to be applied in the specific environment of an experiment. An observer perceives that the experimenter does not behave according to the rules and norms of the experimenter script. The observer experiences a discrepancy between the observed and the expected behavior of experimenter.

*Physiological Reactions to Perceived Discrepancy*

Observers are not receiving a positive or negative resource—they are involved indirectly in the allocation event. Still, they can be morally or otherwise aroused by the perception of the allocation event. These pieces of information may show a discrepancy, which means that the expected behavior from memory (script) and perceived behavior from the visual cortex do not fit. The situation previously described for a recipient's perception of discrepancy between expected and received resource will probably also work for observers experiencing a discrepancy between what they perceive and what they retrieve from memory. So-called predictive coding models propose that this process of cognitive inference "proceeds as an iterative matching process of top-down predictions against bottom-up evidence along the visual cortical hierarchy" (Egner et al. 2010: 16601; see O'Doherty et al. 2003).

*Psychological Reactions to Perceived Discrepancy*

Perceiving a discrepancy between expected and observed behavior will arouse emotions. An emotion that is less likely to occur in observers is frustration. Because observers are not directly involved in the allocation process they do not expect to receive a specific resource: they are not blocked directly in goal-approaching behavior. It is more likely, in that the impolite behavior happens to someone else, that an observer is aroused by moral emotions and less by self-preservation emotions (Mullen 2007). They may feel anger (Modde 2002) in that another is treated badly, and/or they may experience shame of being a witness of inappropriate behavior.

Rubin and Peplau (1973), studying belief in a just world, found that observers evaluated the "losers" of a lottery rather positively: they felt compassion for them, liked them, and felt less resentment towards them. Other studies, however, showed victim derogation when observers rated innocent victims (see Hafer and Bègue 2005; Chapter 2 of this volume) in order to maintain the belief in a just world. Further, in line with self-enhancement, Modde found that observers' self-esteem ratings were higher than recipients' self-esteem ratings, but also higher than those of control participants. These last ratings indicate that observers boosted their self-esteem when confronted with an unfairly behaving actor as well as with the presence of an undeservedly badly treated recipient. Lerner (1980) proposed nine strategies to undo the injustice (and restore the belief in a just world that was challenged by perceiving undeserved suffering). Four of these strategies may be subsumed under psychological reactions to discrepancy: refusal to accept the unfairness; denial of the unfairness; reinterpretation of the elements of the allocation event—derogating the victim, upgrading the character of the beneficiaries (actor); and reinterpreting the outcome (the outcome is not that bad; see also Hafer and Bègue 2005).

Hafer (2002) showed that threat to observers' belief in a just world when viewing tv news portraying a victim of robbery and physical assault was caused by the injustice of the innocent victims' suffering. Hafer also found that the threat of injustice instigate rejection of innocent victims.

*Behavioral Reactions to Perceived Discrepancy*

Observers watching a recipient's unfair treatment have several behavioral strategies for reacting to the bad treatment. Lerner (1980) mentions two strategies: prevention—acting to prevent injustice before it occurs—and restitution—helping or compensating the victim. Reichle and Schmitt (2002) differentiate between action strategies and cognitive strategies. Ellard et al. (2002) studied observers' reactions to perpetrators to restore their belief in a just world. Ellard et al. suggested that observers confronted with severe forms of injustice when it is impossible to restore justice or to cognitively distort the outcome (torture as a bad form of negative service) may denote the perpetrator as a demon, as evil. Modde (2002) found that observers of an injustice are not inclined to engage in inappropriate behavior (stealing) to "punish" the perpetrator—the experimenter - who treated the recipient unfairly and who provided them with the pouch of money. Turillo et al. (2002) found that a larger group of participants punished an actor more who kept more money for self than gave to other than when actor divided the money evenly. Participants rewarded the equal dividing actor more than the uneven dividing actor. It is interesting to note that Turillo's study concerned punishing in kind: money for money, while Modde's study concerned the operation of two types of resources: status and money.

Observers' types of behavioral reactions to perceived injustice may be more specifically assumed by applying Foa and Foa's resource theory (1974), although the theory is not focused on observers. It seems plausible to assume that observers who wish to undo the unfairness also show a preference for actions—helping or compensation—that are best for the victim: undo the suffering. Helping can be subsumed under the Service resource class, while compensation may be subsumed under Status. In the Modde study it is unlikely that observers of a recipient's unfair treatment engage in stealing: Money is too far removed from Status and Service in the circumplex structure of resources to be attractive for compensation or helping. In the case where recipients are treated disrespectfully, observers might have a preference for compensation. It is more appropriate if observers had the opportunity to increase the recipient's status position (Rubin and Peplau 1973) that was threatened by the actor's rude behavior or bad luck.

The findings with regard to observers' reactions to unfair behavior of actors are mixed. Some studies show victim derogation when observers are confronted with innocent victim's suffering. Other studies show reactions directed at the actor (Ellard et al. 2002) or at the self (Modde 2002). A splitting factor to explain these differences might be the presence of specific information about or relationship with the actor or recipient: If observers have only vague knowledge about the perpetrator, to denote the perpetrator as demon is feasible but hardly influences the belief in a just world; vague knowledge about the victim will boost self-esteem ("I am not like the unfairly treated recipient").

If observers are familiar with or have some information about the recipient, their reactions are directed at the recipient. Aderman, Brem and Katz found that observers who identified with the victim did not derogate the victim. And this opens avenue for attempts to help the victim and/or to compensate the recipient of the harm for loss of status. In this respect, Reichle and Schmitt state that observers will help if they are convinced that the help is effective and brings not too much costs with it. The question is what kind of help will observers of the suffering of an innocent victim offer?

*Hypothesis 1*
When observers have the opportunity to compensate (help) or to distort information about an unjustly treated recipient, they will preferably restore justice by a form of compensation or help rather than by distorting information.

All things being equal, offering physical or psychological help (Service) matches more the bad state of the victim (negative Service) than distorting information (Information).

*Hypothesis 2*
The greater the perceived discrepancy between expected and observed treatment, the more intense the observer's motivation is to restore justice or the harder the attempts to distort cognitively elements of the allocation event.

*Hypothesis 3*
Moreover, when an observer has no opportunity to restore justice in an appropriate way, the greater will be the residual unfairness and frustration.

Foa and Foa's (1974) resource theory would predict that when restoring an injustice is not possible, or not fully possible, observers will be left with some amount of unfairness, but also frustration because their goal is not reached. The residual frustration may come out when circumstances are appropriate.

In some respects, observers react differently to unfairness than recipients. Because observers often derogate actors (experimenters) as well as victims (recipients), the findings do support Tyler and Lind's (1992) relational model of authority as well as Lerner's (1980) belief in a just world model. Observers clearly hold a realistic view of the real situation in that they evaluate actors more negatively when they treat others unfairly than in the case of fair treatment. Derogating the victim is an indication that observers also hold a less realistic view of the observed situation in that they evaluate innocent victims negatively.

From these findings, I conclude further that actors in an allocation event not only have to take account of recipients' reactions to allocation behavior and outcomes but should also take notice of observers' reactions. Chapter 3 drew attention to the presence of an audience when a person is punished for wrongdoing, using the example of a class situation in which a teacher tries to behave morally correctly. What is morally correct depends on the justifications the actor uses and the acceptance of the justifications by all involved or by as many people as possible, recipient as well as observer. But as the Lerner studies show, people are not just rational in their evaluation of the allocation event. They also behave in a more or less irrational way in that they construct a situation that is not or is less realistic: derogating an innocent victim in cases where a concrete actor is absent. People put much effort into defending their view that the world is a just place where people get what they deserve. By viewing oneself as a good person, good consequences or outcomes will be part of one's actions. In this way, observers protect their favorable place in the world and thus their esteem. Self-preservation motives thus do play a role in observing allocation events, a statement already made in several previous chapters.

Derogating the victim also implies that the perpetrator is out of sight. In this way, observers keep their belief in a just world intact. In situations in which the just world belief applies, there is often no place for a perpetrator. All that observers perceive is the outcome of the event. The consequences of a car accident, the raped girl, the robbed family are often known, but not the other elements of the allocation event. It is therefore plausible, but not permissible, for the observer to focus on the position and perceived intentions and characteristics of the victim. But as I have indicated, an allocation event consists of more than the allocation outcome. And when these elements are introduced, a more varied picture of the observer's evaluation can be found. In the Modde experiment the additional information leads to derogating the actor, which seems to contradict just world belief hypotheses.

Observers' reactions partly confirm Foa and Foa's (1974) theoretical predictions about preference for reacting in kind. Foa and Foa predicted that reactions to goal-blocking behavior—the recipient does not receive the needed resource—are focused on behaviors to acquire the needed resource and if that is not possible to acquire the resource that resembles the missed resource as closely as possible. The reasoning behind this hypothesis is that frustration will be reduced optimally when the lacked resource or the closely related resource is recovered. From the Modde data I conclude that this reaction—regaining status—is also part of an observer's preferred repertory. But why would observers care about the actor's status? They show reduced respect for the actor, and in so doing judge from a moral point of view: this behavior is not acceptable (see also Folger and Skarlicki 1998; Chapter 3 of this volume). Unfair treatment lowers an actor's status and observers show this moral view by derogating the actor. They do not, in agreement with the Foa and Foa predictions, engage in stealing money, which is in sharp contrast to the recipient's behavior. One explanation is that recipients in these experiments could only react by taking money away to undo the unfairness. For observers, this reaction is inappropriate because they do not experience frustration: they themselves are not treated unfairly, or, in other words, they are not withheld a desired resource.

From the findings described above, I conclude that the roles of observer and recipient show remarkable similarities as well as differences, claiming a distinct role for observers in the allocation event.

## Conclusions

This chapter has outlined the first draft of the fairness-resource theory, integrating justice theories and resource theory. Two important elements of the theory are worth mentioning here. The theory has taken into account the accepted (or neglected) difference between the content of the outcome and the procedure. I infer from social resource theory that the optimal allocation event is one in which outcome and procedure are of the same resource: Service for Service and not Money for Service. Based on this inference, a recipient feels more justly treated when demotion (status) is decided after receiving voice (status) than after receiving a dinner (goods). If this inference is correct, Table 7.1 should be extended with a third axis on which difference in type of focal resource and additional resource is added. There are arguments for constructing a third axis, and there are arguments claiming that an additional axis is not necessary. Taking the content and thus the differences between resource types literally it makes sense to add an additional axis. However, Foa and Foa (1974) explain that actors, recipients, and observers act on the meaning they attach to the allocated resource and less so, or not at all, on its literal content. From this statement I infer that the recipient always experiences an unfair or inappropriate focal and/or additional resource more or less as a status loss. Thus, next to loss of the specific resource, unfair and/or inappropriate resource allocation also brings loss in an element all resources have to a smaller or larger extent in common. If this explanation is correct, it may not be necessary to add a third axis to Table 7.1. In addition, this argument explains why a fair procedure (partly) undoes the unfairness of an unfair allocation outcome (fair process effect; Van den Bos et al. 1998), more or less contrary to what Foa and Foa would predict.

The second element to discuss is the primacy of unfairness or dissatisfaction when a recipient experiences a discrepancy between the amount, respectively type, of resources. The point of departure of the reasoning in this book is that the justice motive is the most powerful drive for allocation actions and decisions—more so than self-interest. In my view, therefore, recipients are more focused on the unfairness of the outcome of the allocation process than on its dissatisfaction. However, the more the allocated resources differ from each other the more dissatisfaction pollutes the fairness evaluation of the outcome and procedure. This argument favors the introduction of a third axis in Table 7.1.

This chapter has shown how important an actor's fair behavior is for the recipient and observer. Unfair treatment often results in a recipient's norm-violating behavior. These reactions are not only detrimental for the relationship between actor and recipient, and between actor and observers, but also for the group to which the three role players belong. In the case where the actor is a supervisor or chief of the group, the ingroup atmosphere and relationships, as well as performance, will suffer from their unfair behavior.

The effects of unfair behavior are stronger if the actor and recipient/observer belong to different groups, or when by some cause the actor (or recipient) comes to stand on the other side of the group fence. Subgroups may form that are now antagonistic towards each other. Behaviors that were advantageous for the whole group now become disadvantageous due to mutual hostilities. When recipients are unfairly treated and classify themselves as different from the actor, two subgroups arise. Performance agreements that the recipients accepted before are now viewed with distrust. These shifts develop suddenly and rapidly. Reactions in an intergroup context are far more detrimental than in the context in which actor and recipient are seen as individuals.

Newcomers—people developing new ideas or behaviors, introduce new norms and values—often experience hostility from those who would keep things as they are. The established adhere to their standards of allocation and evaluate the norms and rules as unfair. The established rapidly go over to derogating the newcomers and making their life difficult. New norms and values often go together with changes in one or more components of the allocation event, such as the allocation rules, or the relevance of the type of resource. For instance, people acquire status based on contribution and not on descent: achieved status versus ascribed status. A change of allocation rules is neither smooth nor easy. It is often accompanied by violence and aggression. But in the course of time, when practice models the new norms and when more and more people practice them, the resistance of the established becomes weaker until they accommodate to the new norms. In the meantime, different rules and standards of allocation exist next to each other, increasing confusion, uncertainty, and even despair.

## References

Adams, S. 1965. Inequity in Social Exchange, in *Advances in Experimental Social Psychology*, edited by L. Berkowitz. New York: Academic Press, 267–99.

Aderman, D., Brehm, S., and Katz, L. 1974. Emphatic observation of an innocent victim: The just world revisited. *Journal of Personality and Social Psychology*, 29, 342–7.

Bargh, J.A., Chen, M., and Burrows, L. 1996. Automaticity of social behavior: Direct effects of trait construct and stereotype priming on action. *Journal of Personality and Social Psychology*, 71, 230–44.

Bies, R.J., and Moag, J.S. 1986. Interactional Justice: Communication Criteria of Fairness, in *Research on Negotiations in Organizations*, Vol. 1. edited by R.J. Lewecki, B.H. Sheppard, and M.H. Bazerman. Greenwich, CT: JAI Press, 43–55.

Brockner, J., and Weisenfeld, B.M. 1996. The interactive impact of procedural and outcome fairness on reactions to a decision: The effects of what you do depend on how you do it. *Psychological Bulletin*, 120, 189–208.

Cloward, R.A., and Ohlin, L.E. 1964. *Delinquency and Opportunity*. New York: Free Press.

Darley, J., and Pittman, T. 2003. The psychology of compensatory and retributive justice. *Personality and Social Psychology Review*, 7, 324–36.

Davis, M. 1983. How to make the punishment fit the crime. *Ethics*, 93, 4, 726–52.

Deutsch, M. 1985. *Distributive Justice: A Social-Psychological Perspective*. New Haven, CT: Yale University Press.

Deutsch, M., and Krauss, R.M. 1965. *Theories of Social Psychology*. New York: Basic Books.

Donnenwerth, G.V., and Foa, U.G. 1974. Effect of resource class on retaliation to injustice in interpersonal exchange. *Journal of Personality and Social Psychology*, 29, 785–93.

Egner, T., Monti, J.M., and Summerfield, Ch. 2010. Expectation and surprise determine neural population responses in the ventral visual stream. *The Journal of Neuroscience*, 30, 49, 16601–8.

Ellard, J.H., Miller, C.D., Baumle, T., and Olson, J.M. 2002. Just World Processes in Demonizing, in *The Justice motive in everyday life*, edited by M. Ross and D.T. Miller. New York: Cambridge University Press, 350–62.

Fararo, T.J., and Skvoretz, J. 1993. Methods and Problems of Theoretical Integration and the Principle of Adaptively Rational Action, in *Theoretical Research Programs*, edited by J. Berger, and M. Zelditch Jr. Redwood City, CA: Stanford University Press, 416–50.

Festinger, L. 1957. *A Theory of Cognitive Dissonance*. Evanston, IL: Row, Peterson.

Foa, U.G. 1971. Interpersonal and economic resources. *Science*, 171, 345–51.

Foa, U.G., and Foa, E.B. 1974. *Societal Structures of the Mind*. Springfield, IL: Charles C. Thomas Publisher.

Folger, R. 1977. Distributive and procedural justice: Combined impact of "voice" and improvement on experienced inequity. *Journal of Personality and Social Psychology*, 35, 108–19.

Folger, R. 1987. Distributive and procedural justice in the workplace. *Social Justice Research*, 1, 143–60.

Folger, R., Rosenfield, D., Grove, J., and Corkran, L. 1979. Effects of "voice" and peer opinions on responses to inequity. *Journal of Personality and Social Psychology*, 37, 2253–61.

Folger, R., and Skarlicki, D. 1998. When tough times make tough bosses: Managerial distancing as a function of layoff blame. *Academy of Management Journal*, 41, 79–87.

Gilliland, S.W. 1993. The perceived fairness of selection systems: An organizational justice perspective. *Academy of Management Review*, 18, 694–734.

Greenberg, J., and Cohen R.L. 1982. Why Justice? Normative and Instrumental Interpretations, in *Equity and Justice in Social Behavior*, edited by J. Greenberg, and R.L. Cohen. New York: Academic Press, 437–69.

Greenberg, J., and Colquitt, J. (eds). 2005. *Handbook of Organizational Justice*. Mahwah, NJ: Lawrence Erlbaum Associates.

Hafer, C.L. 2002. Why we reject innocent victims, in *The justice motive in everyday life*, edited by Ross, M., and Miller, D. New York: Cambridge University Press, 109–26.

Hafer, C.L., and Bègue, L. 2005. Experimental research on just-world theory: Problems, developments and future challenges. *Psychological Bulletin*, 131, 1, 128–67.

Haidt, J., and Graham, J. 2007. When morality opposes justice: Conservatives have moral intuitions that Liberals may not recognize. *Social Justice Research*, 20, 1, 98–116.

Homans, G.C. 1958. Social behavior as exchange. *American Journal of Sociology*, 63, 447–58.

Jasso, G. 1978. On the justice of earnings: A new specification of the justice evaluation function. *American Journal of Sociology*, 83(6), 1398–419.

Jasso, G. 1990. Methods for the Theoretical and Empirical Analysis of Comparison Processes, in *Sociological Methodology*, edited by C.C. Clogg. Washington, DC: American Sociological Association, 69–419.

Koper, G., Van Knippenberg, D., Bouhuys, F., Vermunt, R., and Wilke, H. 1993. Procedural fairness and self-esteem. *European Journal of Social Psychology*, 26, 313–25.

Lerner, M.J. 1975. The justice motive in social behavior: Introduction. *Journal of Social Issues*, 31, 1–20.

Lerner, M.J. 1977. The justice motive: Some hypotheses as to its origins and forms. *Journal of Personality*, 45, 1–52.

Lerner, M.J. 1980. *The belief in a just world: A fundamental delusion*. New York: Springer.

Lerner, M.J., and Whitehead, L.A. 1980. Procedural Justice Viewed in the Context of Justice Motive Theory, in *Justice in Social Interaction*, edited by G. Mikula. New York: Springer Verlag, 219–56.

Leventhal, G.S. 1976. Fairness in Social Relationships, in *Contemporary Topics in Social Psychology*, edited by J.W. Thibaut, J.T. Spence, and R.C. Carson. Morristown, NJ: General Learning Press, 211–39.

Leventhal, G.S. 1980. What Should Be Done with Equity Theory? New Approaches to the Study of Fairness in Social Relationships, in *Social Exchange. Advances in Theory and Research*, edited by K.J. Gergen, M.S. Greenberg, and R.H. Willis. New York: Plenum Press, 27–55.

Lind, E.A., Kulik, C.T., Ambrose, M., and de Vera Park, M.V. 1993. Individual and corporate dispute resolution: Using procedural fairness as a decision heuristic. *Administrative Science Quarterly*, 38, 224–51.

Lind, E.A., and Tyler, T.R. 1988. *The Social Psychology of Procedural Justice*. New York: Plenum Press.

Mikula, G. and Schwinger, T. 1978. Intermember Relations and Reward Allocation: Theoretical Considerations of Affects, in *Dynamics of Group Decisions*, edited by H. Brandstätter, J.H. Davis, and H. Schuler. Beverly Hills, CA: Sage, 229–50.

Modde, J. 2002. *Injustice and norm-violating behavior*. Enschede: Twente University: Dissertation.

Modde, J., and Vermunt, R. 2007. The Effects of Procedural Unfairness on Norm-Violating Behavior, in *Distributive and Procedural Justice. Research and*

*Social Applications*, edited by K.Y. Törnblom and R. Vermunt. Burlington, VT: Ashgate Publishing Company, 111–24.

Montada, L., and Lerner, M. 1998. *Responses to victimization and belief in a just world*. New York: Plenum.

Mullen, E. 2007. The Reciprocal Relationship between Affect and Perceptions of Fairness, in *Distributive and Procedural Fairness: Research and Social Applications*, edited by K. Törnblom, and R. Vermunt. Hampshire: Ashgate Publishing Limited, 15–37.

O'Doherty, J., Dayan, P., Friston, K., Critchley, H., and Dolan, R.J. 2003. Temporal difference models and reward-related learning in the human brain. *Neuron*, 38, 329–37.

Reichle, B., and Schmitt, M. 2008. Helping and rationalization as strategies for restoring the belief in a just world: Evidence from longitudinal change analyses, in *The justice motive in everyday life*, edited by Ross, M., and Miller, D. New York: Cambridge University Press, 127–48.

Rubin, Z., and Peplau, A. 1973. Belief in a just world and reactions to another's lot: A study of participants in the National Draft Lottery. *Journal of Social Issues*, 29(4), 73–93.

Skarlicki, D.P., and Folger, R. 1997. Retaliation in the workplace: The roles of distributive, procedural, and interactional justice. *Journal of Applied Psychology*, 82, 434–43.

Skitka, L.J., and Houston, D. 2001. When due process is of no consequence: Moral mandates and presumed defendant guilt or innocence. *Social Justice Research*, 14, 305–26.

Summerfield, Ch., Egner, T., Greene, M., Koechlin, E., Mangels, J., and Hirsch, J. 2006. Predictive codes for forthcoming perception in frontal cortex. *Science*, 314(5803), 1311–14.

Thibaut, J., and Walker, L. 1975. *Procedural Justice: A Psychological Analysis*. Hillsdale, NJ: Lawrence Erlbaum.

Turillo, C.J., Folger, R., Lavelle, J., Umphress, E., and Gee, J. 2002. Is virtue its own reward? Sacrificial decisions for the sake of fairness. *Organizational Behavior and Human Decision Processes*, 89, 839–65.

Tyler, T.R., and Lind, E.A. 1992. A Relational Model of Authority in Groups, in *Advances in Experimental Social Psychology*, Vol. 25, edited by M.P. Zanna. San Diego, CA: Academic Press, 115–91.

Törnblom, K.Y., and Vermunt, R. 1999. An integrative perspective on social justice: Distributive and procedural fairness evaluations of positive and negative outcome allocations. *Social Justice Research*, 12, 39–64.

Törnblom, K., and Vermunt, R. 2007. Towards an integration of distributive justice, procedural justice, and social resource theories. *Social Justice Research*, 20, 312–35.

Törnblom, K.Y., and Vermunt, R. 2012. Towards Integrating Distributive Justice, Procedural Justice, and Social Resource Theories, in *Handbook of Social Resource Theory*, edited by K.Y. Törnblom, and A. Kazemi. New York: Springer, 181–98.

Van den Bos, K., Ham, J.R.C., Lind, E.A., Simonis, M., Essen, W.J., and Rijpkema, M.J.P. 2008. Justice and the human alarm system: The impact of exclamation points and flashing lights on the justice judgment process. *Journal of Experimental Social Psychology*, 44, 201–19.

Van den Bos, K., Lind, A., Vermunt, R., and Wilke, H. 1997. "How do I judge my outcome when I don't know the outcome of others?" The psychology of the fair process effect. *Journal of Personality and Social Psychology*, 5, 1034–46.

Van den Bos, K., Wilke, H., Lind, E., and Vermunt, R. 1998. Evaluating outcomes by means of the fair process effect: Evidence for different processes in fairness and satisfaction judgments. *Journal of Personality and Social Psychology*, 74(6), 1493–503.

Vermunt, R. 2002. The Dual Position of the Boss, Injustice and Stress, in *Organizational Justice beyond the Organization*, edited by S. Gilliland, D. Steiner, and D. Skarlicki. Greenwich, CN: Information Age Publishing.

Vermunt, R. and Steensma, H. 2001. Stress in Organizations, in *Justice in the Workplace, Volume 2*, edited by R. Cropanzano. New Jersey: LEA, 27–49.

Vermunt, R. and Steensma, H. 2005. How Can Justice Be Used to Reduce Stress in Organizations, in *Handbook of Organizational Justice*, edited by J. Greenberg and J. Colquitt. Mahwah, NJ: Lawrence Erlbaum Associates, 383–410.

Vermunt, R., Peeters, Y., and Berggren, K. 2007. How fair treatment affects saliva cortisol release in stressed low and high type-A behavior participants. *Scandinavian Journal of Psychology*, 48, 547–55.

Vermunt, R., Wit, A., Van den Bos, K., and Lind. A. 1996. The effects of unfair procedure on negative affect and protest. *Social Justice Research*, 9, 109–21.

Wolters, G., and Raffone, A. 2010. Cohernece and recurrency: Maintenance, control and integration in working memory. *Cognitive Processes*, 9, 1–17.

# Chapter 8

# Reactions to Unfair Allocation Behavior. Part II: Actor's Role

## Introduction

The central theme of this chapter is the assertion that experienced injustice increases stress, while experienced justice reduces stress. The resulting stress is moderate under some conditions, but high under other conditions. Specifically, when unfairness is experienced over a long period, chronic stress may result. The roles of the major players of an allocation event are different under conditions of moderate stress as compared to high stress. If the unfairness is evaluated as a challenge, stress is moderate, and recipient and observer make attempts to reduce the unfairness. This was the topic of Chapter 7. If, however, chronic stress is experienced, the recipient becomes immobilized. The unfairness is experienced as a threat. In that case, the actor is the main player who can reduce the recipient's stress. This will be the topic of Chapter 8.

To make the argument, I will first discuss the concepts of social justice and stress, followed by descriptions of the interrelationships between the two phenomena. These preliminary statements and descriptions bring us in a logical way to the art of reducing stress, with an emphasis on the actor's role.

## Social Justice

Theory and research in the social sciences focus on perceived or subjective justice and not on objective justice as in law or economics. In other words, social scientists are interested in the fairness evaluation of an allocation event and not so much in prescribing an ideal fair allocation event. To make it a bit more complex, in the social sciences the term social justice is used to indicate that this type of justice originates in the interaction between social actors like citizens, employees, family members.

Social justice is conceived as the evaluation, in terms of fairness or deservingness: (a) of the distribution of scarce resources by an actor between him/herself and other(s) or among others; as well as (b) of the applied procedure. For instance, a child divides cookies between herself and her friends or among her friends mutually. In this example, the child is said to be engaged in an allocation process during the allocation event. In the allocation event we thus distinguish the distribution (how much of the resource) that the recipients receive from the actor according to specific distribution rules; from the procedure, the treatment applied by the actor to allocate the resource according to specific procedural rules. Distributions are evaluated in terms of fairness, distributive fairness, while procedures are evaluated in terms of procedural fairness. It is interesting to remark that in the justice literature distribution and procedure are distinguished from each other. The foregoing chapters of the present book, and specifically Chapter 7, have focused on another approach to distributions and procedures (see also Ambrose and Arnaud 2005). In my view, procedures are an indication of the distribution of mainly immaterial resources. Giving people voice, for instance, is an expression of the resource Status indicating that the actor is interested in the recipient as a valuable partner in the allocation event. As has already been described, the actor who decides to allocate resources to a recipient allocates a focal resource, for instance, goods, in combination with the allocation of an additional resource, for instance, status. A judge who decides on a fine for a perpetrator allocates a negative resource (imprisonment: status), and in doing so the judge may or may not give voice (status) to the perpetrator. Thus, resources are material, like money or goods, or immaterial, like time or attention; they may be positive, like a financial bonus, or negative, like a punishment or a fine (Törnblom 1992). In the next description I will use the nomenclatura as they are used in the standard justice literature. Moreover, the hypotheses that are tested in the experiments to be described in this chapter are only partly derived from the theory developed in Chapter 7. The resource to be distributed is status—whether a participant passes a test or not—and the procedural (procedure) is also status. In this way, Foa and Foa's (1974) assumption that people prefer reciprocation in kind is followed. Information, however, is held constant throughout the experiments—all participants do not pass—not giving rise to complex hypotheses about the interaction between focal resource distribution and additional resource distribution.

According to standing procedural justice theory (Tyler and Lind 1992), actors apply procedural rules while allocating scarce resources among recipients. Procedural rules are, for instance, the consistency rule: treat all recipients in the same way on every occasion; the accuracy rule: use all relevant information about the recipient to decide how much of the resource he/she will receive. Whether an actor will apply a rule depends on the legal frame of the group, organization, or society, and on the actor's motivation; how an actor will apply a rule is dependent, for instance, on the social context in which the allocation process takes place, and on the actor's characteristics.

Because allocation of resources is part and parcel of everyday social interaction, justice evaluations of distributions and procedures are very central in human lives. It has been shown time and again that justice evaluations influence people's behavior in several different social interactions like encounters with managers in the work situation, legal authorities, police officers, parents, tribal leaders, or educational authorities. Justice phenomena are not only observed in current social interactions in all parts of the world, but also in the past, and are assumed to be relevant even in the earliest development of human existence.

I assume that allocation processes play a role in the early phases of human development (see, for extensive description of this point of view, chapters 1 and 2). Allocation of food among members of the family shows some kind of distribution pattern. Findings indicate that hominins shared food (Enloe 2003). Sharing food may bring social obligations with it, and some form of reciprocity. I assume that these experiences may have developed feelings of rightness or correctness that this distribution is the best way for the survival of the family, and may have resulted in feelings of what we now label as justice.

Feelings of compassion and caring for the other, such as a mother for a child, are seen as the start of moral behavior. The mother gives the child affection, attention, food; in other words, the mother gives the child material as well as immaterial resources. Later in the development of the individual the mother rewards the child for appropriate behavior, appropriate for the family, so that the child learns what appropriate behavior is and what is correct or not. When, in human development, families tied together into groups and communities, ideas and beliefs about right and wrong spread, and implicit applied rules about allocation may have been settled more firmly; for example, they appear in holy books such as the Bible, the Torah, and the Koran.

These moral developments are probably accompanied by developments in the physiological make-up of humans. As has already been stated, justice evaluations are strongly related to the allocation of scarce resources. Because allocating scarce resources was already present in prehistoric groups and families (see Isaac 1978) living some two million years ago, it is plausible to assume that feelings of justice have developed from at least those times on. The hominins of two million years ago had brains that had half the volume of the brains of contemporary human beings. It is, therefore, not inconceivable that these experiences have structured the brains of the hominins and of our more recent ancestors. If that assumption is correct it should not come as a surprise that justice feelings and related cognitions will have powerful positions in our brain and consequently will play a dominant role in our behaviors and interactions with others. These speculations have received some, although indirect, empirical support. Let us describe some of the evidence.

It is assumed that repetition of experiences strengthens connections between relevant neurons or brain cells (see Chapter 5). If justice feelings and cognitions are part and parcel of the development of human behavior, and thus of the human brain, it is conceivable that connections between "justice-related" neurons (see also Allman et al. 2005) and other neurons will be rather strong. When the behavioral repertory became more complex—not only catching or killing animals, dividing the meat, and eating it, but also carrying animals or meat to other places, negotiating, exchanging it for other goods—connections between "justice-related" neurons and the neurons that guide these other behaviors probably became strong. If this assumption is valid we should find remnants of these connections still present in the brains of modern humans. I assume that if the representation of justice is activated, people will react faster to justice-related words than when the representation of justice is not activated. Thus, focusing experimental subjects on justice-related words (like "fair," "unfair") will make them extra alert for subsequent experiences. resulting in faster reactions than experimental subjects who are focused on neutral words (like "blabby"). In a study that was designed to test the importance of justice, Miedema et al. (2000) showed that experimental subjects indeed reacted faster after being primed with justice-related words than when primed with neutral words. The participants first read a description of the allocation of a fair reward (fair scenario), an unfair reward (unfair scenario), or a description about making tapas (neutral scenario). Thereafter, participants performed a lexical decision task in which they had to decide whether a series of letters formed a word. The participants answered the question with a "yes" or "no," while the response time was measured by the computer. Some words were related to justice/injustice, other words were unrelated to justice/injustice. The results showed that participants in the (in)justice conditions reacted faster than participants in the control condition. The authors concluded from these findings that representation of justice makes people alert for experiences that follow. Of course, from these findings it may not be concluded that justice has as prominent a position as stated: it is still circumstantial evidence, because we did not compare it with words of the same relevance.

Although the assumption that feelings of justice have a physiological basis may be valid, research results show that cultural influences also have a great impact on justice evaluations. Lerner (1980) states that individuals develop a sense of entitlement while growing up: a belief that everyone will get what he/she deserves. Lerner connects the sense of deservingness to values of the Protestant Ethic which says that working hard, living a simple life, and devotion to God will reward itself. Those people that live up to these values will be rewarded by God by receiving a high place in heaven. But the signs of a life of hard work and devotion are not only visible in the hereafter. A life of hard work and devotion will show itself in the here and now as well: Those people are more prosperous than others, and are more respected. In living such a life and having success, people develop expectations that a certain type of behavior leads to a certain outcome (see Chapter 2). And when successful, people teach them to their children, and the expectations become integrated into the personality: the justice motive. For those people, good behavior is followed by reward and bad behavior by punishment: they get what they deserve. It has been shown that this belief in a just world strengthens group cohesion and solidarity and helps a group to cope better with environmental threats (Tomaka et al. 1997). For instance, Tomaka and Blascovich (1994) found that individuals who believe strongly that the world is a just place cope better with stress. People who believe strongly that the word is a just place where everyone gets what he/she deserves, performed better when stressed and they showed a physiological pattern that corresponded more with a challenge response than a threat response to stress.

That these values are still part of the cultural heritage of people in many Western countries is shown in research where people were paid less for a certain amount of work than promised (Adams 1965). The people who were paid less felt distressed and worked less hard than the people who were paid fairly, that is, in agreement with what they were promised.

I conclude from this overview that justice is a sort of built-in structure and exerts a great influence on people's behavior and relationships with others. Receiving fair outcomes and fair procedures is beneficial and even helps people when they are in harmful situations. A situation that is highly harmful to people is the stress situation.

## Stress

### *Prevalence of Stress*

Many individuals experience stress at work. The prevalence of job stress is rather high. A survey among European employees showed that 29 percent thinks that their job has negative effects on their health (Paoli 1997). In the Netherlands, a sample of 4,474 working people, interviewed about their daily work (Botterweck 2003), showed a figure of 12 percent stressed respondents, as expressed in having been anxious and worried for at least two weeks on end. The proportion for male respondents was 8 percent, while for female respondents it was 17 percent. From a total working population of 7.5 million working people, a percentage of 12 percent means more than 900,000 people. In a survey study among 751 American workers a vast majority indicated that they are stressed (Seventh Annual Labor Day Poll 2001). From survey data in France, Bejean, Sultan-Taieb and Wolff (2002) estimated the annual costs of work-related stress from 830 to 1656 million Euro. The Health and Safety Authority (2002) calculated that the costs due to stress are for the 15 EU countries 20 billion Euro per year in lost time and health costs. For the US, industry costs are estimated at over $300 billion annually.

Stress, particularly work-related stress, has aroused growing interest across Europe in recent years. The workplace has changed dramatically due to globalization of the economy, use of new information and communications technology, growing diversity in the workplace (e.g. more women, older and better-educated people, as well as increased migration, particularly between the EU Member States), and an increased mental workload (Kompier 2002; Landsbergis 2003). A recent survey in the 15 European Union countries (EU15) showed an increase in stress during the last 10 years (European Agency for Safety and Health at Work 2009).

At the same time, workers are reporting rather high levels of mental health problems. In the 2000 European Working Conditions Survey (EWCS), work-related stress was found to be the second most common work-related health problem across the EU15 (at 28 percent; only back pain was more common). Moreover, work-related stress has also been associated with a number of other health problems, such as cardiovascular diseases (e.g. Kivimäki et al. 2002), musculoskeletal disorders, particularly back problems (e.g. Hoogendoorn et al. 2000) and neck/shoulder/arm/wrist/hand problems (the so-called RSI—repetitive strain injuries;

e.g. Ariëns et al. 2001), as well as absence from work (e.g. Houtman 1999). The potential outcomes of stress at work are thus rather diverse, and not only pertain to health but also to actual participation in the workforce. That is the reason why this topic report highlights work-related stress (European Foundation for the Improvement of Living and Working Conditions 2007).

The prevalence of stress in European countries is rather high as compared to other negative consequences of work. Moreover, stress and stress-related problems have shown an increase since the 1990s which has not yet stabilized.

There are several risks for stress, but the main risks are working at too high a speed and working according to too-tight deadlines; these risks became more prevalent from the 1980s.

Karasek's (1992) job demand-control model posits that people experience stress mostly when the demands of the job are high and their control, or ability to do the work autonomously, is low. Workers in the United Kingdom, Greece, Germany, and Ireland experience high tension in their work as a consequence of relatively high job demand and low control. Workers in countries like the Netherlands, Sweden, and Finland have relatively high job demands but also much more autonomy in doing their job. According to the demand-control model, workers in several countries in Europe should move to the active part of the dimensional structure, the top-right quadrant: relatively high job demands and relatively much autonomy. Workers in the active part of the structure experience some stress but this stress is probably not detrimental in the long run. Small levels of stress are necessary to do the job well.

### *Stress Model*

Stress is a serious matter: long-term stress has detrimental effects on health. It is therefore not surprising that much research is conducted to search for the main causes of stress as well as the best ways to reduce stress. This chapter will outline a justice-based stress approach to shed new light on the causes of stress and on stress reduction. Furthermore, experimental data will be presented to underline this line of reasoning, and strategies to reduce stress will be discussed.

Stress is the experienced discrepancy between demands from the environment and an individual's capacities (Carver 1995; Cropanzano et al. 1997) or needs (Siegrist 1996). If the demands exceed the capacities of the individual, the demands constitute a stressor (Allegro and Veerman 1992; Schaufeli and Van Dierendonck 1993), which, in turn, causes stress and strains (with symptoms like absenteeism, burnout, illness, physical impairment). In this view, there are two aspects of stress that merit attention: the demands of the environment on the one hand and the capacities or needs of the individual on the other. In research on stress and stress reduction two approaches can, therefore, be distinguished: one approach focuses on the capacities and needs of the individual and how to strengthen these capacities; in other words, this approach aims at improving individual coping strategies to reduce stress. Examples of improving individual coping strategies are seeking social support (see Buunk and de Wolff 1992), or teaching the individual to make a more efficient timetable or to learn to say no to requests to do an assignment that is beyond their capacities (Quick and Quick 1984). A common characteristic of this approach is that it operates primarily on the individual, psychological, level: the individual learns strategies to cope with stress. However, it has been shown time and again that strategies directed at the individual level are only moderately effective in reducing stress (Le Blanc et al. 2000). Reducing stress due to psychological stressors aims at improving the capacities of the individual—the individual psychological approach—and is less focused on reducing the demands (see also Quick and Quick 1984).

The other approach emphasizes the importance of the environmental demands under which people work (Elovainio et al. 2002). With regard to stress due to hardship in the work environment, the so-called physical stressors like working in heat, cold, and rain, trade unions have done a lot to improve the work situation. The Dutch Work Safety Regulations (ARBO) set limits on the physical environment in which people work by accommodating, for instance, air circulation, the sitting position of employees, or the altitude of the work table or desk.

The approach presented here emphasizes the importance of the environmental demands as well, but focuses on environmental psychological demands instead of environmental physical demands. Tackling the psychological demands can be achieved by taking into account the relationship between the employee and the organization. The organization provides resources to employees to do their job well, such as materials and equipment. In many work situations it is the supervisor who provides or allocates these resources. As has already been shown, employees evaluate the distribution of resources and the applied procedure in terms of justice or fairness.

## Injustice and Stress

In the justice-based approach to stress advocated here, demands from the environment—possible stressors—are conceived of as part of an allocation event in which resources are allocated by an actor (supervisor, father). For example, individuals have to perform assignments and receive appropriate equipment and adequate time to complete these tasks. The demand is to complete a task with the equipment and within the given time period (see also Van Yperen and Hagendoorn 2003). If individuals experience that the quality of equipment or the amount of time required to finish the task do not meet their standards with regard to what they think they need and are entitled to, they may judge the allocation of equipment and time as unfair. Because justice is of fundamental importance in people's lives, and because inappropriate allocations block individuals' goal attainment (Foa and Foa 1974), they become stressed. Moreover, the way material and immaterial resources are allocated—with voice or not—is of crucial importance in the experience of (additional resource) justice.

*Distributive Injustices, Procedural Injustices, and Stress: Empirical Evidence*

In the literature, two models appeared dealing with the issue of how distributive justice and procedural justice combine to affect subsequent attitudes and behavior. One is a model proposed by Tepper (2001), and the other is proposed by Vermunt and Steensma (2003). Both models apply Lazarus and Folkman's (1984) appraisal model in which a stimulus is perceived and evaluated as a threat, a challenge, a benign one or as a neutral stimulus. This primary appraisal process is followed by a secondary appraisal process which is intended to evaluate the options for coping with the threat. Vermunt and Steensma (2005) wrote:

> Tepper (2001) assumes that unfair outcomes are evaluated as a threat (harm/losses) by the primary appraisal process. Because distributive unfairness also affects negatively self-esteem and self-efficacy, the secondary appraisal process evaluates distributive unfairness as a threat to self-esteem. Both threats, triggered by distributive injustice, will be regarded as stressors, producing psychological stress. In addition, Tepper assumes a relationship between procedural justice and the primary and secondary appraisal process. The author makes the distinction between the instrumental component of procedural justice and the non-instrumental component. The instrumental component of procedural justice indicates that a fair procedure is valued because a fair procedure is more likely to produce favorable outcomes. The non-instrumental component of procedural justice indicates that a fair procedure is valued because a fair procedure gives an indication of one's status in the group or in relation to others. According to Tepper, unfair procedures: 'robs the employee of two vital coping resources—a social support system and a sense of self-efficacy' (200). (Vermunt and Steensma 2005: 398)

Vermunt and Steensma offer another explanation of the relationship between distributive and procedural justice and stress (Vermunt 2002; Vermunt et al. 2007; Vermunt and Steensma 2001; Vermunt and Steensma 2005):

> They also apply the Lazarus and Folkman model of psychological stress. In their view, distributive injustice or procedural injustice will be evaluated as a threat only if additional information gives reason to it. Otherwise, it will be evaluated as a challenge or as irrelevant or even as benign. If the combined injustice is evaluated as a threat, the second appraisal process will be triggered in which the available resources and options are evaluated to cope as effectively as possible with the threat. For instance, when employees perceive distributive injustice, the injustice will be evaluated as a threat as the information is available that the procedure with which the decision to cut their salary is experienced as unjust as well, ending in a stressful situation. Effective coping behavior could be to criticize the applied procedure. When, however, the employee experiences that the applied procedure was just the injustice will hardly be evaluated as a threat, but more as a challenge. An effective coping strategy would be to put more

> effort in the job and if that will not work in the short run, then the employee may become stressed. In many situations individuals receive distributive information, procedural information and information about the type of resource at the same time: information about the allocation event. This information forms a 'Gestalt.' Recipients process the information on line and on line processing is most likely when interactional justice is involved (Vermunt and Steensma 2001). In on line processing it is most likely that the information about procedure, distribution and resource type are combined to form a primary appraisal. (Vermunt and Steensma 2005: 399)

*Experimental evidence*

Vermunt and Steensma (2003); (Vermunt 2007; Vermunt, Peeters, and Berggren 2007; Vermunt, Berggren, and Peeters forthcoming) induced stress and unfairness experimentally. The dependent variables are the physiological responses heart action and blood pressure. Participants were brought into a high or low time pressure condition while performing a relevant task and were treated fairly (participants got the opportunity to give arguments for their performance) or less fairly (participants did not receive that opportunity). Physiological responses were assessed before and after testing. The results showed that participants in the high and low stress conditions showed significant decreases in heart action only after fair treatment, and not after unfair treatment.

We may conclude from these findings that participants are able to recognize and experience stressful situations and that workload and mental load (distributive injustice) lead to stress which is moderated by fair treatment (procedural justice).

Many studies show that people react differently to stress (see, e.g., Vermunt et al. 2007; Vermunt and Steensma 2003). In particular, it is assumed that individuals who differ in self-esteem react differently to stress. In reviewing the literature it was found that several studies have been done to correlate self-esteem and stress (Tepper 2001). It was found that self-esteem appears to moderate the effects of stress on psychological functioning. Individuals with low self-esteem exhibit more distress from negative events than those with high self-esteem. High self-esteem protects the individual from distress by allowing the individual to feel less vulnerable and deal with stressful situations. High self-esteem may also result in more active and effective coping and in enhanced motivation in response to stress (Abel 1998). In an article by Kreger (1995), it was hypothesized, after reviewing some studies, that scores on self-esteem may act in an attributional style manner as predictor of the effects of stress, and that perceived stress may be more related to self-esteem than to the actual stressfulness of a situation. After conducting a study to test the hypothesis, Kreger found support that stress is inversely correlated with self-esteem (Kreger 1995). According to another study, researchers found that there is a strong relationship between how someone copes with stress and self-esteem. It was also found in the same article in another study that people with low self-esteem are more likely to view their behavior as being dependent on the situation while people with high self-esteem have a greater capacity to engage in a wide range of coping behaviors. This article also asked the question, why people with low self-esteem tend to make their coping responses so situation-dependent. It has been suggested that self-esteem influences coping because it is so strongly related to personal attributions for different events and outcomes. The situation dependency of low self-esteem individuals versus high self-esteem individuals is measured by the state self-esteem scale developed by Heatherton and Polivy (1991). The two subscales most used are the performance self-esteem subscale and social self-esteem subscale. The performance self-esteem subscale measures how an individual performs compared to others, while the social self-esteem subscale measures how positively the individual thinks others view him/her. The performance self-esteem scale consists of seven items, the social self-esteem scale of six items.

*Overview and hypotheses*

To investigate whether fair treatment reduces stress, participants first work on an arithmetic task experienced as aversive due to time restriction (Hedman et al. 1990; Lovallo 1997). I expect that participants, who are students and therefore are motivated to do well, will experience doing tasks with high expectations of good performance as a stressful event. Stress was assessed by measuring saliva cortisol release before and after testing. Half of the participants received a high mental pressure treatment while the other half received a low mental pressure treatment. Immediately after the mental pressure treatment, half of the participants in each of the mental pressure conditions got the opportunity to voice (fair treatment: voice condition) their opinion, while the other half of the participants was not informed about getting voice (neutral treatment: no-voice condition).

Based on the above-mentioned theoretical arguments and previous findings, I predict that high self-esteem individuals will react more positively to fair treatment subsequent to a high mental pressure situation than low self-esteem individuals. More specifically, I predict that saliva cortisol release will be lower for high self-esteem individuals in the high mental pressure condition after voice than after no voice, and that saliva cortisol release will be lower for low self-esteem individuals in the low mental pressure condition after voice than after no voice (hypothesis 1). Because the task situation elicits rather strong performance motivation, I predict that performance self-esteem will show stronger effects than social self-esteem on cortisol release (hypothesis 2). Moreover, I predict that cortisol release scores will correlate positively with negative affect scores, and correlate negatively with positive affect scores (hypothesis 3).

Participants performed a difficult arithmetic task. Half of the participants received barely enough time to perform the task; the other half had enough time for it. No participants passed the test. Half of them got the opportunity to voice their arguments for not passing, the other half received no opportunity. Before testing and after testing and receiving information about test performance, cortisol samples were taken from each participant. Before they were tested, but after the first assessment of cortisol, participants filled out a self-esteem measure

(Heatherton and Polivy 1991) and two questions about how stressed they felt at that moment. These questions were repeated after the test and information about (not) passing the test.

*Effects of social self-esteem*

Analysis of covariance (ANCOVA) on the cortisol scores was done with the pre-measure of cortisol level as covariate, and social self-esteem (low versus high), mental pressure (high versus low), and voice (voice versus no-voice) as independent variables, and with the post-measure of cortisol as dependent variable. A strong main effect was found of pre cortisol scores on post cortisol scores ($F(1, 64) = 187.5$; $p < .001$; $\eta = .75$). More importantly, the expected three-way interaction (hypothesis 1) between social self-esteem, mental pressure, and voice tended to be significant ($F(1, 64) = 3.7$; $p < .06$; $\eta = .06$). The mean values and standard errors are displayed in Table 8.1.

**Table 8.1 Mean values and standard errors of post cortisol levels, corrected for pre cortisol levels, for low and high social self-esteem (SSE) participants in the mental pressure and voice conditions**

| Social self-esteem | Mental pressure | Cortisol | | | |
|---|---|---|---|---|---|
| | | Voice | | No voice | |
| | | M | SE | M | SE |
| High SSE | High | $4.46_b$ | .21 | $4.59_b$ | .24 |
| | Low | $4.59_b$ | .22 | $4.36_b$ | .33 |
| Low SSE | High | $4.40_b$ | .30 | $4.22_b$ | .23 |
| | Low | $3.77_a$ | .27 | $4.60_b$ | .20 |

*Note:* Entries of mean cortisol scores are in nmol/l, the higher the score the more cortisol. Entries with different subscripts differ at $p < .05$, tested with the protected LSD test.

Pair-wise comparisons of the cortisol means of Table 8.1 with the protected LSD procedure (Huitema 1980) yielded only a significant effect for low social self-esteem individuals in the low pressure conditions between voice and no-voice conditions ($t(34) = 1.9$; $p < .04$). Low self-esteem participants in the voice conditions showed lower cortisol release in the voice condition ($M = 3.77$) than low self-esteem participants in the no-voice condition ($M = 4.60$). These differences between voice and no-voice conditions in cortisol release for high self-esteem participants were absent in the low mental pressure conditions ($t(34) < 1$: *ns*). The differences in cortisol release of high self-esteem participants between voice and no-voice conditions in the high mental pressure condition were not significant.

*Effects of performance self-esteem*

ANCOVA on cortisol scores was done with the pre measure of cortisol level as covariate, and performance self-esteem (low versus high), mental pressure (high versus low), and voice (voice versus no-voice) as independent variables, and with the post measure of cortisol as dependent variable. A strong main effect was found of pre cortisol scores on post cortisol scores ($F(1, 64) = 200.7$; $p < .001$; $\eta = .75$). More importantly, the expected three-way interaction (hypothesis 1) between performance self-esteem, mental pressure, and voice showed a significant effect ($F(1, 64) = 8.2$; $p < .001$; $\eta = .11$). The mean values and standard errors are displayed in Table 8.2.

**Table 8.2 Mean values and standard errors of post cortisol levels, corrected for pre cortisol levels, for low and high performance self-esteem (PSE) participants in the mental pressure and voice conditions**

| Performance self-esteem | Mental pressure | Cortisol | | | |
|---|---|---|---|---|---|
| | | Voice | | No voice | |
| | | M | SE | M | SE |
| High PSE | High | $4.14_a$ | .24 | $4.66_b$ | .24 |
| | Low | $4.51_b$ | .20 | $4.48_b$ | .24 |
| Low PSE | High | $4.74_b$ | .24 | $4.16_{ab}$ | .22 |
| | Low | $3.79_a$ | .29 | $4.59_b$ | .24 |

*Note:* Entries of mean cortisol scores are in nmol/l, the higher the score the more cortisol. Entries with different subscripts differ at $p < .05$, tested with the protected LSD test.

Pair-wise comparisons of the cortisol means of Table 8.2 with the protected LSD procedure (Huitema 1980) yielded a significant effect for high performance self-esteem individuals in the high pressure conditions between voice and no-voice conditions ($t(34) = 1.6$; $p < .05$). High self-esteem participants in the voice conditions showed lower cortisol release in the voice condition ($M = 4.14$) than high self-esteem participants in the no-voice condition ($M = 4.66$). These differences between voice and no-voice conditions in cortisol release for high self-esteem participants were absent in the low mental pressure conditions ($t(34) < 1$: *ns*). Pair-wise comparisons of the cortisol means of Table 8.2 with the protected LSD procedure (Huitema 1980) yielded a significant effect for low performance self-esteem individuals in the low pressure conditions between voice and no-voice conditions ($t(34) = 2.6$; $p < .02$). Low self-esteem participants in the voice conditions showed lower cortisol release in the voice condition ($M = 3.79$) than low self-esteem participants in the no-voice condition ($M = 4.59$). These differences between voice and no-voice conditions in cortisol release for high self-esteem participants were absent in the low mental pressure conditions ($t(34) < 1$: *ns*).

*Affect results* To test hypothesis 3 about the relationship between cortisol release and positive affect and negative affect, partial correlations were calculated between post cortisol scores (corrected for pre cortisol scores) and positive affect scores, respectively negative affect scores. The partial correlation between post cortisol scores and positive affect was ($pr = -0.27$; $p < .05$) and between post cortisol and negative affect ($pr = 0.08$; $p < .23$). The mean positive affect score is ($M = 2.4$; $SD = 0.64$), the mean negative affect score is ($M = 1.6$; $SD = 0.66$). From the mean affect values I infer that participants reported moderately high positive affect and rather low negative affect.

In this study, participants were brought into a high or low mental pressure condition, followed by fair treatment manipulation. Saliva cortisol as an indicator of stress was measured before the manipulations took place as well as after the manipulations. State self-esteem, with the subscales social self-esteem (SSE) and performance self-esteem (PSE), was used as a moderator. The results showed that low SSE participants under low pressure showed lower cortisol release in the fair treatment condition than low SSE participants under low pressure in the neutral treatment condition. High PSE participants in the high mental pressure condition showed lower cortisol release after fair treatment than after neutral treatment. In addition, low PSE in the low mental pressure condition showed lower cortisol release after fair treatment than after neutral treatment. Moreover, these findings were complemented with data about the affective state of the participants, but only the (negative) correlation between positive affect and cortisol was significant. That is to say: high levels of cortisol release go together with low levels of positive affect. The combination of a high level of cortisol with a low level of positive affect is an indication of a stressful situation (Lovallo 1997). Although the data are not as strong as one would like them to be, one may conclude that there is a strong tendency in the data that points to the beneficial effects of justice on stress levels. That is to say that high self-esteem individuals in the high mental pressure condition benefit from fair treatment in having lower cortisol release, and more positive affect, while low self-esteem individuals in the low mental pressure condition benefit from fair treatment in having lower cortisol release, and more positive affect.

I conclude that fair treatment (voice) has beneficial effects on cortisol levels. Fair procedures reduce stress, as shown by lower cortisol levels as well as increased positive affect. These findings, combined with results from previous experiments (Vermunt and Steensma 2003; Vermunt et al. 2007), open opportunities for remedying subordinates' stress by authority's fair behavior.

The present experiment was set up from the basic assumption that stress can be reduced by appropriate actions of authorities who have the power to allocate resources to recipients and thereby apply certain procedures. Starting from injustice-stress theory (Vermunt and Steensma 2001), it is assumed that unfair treatment (distributive or procedural) can operate as a stressor that may cause stress, ending up in aversive psychological symptoms, like sick leave and absenteeism. It is also assumed that fair treatment may, however, reduces or even prevents stress. The mechanism that is assumed to operate, according to the injustice-stress theory, is that by being just the perceived threat value of an event will be reduced (see Lazarus and Folkman 1984). The reappraisal of the perceived threat value of the event takes place in the frontal cortex, setting in motion a cascade of physiological processes in the hypothalamus and other glands. (see for a detailed description of the neuro-physiological pathways from appraisal to cortisol release, Chapter 5, paragraph: Stress).

## Justice and Stress Reduction

The similarities between theories of justice (i.e. equity theory) and stress theories (i.e. appraisal theory) have stimulated researchers to develop a theoretical framework that encompasses the two approaches to stress. An interesting similarity is that both approaches start from the assumption that a discrepancy between two cognitive elements (e.g., between perceived effort and reward, or between perceived demands and capacities; see also Folger 1987) may upset individuals. The other similarity between the two approaches to stress is the role of the social environment in relation to stress. According to equity theory, a fair reward offered by an allocator (supervisor) results in low levels of (dis)stress. In the stress literature it is emphasized that seeking social support from a supervisor and colleagues may be important in reducing stress. Combining the two approaches to stress, Vermunt and Steensma (Vermunt 2002; Vermunt and Steensma 2003; Vermunt et al. 2007) have developed the injustice-stress theory (IST). The most important element in IST is the assumption that the discrepancy that people experience between the demands of the environment and their own capacities is attributed to the actor's allocation decision (supervisor, manager, leader). In many situations, the demands of the environment can be conceived as a lack of necessary resources compared to what the employee needs to do the job well. The demands of the environment may, thus, exceed the capacities of the employee and in that case one may speak of an inequitable allocation of scarce resources. Work load, for instance, can be a stressor, and can be viewed as the result of the inequitable allocation of a resource, such as time or equipment. Subordinates may attribute a heavy work load to the allocation decision of their supervisor of the scarce resource time in which to do the task. From the justice literature, we know that an allocation decision is evaluated in terms of fairness; distributive fairness is the evaluation of the outcome of the allocation decision (Törnblom 1992), and procedural fairness is the evaluation of the procedure to arrive at the outcome (Thibaut and Walker 1975). In allocating a scarce resource, the actor induces feelings of fairness or unfairness. Allocations that are in agreement with the individuals' capacities will be viewed as fair, while allocations that are not in agreement with their capacities will be evaluated as unfair.

As described earlier, in many allocation decision processes individuals are affected not only by the outcome of the allocation decision (e.g., the allotted time to perform the task), but by the applied procedure as well (e.g., participation in the allocation decision process). According to Lind and Tyler (1988) and Tyler and Lind (1992), an unfair outcome, but far more so an unfair procedure, is an indication of disrespect for the individual by the actor.

Individuals who are treated unfairly may conclude that the actor has insufficient knowledge of their capacities and abilities, and is clearly not interested in them. Allocation of a scarce resource will be evaluated as unfair if the actors lack the necessary knowledge about the individual on which to base their decision. Moreover, not receiving voice in a decision process that affects her or him greatly may be viewed as an indication of the actor's low regard for the recipient. The disturbed relationship may become a heavy burden for the individual. Consequently, the allocation of an insufficient amount of a resource—e.g., time or equipment—is not the only factor that causes stress. Disrespectful treatment by the actor is another, and probably even more important. The allocation of insufficient resources (unfair distribution), combined with the perceived disturbed relationship with the supervisor (unfair procedure) are, in my view, important causes of stress. An unfair outcome—that is an outcome that is not based on the capacities of the individual—can cause stress, and this stress can be increased by an unfair procedure.

In several studies, the effects of distributive and procedural fairness on the physiological reactions of individuals working on a stressful mental task have been investigated, because physiological responses give us an accurate view of the health effects of stress and also of stress reduction. For instance, Markovsky (1988) found that participants who received an inequitable outcome for task performance produced more sweat then equitably paid participants (see also Tomaka and Blascovich 1994). Lovallo (1997) describes psychological stressors as "challenges that can alter the workings of the body, and perhaps affect health, because of their meaning to the person and the effects of these meanings in the person's daily life" (65). According to Lovallo, psychological stressors do not pose a threat because they are physically harmful, but because the challenges may bring tears and sorrow, loss of faith in the future, and even illness. Evidence of the consequences of psychological stressors may be found in organisms anticipating exercise. These studies are interesting because it shows us the possibilities that changes in physiological reactions can occur because of changes in brain activity associated with thinking about and preparing for movement. Records of physiological activities and the behavior of monkeys show substantial rises in heart rate and blood pressure when sitting still but preparing to attack another monkey.

If an unfair outcome and an unfair procedure may cause stress, the opposite may also be true: a fair outcome and a fair procedure may decrease the amount of stress. In many situations individuals may perceive a task as stressful. A supervisor can be well aware of the stressful task he puts on the shoulders of the subordinate. With some well-chosen words the supervisor may lighten the burden for the subordinate. Not being able to decrease the stress caused by unfair allocation of resources, the supervisor can be helpful in decreasing stress by applying a fair procedure. The justice literature offers sufficient evidence that an unfair outcome will be viewed as more fair if the procedure that is used is seen as fair. Van den Bos et al. (1998) found that giving voice to subordinates while taking an allocation decision increases the perceived fairness of the outcome decision. Stress research shows that support given by colleagues and others improves people's ability to cope with stress.

We may infer from the foregoing analysis not only that injustice leads to stress, but also that justice may reduce or even prevent stress. In other words, authorities allocating just distributions or applying just procedures may help to reduce stress. Tepper (2001) assumes that a situation without injustice and without stress is hard to accomplish. In every encounter between people with different amounts of power, injustices are nearby. Authorities who are familiar with the continuous struggle with allocation decisions will also be aware of the beneficial effects of treating individuals fairly.

An actor reduces stress caused by unfair resource allocation through the application of instruments that recipients also apply. The actor may apply compensation, justification, appreciation, and mitigation (see also Chapter 5). A salary cut may be compensated by extra bonuses. Performing tasks under difficult conditions (focal resource; Status) may be justified by giving good reasons for taking the decision (additional resource; Information). Stress caused by unfair procedures (discrepancy between expected and received additional resource; being rude) may be reduced by a fair distribution (focal resource; appreciation) or by another, fair, procedure (mitigation). Refusing to let a recipient participate in the decision-making process can be redeemed with a bonus. Refusing to let a recipient participate in the decision-making process may be mitigated by a closer personal relationship. In short, the justice literature offers many methods for authorities to handle stressful situations for individuals.

Stress reduction is of the utmost importance, not only to reduce a recipient's stress level, but also because chronically stressed recipients evaluate the work situation as threatening. And we know that threat-induced fear reduces the operation of justice-motivated behavior.

## Identification of Stressed Individuals

Reduction of stress in other individuals, such as subordinates and colleagues, starts with the recognition or identification of those individuals as being stressed

(Vermunt 2007). There are several ways to approach the problem of identification of stressed individuals. One way is to ask others whether they feel stressed. Supervisors as well as colleagues can use this method. It is easy to do, but for several reasons the answers to the questions must be treated with caution. People's self-perception of stress may be inaccurate. A study by Lerner et al. (2007) showed that the relationship between self-reported emotions and physiological correlates of stress emotions was not high, indicating that individuals are not accurate in identifying their own stress level. Moreover, people may be reluctant to admit that they are stressed, because it may make them weak or vulnerable, eventually resulting in perceptions of being exploited (see Lind 2001). These perceptions will decrease eventual opportunities to reduce stress by being fair. So, questioning may lead to a more or less accurate picture of a stressed other, but it should preferably be done in a non-obtrusive way, reducing the chances that the other might feel exploited.

### *Art Theory*

Another way to identify stressed individuals is to pay close attention to their facial expression, bodily posture, and speech. The emphasis is on the observer's ability to watch and to listen carefully to the other. In art, and later also in psychology, artists and scientists have done much theoretical and empirical work to know more about how people perceive emotions in others. In art (Barasch 2000), several theories have been developed on how artists express or should express emotions in sculpture, painting, and music. In the second part of the seventeenth century, Le Brun was director of the Academy of Art in Paris and emphasized in his teachings how to depict emotions. For Le Brun, the expression of emotions was as important for the art of painting as perspective and proportion had been in earlier times. Earlier in that century, around 1630, Descartes (1989) developed a theory of how emotions are formed and transformed to bodily and facial expressions. For Descartes, mind and body are separate entities. He could not deny that the mind affects the body and thus he postulated an organ in the brain, the pineal gland, the go-between of mind and body. The starting point is the neutral emotion causing no operation of the pineal gland. A positive emotion causes the pineal gland to make upward correction resulting in lifted eyebrows, lifted corners of the mouth, an erect bodily posture, and correct speech, while a negative emotion causes the pineal gland to make downward correction resulting in lowered eyebrows, lowered mouth corners, slack bodily posture, and incorrect speech. In line with the Cartesian art theory, Le Brun differentiated between several emotions, added emotions to the list Descartes had made, and focused on the human face as a medium for the expression of emotions. Le Brun spoke of the following emotions in his lectures in the Academy: admiration, love, hatred, joy, sadness, fear, hope, despair, audacity, fury, respect, veneration, rapture, disdain, horror, anxiety, jealousy, depression, pain, laughter, weeping, and rage. Le Brun believed that all these emotions could be distinctly conveyed by visual depictions (Barasch 2001: 334). One of the paintings shows the salute but also the subjection of the women in the household of Darius III, king of Persia, to Alexander the Great of Macedonia, after Darius was defeated by Alexander and died shortly after. Each of the women has her own individual attitude toward Alexander which is clearly expressed in their facial expression and bodily posture. It is a one-to-one translation of what is in the mind of the women and what their faces and bodies show.

In the picture, we see Alexander and his captain visiting the tent where the mother of Darius III, his wife and child, and members of the household are gathered. The second standing person to the left is Alexander. Alexander is not wearing a sword, but the captain's sword is visible and his hand is open but near to the hilt. Alexander's bodily composure is one of respect for the family and household of the defeated Darius and is reassuring: it expresses the presence of a benevolent king. His left hand is open to the family, his right arm is stretched out in a gesture that is directed to hold back the captain. His head is slightly bent to the left to express kindness. The family members of Darius III are not standing before Alexander, but they are kneeling, expressing subjugation. Darius' mother, the person with the yellow robe, bends forward to hold Alexander's feet, but because she does not know who Alexander is, approaches the captain instead of Alexander. The woman with the child, Darius' wife, is aware of the mistake and tries to correct the mother by slightly touching the mother's back. Each of the faces of the kneeling women expresses an emotion such as sadness, fear, anxiety, despair.

Purely artistic, the above painting is of great value, but for me there is another reason for the importance of the picture. The family of Darius is in great distress, not only because their beloved emperor and protector is dead, but they also must fear for their life. In those periods it was not uncommon that the family of the defeated, and especially their heir, was killed. The members of the family and of the household must have been very frightened and stressed about what kind of decision Alexander would take in these matters. It must have been a relief—and in the face of Darius' wife one can see a faint hope—that Alexander presented himself as a benevolent ruler who clearly had no intention of murdering the members of the family. In other words, Alexander reduced distress by being fair and morally correct.

In later disputes on the relation between emotion and facial expression and bodily posture, as well as in psychology, this view of the internal origin of emotions is challenged. For instance, Diderot, the French author and philosopher, explained that the facial expressions could also be the result of deliberate action by the person. People could look sad without feeling sad. This was the onset of a new theory of art in which the facial expression is related to what the person would like to achieve with the expression. And because this almost always regards other people, facial expression, bodily posture, and speech are viewed as relational. More generally, emotions are viewed as having evolved through their adaptive value in dealing with fundamental life tasks. Each emotion has unique features: signal, physiology, and antecedent events. Each emotion also has characteristics in common with other emotions: rapid onset, short duration, unbidden occurrence, automatic appraisal, and coherence among responses. These shared and unique characteristics are the product of our evolution, and distinguish emotions from other affective phenomena.

### *Psychology*

In general, facial expression, bodily movements and speech are ways to communicate with others (Allwood 2002). The content of the communication one would like to convey might be physiological states like hunger, stress, fatigue, or illness, but also emotions and attitudes, factual information and the like. Stressed individuals can be identified not only by focusing on their facial expression but also by focusing on their bodily movements and speech. This multidimensional medium of expressing emotions and/or physiological states (stress) can be studied by focusing on one of the dimensions at a time, or on a combination of dimensions. Let us consider a brief description of the theory and research for cacial expression and bodily movements.

#### *Facial expression*

Psychological research is concerned with the measurement and communicative value of facial movements. The aim is to measure facial movements and to categorize them in terms of basic emotions. Results show that facial movements can be categorized according to six basic emotions: happiness, sadness, anger, fear, disgust, and surprise. Furthermore, a coding system was developed to measure facial movements (Ekman and Friesen 1978). In my view, this coding system may be used to identify facial expressions in stressed individuals. In the study cited here already, Lerner et al. (2007) coded the facial expressions of participants during a stress task as well as during a recovery period. As predicted, participants displayed greater fear, anger, and disgust during the stress task than during the resting periods. From these results one may infer that stress in individuals can be identified by focusing on facial expressions displaying combinations of fear, anger, and disgust. Several examples of faces showing the basic emotions and combinations of these emotions were produced. Participants, confronted with the faces, were asked to indicate the emotion(s) the faces conveyed. Data from neurologically intact participants show that stimuli that contain 90 percent and 70 percent of an expression are consistently identified as the intended emotion.

#### *Bodily movements*

Research on the relationship between stress and bodily movements is scarce. It is assumed by some that muscle tension, pounding heart, raising voice, irritation, dry mouth, or erratic movements are symptoms of being stressed. Others add to this list symptoms like clenched teeth and cold or clammy hands. It is not easy for an observer to recognize these symptoms separately, but the posture of a stressed individual is one that conveys tension and not relaxation.

## Conclusions and Discussion

By integrating justice theory, stress theory, and theory of perception of faces and bodily movements it is possible to start a program to train people to identify stressed individuals. The justice approach to stress starts from the assumption that stress is the result of unfair allocation of resources and/or disrespectful treatment. It is assumed further that in a work relationship a supervisor is the actor who allocates scarce resources to subordinates. Moreover, the supervisor interacts with the subordinate in order to allocate the resources (see also Vermunt 2002). Allocated resources evaluated as unfair may become stressors, resulting in stress and consequently in strain symptoms. The stressor in this view—the justice approach to stress—is not something that simply happens to people in a work situation and with which one has cope. In the justice approach to stress there is a responsible actor, and this actor may cause stress by behaving unfairly. But the actor is also able to reduce stress by reducing the impact of the stressor and thus influencing the primary appraisal process, that is, whether the situation is evaluated as threatening, challenging, or benign. In this view, behaving fairly does not affect the other person's secondary appraisal process but the primary appraisal process—see, however, Tepper (2001) for an alternative interpretation. And this line of reasoning brings us to instruments or methods that actors can use to reduce stress.

### *Remedies*

When the supervisor has identified a stressed subordinate, the social justice literature describes several instruments that he/she can use to actually reduce stress. In the distributive justice and the procedural justice literature several instruments are mentioned to reduce stress. In the distributive justice (equity) literature (Adams 1965), measures can be inferred such as giving more and better equipment, more time, higher compensation, skill training. In the procedural justice literature, procedural rules like those mentioned by Leventhal (1980), Bies and Moag (1986), and Tyler and Lind (1992) can be applied to reduce stress. Tyler and Lind (1992) defined the procedural rules in the most abstract way. An actor is evaluated as fair if he/she shows respect for the other person, is impartial when making decisions, and is trusted. These abstract procedural rules can be made concrete by referring to Leventhal's procedural criteria and Bies and Moag's rules for correct communication. Leventhal mentions six criteria or rules. Here, I refer to the consistency rule: in making allocation decisions, one should be consistent across people (equal treatment) and time (same rule each time); the bias suppression rule, which dictates that personal interests shall not play a role in making allocation decisions; the accuracy rule: base allocation decisions on as much information as possible; and the correctability rule: offer possibilities to modify and reverse decisions. Bies and Moag (1986) mention communication rules like being ethical, being polite, asking no inappropriate questions, not being intimidating. In our view, it will not be difficult to acquire the skills to apply these instruments. It is surprising that supervisors do not follow these rather simple instructions with which they can simply reduce stress.

The fair behavior of a supervisor can reduce stress, but there is one important condition that has to be fulfilled before a supervisor's behavior will be effective. This condition is that the supervisor is able to identify a (potentially) stressed subordinate. The psychology of facial expression, bodily movements, and how people perceive them can help to teach the supervisor to identify stressed subordinates. As described above, it is possible to recognize stressed individuals: look at their facial expression, bodily movement, and speech. Pictures of individuals teach supervisors how to distinguish stressed individuals among other individuals. Supervisors should be attentive to subordinates' faces as expressing a combination of fear, anger, and disgust, accompanied by a tensed posture and erratic movements as well as raised voice.

It is not a difficult skill that supervisors have to acquire, and I am convinced that people can master the skill, although I have to admit that things are even more complex than described here. As you will probably remember from the results of the summarized experiments, self-esteem has a moderating role in stress reduction. Low self-esteem individuals react differently to stressors than high self-esteem individuals. As with identification of stressed individuals, facial expression with regard to self-esteem is an important clue. A study by Chesney et al. (1990) showed that glare and disgust differentiated type-A behavior individuals from type-B behavior individuals (see Chapter 5).

Stress at work is an important cause of absenteeism, has severe individual psychological consequences, and has a strong impact on the economy and the health of organizations and society. Therefore, all decisions and arrangements that can be taken to reduce stress are welcome—ones that reduce stress by focusing on improving the coping mechanisms of employees as well as those that focus on the psychological environment at work.

So far, this chapter has focused on the work situation and the supervisor's behavior causing stress. The work situation is a specific social environment in which the group size is not large. Even in large companies, people work in relatively small groups supervised by one person. Higher up in the organization, superiors supervise their subordinates. The pyramid goes up to the top of the organization. Supervisors occupy a dual position (Vermunt 2002). They allocate resources—material and immaterial—which they receive from their superiors. They are actor as well as recipient. A supervisor's allocation behavior toward their subordinates is steered partly by the allocation behavior of their superior. The dual position of the boss may end up in stress for the subordinates because supervisors have to keep in line with received resources.

However, it is not only in organizational life that stress is abundantly present. In family life, public life, and political life people experience stress, sometimes short-term stress but also long-term stress. The family is a small group in which resources are allocated: love, service, goods, money, information. Do I really love one child more than the other? If I give a small pet to my daughter, what should I give my son? Shall I help my children with homework from school? The neighborhood is larger than the family, but still small. People can do tasks for the benefit of self and neighbors. Neighborhoods are part of a community or municipality, the city, and so on. On each level—micro, meso, and macro—actors can fulfill important supervisory roles to comfort and help people. All these actors find themselves in the position of the actors in the waiting room before one of the doors opens. They have to be alert to the condition of the people in the subgroup, but also keep in mind the whole group in the waiting room.

Uncertainty about economic prospects also causes stress. House owners who are not able to sell their house and are confronted with costs that are too high because of unemployment develop stress. Political upheaval resulting from power struggles between the most important factions causes stress because the struggles prevent the solution of fundamental societal problems. At the macro level, an actor's skills in detecting stress from faces or bodily movements are less appropriate. They use information from intermediate levels to detect distress in people: newspapers, TV shows, civil initiatives, civil organizations. Policy makers and family heads should be aware of the negative consequences of their actions. In other words, actors in all types of societal circles have a huge responsibility with regard to the consequences for recipients of the allocation decisions they take. Sensitivity about these consequences is the start of a remedy process to de-stress people. As indicated in Chapter 3, being sensitive is a necessary condition for remedy, but not a sufficient condition. Actors should also possess the qualities necessary to make fair allocation decisions even when they run counter to general public attitudes and opinions. An actor should not only be a Humian actor (showing compassion) but also a Machiavellistic one (wielding power). The Humian and Machivellistic actor can best realize Rawls' maximin principle. The Machivellistic actor is able to accomplish the highest satisfaction and justice in the group, while his Humian part is able to promote the highest equality.

An educational system in which actors are trained for each level of the societal structure will be beneficial for all involved, as well as for society.

## References

Abel, M. 1998. Interaction of humor and gender in moderating relationships between stress and outcomes. *The Journal of Psychology*, 132, 267–76.

Adams, J.S. 1965. Inequity in Social Exchange, in *Advances in Experimental Social Psychology*, Vol. 2, edited by L. Berkowitz. New York: Academic Press, 267–99.

Allegro, J.T., and Veerman, T. 1992. Ziekteverzuim, in *Nieuw handboek arbeids- en organisatiepsychologie*, edited by P.J.D. Drenth, Hk. Thierry, Ch.J. de Wolff. Houten: Bohn Stafleu Van Loghum, 497–537.

Allman, J.M., Watson, K.K., Tetreault, N.A., and Hakeem, A.Y. 2005. Intuition and autism: a possible role of Von Ekonomo neurons. *Trends in Cognitive Sciences*, 9(8), 365–73.
Allwood, J. 2002. Bodily Communication Dimensions of Expression and Content, in *Multimodality in Language and Speech Systems*, edited by B, Granström. Dordrecht: Kluwer Academic Publishers, 7–26.
Ambrose, M., and Arnaud, A. 2005. Are procedural justice and distributive justice conceptually distinct? in *Handbook of Organizational Justice*, edited by Greenberg, J., and Colquitt, J. Hillsdale, NJ: Erlbaum, 59–84.
Ariëns, G., Bongers, P., Van Mechelen, W., Hoogendoorn, W., and Van der Wal, G. 2001. High qualitative job demands and low coworker support as risk factors for back pain, results of a prospective cohort study. *Spine*, 26, 1896–903.
Barasch, M. 2000. *Theories of Art. Part 1: From Plato to Winckelmann*. New York: Routledge.
Bejean, S., Sultan-Taieb, H., and Wolff, N. 2002. *Modelling the social cost of work-related stress*. LATEC, University of Burgundy, Dijon.
Bies, R.J., and Moag, J.S. 1986. Interactional Justice: Communication Criteria of Fairness, in *Research on Negotiations in Organizations*, Vol. 1, edited by R.J. Lewecki, B.H. Sheppard, and M.H. Bazerman. Greenwich, CT: JAI Press.
Botterweck, A.A.M. 2003. Psychische werkbelasting en gezondheidsklachten. *Sociaal-economische Maandstatistiek*. Voorburg: CBS, 23–7.
Buunk, A.P., and Wolff, Ch.J. de 1992. Social Psychological Aspects of Stress at Work, in *New Handbook Work and Organization Psychology*, edited by P.J.D. Drenth, Hk. Thierry, and Ch.J. de Wolff. Houten: Bohn Stafleu Van Loghum, 447–96.
Carver, C.S. 1995. Stress and Coping, in *The Blackwell Encyclopedia of Social Psychology*, edited by A.S. Manstead, and M. Hewstone. Oxford: Blackwell Publishers, 635–9.
Chesney, M.A., Ekman, P., Friesen, W.V., Black, W.V., and Hecker, M.H.L. 1990. Type A behavior pattern: Facial behavior and speech components. *Psychomatic Medicine*, 53, 307–19.
Cropanzano, R., Howes, J.C., Grandey, A.A., and Toth, P. 1997. The relationship of organizational politics and support to work behaviors, attitudes, and stress. *Journal of Organizational Behavior*, 18, 159–89.
Descartes, R. 1989. *The Passions of the Soul*. Indianapolis: Hackett Publishing Company.
Ekman, P. and Friesen, W.V. 1978. *Facial Action Coding System: A Technique for the Measurement of Facial Movement*. Palo Alto, CA: Consulting Psychology Press.
Elovainio, M., Kivimäki, M., and Vahtera, J. 2002. Organizational justice: Evidence of a new psychosocial predictor of health. *American Journal of Public Health*, 92(1), 105–8.
Enloe, J.G. 2003. Foodsharing past and present: Archaeological evidence for economic and social interactions. *Before Farming*, 1, 1–23.

European Agency for Safety and Health at Work. 2009. Annual Report.

European Foundation for the Improvement of Living and Working Conditions. Report 2007.

Foa, U.G., and Foa, E.B. 1974. *Societal Structures of the Mind.* Springfield, IL: Charles C. Thomas Publisher.

Folger, R. 1986. A Referent Cognitions Theory of Relative Deprivation, in *Social Comparison and Relative Deprivation: The Ontario Symposium*, Vol. 4, edited by J.M. Olson, C.P. Herman, and M.P. Zanna. Hillsdale, NJ: Lawrence Erlbaum Associates, 35–55.

Folger, R. 1987. Distributive and procedural justice in the workplace. *Social Justice Research*, 1, 143–60.

Heatherton, T., and Polivy, J. 1991. Development and validation of a scale measuring state self-esteem. *Journal of Personality and Social Psychology*, 60, 895–910.

Hedman, A., Hjemdahl, P., Nordlander, R., and Åström, H. 1990. Effects of mental and physical stress on central haemodynamics and cardiac sympathetic nerve activity during QT interval-sensing rate-responsive and fixed rate ventricular inhibited pacing. *European Heart Journal*, 11, 903–15.

Hoogendoorn, W., Van Poppel, M., Bongers, B., Koes, B., and Bouter, L. 2000. Systematic review of psychosocial factors at work and private life as risk factors for back pain. *Spine*, 25, 2114–25.

Houtman, I. 1999. Monitor stress and bodily load: Employers and employees about risks, consequences and remedies. *Behavior and Organization (Gedrag en Organisatie)*, 12, 364–83.

Huitema, B. 1980. *The analysis of covariance and alternatives*. New York: Wiley.

Isaac, G. 1978. The food-sharing behavior of protohuman hominins. *Scientific American*, 34, 90–108.

Karasek, R. 1992. Stress Prevention Through Work Reorganisation: A Summary of 19 International Case Studies, in *Conditions of Work Digest: Preventing Stress at Work*. Geneva: ILO, 11(2), 23–42.

Kivimäki, M., Leini-Arjas, P., and Luukkonen, R. 2002. Work stress and risk of cardiovascular mortality: Prospective cohort study of industrial employees. *BMJ*, 325, 1–5.

Kompier, M. 2002. The psychosocial work environment and health—What do we know and where should we go? *Scandinavian Journal of Work, Environment, and Health*, 28, 1–4.

Kreger, D. 1995. Self-esteem, stress, and depression among graduate students. *Psychological Reports*, 76, 345–6.

Landsbergis, P. 2003. The changing organization of work and the safety and health of working people: A commentary. *Journal of Occupational Environmental Medicine*, 45, 61–2.

Lazarus, R.S. 1999. *Stress and Emotion: A New Synthesis*. New York: Springer Publishing Company.

Lazarus, R., and Folkman, S. 1984. *Stress, appraisal and coping*. New York: Springer.

Le Blanc, P., de Jonge, J., and Schaufeli, W.B. 2000. Job Stress and Health, in *Work and Organizational Psychology*, edited by N. Chmiel. Oxford: Blackwell Publishers, 148–77.

Lerner, M.J. 1980. *The Belief in a Just World. A Fundamental Delusion*. New York: Plenum Press.

Lerner, J.S., Dahl, R.F., Hariri, A.R., and Taylor, S.E. 2007. Facial expressions of emotion reveal neuroendocrine and cardiovascular stress responses. *Biological Psychiatry*, 61, 253–60.

Leventhal, G.S. 1980. What Should Be Done with Equity Theory? New Approaches to the Fairness in Social Relationships, in *Social Exchange Theory*, edited by K. Gergen, M. Greenberg, and R. Willis. New York: Plenum Press, 27–55.

Lind, A. 2001. Fairness heuristics theory: Justice judgments as pivotal cognitions in organizational relations, in *Advances in Organizational Justice*, edited by J. Greenberg, and R. Cropanzano. Stanford: Stanford University Press, 56–88.

Lind, E.A., and Tyler, T.R. 1988. *The Social Psychology of Procedural Justice*. New York: Plenum Press.

Lovallo, W.R. 1997. *Stress and Health. Biological and Psychological Interactions*. London: Sage, 57–71.

Lovallo, W.R., Pincomb, G.A., and Wilson, M.F. 1986. Heart rate reactivity and high type-A behavior as modifiers of physiological response to active and passive coping. *Psychophysiology*, 23, 105–12.

Markovsky, B. 1988. Injustice and arousal. *Social Justice Research*, 2, 223–33.

Miedema, J., Van den Bos, K., and Vermunt, R. 2000. Rechtvaardigheid, onrechtvaardigheid en tapas: Perceptie van (on)recht roept alertheid op, in *Fundamentele sociale psychologie 14*, edited by C. Martijn, C.G. Rutte, D.A. Stapel, and E. van Dijk. Delft: Eburon, 89–99.

Milczarek, M., Schneider, E., and Gonzalez, E.R. 2009. *OSH in Figures: Stress at Work—Facts and Figures*. Luxembourg: European Agency for Safety and Health at Work.

Montada, L. 1998. Belief in a Just World: A Hybrid of Justice and Self-Interest? in *Responses to Victimizations and Belief in a Just World*, edited by L. Montada and M.J. Lerner. New York: Plenum, 217–46.

Paoli, P. 1997. *Second European Survey on the Work Environment 1995*. Dublin: European Foundation for the Improvement of Living and Working Conditions.

Parent-Thirion, A., Macias, E., Hurley, J., and Vermeylen, G. 2007. Fourth European Working Conditions Survey. Luxembourg: European Foundation for the Improvement of Living and Working Conditions.

Quick, J.C., and Quick, J.D. 1984. *Organizational Stress and Preventive Management*. New York: McGraw-Hill Publishing Company.

Schaufeli, W. and van Dierendonck, D. 1993. The construct validity of two burnout measures. *Journal of Occupational Behavior*, 14, 631–47.

Siegrist, J. 1996. Adverse health effects of high-effort/low-reward conditions. *Journal of Occupational Health Psychology*, 1(1), 27–41.

Tepper, B.J. 2001. Health consequences of organizational injustice: Tests of main and interactive effects. *Organizational Behavior and Human Decision Processes*, 86(2), 197–215.

Thibaut, J., and Walker, L. 1975. *Procedural Justice: A Psychological Analysis*. Hillsdale, NJ: Lawrence Erlbaum.

Tomaka, J., and Blascovich, J. 1994. Effects of justice beliefs on cognitive appraisal and subjective psychological, and behavioral responses to potential stress. *Journal of Personality and Social Psychology*, 67, 732–40.

Tomaka, J., Blascovich, J., Kibler, J., and Ernst, J.M. 1997. Cognitive and physiological antecedents of threat and challenge appraisal. *Journal of Personality and Social Psychology*, 73, 63–72.

Törnblom, K.Y. 1992. The Social Psychology of Distributive Justice, in *Distributive Justice from an Interdisciplinary Perspective*, K.R. Scherer. Cambridge: Cambridge University Press, 177–284.

Tyler, T.R., and Lind, E.A. 1992. A Relational Model of Authority in Groups, in *Advances in Experimental Social Psychology*, Vol. 25, M. Zanna. New York: Academic Press, 115–91.

Van den Bos, K., Wilke, H., Lind, E., and Vermunt, R. 1998. Evaluating outcomes by means of the fair process effect: Evidence for different processes in fairness and satisfaction judgments. *Journal of Personality and Social Psychology*, 74(6), 1493–503.

Van Yperen, N.W., and Hagendoorn, M. 2003. Do high job demands increase intrinsic motivation or fatigue or both? The role of job control and job social support. *Academy of Management Journal*, 46, 339–48.

Vermunt, R. 2002. Employee Stress, Injustice, and the Dual Position of the Boss, in *Emerging Perspectives on Managing Organizational Justice*, edited by S. Gilliland, D. Steiner, and D. Skarlicki. Greenwich: IAP, 157–76.

Vermunt, R. 2007. *Social justice and the art of reducing stress*. Leiden University: Farewell lecture.

Vermunt, R., and Steensma, H. 2001. *Stress and justice in organizations: An exploration into justice processes to find mechanisms to reduce stress, Justice in the Workplace*, edited by R. Cropanzano. Mahwah: Erlbaum, 27–48.

Vermunt, R., and Steensma, H. 2003. Physiological relaxation: Stress reduction through fair treatment. *Social Justice Research*, 16(2), 135–50.

Vermunt, R., and Steensma, H. 2005. How can justice be used to manage stress in organizations? in *Handbook of Organizational Justice*, edited by Greenberg, J., and Colquitt J. Mahwah: Erlbaum, 383–410.

Vermunt, R., Berggren, K., and Peeters, Y. (forthcoming). *Fair treatment affects saliva cortisol release in stressed low and high self-esteem individuals*.

Vermunt, R., Peeters, Y., and Berggren, K. 2007. How fair treatment affects saliva cortisol release in stressed low and high type-A behavior individuals. *Scandinavian Journal of Psychology*, 48, 547–55.

# Epilogue

## Introduction

Having described the four components of the justice model in the Prologue, and their elaboration in the later chapters, reflection on the main content is appropriate. The epilogue is a term from drama and literature and its aim is to tie up loose ends and understand the main characters of the play. I use the term here to describe the main features of the justice model (Demonstration), to sum up its strengths and weaknesses (Evaluation), and to speculate on steps to improve the model (Speculation). The aim of the epilogue is therefore to give the reader an insight into the state-of-the-art of resource allocation theory and research as I see it now.

## Demonstration

Life is devoted to the allocation of resources, whether they concern love, service, goods, money, information, or status. A resource allocation event consists of an actor who takes the allocation decision, a recipient, and an observer. The decision concerns allocation of a focal resource and an additional resource: the means to allocate the focal resource. Actor, recipient, and observer evaluate the resulting type and amount of the allocated resource in terms of fairness and satisfaction.

Resources have meaning for living beings and allocation is a primordial activity: it relates to the survival of an individual living being as well as to that of the group (species). The survival urge finds its operation in self-directed allocation motivation (egoism) as well as in other-directed allocation motivation (altruism). In the evolution of the species, these motivations have—specifically in human beings—evolved into a more balanced allocation motivation: the justice motivation.

In human beings, cognitive brain evolution has made the operation of the motivations more dependent on deliberate decision-making than in other primates.

The meaning that human beings attributed to resources changed continually. An important change in meaning took place when they became domesticated and created villages and towns. A person who contributed much to the group was admired and was allowed to allocate more resources to himself than someone who did not. However, the creation of more goods has resulted in the disproportionate wealth of a few people. Thus, people have come to base relationships more and more on what a fellow human being has rather than on who that person is.

The growing complexity of social relationships within the community is experienced like the physical environment once was: as a limit-setting edifice. The created social edifice strongly influences people's opinions and behaviors. Changes in the physical and social environments, and the appearance of new goods, create newcomers who challenge the position of the people settled in the community. Once settled, the newcomers force the settled to adapt their beliefs about resource allocation rules and principles, and thus change the social edifice. Parents teach their children alternative behaviors and attitudes to increase their children's chances of a successful future. These learned behaviors become part of the individual's cognitive, emotional, and behavioral repertory.

People are justice motivated, and under influence-free conditions allocate resources (primary goods and civil liberties) equally. But the waxing and waning of social groups affects the balance between self-directed allocation motivation and other-directed allocation motivation. The resulting unequal division of primary goods and civil liberties is only acceptable (permissible) if appropriate justifications are given and accepted with love and respect by all, or by a majority of the group members. In some periods culture has supported the operation of the self-directed motivation with created and accepted justifications, while in other periods the other-directed motivation was dominant. When fear is imminent as in the state of nature or behind the veil of ignorance, group members are inclined to allocate resources unequal. Dedicated leaders with compassion are needed to on all levels of the social edifice to regulate inequality. They can teach others humility and induce forms of complex inequality.

Moral behavior is subsumed under just behavior and is primarily directed at equal status (respect) allocation between self (actor) and other (recipient): Treat others as you treat yourself. Unequal status allocation is only acceptable (permissible) if appropriate justifications are given and accepted with love and respect. Justice is primarily directed at equal allocation of all other resources between self and other, as well as among others. Unequal resource allocation is only acceptable (permissible) if appropriate justifications are given and accepted with love and respect.

The individual actor is also subject to internal forces—psychological ones—that distort the justice (morality) balance. The justice urge, developed as part of the new cortex, has to compete with urges in the older layers of the brain, the egoistic and altruistic urge.

A crucial psychological force is anxiety or fear caused by threat of physical and social changes. In the modern era, this anxiety takes the form of existential anxiety that each individual experiences and has a disturbing effect on fair allocation motivation. Moreover, cyclical fear, accompanying economic and social upheaval, increases the already present existential anxiety. Fear caused by the presence of other group(s) also has disturbing effects on the balanced justice motivation. Intergroup fear reduces just allocations abruptly.

Self-preservation as well as moral emotions are triggered during resource allocation processes. The actor strives to reward himself/herself with positive self-preservation and moral emotions. Negative self-preservation and moral emotions alert the actor, recipient, and observer engaged in resource allocation. To prevent or reduce experience of negative emotions like guilt, shame, or unhappiness, the actor engages in justifications when unfair allocation is inevitable or desired. If the actor, recipient, and observer accept the justifications they may become guidelines (norms and rules) for the behavior of community members and will result in positive self-preservation and moral emotions. Actors strivings for just allocation of resources and his struggle with other psychological forces can be traced by assessing their neurological and psycho-physiological correlates.

Recipients and observers react to an actor's unfair and inappropriate allocation decision. The kind and strength of the reactions is dependent on the discrepancy (inequality) between the type and amount of expected and received resources. Recipients prefer working on an actor with attempts to get compensation or justification, or work on themselves with attempts to (de)appreciate components of the allocation process and/or mitigate their consequences. When "legal" attempts do not succeed, recipients turn to rule-violating and norm-violating behaviors.

A major response to unfairness is experienced as distress which, on a chronic basis, causes severe psychological and physical damage to recipients and observers. Sensitive and trained actors are able to reduce recipients' and observers' distress. If they do not succeed in reducing distress and giving recipients and observers satisfaction, new behaviors may be developed which may end in new beliefs and attitudes about what is appropriate resource allocation. The newcomers' attitudes give rise to a new social edifice.

## Evaluation

The phenomena the justice model describes are actors', recipients', and observers' resource allocation actions. For actors, the actions exist of decisions to allocate resources fairly. In this book, allocation decisions are described that mainly concern material resources, for example money, and immaterial resources, for example status. Less attention is paid to other material and immaterial resources, like goods, love, service, and information. Focus on the allocation of money and status, although instigated by individual motivation, directs attention to higher-order phenomena like (un)equal allocation of primary goods (money), civil liberties, and societal norms (status). On the psychological level allocation decisions are related to motivational, emotional, and cognitive processes and their physiological counterparts.

Each of the chapters describes these levels of inquiry in a way that generates hypotheses as to the origin, process, and consequences of resource allocation. In this section, the most important features of the justice model are described, explained where possible, and the statements (description and explanation) are evaluated. Each feature has its *description*, *explanation*, and *evaluation*.

*The Justice Model*

*Description*
The presented justice model consists of four components: motivation, morality and justice, psychological processes, and reactions. The chosen components provide the possibility of describing and explaining justice phenomena on the individual psychological level, on the interpersonal level, and on the social and societal level.

*Explanation*
Applying the allocation model and the concept of figuration allows us to switch from the individual level to the group and societal level and back, emphasizing the complexities of human interactions.

*Evaluation*
The chosen components proved their value but the choice is more intuitive than based on theory. The order of priority of the components could not be determined.

*Survival and Group*

*Description*
Hominins could only survive in the worsening conditions caused by climate change by protecting scarce food sources and eliminating competing groups of primates, other animals, and fellow hominins, thus enabling them to allocate food to their own group only.

*Explanation*
Groups have more chance of survival than individuals.

*Evaluation*
Simulation studies give indications of this line of reasoning but archeological findings are not conclusive. It cannot be excluded that it is not climate change that is the primary cause but the worsening of already existing conditions.

*Morality and Justice*

*Description*
Justice is defined here as evaluation of allocation of resources between self and other, as well as between others mutually. Morality is defined here as the evaluation of allocation mainly of the resource status between self and other. In moral issues, the content of status is related to the other as a human being as an end in itself. Treat others as you treat yourself.

*Explanation*
Justice is the more encompassing concept than morality because justice concerns allocation of all resources while morality is confined to allocation of status.

*Evaluation*
The term "human being as an end" is not specific. Some authors refer to individual well-being, others refer to more specific qualities, as in life-and-death issues.

*Social Mass*

*Description*
In the material world as well as in the world of living beings, "mass," keeping one's "mass," or increasing one's "mass" is crucial. Resource allocation through interpersonal behavior affects an individual's social "mass." In the case of food, resource allocation affects physical "mass" as well.

*Explanation*
Just as physical mass attracts other physical mass and affect each other, so social mass affects other social mass as well. People accept being close to another, but accept to a lesser degree another coming close to them. "Strong" people attract others more easily than "weak" people do.

*Evaluation*
There is not much direct evidence for this statement. However, experimental data on the asymmetry phenomenon show that individuals view others as objects to approach or from which to distance themselves.

*Equality*

*Description*
Creating equality is intrinsically good; it is an end in itself. It regards resource allocation between self and other as well as among others.

*Explanation*
Equality fosters humanity.

*Evaluation*
Philosophers define a trait, a duty, or a virtue as a good. The question is whether a quality like equality is a good.

*Inequality*

*Description*
Increased wealth leads to growing inequality of material resources, but results in reactions to restore equality *or* to increase inequality. People developed value systems to justify large or small inequalities in material resources. Individuals in the original position being rational, reasonable, and anxious allocate material resources unequally, justify the inequality, and try to convince themselves, recipients, and observers to accept the justifications.

*Explanation*
Rational, reasonable, and anxious individuals seek a balance between their own and others' interests by using justifications, and thus restore justice.

*Evaluation*
Inequality is the ultimate consequence of Rawls' ideas of people in the original position deprived from their identity.

*Civil Society*

*Description*
Individuals in the original position, being rational, reasonable, and anxious, allocate immaterial resources unequally, justify the inequality, and try to convince recipients to accept the justifications. Value systems were developed to impose equality of immaterial resources.

*Explanation*
Anxiety about one's own position drives people to deviate from fairness and equality in immaterial resource allocation. Human rights agreements are necessary to provide a justice framework to guide people to the right path.

*Evaluation*
This reasoning follows directly from the justice model developed here. It is contrary to Rawls' ideas of a civil society.

*Justification Process*

*Description*
The fundamental assumption is that an individual person has an urge to allocate resources fairly between self and other. The fair motivation is modulated by psychological factors (e.g., anxiousness, fear, egoism, altruism) as well as social factors (e.g., intergroup relations or culture, such as individualism, capitalism, collectivism). Cognitive and emotional sources are tapped to justify unfairness

and to convince others to accept the justifications. The individual's struggle for justice can be measured using central or peripheral physiological correlates.

*Explanation*
During evolution, balanced allocation of resources was a successful survival strategy. Brain structures seem to show remnants of evolutionary development. Older structures as well as new social conditions modulate the urge for fairness.

*Evaluation*
Although evolution of the brain is generally accepted by scientists, the fairness structure is less so. Also, the idea of older structures that encompass egoism and altruism needs more experimental evidence.

*Intergroup Relations*

*Description*
A crucial social factor of fair allocation is ingroup–outgroup perception. If the other is perceived as belonging to the outgroup instead of the ingroup, fair allocation changes dramatically and suddenly to unfair resource allocation. This shift has the characteristics of a catastrophe.

*Explanation*
Discrimination, outgroup derogation, and ingroup favoritism, though functional once, are no longer functional for many human relations.

*Evaluation*
There is a huge amount of evidence about intergroup behavior and attitudes, and the detrimental effects of ingroup–outgroup differentiation. The catastrophe idea has not yet been tested.

*Reactions to Unfairness*

*Description*
Unfair and inappropriate resource allocation is viewed as a discrepancy between the expected and received types and amounts of resources. Discrepancy is experienced not only with regard to the focal resource but also with regard to the additional resource: the resource needed to get the focal resource. The recipient and observer who experience discrepancy react to restore justice and satisfaction by working on the actor—attempting to get compensation and/or justification—or on the self, by mitigation and appreciation. Recipients prefer compensation to justification, mitigation to appreciation.

*Explanation*
Changes in the natural but also in the psychological environment are detected quickly (vigilance). A discrepancy between the expected and received amount or type of resource causes distress, leading to action. The recipient prefers actions reflecting a high amount of moral and self-preservation emotions.

*Evaluation*
The allocation model differentiates between the amounts and types of focal and additional resources. Simpler versions have been formulated and accidental testing showed some support for the hypotheses. The complex model developed here is not yet tested.

*Stress Reaction*

*Description*
The actor's unfair and inappropriate resource allocation results in the recipient's distress. Stress may be moderate or high. The recipient reduces moderate stress by undoing unfairness and frustration. High stress reduction can only be accomplished by a sensitive actor who compensates, justifies, mitigates, or re-appreciates adequately the original unfairness and frustration. Thus, the actor reduces the recipient's stress by appropriate action, and we are back where we began: the crucial role of the actor in the allocation process.

*Explanation*
Unfair treatment decreases the recipient's status and instigates a reaction to the threat of status loss. The stress experienced following loss of status sets in motion a cascade of physiological, cognitive, and behavioral reactions so heavy that the recipient is not able to cope with it effectively.

*Evaluation*
The physiological paths of detecting discrepancy—a perceptual process—leading to immobilized reaction in animals are well documented.

## Speculation

Justice is defined as the evaluation of balanced resource allocation between self and other or between others mutually. If the resource is allocated with a high degree of balance between the parties, the final outcome will be evaluated as just. If the allocation is unbalanced, the outcome will be judged as unjust. Thus, the actor is motivated to allocate resources in a balanced way, but social and psychological forces (anxiety, egoism, altruism, culture, relationships) modulate a balanced allocation. In the economic area, much research has been done with regard to allocation of money and goods. Far less research has been done with regard to other types of resources.

For recipients, a balanced allocation of resources is derived from their outcome expectation in relation to the actual received outcome. If there is no discrepancy between the expected and received outcome, the outcome is balanced and will be evaluated as neutral or fair. The recipient's evaluation is influenced by psychological as well as social factors (emotion, ideology, culture). Research about the effects of mental states on justice evaluations and subsequent reactions is abundant in the literature, but what is missing is knowledge about the type, strength, and extent of the evaluations and subsequent reactions. In the sociological literature, theoretical models have been developed to fill this gap, but empirical support is scarce. More research needs to be carried out to connect sociological and psychological models of recipients' reactions.

Morality is defined here as the balance between allocating the resource status (respect) to the self as compared to the recipient. In this general definition, morality cannot be distinguished from justice. This confusion is visible in the justice literature. Evaluation in terms of just or unjust is also used in the procedural justice literature when an actor treats a recipient disrespectfully (status) by, for instance, asking inappropriate questions. One can also define this behavior as unethical because it affects the recipient's integrity. In the same procedural justice research, treating the recipient according to ethical rules (being concerned about the health of a person) is evaluated in terms of justice. Both terms are used under these conditions interchangeably. However, with regard to the allocation of money or goods, the actor, recipient, and observer evaluate the final outcome as fair or unfair, but not as ethical or unethical. In the case, however, where there are neither specific recipients nor observers, the term unethical is used, as was done in the evaluation of bankers' very risky financial decisions affecting large groups of people.

In the case of a dilemma such as whether to save someone's life or those of five others, the dilemma is defined as a moral one and not as a justice one. The morality of the dilemma is derived from the fact that the dilemma concerns a life-and-death issue. A life-and-death issue is, in fact, a severe status issue. The question becomes more complicated as one observes that a medical treatment to save a patient's life is refused because the treatment costs are too high. Is the refusal a question of injustice (expensive service is not given), or is the decision an immoral one (the recipient's life can be saved but one does not do it)? How one defines the dilemma depends, among other things, on the perspective taken. The actor—for instance, the hospital—judges the issue as one of costs, and as such they evaluate the very expensive treatment of this patient as unfair because it takes too much of the financial resources for the rescue of one person (status). The hospital would say that the expensive treatment is unfair toward other patients in need who deserve the best treatment as well: the hospital makes a comparative judgment. The recipient and observers will be inclined to evaluate the hospital's decision as unethical because they emphasize the patient's life—these people make an absolute judgment: life or death. In other words, whether the dilemma is a justice one or a moral one depends also on the perspective taken.

The debate on (in)equality in society is old and not settled. Scientific hypotheses are set up to explain (in)equality, ideologies have been put forward to justify it, while policy makers, from a pragmatic point of view, take measures to affect (in)equality. There are periods and countries where (in)equality is more accepted than in others. Studies have revealed the history of (in)equality from archeological and anthropological findings. Although we know much about (in) equality in society, the optimal degree of (in)equality is still the subject of debate. Some findings suggest that the lower the inequality the more people are happy and healthy. These studies are correlational and lack precision. But let us assume that the findings about a moderate inequality can be replicated; questions arise as to what is an acceptable inequality? Does the moderate inequality count for every citizen or do we allow that some people are very poor and some are very rich? Is it acceptable, for instance, that 90 percent of the population differs moderately in income while 10 percent deviates extremely at both ends?

It is important that a large part of the population has moderate differences in income: the reason is that people of each income level have an accurate view of the next level up as well as of the next one down. This constellation motivates people to try to approach the next level and to distance themselves from the lower one. This upward–downward intention motivates people to move but also to keep the social network intact. The precise extent of the inequality is therefore of crucial significance to improving happiness and health in society.

There are strong indications that climate change was and still is a crucial condition for social, economic, and psychological change. Scientists have related climate change in several periods in unwritten and written history to changes in the social edifice of society. But it is difficult to disentangle the several causes and effects of the changes: what caused what? Was the end of the Mayan culture around 800 AD a consequence of drought, as some scientists suggest, or was Mayan society already in such turmoil that drought could not be counteracted properly?

The justice model would gain in strength if an improved and better-tested model of the consequences of climate change could be used. Improving the model is feasible, in that contemporary society is confronted with climate change. The International Panel on Climate Change, in which climatologists from nearly all countries in the world are working together, has confirmed that all climate indicators point in the direction of irreversible changes in global temperature, rainfall, and weather. This generation is the first in history that has knowledge of climate change and has a theory of the causes and possible consequences.

We can already perceive alteration of attitudes and behaviors in relation to the climate: less energy consumption, more energy from sun and wind, people willing to pay higher prices for green energy. I need not be specific but it is clear that social, economic, and psychological changes occur in relation to climate change. To counteract the consequences of climate change effectively, governmental agencies and the public try to introduce new behaviors.

Allocation behavior is changing as well. More and more people are prepared to pay more for food and other products when they know that the production is climate friendly. Nations are (reluctantly) willing to help other nations to protect inhabitants from flooding caused by a rise in the sea level as an effect of rising global temperature. There are many initiatives to improve energy production and reduce energy loss during production and consumption. These newcomers on the energy market invent new energy-saving apparatus and challenge the settled, who will continue to produce in the energy-consuming way.

Alternative moral standards are developed prescribing how to treat animals and how to live alongside the natural environment. People are prepared to separately collect household garbage (plastics, paper, glass) to recycle and reuse. And as these behaviors become more and more general practice, it is increasingly viewed as unethical to waste products and to pollute the natural environment.

Are these actions in relation to the natural environment directly and solely due to climate change? Or were the behavioral and social changes already operative, and has the prospect of climate change only accelerated these processes? In my view, climate change has a pivotal role in human existence, its continuity, and change, as well as in the structure and culture of human relationships. Its influence on allocation behavior and justice beliefs is inevitable. Theorizing and research in all these areas are of crucial importance for the fate of humanity.

# Index